BETWEEN OLD WORLDS AND NEW

BETWEEN OLD WORLDS AND NEW
OCCASIONAL WRITINGS ON MUSIC BY
WILFRID MELLERS
EDITED & INTRODUCED BY JOHN PAYNTER

cygnus arts

London **Cygnus Arts**
Madison & Teaneck **Fairleigh Dickinson University Press**

UNITED KINGDOM BY
of Golden Cockerel Press
r Street
London
WC1A 2AH

PUBLISHED IN THE UNITED STATES OF AMERICA BY
Fairleigh Dickinson University Press
440 Forsgate Drive
Cranbury
NJ 08512

First published 1997

ISBN 1 900541 45 9
ISBN 0 8386 3798 1

© 1972–74, 1981, 1984–97 Wilfrid Mellers
Introductions, selection, notes, and reference material © 1997 John Paynter

Wilfrid Mellers and John Paynter have asserted their right under the Copyright, Designs and Patents Act 1988 to be identified as Authors of this Work

CATALOGUING-IN-PUBLICATION DATA

Catalogue records for this book are available from the British Library
and the Library of Congress

PRINTED BY BOOKCRAFT (BATH) LIMITED IN THE UNITED KINGDOM

And all sway forward on the dangerous flood
Of history, that never sleeps or dies,
And, held one moment, burns the hand.

W. H. AUDEN

CONTENTS

FOREWORD

by Wilfrid Mellers

W RITING ABOUT MUSIC IS OFTEN CONSIDERED A MUG'S GAME, SINCE although music is a language it uses none of the counters we employ in verbal conversation or in writing, nor does it have the relationship with the visual world such as is possessed by painting and sculpture, even when ostensibly 'abstract'. In aural terms the henniness of Rameau's *poule* or the cuckoodom of Beethoven's cuckoo make only the crudest reference to what hens and cuckoos do much more expertly, while railway trains and factories, noise-makers once emulated by fairly modern orchestras, make little effect that may be called musical.

Even so, the language of music does function, and communicate, by way of physiological and psychological factors inseparable from our minds and nervous systems, and, though difficult, it is not impossible to define what these factors are. On balance, I believe that this task of definition is feasible, for I have been writing about music—getting satisfaction from doing so and perhaps affording some satisfaction to others—for over half a century. I have written big or biggish books about 'significant' subjects—such as Couperin, Bach, Beethoven, American music, and Vaughan Williams—and smaller books about smaller composers, such as Poulenc and Grainger. I have also made several assays into the worlds of pop music and the media, including books on the Beatles, Bob Dylan, and women pop and jazz singers—in which fields the criteria for valid comment may be different in application though not in principle. I've also, over the past half-century, functioned as a music journalist, producing material that, in sheer quantity, causes me momently to blench.

The first piece reprinted in this volume—an address given on my eight-ieth birthday to students of the University of York, of whose music depart-ment I was founding professor in 1964—suggests that I've devoted so much time to teaching and writing about music because I believe it to be not just 'relevant' but essential to human society. I see no real distinction between writing books that modestly presume to make statements about music that are worth the carrying, and producing music-journalism that seems, by definition, to be ephemeral. I'll hazard the view that journalism involves making quick but not mindless judgements about the aural arts; whereas criticism consists in the analysis and exposition of such judgements. Both activities may be justifiable if they provoke thought and feeling: and mine seem to have done this to the extent that, over the years, people have often asked me how they could get hold of one of my out of print books or even an article fortuitously lighted on in one of the journals to which I've contributed—principally the *New Statesman* in early years, and later *The Times Literary Supplement* and the *Musical Times*, with occasional incursions into the *Guardian, The Times,* the *Independent,* and the American *Atlantic Monthly* and *New Republic.* Grateful acknowledgements to sources are made for permission to reprint; but my main debt is to my friend and one-time colleague John Paynter who, in his editorial capacity, has assembled and ordered these hopefully not-totally-ephemeral miscellanea with imaginative percipience and skill.

York, April 1997

Acknowledgements

Reviews and lectures reproduced in this book are the copyright of Wilfrid Mellers and were first published in *The Times Literary Supplement, The Musical Times, The Atlantic Monthly,* and *Music and Musicians* (identified, as appropriate—*TLS, MT, AM, MM*—with dates of publication, at the end of each article). Thanks are due to the publishers and editors of these journals for their co-operation in the assembling of this selection.

The Introduction incorporates some material from my article, 'Renewal and Revelation: Wilfrid Mellers at York', published by Cambridge University Press in *Popular Music* (vol. 13, no. 2, May 1994).

I am grateful to the University of York Department of Music for providing photocopying facilities, and to The Sir Jack Lyons Charitable Trust for generous financial assistance for word-processing and other initial costs in the preparation of this book.

JP

BETWEEN NEW WORLDS AND OLD

INTRODUCTION

by John Paynter

A
S I WRITE, THE BBC HAS JUST BEGUN TO PUBLICISE ITS PLANS FOR THE 1997 season of Promenade Concerts. Much is being made of the decision to include songs by the Beatles—"acceptable now", we are told, "as 'classical' music". But a quarter of a century ago, when Wilfrid Mellers published his retrospective study of the Beatles, *Twilight of the Gods,* it caused a not inconsiderable rumpus. On the one hand there were those scornful of what they regarded as academic trendiness, while on the other, pop musicians, journalists, and sociologists joined forces to berate him for even thinking of writing about the structural niceties of those famous '60s songs—pop music was not meant to be analysed by university professors. (It didn't seem to occur to them that no music was ever *meant* to be analysed, notwithstanding which, it doesn't hurt us to know a bit about how it works.) Wilfrid was mystified by the outcry, and I well remember his comment: "If it behaves like music why shouldn't I write about it as music?"

It is his total commitment to music *as music* that has made Wilfrid Mellers, throughout a long and active life, such a significant figure: a resolutely individual composer, an inspired teacher and a critic of powerful insight. Above all, he has shown that it is essential to discriminate only in matters of musical excellence, and not between different kinds of music. At the age of eighty-three, his writing, marked as ever by a compassionate vision of humanity, and reflecting his facility for teasing out subtle relationships between ideas, techniques, and musical experience, is as vital and refreshing as it was when his first books, *Music and Society* and *Studies in Contemporary Music,* appeared in 1946 and 1947.

At Cambridge in the 1930s, he graduated first in English and then in music, and also during that time studied composition with Egon Wellesz and Edmund Rubbra in Oxford. He became music editor of *Scrutiny*—a leading critical journal of its day—and began to write for *The Listener* and the *New Statesman.* Eloquently, he developed an entirely new approach to music criticism; one which would make sense of the vast range of musical expression flowing, world-wide, from varied lifestyles and strongly held beliefs. Thus, to 'understand' music, it is necessary first to acknowledge its ethnic, social, and psychological significance. Persistently he asks, "What is music *for*? What does it *mean*?"

This theme—the nature and function of music—is evident in everything Wilfrid Mellers writes. While not denying that music has many *uses* or "may merely wile away empty time", its prime *function* is to "reveal what we live for"—it is a manifestation of thought which allows us to "live momently in eternity's sunrise and to become more aware of human potentiality". Always it is always within this context that he explains technical development; for example, when he points to stylistic changes in Monteverdi's music which indicate a "shift from Renaissance description and illustration . . . to Baroque re-enactment, whereby music becomes *process*: aural synonyms for the ways in which people, here and now, feel, think and act." On the final page of his masterly study *Bach and the Dance of God*—itself the outcome of no less than thirty years of thinking and teaching about Bach's music—he writes, "Without historical knowledge sensitivity may mislead; but without sensitivity historical knowledge is impotent". Understandably, then, he is wary of writers who give the impression of pursuing historical or technical information for its own sake. Although he never hesitates to praise "technical analysis of the kind that promotes experiential understanding", and welcomes even "the journalistic approach one might expect in writing about show-biz people" so long as it is "agreeably toughened with musical commentary", he deplores the tendency to write about music as though it were "merely a commodity to be quantitatively catalogued and has nothing to do with the nature and quality of living"; increasingly, he argues, "we have become better and better at analysis of tiny details—account-driven and accountable—but less good at seeing the whole picture".

That "whole picture" is a recurring feature of Mellers's journal articles, each new topic, in its own way, leading him to focus afresh on the power and purpose of music, highlighting both our shortcomings and our continuing need for renewal. There are indeed signs that our time is out of joint, and that "the criminal imbecility of the human race (to which we all belong) seems hell-bent on self-destruction" and that "We have become, or are in the process of becoming, a society of lemmings whose disaffection with post-Renaissance consciousness has reached a point of no return". Yet he urges us to "recognise life when we see and hear it, whether in other people's artefacts or in the still small voice within our minds and senses . . . Whatever the nature of the experience proffered, we must attend to it wittingly, for while there is life there is hope." And he instances the character of Captain Vere in Britten's opera *Billy Budd* as "the potential *reconciler of opposites, which we call civilisation*" (my italics). To so many of those who have been taught by him, heard him lecture, and read his books and articles, Wilfrid Mellers too is a reconciler of opposites, drawing things of lasting value from even the most negative circumstances. Thus he speculates that, although the 'mindless' monotony of 'tribal pop' and noisy minimalism may threaten our hearing and our nerves, it may be "a risk worth taking, since relinquishing

Western materiality may paradoxically bring immense material rewards . . . mindlessness, after many centuries of mind obsession, may be momentarily a positive need"; and *that* may help us "to survive and even flourish in our asphalt jungle, much as indigenous peoples used art to habituate themselves to the fright of the forest."

Speculation about, and reflection upon, the grand scheme of things is the lifeblood of creativity. Artists, like children, continually ask, "why?"— not so much about the mechanics of existence but rather about feelings and attitudes of mind, and what is *meant* by the various ways in which we attempt to shape our lives. Undoubtedly, Wilfrid Mellers's literary training, and especially his scholarly work on Shakespeare, has influenced the questions he asks as a composer. A characteristic composition is *Rose of May*, subtitled *A Threnody for Ophelia*, for speaker, soprano, flute, clarinet and string quartet. Commissioned for the 1964 Cheltenham Festival, it is a setting of the Ophelia texts from *Hamlet* framed by the Queen's account of finding the drowned Ophelia: "There is a willow grows aslant a brook . . ." The speaker is instructed to "begin very lazily and slowly", to move gradually to a normal narrative style and then to "return to the dreamy manner of the opening, softly floating out as the invocation music subsides and Ophelia's 'presence' enters". There are similar 'stage directions' throughout the work, not only for speaker and singer but also for the instrumentalists. For, although it is organised as chamber music in a neatly sectionalised form (an 'Invocation' beginning with the solo clarinet and leading to three 'Ballads'—each culminating in a cadenza, for clarinet, flute, and singer respectively—and a coda in which the speaker returns with the Queen's concluding lines), this music is also 'theatre', a point of some importance to the composer:

Its extra-musical connotations are very clear. First of all, I'd known *Hamlet* all my life, and had been obsessed by Ophelia—another of those innocent creatures who's not so innocent; and a victim—and particularly by the mad-songs. Indeed, I'd set them before, in 1944, for three girls' voices. The genesis of this piece is connected with what was in my mind through all those years; also with this particular commission for a concert in honour of the Shakespeare quatrocentenary for which there were to be actors from the Shakespeare Memorial Theatre as well as musicians [Diana Rigg, April Cantelo, and the Wigmore Ensemble]. The clarinet I wanted because it's a solo voice; a marvellously expressive instrument with great variety and range which can be like a speaking voice—as we know from jazz clarinet, which is so close to the jazz *singing* voice. The flute I wanted because of its association with Ophelia and with innocence in general. I didn't want to begin with the voice: I wanted the clarinet to come out of the silence but to be related to the actual situation. So, when the first 'Ballad' occurs there is a direction: "Simply: not slow but hesitant", and then there's a note that explains why it's to be performed like this—"Ophelia sings as she drowns: but this prelude is also meant to evoke her 'distracted' entry in the Mad scene. The clarinet phrases should suggest hesitant movement, perhaps vaguely outstretched arms and hands." Now this is corporeal music, isn't it? The music is *doing the action*, and I wanted the singer to feel this, if not exactly to act it.* [*see Notes on p. 305*]

Spells (to words by Kathleen Raine) is another piece which "directly involves music as a *function* rather than merely as a communication from A to B", as is also his setting of the runic poem, *The Key of the Kingdom*, for a soprano who must also dance and play on small bells.

A preoccupation with Edenic innocence is present in many of Mellers's compositions, and not infrequently this leads him to incorporate traditional musics and elements of jazz—for example, *White Bird Blues* (1975) for miming, dancing soprano and free bass accordion; a solo guitar piece, *A Blue Epiphany for J. B. Smith* (1976); and the *Shaman Songs* (flutes, saxophones, keyboards, electric bass, and percussion) composed in 1980 for Barbara Thompson and her Jazz Paraphernalia. The title of an earlier work, *Yeibichai*, alludes to a Navaho Indian Night Chant which is also a masked dance by the Grandfather of all the Monsters and the Principle of Female Divinity. Scored for unusually large forces—coloratura soprano, scat singer, mixed chorus with soprano and baritone soloists, two speakers and large orchestra—this is a setting of texts by the Black Mountain poet, Gary Snyder, and was commissioned by the BBC for the 1969 season of Henry Wood Promenade Concerts. The composer describes it as "a parable about the intermittent necessity for a return to the instinctual life", and he sees the fusion of contrasting musical genres as a natural "incarnation of the poetic theme". Since then, others have developed—perhaps, rather more self-consciously—amalgamations of techniques in what we now call 'crossover' styles, a phenomenon which Wilfrid Mellers discusses in Part 2 of the present volume in relation to the music of Bernstein, Sondheim, and Lou Harrison, and also in Part 5, where he traces hybrid forms back to Gottschalk.

Life Cycle (1967), *Yeibichai* (1969), and *The Word Unborn* (1970) form a trilogy of large-scale works concerned with 'the savage state' and its relevance to the modern (decadent) world. And there is further exploration of the Eden theme, first, in another 'big' piece (which again reveals the importance of the composer's literary interests), *Sun-flower: the Divine Quaternity of William Blake* for chorus, solo voices and orchestra (1972), and secondly, in the violin concerto entitled *The Wellspring of Loves*.

Whilst commissions and other opportunities to compose vocal works, both solo and choral, have encouraged Mellers to develop techniques appropriate to his interests in the 'corporeality' and 'theatre' of improvised musics, instrumental works such as the String Trio and the Viola Sonata (both from 1946), *Natalis Invicti Solis* for piano (composed in 1968 for Malcolm Troup), the *Threnody in Memoriam E. W.* [Egon Wellesz] for eleven solo strings (1975), and the 1981 *Glorificamus* for double brass choir, remind us that the European heritage has been the cornerstone of his writing and teaching for more than fifty years. In books such as *François Couperin and the French Classical Tradition* (1950), *Man and his Music* (1957), *Harmonious Meeting* (1965), *Bach and the Dance of God* (1980), and *Beethoven and the Voice of God* (1983) he explores with characteristic insight the development of European 'consciousness' as revealed in musical history. Elsewhere—for example, in *Music in a New Found Land*, his comprehensive study of American music, and in *Caliban Reborn: Renewal in Twentieth Century Music*—he applies a similar approach to the work of later composers, within or outwith Europe, who either cultivated in new ways that same 'consciousness of being conscious' or who, to a greater or lesser degree, eschewed it and followed other paths. The books on Mompou, Poulenc and, most particularly, that on Percy Grainger, reflect Mellers's abiding interest in the links between folk music, art and entertainment.

Teaching has been an important part of his life. After three years as supervisor of English and music at Downing College, Cambridge, he became staff tutor for music in the extra-mural department of Birmingham University, and there he began to evolve his unique style of analysis and comment from the *heard* music.

I was lecturing to people who were not musical specialists, and in some cases—quite a number of cases—people who couldn't read music. I was putting over history, and I found that, more and more, as I went on, I was tending to devote my lectures to particular works—works which were going to be performed.

For thirteen years—throughout his time in Birmingham—he organised an annual Summer School at Attingham Park near Shrewsbury, to which he invited, as guest lecturers, important English and American composers, among them, Aaron Copland, Virgil Thomson, Marc Blitzstein, Alan Bush, Edmund Rubbra and Egon Wellesz.

In 1960 he was appointed Visiting Andrew Mellon Professor of Music at the University of Pittsburgh, and experiences there further developed his interest in musical education. A much earlier enthusiasm for jazz was reawakened, and at the same time he found himself fascinated by the other kinds of music he encountered, often from very different ethnic backgrounds. In association with Jacob Evanson, an unusually adventurous schools music supervisor, Mellers worked in the Pittsburgh Public Schools, and for one particular school—"an all-Black school, in a relatively 'low' area"—he composed a liltingly jazzy setting of e. e. cummings's 'A Ballad of Anyone'. As he later recalled it, "This Pittsburgh 'scene' was all my ethnic interests come together in a big industrial city, and I suppose that gave me an idea of the way in which things ought to be inter-related."

He returned to England in 1964, having accepted an invitation to initiate joint English-Music courses at the University of York, founded in the previous year. But by the time he arrived in York his involvement with a variety of folk music, theatre and dance had radically altered his views on what a university course in music should be about:

The first thing that happened was my emphasis upon 'theatre': the course which I call Musica Poetica. And now I see that it *does* imply all my interests in ethnic musics, in folk musics, in African musics, and of course in jazz too. Trying to create a course in which all these kinds of music would be incorporated really grew out of that Musica Poetica venture.

It was soon apparent that such a programme could not be covered adequately as part of the English degree. Music became a separate Department with Professor Mellers as its head. This was an appointment which made the newspaper headlines: "FROM BACH TO THE BEATLES AND BACK", one of them shouted. Journalists were aware that something unusual was going on, and some, attracted perhaps by a whiff of sensation, seemed determined to milk for all it was worth the image of a trendy 'Beatles Professor' and his decision to include popular music in the new department's curriculum. But many more greeted with eager anticipation what was clearly going to be a renaissance in university music studies.

Over the next few years Mellers published several articles on musical education and, in particular, his thoughts about new possibilities for music in modern universities. This had been for him (as, indeed, it would have been for anyone at that time) a rare privilege—to be given an entirely free hand to found a new department, unhampered either by tradition or by the preconceptions of others. It would have been very easy to have come in with a detailed and inflexible scheme, but that would have allowed for only one point of view—and that is not Wilfrid Mellers's style. He knows that, if his students are to become *thinking* musicians rather than mere copies of their teachers, paying lip-service to a vague belief in a student's potential is pointless—they must be encouraged to aim high, and there have to be real opportunities for them to cultivate the talents and enthusiasms they bring with them to university. The teacher's task is to provide a stimulating atmosphere of inquiry that challenges with the immediacy of musical experience, and which respects and makes full use of the students' skills, whatever those may be. Naturally, Mellers brought to the new degree courses the product of his own musical enthusiasms, wide experience, literary and creative skills and scholarship, but not merely as something to be 'passed on' to students. Rather, this would be the base from which he could react—as it puts it, modestly—to "whatever came along". And, as always, the emphasis was upon music *as music* and as a manifestation of our humanity:

I don't think I had any idea what was going to happen . . . I merely started teaching English and Music conjointly and trying to do it more or less as I'd been taught at Cambridge, but putting right the more idiotic anomalies, as it seemed to me. I don't think you can separate teaching performance from teaching music history . . . therefore it does seem to me to be a nonsense to have a department which professes to educate in music if you don't perform it.

There is still a tendency for the self-regarding world of academic politics to stifle the originality of younger members of staff, even when the fashionable 'mission statements' profess to encourage it. But Wilfrid Mellers has never been an empire-builder: always he is excited by other people's ideas and immensely supportive when anyone is trying to break new ground. As the York department grew, he chose his colleagues carefully, for what they were, as people, and for their musical enthusiasms regardless of whether these would or would not fill gaps in the curriculum. He was not aiming to fulfil some grand academic plan, nor even to ensure that what others might regard as essential areas of study were covered. Yet, although he never attempted to make the department in his own image, he engendered a quality of co-operative musical and scholarly enterprise which, in spite of inevitable changes since his retirement in 1981, persists and makes it a unique institution still. Whenever he returns to the department to lecture—as he does from time to time—it is as though he has never been away.

It is as a most stimulating lecturer (*the* most stimulating!) that Wilfrid Mellers's students will most likely remember him. Now a lively octogenarian, he is much in demand as a lecturer. He is a regular contributor to the Dartington International Summer School of Music and still makes occasional visits to universities overseas. His style is animated and quickly raises the level of intellectual expectation. The range of reference is wide, the ideas are challenging, and the pace is fast. Clearly, he respects his audience. Frequent asides are a characteristic feature as he warms to a subject and further evidence or other views spring to mind to support his argument. More often than not he starts with a piece of music (preferably in live performance), exploring the paths that lead from it and revealing, along the way, alternative routes with unexpected and surprising links between them—a process which carries over into his writing. A new book, *Singing in the Wilderness: Music and Ecology in the Twentieth Century* will appear shortly, together with a revised edition of *Vaughan Williams and the Vision of Albion*. Much of his current thinking about music, however, goes into journal articles and reviews.

Wilfrid Mellers's journalism spans five decades, but although some pieces have been incorporated into books, most are no longer available in permanent and easily accessible form. This is a pity because they contain a wealth of scholarship and ideas that would be valuable to both students and general readers today. The present selection has been made largely from recent lectures and from articles written since 1980, with just a few from the 1970s. It is in these relatively short pieces of writing that we find the most direct transfer of his invigorating, dynamic style of lecturing; a style which invites us to *experience* the music—to live dangerously (he likes to remind us that the origin of 'experience' is the Latin *ex periculo*, meaning 'out of trial or peril'). As that great jazzman, Miles Davis, once remarked: "Music isn't about standing still and becoming safe".

PART ONE

MUSICAL MEANS AND MEANING

Culture, the acquainting ourselves with the best that has been known and said in the world, and thus with the history of the human spirit.

MATTHEW ARNOLD, *LITERATURE AND DOGMA*, 1873

The arts exist to fashion aesthetically compelling images of existence, of human meaning and human possibility.

PETER ABBS, *ESSAYS ON CREATIVE AND AESTHETIC EDUCATION*, 1989

Felix qui potuit rerum cognoscere causas.
Happy the person who has been able to find out the causes of things.

VIRGIL, *GEORGICS*, 490

Introduction

I N THE NORMAL COURSE OF EVENTS, IT IS DIFFICULT TO GET THROUGH A DAY
without hearing music of one kind or another. Good, bad, or indifferent,
it comes to us from loudspeakers almost everywhere we go. Yet although
the technology of recording and broadcasting may be responsible for an
increase in the variety of what we hear, the incidence of music in everyday
life, relative to the size of the population, has probably changed very little
over the centuries. Whether or not we choose to listen to it, music is *there*,
and doubtless it has been *noticeably* there ever since human beings started to
live together in communities. Curt Sachs observes that, "However far back
we trace mankind, we fail to see the springing up of music. Even the most
primitive tribes are musically beyond the first attempts."* Closer to our own
time and culture, Hogarth's engraving of 'The Enraged Musician', depicting
the frustration of a professional violinist whose practising has been inter-
rupted by the cacophony of street music outside his window—an oboe
player, a ballad seller, a boy with a drum, and a man blowing a cow's horn—
suggests that "music in the background"* was as prevalent in the 1740s as it
is in the 1990s. Although, at times, it may irritate us and we may try to ignore
it, there would appear to be no end to ways of making music and no
diminution of people's need for music. Were it to suddenly disappear ,
doubtless even those who regard themselves as *un*musical would miss it.

What, then, is it doing in our lives? Why does music persist? What does
it represent? These questions are fundamental in Wilfrid Mellers's writings, and in his thinking about the role of music in a university. His
starting point for the York music degree was the old concept of *musica
poetica*, relating text, sounds, structure, and meaning. From this, there
developed, among other things, an exploration of corporeal rhythm and
melismatic monody in the music of Carl Orff, which in turn led to an
interest in the spontaneity of children's music-making—reflected in certain of Wilfrid Mellers's own compositions, such as *The Happy Meadow*
(1964) and *Runes and Carolunes* (1967). These things relate also to his preoccupation with the social background of music—the subject of one of his
first books, *Music and Society* (1946)—evident here in reviews of books on
the origins of the Blues, the ubiquitous muzak, public music-making in
Victorian England, the instruments we've evolved for making music, and
the musicians we choose to write about. These seemingly diverse topics are
united by those same basic questions, also explored in some detail in the

opening lecture. This is not an attempt to find once-and-for-all answers—because, in the final analysis, the questions are probably unanswerable. Principally it is an affirmation of music's *revelatory* nature as it can be observed in the magical ritual of children's game-songs; the appeal to reality "not without us but in our minds"; the formal, logical processes, analogous to human life; and the mysterious marrying of words and melody. All of which reminds us that art educates: it sheds new light on age-old problems. So that when we ask what this or that music *means*—what it *is* for, or *was* for, here and now or in some distant time or place—we are also asking, "What do we learn from this?"

JP

WHAT IS MUSIC FOR?

This is a revised version of a talk—entitled 'What is music and what is it for? An address to young musicians'—given in the Music Department of the University of York on the occasion of Wilfrid Mellers's 80th birthday, 26 April 1994.

THIRTY YEARS AGO, UNIVERSITIES AND SCHOOLS ALIKE WERE ANIMATED by what was called Creativity: the arts, we believed, were not specialized pursuits but activities that almost anyone might indulge in, and sometimes did, without conscious awareness that this is what they were doing. Children, from infancy, draw, paint and model what they see out there in the world, along with what they see in the mind's eye. Slightly less immediately, they use words such as we all speak in normal converse to explore, if not define, their place in the world; and although music is a pursuit more circumscribed by conventions that have to be 'learned', it is possible to create in sound-materials on principles similarly empirical.

To this triumphant empiricism there have, as always, been adverse reactions, more or less contiguous with what we now think of as the Thatcher Years. As the pendulum has swung back, the music educators of the 1960s have been accused of undermining a sound musical grammar, substituting *ad hoc* abilities for trained skills and crafts. It is true that for the full enjoyment and experience of music, skills (some of them difficult) are essential, and that vaguely benign intentionality has sometimes been substituted for devoted work and comprehensive knowledge. Even so, though it is right that we should reinstate the 'rudiments' of music both in performance skills and in compositional craft, we should never forget that the primary impulse to creation comes from within, and that no prescriptive laws and rules, from wherever derived, can be ends in themselves. William Blake was characteristically *basic* in pointing out that 'Jesus Christ *is* the Human Imagination', and in reminding us that

> He who bends to himself a joy
> Doth the winged life destroy;
> But he who kisses the joy as it flies
> Lives in Eternity's sun rise.

So the prime incentive to excellence in any area is the awakening of the creative imagination, whether through per-form-ance—making *forms* by working things *through*—or whether through experience of already created artefacts, most though not all of which will already have stood the test of time. Only thus may one discover what music *is* and what it is *for*. We may not think, as did and do some so-called 'primitive' peoples, that without music the sun would cease to promote life, the moon to control the tides, nor can we understand why, some 26,000 years before Christ, the Chinese Emperor Chuan Hao "struck the bell and called the attention of the people, so that music could teach them righteousness".* Yet even we in Western Europe still dimly recognise that music, which may merely wile away empty time, may also, fulfilling the offices of King and Priest, reveal what we live for. Let us consider a few examples: and faced with the multiplicity of choices proffered by the musics of the wide world, we may as well start by reflecting on the three composers whom most people think of as the apex of European music: Bach, Mozart and Beethoven.

Bach, in Lutheran Germany in the early eighteenth century, defined music as "an Harmonious Euphony for the Glory of God and the Instruction of my Neighbour".* What an awe-inspiring definition, stressing music's simultaneously religious and social functions, while paying no deference at all to its capacity amiably to fill in time. The contrapuntal and architectural unity of Bach's structures, the consistency of his figurations, the regularity of his pulse themselves amount to a faith rendered audible. If Bach was in this philosophical sense 'monistic', concerned with fundamental unities, Mozart—living in late eighteenth-century Vienna, a humanistic society in process of creating what we now call democracy—was in essence dualistic. Unsurprisingly, he made operas that were imitations of human action because he believed that human actions were worth imitating; in so doing he mirrored the dualistic contradictions inherent in life-in-process, compromising between the aristocratic and the emergently democratic, between the tragic and the comic, between art and entertainment and, in technical terms, between the closed forms of the old heroic opera and the open process of the new sonata, which was concerned with growth *through* conflict. This is why he was equally distinguished as a composer of social music in theatrical terms, and as a composer of instrumental sonatas, in which conflict was interiorised within the mind. The two struggles—that in the world 'out there' and that unfolded within the psyche—were inseparable; and by the time of Austro-German Beethoven the process of interiorisation is complete. True, he created in *Fidelio* one sublime operatic imitation of human action: which turns out, however, to be a projection of the inner dualism manifest in his sonata forms, as the democratic ideal was painfully born from the disintegration of traditional notions of order. Beethoven's 'process' is religious as well as social, for his sonata forms, especially in later years, seek an undivided whole. One might almost say that for Bach music was a religious rite, for Mozart a social activity, and for Beethoven a psychological event.

Now it is patent that these three views of music's nature and purpose—originally topical and local but now so proven by intensity and durability that we call them 'universal'—all depended on a hierarchy of values. God's Law, however difficult to understand, let alone obey, was for Bach a yard-stick applicable to human behaviour. Mozart, though living in a transi-tional society, still had no doubt that private needs and public responsibilities must be interdependent if civilisation were to endure, let alone prosper. Even Beethoven, consciously a revolutionary genius, believed that his music remade the world in the interests of human better-ment, magisterially remarking that "he who truly understands this music will be free thereby from all the miseries of the world." That's a breathtaking statement, even more than Bach's "harmonious euphony for the glory of God"; and one suspects, moreover, that it is *true*—given the rub of that little adverb 'truly'. Beethoven didn't think that comprehension was easy, but he believed that, for men of good will, it was possible; and we're apt to forget how relatively large his public was: 28,000 people turned out for his funeral in his (by our standards) small city. Today only a media idol or perhaps a football star could compete.

It would seem that we have to admit that the paradox in the democratic idea is that if all people are equal *in potentia,* the concept of value becomes meaningless. A limitless plurality of values is indistinguishable from no values at all; and if we can accept no criteria established by God or State, or can ourselves formulate none that we think appropriate to absolutes like Reason, Truth and Nature, we can have little choice but to substitute for moral and ethical value the concept of Price. This concept accorded readily with the vast expansion of democracy that accrued in the wake of industrial technology, for industrialism was both a consequence of democracy and part of its cause. It made for communities that could be quantitatively, but not qualitatively, measured; both industrialized totalitarian states and capi-talist America produced such societies, and we in post-Thatcherite Britain are doing our best to catch up. Perhaps the most depressing among many depressing incidents I recall from the 1992 election campaign was a televised interview between John Major and an equally grey man in the street: wherein the Prime Minister expressed incredulous bemusement that this particular representative of Us the People seemed unlikely to support the Tory party. Why, stammered Mr Major, goggle-eyed, "don't you realise that I'll be putting down your taxes . . . just think you'll be able to . . . to BUY A NEW CAR"—and perhaps, we might add, gallivant off to Europe's then-embryonic Disneyland! Never mind that in fact Mr Major has put our taxes not down but up; never mind that Euro-Disney is losing a million and a half a day! For if there can be no criteria of value, there is no answer to Mr Major's ultimate vision of bliss; any more than there can be any refutation of the case that Bob Dylan, being politically correct, has rendered Keats obsolete. In this case Bob

Dylan happens to be a good poet: certainly a better poet than John Major is a politician. This doesn't, however, mean that such disparate phenomena as Dylan and Keats are validly comparable; for although values can never be absolute, human life depends on our behaving as though they were, or could be. If God made man in his own image, we have certainly made Him in ours; and our images, being limitlessly multifarious, can beget only confusion.

Bearing on this there's a true story about Stockhausen, who thirty years ago was perhaps the most élitist and mathematically abstruse of modern masters. Over the last twenty years, however, he has intermittently veered away from preconditioned intellectuality towards a Cage-like instinctual mysticism, even producing musical compositions that include no notated sounds, only a set of verbal instructions. In one of these works the performers are at one point instructed to "vibrate with the rhythm of the universe". At a rehearsal, the story goes, someone (probably in the back row of the second fiddles) raised a timid hand to enquire: "Please, Herr Stockhausen, how shall I *know* when I'm vibrating with the rhythm of the universe?" To which the composer-scientist-priest witheringly retorted, "*I* will tell you". Well, yes, a funny story; but, if you think about it, one with alarming implications. We know that God works in a mysterious way and we are sometimes dubious about his wonders; but can those of Stockhausen, a mere man, inspire *total* confidence?

The disintegration—indeed the deliberate dismissal—of concepts of value in our society, and therefore in its arts, has potent economic and political consequences. In the days when a composer worked, as did Bach, for an established Church, he knew what his job was and to whom he was responsible; he also knew where his living came from, if he fulfilled his obligations with reasonable competence. The same was true when a composer lived under a system of patronage by the state or by Very Important Persons willing to promote art for a variety of reasons, not excluding vainglory. Such was the position of a Monteverdi, a Mozart, even a Beethoven and a Wagner. None of these roles is readily available to a composer today, and relatively few Western composers who regard themselves as Artists support themselves solely by making artefacts. Some, somewhat grudgingly, teach; more teeter between the concert hall and the film or television studio, legitimately claiming that techniques offered by the media are a morally acceptable extension of their range, since through them they contact a more widely democratic (and politically correct) public. Others manage to reconcile artistic pretension with commercial enterprise in the field of the advertising jingle, finding justification in the anti-aesthetic 'philosophy' of an Andy Warhol, who became simultaneously an immensely successful businessman and a revered leader of an artistic avant-garde.

Today we have visual artists who earn fame and fortune by pickling sharks, or by allowing the sea to wash away a laboriously erected pillar of salt.

While one shouldn't enviously resent the material comfort afforded to artists by such literally amphibious activities, they are in sharp contrast to the plight not only of the old-fashioned Dedicated Composer, but also to the folk musician, including the jazzman. Generically, he belongs to the tribe of ethnic music-makers who, in African and Latin-American communities, are engaged not in 'high' art but in music as a functional aid to living. During the 1960s some people thought that it was philosophically nonsensical, in our technological society, that a body designated as the Scratch Orchestra should have received substantial support from an élitist Arts Council in order that unskilled people should scratch musical or unmusical sounds for their own delectation. At a more serious level one can claim that even a highly talented jazzman is a 'performance artist' who makes a 'music of necessity' for himself and his friends, rather than a maker of artefacts to be bartered in a commodity-producing market. The pop musician's status is even more ambiguous. He may be merely a money-machine, promoting daydreams that many of us—perhaps at times all of us—momently prefer to reality; alternatively he may seek fame and fortune by smashing to smithereens the 'established' world while having nothing to offer in its place. More hopefully, he may be an electrophonic compromiser who *manufactures* a fabricated 'music of necessity' as appropriate to our industrialized society as are African and Latin-American pop musics to their still-emergent communities: in which case he will have much in common with a minimalist composer like Steve Reich or Philip Glass. Progressive pop and minimalism often share the racks in record shops, for the barriers between the genres have broken down.* It is still even possible that a pop musician might—like the Beatles, Bob Dylan, Joni Mitchell, David Bowie or (at least until recently) Michael Jackson—be a money-spinning idol and at the same time an artist in the old sense, making a personal contribution more valuable than much that is esteemed in the world of Art with a capital A.

A 'dedicated composer', such as is supremely represented by Beethoven, will be preoccupied with tension between the human will and ego—his own—and the world in which he operates, including the people in it; implicitly, he wants to change us in 'expressing' *himself*. A folk or jazz musician, who makes 'music of necessity', has a different but related function: a Shetland folk fiddler, for instance, uses his bowing arm to promote energy that keeps his fellows *going*; at the same time it asks questions as to where they're going and why: so that a good folk fiddler is at once a servant of his community and the voice of its morality and conscience. The "marriage of instrument and bow"* is at once a festivity and a sacrament. Perhaps the distinction is one of degree rather than of kind; in any case it reminds us that we shouldn't too stringently categorize the categories. There is usually a reason beyond mere commercial manipulation why some of the Top Twenty stay tops: while we all know that in the élitist art world the fashionably lauded often have feet of clay. Whatever musical and social group we live in, we have to face the fact that one day the computer will make working for our living an anachronism; as a consequence of which we'll have to consider how best we may fill in the deserts of our leisure. To this there is no answer except creative activity of one kind or another: which is why, in any tomorrow music may have, amateur and professional and artistic and commercial interests must needs become ever more closely integrated. One might even say that to assist or to block this integration is to choose between life and death: which prompts me to return to the educational theme I started from, even though education, like value, has almost become a dirty word.

One of the paradoxes inherent in industrial technocracy is that, while offering opportunities for radical metamorphoses in our potential, it at the same time presents us with unwontedly efficient means of preserving the past on disc, video tape, and computer. This gives us a chance to keep our options open, safeguarding us from despair on the one hand, and from an inanely euphoric reliance on our technical expertise on the other. Although both tribal rock and minimalist musics betray their slavery to history by pretending to abolish it, we still have a chance to keep our ears, hearts, and minds open, in that order. If we do, we recognise that George Gershwin (or for that matter Leonard Bernstein or even Stephen Sondheim) is a finer composer than Andrew Lloyd Webber, both in emotional and intellectual commitment and in technical competence, though if the market were the only arbiter of excellence, Lloyd Webber ought to be the best, because richest, composer who ever lived. It is a matter of comparing like with like, not of assessing a Lloyd Webber by criteria appropriate to Bach or Beethoven. Similarly, given eager and responsible ears, we can recognise that the Beatles were 'better than' the Monkees, Duke Ellington's band 'better' than Paul Whiteman's, Beethoven better than fashionable Hummel, Mozart better than J. C. Bach, J. S. Bach better than Telemann—though in this case the burghers of Leipzig may, *at the time*, have had a point in thinking that the talented and versatile Telemann was better value for their money in that he better answered their immediate needs.

None of these value judgements can, of course, be proven; but we can modestly hazard that, looking back on the past and around at the present, we may spot what is truly *alive*, whatever category it may function in. This is the more urgent because we have produced in muzak music's embalmed and titivated corpse. For muzak is meant to be *not listened to*; as wallpaper music it serves, among many extra- or anti-musical purposes, to lower resistance to sales pressure in supermarkets, or to assuage frazzled nerves in terrorist-afflicted airports. The mind boggles at the mind-bending of which we are capable; and we're left reflecting that although all music, in so far as it orders sounds and channels experience, is in a sense propaganda, nonetheless propaganda for life is preferable to propaganda for death— such as is proffered by some heavy metal rock and perhaps by the minimalism of a Philip Glass.

Moreover, academic education in music may itself encourage rather than discourage this cult of death. A few years ago I attended a university conference on the place of music in American society. Half-hour papers were given over two days on a variety of topics, one of them being 'Parlour music in Pittsburgh between the years 1837 and 1842'. This paper consisted exclusively of a list of the titles of all the pieces known to have been played in Pittsburgh parlours during those years, the names and dates of their composers and of the performing artists, and the names and addresses of the venues wherein these events occurred. When I enquired what, roughly speaking, these musics were like—not how 'good' they were—the lecturer retorted: "That is not my concern. I am not interested in the slushy side of music".

Perhaps that was meant as a grotesque if not very risible joke; even if it was, its implications are scary indeed. For if music is merely a commodity to be quantitatively catalogued and has nothing to do with the nature and quality of living, why should we expect our children to give it a caring ear, or why should we deplore their attempts to obliterate consciousness in submitting to visual-aural electrophonic rites commercially affiliated to the drug-culture that usually accompanies them? Of course, pop music rites and festivals are not necessarily a bad thing; some of them, especially in those distant 1960s, have been profoundly as well as powerfully indicative of the fact that the times they are a-changing, and that change is both necessary and inevitable. Even so, in the complex, bewildered and bewildering world we live in, it is important that we recognise life when we see and hear it, whether in other people's artefacts or in the still small voice within our minds and senses. Whatever the nature of the experience proffered, we must attend to it wittingly, for while there is life there is hope. Since the prescription works the other way round, we may understand why the American poet A. R. Ammons* wrote, in the late 1970s, that

> our young don't believe in time as future and, so
> suffer every instant, death: they don't believe
> in the thread, plot, the leading of one thing into

another, consequence, developed change: without retrospect
or prospect, they seek the quality of experience
a moment's decision allows: thrill replaces

goal: threat lessens and fractures time, shortening
the distance to the abyss, immediate, a step away:
without calm they can't see tomorrow unfolding ...

hell is the meaninglessness of stringing out
events in unrelated, undirected sequences: remove danger
(holocaust, suffocation, poisoning) from the young and

their anxieties will unwind in long reaches of easeful seeking:
we now have a myth of Despair, and that's harder
than some other kinds of myth.

Think of those words as you perform or listen to your Bach, Mozart, Beethoven, Stravinsky, Bartók, Shostakovich, Ives, Lutosławski or whomever, not eschewing any composer, however 'light', who enhances rather than stifles the mind and senses; hang on for dear life to "the thread, the plot, the leading of one thing into another"—the qualities that balance that 'momentary thrill' with the possibility of 'goals'.

So you young people, as you go out from these cloisters into the wide and wild world, should think again about what you're doing when you make music, and why you do it. If you're likely to be a performing musician, remember that the differentiation between performing and composing musicians is of comparatively recent invention; and that performers are inevitably creators since they refashion already existent artefacts, in the process giving, to things presumptively dead, new life. We all live in and on the company of the dead, to which we all contribute—me predictably quite soon, you sooner or later.

If on the other hand you think of yourselves as composing musicians—people who put sounds together—you'll have to recognise that in our pluralistic world the mere fact of creation opens unanswered questions, for you have to decide what kind of composer you are, as a Palestrina, a Handel, or even a Beethoven didn't need to, since they all accepted criteria of what was right, whether or not it was attainable. Today, it is unlikely that you'll be able, with Schoenberg, to invent or evolve a new system or theory of composition which will settle the destiny of European music for the foreseeable future—if only because you come late enough to see that in that prognostication Schoenberg himself was simply wrong. Nor is it probable that you'll have the dazzling multifarious talents of a Stravinsky who, throughout more than half of this century, shored such fragments of the past as he could against our ruins, creating order from apparent chaos. But even if you're content to accept your lowlier status as an averagely representative composer, that still leaves an open question, for what can be representative of multifariousness? Can you still be conservative, hopefully conserving what's left of the past? Or if you are aiming to 'make' the present, which bit of it do you want to tune to? Are you an old-fashioned avant-gardist, which is a paradox? Or a new minimalist, pretending to be a city savage?—in which case your creation will overlap with some of the small savageries recreated in some brands of pop music; except that real savages know what their rites are for, whereas today's young, through no fault of their own, for the most part don't know. Perhaps, baffled, you will favour compromise, which the British are said to be partial to. Even so, 'between-worlds' composers have been more common in the New World than the Old: think of George Gershwin, reared on Tin Pan Alley, yet the creator of an opera that is not only generically grand but also great on any count, being about the plight of industrial man, whatever the colour of his skin. Or think of Duke Ellington, who didn't know whether he was an artist or an entertainer but did know that this ambiguity was his very heart. Or think of Heitor Villa-Lobos who, in distant Brazil, spawned a vast amount of music in all genres, never asking dangerous questions about Value, but satisfied so long as the music served a purpose while it lasted.

Nor are barriers between media more clearly defined than those between genres. Electrophonics have been used by Milton Babbitt and his disciples to make the most mathematically rigorous music yet invented: which has had its effect on the composers of the New Complexity, some of whose works are meant to be audibly unintelligible, and perhaps physically unperformable; whereas at the opposite pole of the New Simplicity a Górecki, a Pärt, and a Tavener go Back to Basics with a single-mindedness that may sometimes be mistaken for simple-mindedness. Yet electrophonics are natural allies of the televisual media and of Virtual Reality, which substitutes ghosts for flesh and blood. In this context, the case of Milton Babbitt is both instructive and amusing: for he, a trained mathematician, made music so complex that he came to suspect that any performance could only sully its mathematical perfection! At the same time he nurtured a passion for the escapism of early American musical comedy, and even confessed to me that he sometimes wished he'd been born as Jerome Kern! Admittedly, that was at a party, after Babbitt had given an elaborately portentous, almost impenetrable lecture about his own music. Party-wise, however, he proved an endearing companion who, when teased by me on the grounds that in being named Milton Babbitt he indeed got the best of both worlds, retorted that the full truth was far richer: "Do you know what my parents gave me for a second name? Milton Byron Babbitt"—nothing left out, moral probity and religious austerity, romantic glamour, and filthy lucre, fusing the seventeenth, nineteenth and twentieth centuries.

Well, your divisiveness is not likely to be as extreme as that; but I suspect you will, as you ask yourselves what you're doing when you make music, come to realise that to ask what music is for is to ask what human life is for—a question unanswered because it is unanswerable. Nowadays one cannot escape televisual chat-shows and discussion-groups that battle in fervour and sometimes anguish with questions as to whether or not one 'ought' to be artistically avant-garde, conservative, élitist, populist, or what-else: as though deciding on the right label is all that is necessary. In fact the label means nothing; in the immensely varied activity of today's cultural worlds, some will be good, some bad, most indifferent; inevitably one makes value-judgements in deciding what is worth one's time in any category. A telling example came up very recently when a young composer of one ilk organised a claque to boo Harrison Birtwistle's *Gawain* because it belonged to a category he disapproved of. I, who have been listening to music for around seventy years, have little doubt that within its category Birtwistle's opera is GOOD because alive and enlivening: whereas Mr X's music, on the evidence of the fragment he presented on the telly, is not so much bad as non-existent, since it is not alive except as muzak, background noise in a cocktail lounge. It is not the category or label but—as Henry James pointed out long ago—the quantity and quality of *felt life* that counts; and in deciding on that no teacher, no role-model or even prophet can make decisions for one. When I became a student more than sixty years ago choices were not as bewilderingly contradictory as they are now, but they still had to be made. In those distant days the 'right' kind of composer to be was a Schoenbergian serialist; it was good to feel that one knew all the answers. Yet that this is a dangerous belief is testified not merely by the example of Schoenberg but also, in wider contexts, by the fate of Russian communism and the horrors daily perpetrated, world-wide, in the name of religious creeds, including our own. There is only one thing more dangerous than thinking one knows all the answers, and that is refusing, because one might be wrong, to make choices or judgements at all.

In Stephen Sondheim's 1984 musical, *Sunday Afternoon in the Park with George* (inspired by the French impressionist painter Seurat), the heroine, appropriately called Dot, puts the matter neatly in saying: "I chose, and my world was shattered. So what? The choice may have been mistaken, the choosing was not". Well, all those years back I think that, for me, I was right in not choosing Schoenberg, even though one of my teachers had been a pupil of his. But I certainly made other choices that were wrong: yet also right in so far as they were an impetus to self-discovery, which is what education

24

is. We have to have the courage of our convictions, which means knowing what they are: until ultimately we do what we have to do, for better and for worse. The world goes on, rendering success or failure optional: which gives me a cue to end with another quotation from A. R. Ammons, this time his noble defence of art in his long ratiocinative poem about poetics.* A work of art, he points out, is

> symbolic representation of the ideal organization whether the cell,
> the body politic, the business, the religious
>
> group, the university, the computer, or whatever: I used to wonder
> why, when they are so little met and understood, poems [and music]
> are taught
>
> in schools: they are taught because they are convenient examples
> of the supreme functioning of the one and the many in an organization
> of cooperation and subordination: young minds, if they are to 'take
> their place in society', need to learn patience—that oneness is
>
> not useful when too easily derived, that manyness is not truthful when
> thinly selective. Assent, that the part can, while insisting on its own
> identity, contribute to the whole, that the whole can
>
> sustain and give meaning to the part: and when these things are
> beautifully—that is, well-done, pleasure is a bonus truth-functioning
> allows: that is why art is valuable: it is
> extremely valuable: also, in its changing, it pictures how organisations
> can change, incorporate innovation, deal with accidence
> and surprise, and maintain their purpose—increasing the means and
>
> insuring the probability of survival.

MT, JUNE 1994

SINGING AND DANCING IN THE UNKNOWN

Iona and Peter Opie, *The Singing Game* (Oxford: Oxford University Press, 1985)

MAGIC IS ENDEMIC IN THE EXPERIENCE OF THE CHILD WHO, A SMALL savage, resembles his primitive forebears in making song and dance to bolster the security threatened when he left the womb. Once out in the world, he sings and dances with his peers, both as an attempt to recapture his lost condition and as a means of making the unknown amenable, or at least less inimical. Erik Erikson has described children's games as "an infantile form of the human ability to . . . master reality by experiment";* and has indicated how melody and dance, usually associated with verse, provide for children a free activity outside ordinary life. Temporarily, normal life is suspended as the children enter a "sacred place" within which they play under the fixed, unalterable rules, often with disguise that separates the in-group from the world outside. In a sense, this activity is not 'serious' since it is an illusion: the very word illusion derives from *in lusione*, 'in play'. Yet in another sense it is the most significant activity there is, to the children intensely and utterly absorbing. We speak of 'playing' music; and playing children create if not 'works' of art—which can occur only when we accept the burden of consciousness unequivocally—at least 'art in process', which constitutes ceremony and fiesta. The work metaphor makes a point, in contrast to the ever-present activity of *homo ludens*.

The recovery and collation of children's singing games in Britain was initiated at the end of the last century by Lady Gomme,* who was the wife of an anthropologist and therefore eager to rescue the games from the veneer of Victorian sanctimoniousness. Since then, rescue operations have been widespread, and few would question that Iona and Peter Opie have done more than anyone to remind us if the heritage children have bequeathed and are bequeathing. Of their compilations *The Singing Game* is the finest: a model anthology. It presents the words, tunes and (usually in the children's own description) attendant actions, of about 150 games still played in Britain. The games, collected over a wide geographical area, are offered in sundry variants, with comments on mythological and historical analogies, and with an appendix to each.

Games function on at least four levels. At bottom is the Jungian archetype which children admit without the prevarications of guilt or remorse. A bit nearer the surface are survivals of the archetypes transmitted in folk plays, festivities and ballads, the stylized language of which—lily-white hands, silver cups, long golden hair—crops up, often in reference to film stars and pop stars, even in the dreariest industrial suburb. With these legendary elements meld specific historical events which seemed significant when they were contemporary, but which with the passage of time have become entangled, wildly inconsistent with chronology, and are in effect often legendary themselves: a mythical king-figure merges into historical Bonnie Prince Charlie, who has a peer in Johnny Smith who lives down the road. This brings us to the fourth level, that of here and now, in our village or street; the process works both ways, for the everyday experience of Johnny Smith is rendered magical when seen in relation to mythology and history—which it at the same time cuts down to size.

One doesn't need to look further than some of the best-known, still current, singing games to realise that they embrace most aspects—high and low, broad and deep—of human experience. Children luminously confront the facts of love and death even when they're very young, acting out 'Poor Jenny [or Mary or Sally or Sarah] lies a-weeping':

> They propped her against a bank ("She's supposed to be in a coffin"), and came back to join in the finale:
> > Now Jenny is de-ad, de-ad, de-ad,
> > Now Jenny is de-ad,
> > On a bright sunny day.
> "And now it's somebody else's turn", they said matter-of-factly.

When they're only a little older they are intuitively more aware of how delicate and precarious is the balance between creation and destruction. The mysteriously titled 'Green gravel', which so mesmerized Thomas Hardy, equivocates hauntingly between the gravel as grave and as ceremonially scattered ashes, possibly life-promoting:

> > Green gravel, green gravel, the grass is so green
> > The fairest young lady that ever was seen,
> > We'll wash her in milk, and dress her in silk,
> > And write down her name with a gold pen and inky.
> > Oh *Mary*, oh *Mary*, your true love is dead,
> > He sent you a letter to turn round your head.

Similarly, 'Wallflowers, wallflowers' seems to be a funerary rite for maidens who are "sure to die"— "Wallflowers, wallflowers, growing up so high, / We are all maidens, and we shall all die"—yet is also, having assimilated a game with the doubly aqueous title of 'Sally Waters', both a well-building and a 'well-flowering' ceremony, evoking the watery wellsprings of life. Death is symbolized by the magic circle in which the children dance, rather sedately, with their backs to the dying maiden; but the resurrection at the end, facing forwards, is spiritual renewal rather than wish-fulfilment. That the death-dance and well-blessing had separate origins only makes their marriage in the children's game more mysterious.

These games are now played almost exclusively by girls; boys are even reluctant to participate in the innumerable courtship and wedding games, of which the most widespread are 'Nuts in May' and the many rites involving (often ribaldly) cushions. Anthropologists and folklorists sound pretentious when pointing out the relationship of these games to commu-nally sanctioned matchmaking and to primitive fertility rites; yet the chil-dren must know in their minds and senses what they are doing, or they would hardly have found the games worth preserving. For 'unconscious' children, those different levels of experience coexist. In 'Oats and beans' they recognise, if not that they are prancing around in a spring festival, at least that they're involved in something strangely life-enhancing. In the related game 'The farmer's in his den' thoughtful children may be puzzled by that den; oblivious of its medieval meaning, they tend to relate it to Daniel and his lions, thereby adding a layer to the story which, if irrational, is not nonsensical.

Similarly, in playing the contest-game 'Romans and English', children might giggle or scoff at the historian's gloss that the contest is that of the Roman and Anglican Church, which is supposed to explain the reference to bread and wine; but they would have no doubt that contest between goodies and baddies is a basic human instinct which may for a while be absolved in mirth and buffoonery, as well as acted out in acrimony and vio-lence. Crazy comedy is often a child's way of dealing with things he is con-scious enough to know he cannot consciously assimilate: for instance the farcical doctors carrying out horrendous operations but usually promoting resurrections, figures shared with medieval folk drama; or the rude sexual jokes about puddings shared with the Black blues. How and when did that 'Jew from Spain' (originally 'Three Brethren out of Spain') corruptly insin-uate himself into what seems to be a simple game of courtship? What his-torical pogrom or darkly unconscious depths stain their funniness with fear, while still allowing us, slightly nervously, to laugh them off?

On the whole children have a healthy suspicion of transcendentalism. The Opies recall a little girl who, playing 'Fair Rosie' (a version of the sleeping beauty story), chanted the title with poetic relish yet didn't hold with the suggestion that the prince ought to kiss the princess awake: "Nope; we just gives 'er a shove". There's a similar deflatory element in many of the mating games; "you shall get a duke, my dear, and *you* shall get a drake" is a pun genuinely witty because unexpected. A child could invent it any day, and it would be 'modern' yet also applicable to days when dukes were Dukes, and it is perhaps related to many nun- and monk-mocking games which may—since nowadays children are indifferent to ecclesiastical hierarchies—hark back to the medieval Feast of Fools. Many nonsense refrains manage simultaneously to debunk and to open vistas. Mostly they are gibberish because they belong to an oral tradition which, in the nature of things, is bound to be 'corrupt'. A wedding game, 'Merry-ma-tansie', sung to the tune of 'Nuts in May', offers a literally enthralling instance. According to the etymologists, "merry ma tansie" is a corruption of "merry maids dancing", or of the German "Mit mir tanzen", or even of "matanza", a ceremonial pigsticking in Spain. These anthropological derivations have a cosier Glasgow complement relating them to Christian practice, if one translates "And round about Mary Matansy" as "round about Mary, matins say"; though this seems fanciful, it's true that Glasgow girls often curtsy (in homage to God's mother) instead of clumping to the ground. The poetry lies in the fact that the children know, even if etymologists don't, that these and many other 'meanings' are not mutually exclusive.

Of course, not all children's games have mythic dimensions. Many are simple action games, serving to release adrenalin; many deal with the humdrum realities of everyday life—drunken fathers and cantankerous mothers in relation to (especially) teenage girls. Some pantomime songs, such as 'Mary is a bad girl', accept the grim facts of life and death with brusque insouciance; others (therapeutically?) dramatise petty dissensions. A few are glumly educational, as the ubiquitous 'Here we go round the mulberry bush' became in Victorian times, whatever it may once have been as a tree-circling ceremony. At any level, one is left, having browsed through this book, grateful that children may still be children, notwithstanding the criminal imbecilities of the adult world: which, quite recently, wanted us to believe that the 'Ring o' roses' in the best-loved of all round games was not a holy circle of the flowers of love, but a reference to plague sores, the tishoo being the sneeze alleged to accompany the seventeenth-century disease, the falling down the ultimate declension to death. The twentieth century shows up a shade worse than the seventeenth century, whose puritanic adults, serving their monstrous god, forbade children to play games such as 'Green gravel' on the grounds that the backward-facing circle must be a witches' sabbath, conducive to licentiousness.

The tunes for these games, being of a pristine simplicity that has no need of notation, are less subject than the words to adult violation. True, a few have been aurally transmitted from notated music-hall tunes of the Victorian and Edwardian eras, and from pop songs of yesterday and today; jingles associated with Shirley Temple have hung on long after that precocious child can have any meaning to those who emulate her, and the same may soon be true of the Elvis and Beatles tunes that have percolated into childhood tradition. It is interesting that not only these once-notated importations but also the majority of traditional tunes, of uncertain antiquity and usually orally transmitted, are plain diatonic major. This indicates not so much that they are corruptions of modal originals as that the Ionian mode (equivalent to our major scale) is most apposite to childhood's childishness. Even the briefest chant has survived because it is memorable; the songs with the profoundest overtones and undertones, like 'Wallflowers', tend to have the most haunting melodies. The magical effect of the bride-song, 'Rosie apple', for instance seems to be due to the way in which the tune, at first confined within tonic, third and fifth of a major triad, opens out to waft skywards in a triad of the subdominant, to the "lily-white maid", leading her "across the water". We can see this illustrated in a marvellous action photograph, taken as late as 1968, near the gasworks at Leyland; and the book includes many such photographs, tellingly juxtaposed with reproductions of paintings or engravings of the same game performed, with astonishing equivalence, by children and young people at various times from the Middle Ages onwards, in various places throughout Europe and America. The production of the book is worthy of the text and illustrations, paper and print being of fine quality, the music engraving exceptionally elegant. This wonderful book is cheap—a mere £15 for more than 500 pages of intellectual stimulation and emotional delight. All praise, in ascending order of merit, to the Oxford University Press, the Opies and the children: who, being products of fallen Adam, may be greedy, grasping and grabbing, but who—as Gavin Ewart puts it—"do speak true, what they feel they certainly show / They're not divine – but they're not hypocritical swine".

TLS, NOVEMBER 1985

HIGHER SATISFACTION IN SYDENHAM
THE CRYSTAL PALACE AND THE RE-CREATION OF
THE HANDELIAN MUSICAL IDEAL

Michael Musgrave, *The Musical Life of the Crystal Palace*
(Cambridge: Cambridge University Press, 1995)

THE CRYSTAL PALACE WAS BUILT IN HYDE PARK IN 1851 TO HOUSE PRINCE Albert's visionary project for a Great Exhibition of the Victorian age's power and glory in scientific invention and industrial achievement. The building itself provided evidence of that power and glory, the more so because it was erected in seven months, two months inside its deadline. Statistical quantification is unavoidable; as Michael Musgrave informs us in this intelligent piece of social history, the Palace had "a ground size of 1,848 feet long by 408 feet wide; a transept of 72 feet wide by 108 feet high; and a total of 293,655 panes of glass weighing over 400 tons—a building of unique size and shape". It was designed by Joseph Paxton, not a professional architect but head gardener at Chatsworth House, and therefore an expert on greenhouses. Over six million visitors from all over the world congregated at the Exhibition (a daily average of 43,000); so remarkable was its success that, although the Palace had been intended to last merely for the duration of the Exhibition, it was immediately decided that a permanent version should be erected on the modest heights of Sydenham, in south London. Paxton's original plans were ingeniously adapted, and the scheme completed in two years.

Although the Crystal Palace was not a musical enterprise, ceremonial occasions and commercial display called for musical support, and a musical director was appointed in the person of Sir Michael Costa, conductor of the Sacred Harmonic Society, the biggest choral institution in the capital. Brass bands and choirs of six or seven hundred provided fanfares, patriotic pageants, and national anthems; famous opera singers were introduced at numerous galas. Almost fortuitously, these circumstances led to the Palace becoming a centre for choral music.

In effect, this also meant a centre for the music of Handel, who, 140 years previously, had been given the sack by his Hanoverian court employers, on the grounds of his too frequent absences abroad. He sought succour in a Hanoverian home-from-home in London. Artistic ambition fused with business enterprise, for his aim was to sell Italianate opera to Britain's rising middle class. While seeking patronage from the English nobility, Handel also established himself in the commercial market, producing his operas in city theatres, to Italian libretti, with imported Italian singers. For some years, Handel's Italian and English veins of influence flowed collaterally; gradually, he abandoned Italian opera in favour of English oratorio, preserving the conventions of *opera seria* but taking his themes from the Old Testament—the one book the English middle class knew intimately—while giving to the chorus a far more substantial role than it had enjoyed in Italian opera. Although infrequently staged, Handel's oratorios were usually presented in theatres, not churches.

Unlike Bach in his Passions, Handel in his oratorios is not so much a religious composer as a music-theatrical moralist. The position occupied by *Messiah*, the most loved and lauded of the oratorios, is inseparable from the fact that it is the only one that takes its text from the New Testament and the Book of Common Prayer as well as from the Old Testament. Significantly, it soon came to be associated with charitable causes, especially the dolefully titled 'Society for Decay'd Musicians'; it is also the least operatic of Handel's oratorios, in that it is built around the chorus, and has no defined characters among its soloists—no regal potentates or tyrants—and tells no story, though that of Christ is enclosed within it.

Messiah proved congenial to the humanitarian ideals of Prince Albert in Victorian England because the music's melodic appeal, metrical simplicity, tonal stability, and ceremonial nobility ensured that, although not intended for performance by massed choirs and instruments, it could be thus presented, as Bach's church music could not. This is why *Messiah*—and a few other pieces, such as *Israel in Egypt*, that were ostensibly public in reference to imperial ambition—became the staple diet of the Handel Festivals celebrated at the Crystal Palace from 1857 onwards, at first under Costa's enthusiastic direction. Controlling choruses of thousands—along with orchestras in which Handel's modest forces were multiplied and reinforced by batteries of percussion and several instruments unknown to Handel or his age—can hardly have conduced to subtlety. Yet the visceral thrill of the sound might justifiably be called sublime, and was certainly relished by the Festival audiences, which were far more democratically constituted than those for Handel's operas. The number of seats available, and the demand for them, meant that prices stayed low.

Costa's talents were those of a charismatic and intelligent circus ringleader, rather than a profound musician. If the Festivals were to survive and develop, however, they called for an energy and application capable of serving both the demands of popular taste and of the music. Costa's successor, Sir August Manns, was ideally suited to the post, for, trained as a military bandsman, he had, as Musgrave puts it, "very sound musicianship, wide experience and total commitment to a vision of the musical possibilities of the Palace". If he never ranked as a conductor alongside Richter or von Bülow, he was nevertheless a fine disciplinarian, who insisted on dedicated rehearsal; his performances, at least in the repertory he understood, seem to have been remarkable for their quasi-electrical charge, as well as their precision. He re-created the Handelian ideal for the British middle class, to their advantage and to his own, in that thousands of people enjoyed the composer's music who had previously been ignorant of or indifferent to it. Mann also established a permanent orchestra, dedicated to the performance of the Teutonic classics on which he, as a German, had been nurtured. He moulded much of the repertory still current in our concert halls; in particular, he persuaded British audiences to relish Beethoven's 'progressive' symphonies and introduced them to works by Schubert, Schumann, Mendelssohn, and Brahms. German hegemony was occasionally dented by performances of French music, especially that of Berlioz, in whose dynamism Manns may have recognized a kindred spirit, and to whose *Grande Messe des Morts* he ungrudgingly accorded the 'Babylonian' forces Berlioz had dreamt of. Modernists like Liszt and Wagner, and eventually Richard Strauss, were discreetly admitted, and Manns generously supported new British music by, for instance, Sterndale Bennett, Sullivan, Hamish MacCunn and—since Manns was agreeably sympathetic to the feminist cause—Ethel Smyth. Nor did Manns neglect concert performances of operas, both in the original language and in translation; while he further established a tradition, still not wholly extinct, of performing operatic 'excerpts' with international singers accompanied by the local orchestra. Celebrity recitals attracted artists (particularly pianists and violinists) from Europe and America, a few of whom (notably Busoni) presented tough programmes. More representative of the Palace were the regular recitals on the mammoth 'Handelian Organ'—so styled, but in fact anti-Handelian in its construction. These were pot-pourri programmes with a number of stunt pieces, some of them not far from farmyard imitations. Concerts of light orchestral music in the manner of the Boston Pops were equally well received.

But Manns's Crystal Palace regime also encouraged what Musgrave calls "a broader educational dimension". Plans for a well-staffed conservatory for the young sowed the seeds for the Royal College of Music, while a more general approach to 'musical appreciation' was initiated by Sir George Grove, who wrote the first ever programme notes for the 'serious' concerts. Tonic solfa and the brass band movement were alike directed at people of limited literacy who had learned that they might yet display technical prowess in musical performance, and thereby share in the 'higher satisfactions' of which Prince Albert believed them capable and worthy. During the last decades of the century, signal advances were made both in the quality of musical performance in Britain, and in the public's response to it; enhanced refinement in the audiences' taste developed in tandem with the drive to popularise the classics. In these transitional years, this interaction of 'higher' education with conscious vulgarization sometimes led to bizarre effects somewhere between tragedy and farce.

Having begun with a reference to quantification in the Palace's cult of the colossal, it seems appropriate to close with a reference to the Grand Salvation Army Festival of 1891, which featured

the biggest band in the world, comprising 10,000 of brass, concertinas, and tambourines, selected from Belfast, Kilmarnock, Pentre, London, South Shields, Northampton, Bristol, Brighton and Norwich. The effect was far more stupendous and magnificent than had ever been heard before, and we see how by the grace of God a vast force is spreading all over the country to bear on the wings of music the message of Salvation.

Today, we are apt to claim that small is beautiful; to be mistrustful of moral improvement, let alone salvation. Yet was Sir Thomas Beecham quite on the mark when, the Palace having been destroyed by fire in 1936, he called the event "the end of an era"? Though the Palace had declined in social and musical importance since its heyday, the "message of Salvation" purveyed by the Salvation Army Festival surely contained a kernel of truth. The Palace's campaign of musical and educational advancement achieved a great deal; Beethoven, Mendelssohn, and Brahms are still with us, even though our contemporary composers are, ironically, less flourishing. Perhaps we need a new Crystal Palace with which to confront the approaching millennium.

TLS, MARCH 1996

IN THE MOOD

Joseph Lanza, *Elevator Music: A Surreal History of Muzak, Easy-listening and Other Moodsong* (London: Quartet, 1995)

W E IN THE WESTERN WORLD, AT LEAST SINCE THE RENAISSANCE, TEND to identify music, although it is the most abstract of the arts, with identity itself—with personal fulfilment. It also has social implications, since most identities live in societies, veering between the extremes of a Handel, a public composer who explored rather than denied private differences, and a Beethoven, an aggressive identity who none the less believed that his art could and should have (beneficial) public consequences. Yet this view of music, notwithstanding its centrality to us, is a relatively recent notion, restricted to a comparatively small area of the globe. In most so-called primitive societies, and in the great oriental cultures, music has been concerned not so much with identity as with identification, providing a continuum within which individual identities seek oneness with the tribe and with nature, the unchanging backcloth to our ephemeralities. Today, when Western 'consciousness' is regarded with increasing scepticism, political correctness extols the identifiers at the expense of the identities: as is evident in this book, which claims that the media people who link art unequivocally with commerce offer a life alternative to the West's long nurtured and much-vaunted 'consciousness'. In this sense, muzak is our 'music of necessity', though the term needs defining with a precision greater than that displayed in Joseph Lanza's lively prose.

In a preludial section of *Elevator Music*, Lanza surveys what, more than sixty years back, Constant Lambert called "the appalling popularity" of music in our century.* Since those days, background music has become foreground: "avant garde sound installations permeate malls and automobile show-rooms, quaint piano recitals comfort us as we wait in banklines, telephone technotunes keep us complacently on hold, brunch Baroque refines our dining pleasures, and even synthesized 'nature sounds' further blur the boundary between our high-technic Platonic caves and real life". All this, Lanza reminds us, was prophesied more than half a century ago in satirical utopian books by Aldous Huxley and George Orwell; but he also points out that there is nothing new under the sun, since Sir Francis Bacon, in his non-satirical Renaissance utopia, had prefigured today's Disneylands and theme-parks in describing "perspective houses representing all colorations of light, all delusions and deceits of figures, magnitudes, motions, colours and demonstrations of shadows"—and conveying, moreover, "sounds in trunks and pipes, in strange lines and distances".

35

In another introductory skirmish, Lanza reviews concepts that emerged both within and in reaction to then current artistic traditions; notably Hindemith's *Gebrauchsmusik*, which tried to define music's utilitarian functions in the industrial environments of the 1920s; and Satie's *musique d'ameublement*, which countered Wagnerian egomania and Debussyan introversion with 'furniture music', tunefully metrical and blessedly predictable, to be eaten to and chattered through—music appropriate alike to factories and to the deserts of our leisure. The purpose of Hindemith's and Satie's musical commodities was not, however, to dethrone the self, but rather to admit that much of modern life was routine behaviourism, which allowed no scope for self-probing. Factory conditions, music while you work, the war effort, evolved in duo with radio and the record industry, abetting the evolution of wallpaper or elevator music that was meant to be *not listened to*—an ear-boggling mind-manipulation to which, thirty years later, John Cage made a devastating riposte in his 'silent' piece, *4'33"*.* In this non-composition a pianist sits at a keyboard for the designated period of time, producing from his instrument not a single sound. The 'purpose' of this non-activity turns out to be precisely the opposite of that of muzak, since the audience, confronted by silence, finds itself listening with unwonted intensity; and begins to create, from what isn't 'really' silence, its own patterns of sound, heard and half-heard among the amorphous aural occurrences of the world. Far from muffling our ears, Cage's joke, if that's what it is, syringes them, enabling each of us democratically to become his or her own composer.

The main sections of Lanza's book are devoted to a chronological survey, always effervescent and often amusing, of muzak's sundry ear-mufflings, beginning with the engineering mastermind who made piped music feasible, George Owen Squier. Now a generic term, Muzak was originally the name of the first commercial firm to patent the product; a March 1939 issue of *Newsweek* boasted that the firm served 360 businesses, a figure that increased to well over 1,000 over the next five years. The big musical names of the industry, some of them still surviving, emerged during those halcyon days: for instance, the syrupy late-romantic strings that tugged at the heartstrings in Percy Faith's *Music by Faith*; Paul Weston's *Music for Sleeping, Dreaming and Smoking to*; or Jackie Gleason's *Lush Life* of "Music, Martinis, and Memories". Capping them all, and still addicted to soaring and sobbing strings, the globally operative Mantovani succeeded in pleasing, not the twenty-five per cent who liked classical music, nor the twenty-five per cent who adored the Beatles, but the fifty per cent in the middle, in the process mating business acumen with streamlined technical expertise. Complementarily, André Kostelanetz sanitized the pop classics in a way he compared to cheap colour prints that "enabled millions to see, enjoy and own fine repro-ductions of paintings by Renoir and Degas". The scrabble for pecuniary reward may, in some of the earlier and more naive promoters of muzak, have been to a degree modified by a certain missionary zeal—and not merely in the 'Gregorian cocktail' of sometimes wordless amplified choral groups that marketed a fusion of churchy sentiment with family sentimen-tality, offering balm to folk who, not necessarily in a discreditable sense, knew what they wanted and wanted what they knew. This could also happen in unabashedly secular contexts, such as Laurence Welk's bubbly *Champagne Music*, though not in the hyper-sophisticated and technically dazzling concoctions of Nelson Riddle, who fused soothing strings with the bland eupepticisms of commercialized jazz. Cocktail-lounge piano trav-elled a similar course, from a tinkling of the ivories a long way 'after' Fats Waller to the grotesque show-business of Liberace.

Gradually, muzak closed the gap between art and commercial tech-nology. The *101 Strings* functioned (and still function) on principles pre-cisely analogous to advertising, 'producing', for instance, a series of sound-capsules of Foreign Travel as we the people increasingly holiday abroad—a music literally synthesized from "Hollywood-Broadway stock-piles of colour-treated sunsets, papier mâché pyramids, and Polystyrene Parthenons . . . letting it all stand out in all the theme-park charm imagined by second generation immigrant offspring". The technical virtuosity mani-fest in these evocations of the world-as-cliché is undeniably impressive; and it is only a step from here to the Virtual Reality promulgated by the Mystic Moods Orchestra, which calls on advanced technology to meld musical sounds with the noises of the world 'out there', so that we don't always know what is real and what is illusory. Lanza recounts a silly-sad anecdote of a Mystic Moods disc which, played by a man hoping to seduce a young woman, backfired because an intrusive 'natural' sound caused the girl con-federate or victim to collapse in a fit of the giggles. Illusion may be perilous, the trouble with Virtual Reality being that it substitutes spooks for human flesh and blood. This applies still more when the 'Sex behind the Gauze' musically savoured by the *101 Strings* and the Mystic Moods Orchestra begins to be superseded by phenomena like Space-Age Bachelor-Pad Music, in which 'musical' sounds exist mainly to put the hi-fi equipment through its paces, so that the medium is the non-message. Of course a lot of New Age music ('Violins from Space', 'Elevator Noir') claims to deal in rediscovered spiritual or magical realms remote from entertainment and industry; the famous score for television's *Twin Peaks* series owed much of its appeal to qualities shared with Górecki's Third Symphony, a 'serious' classical work that, to its composer's amazement, attained a fabulous commercial success on the charts, perhaps because it got the best of both worlds in being serene, super-natural, yet 'about' the dire reality of the Holocaust. Lanza justifiably queries how far such 'spiritual' experiences are radically distinct from the Easy Listening of the 101 Strings, or even of faithful Percy Faith.

Brian Eno's elevation of Airport Music, Mall Music, Freeway Music and the like to an electrophonic pseudo-art may be comparably a cheat; and that Lanza doesn't commit himself on such matters explains why his book, though incidentally fascinating and factually illuminating, confuses the reader about its 'message'. It seems to equate muzak with the physical music of necessity used by primitive peoples when they dance and sing, to propitiate the gods, and thereby to encourage the sun to persist in its diurnal cycle, the moon to control the tides. It even hints that muzak may release us from temporality in ways collateral with the meta-physical musics of ancient India or China, not to mention medieval Christian chant; more justifiably, it suggests that some jazz and pop music, in borrowing techniques from Bach, may betray an experiential, if hardly philosophical, affinity with him. Even so, the crux that Lanza never confronts is the profit motive. When 'savages' sing and dance, when 'civilized' worshippers engage in audible ritual, their purpose is, strictly speaking, disinterested and non-commercial, if not necessarily non-utilitarian. There is surely a difference between the heavens evoked by Gregorian chant or Bach and those evoked by Mantovani or the Mystic Moods Orchestra; and although one cannot define that difference without making value-judgements such as are currently discounted, it is none the less inescapable that, in the absence of such judgements, Lanza's argument carries little weight.

On his final page he asserts that "elevator music (besides being just good music) is essentially a distillation of the happiness that modern technology has promised". One up for modern technology; but what does Lanza mean by his phrase "just good music"? If he means good because technically proficient, that will pass, for much of this music displays remarkable technical ingenuity, and even care, in realizing its sometimes dubious ends, and is, moreover, usually played by top-notch professionals who think they deserve a share in the lolly. Yet it's difficult to credit that music deliberately dedicated to amnesia and to 'manufactured' feelings can be 'good' in the sense usually applicable to art, which makes us more rather than less aware of the nature of ourselves and of the world we inhabit. Perhaps one might claim that muzak promotes the Good Life among the Beautiful People: but few of us will make that grade nor, if we did, would we know what to do with our fleet of Rolls-Royces, convoy of yachts, and drawer-full of diamond-studded wrist watches, mouldering in elegant mansions scattered over the pleasanter areas of the earth. We'd have to come back to the amount of 'felt life' (Henry James's expression) we'd achieved within ourselves, to which 'good' music testifies. For this reason, I suspect that although improbable millions of people have bought discs of the *101 Strings*, muzak hasn't changed us radically. Those who need dreams as escape—which means many of us all the time and most of us some of the time—will continue to relish such evasions, without doing much harm to anyone except possibly themselves; those people who are musically aware (including of course you and me) will welcome dreams and even nightmares as aids to maturation, but will tend to develop imperviousness to, even obliviousness of, muzak *per se*. I don't think I 'hate' or feel 'fury' over muzak, as Lanza thinks musicians of my ilk (educated, professional, even—dread word—academic) are prone to. Since the subject of this review seems to have elicited so unseemly a plethora of inverted commas, I nearly put them around the word musicians in the above sentence. That would have been the ultimate betrayal, from which I rescued myself in the nick of time.

TLS, JULY 1995

COMPOSERS' THOUGHTS

Victor Zuckerkandl, *Man the Musician*
(Princeton: Princeton University Press, 1973)

D R BURNEY, GRAND PANJANDRUM OF EIGHTEENTH-CENTURY MUSIC, defined his art as "an Innocent Luxury, unnecessary indeed to our Existence, but a great Improvement and Gratification of the Sense of Hearing". The definition was inadequate even to conventional eighteenth-century practice, which so elaborately codified music's 'affective' properties; it would have appalled Bach, for whom music was "for the glory of God and the instruction of my neighbour", and would no less have horrified Beethoven, who rightly believed that his music was a moral force capable of changing the world. Even if one leaves out of account men of genius it would seem, from the evidence of history, that there must be a sense in which music *is* necessary to our existence. In what, then, does music's 'necessity' consist? *Man the Musician*, by a Viennese refugee who taught in the United States from 1940 until his death in 1965, is a courageous attempt to provide an answer. It could have been written only by a trained musician who was also reasonably proficient in philosophy, mathematics, psychology, and the physical sciences. Not surprisingly, the breed is rare.

Man the Musician is the second volume of a work entitled *Sound and Symbol*. In the first volume, published in 1956, Victor Zuckerkandl outlined "not so much a philosophy *of* music as a philosophy *through* music".* Starting from the basic properties of sound, he arrived at a set of concepts that would help us to understand the world and our place in it, these concepts being remarkably similar to some of the concepts behind modern science. The present volume starts not with the world but with us: and specifically with the fact of music's universality referred to above. That all peoples have needed music suggests that it must have human attributes; if it is a language, what kind of language is it? So Zuckerkandl begins with a distinction between language as speech and the language of musical tones. Speech defines separateness, the I-and-he or the I-and-it; music concerns togetherness, and in savage societies and peasant communities is the natural expression of the group. The musical 'treatment' of words in folksong suggests that music provides a solvent of the boundaries between the self and others; and Wittgenstein was off the mark in saying, "what we cannot speak we cannot consign to silence". On the contrary, what we cannot speak we sing about. But the otherness of tones does not belong to an *other* world. Speaking, rational man (Zuckerkandl does not include the poet in this category) complements apparently irrational singing man. One does not supersede the other.

40

So Zuckerkandl discounts the often canvassed theory that the magical precedes the mythical stage in man's story, the two stages being epitomized respectively in the ear and the mouth. He rather holds that music originated in the *loss* of magic: and that in so doing it prevented the world from being entirely transformed into language (becoming nothing but object), while at the same time it prevented man from becoming nothing but subject. When everything namable, including God, has been named, there remains "a void to be filled, a darkness to be lit". Music answers the question that language cannot answer.

The author then turns from the abstract to the audible, calling on Gestalt psychology to explore the ways in which we hear music. He finds this a valid starting-point because Gestalt analytical techniques demonstrate that it is not ratios of pitch and duration that we hear in music, but relationships of tonal direction and tension. None the less he considers Gestalt theory inadequate because what takes place when we hear music cannot be assessed in terms of past, present and future. In listening to music we are flowing *with* time, and are aware of past and future only as characteristics of a moving present. The Gestaltists cannot grasp music's structure except by invoking recollection and anticipation. They "fail to account for the extraordinary fact that the ear receives dynamic tone qualities directly, as forces in action, and interprets their meaning at the same time".

As Gerard Manley Hopkins put it, "Meaning motion fans my wits with wonder and awe". In the temporal aspects of music, a law governing life becomes audible, for musical motion is "freedom in prospect, necessity in retrospect". Tones do not 'stand for' emotion but are themselves *in* emotion, which is that of the tones. The art of hearing is itself an art of feeling (of being in emotion) and of understanding (perceiving the dynamic qualities of the tones). A piece of (good) music is a "meaningful entity of tones because its deep structure is organic in the exact biological sense of the term. To hear a composition is therefore directly to perceive organic structure; the act of hearing is itself organic."

Zuckerkandl pays tribute to Heinrich Schenker, whose methods of analysis, unlike conventional academic techniques, demonstrate how music functions organically; and can therefore indicate why (for instance) the tune of Schubert's 'Forelle' is more humanly fulfilling than a modern pop tune that superficially resembles it. It would seem that the 'inspiration' of Schubert's melody is inseparable from what is normally called thought; and both inspiration and thought co-exist not merely in a self-contained tune like Schubert's, but also in compositions, such as a Palestrina motet, in which there is no evident 'theme' at all.

Following this argument, Zuckerkandl analyses a sequence of Preludes

41

from Bach's 'Forty-eight', in one of which there is theme and extension, whilst in others there appears to be only figuration, possibly triggered off by the behaviour of the hands at a keyboard. Physiological factors may apply to the composer's 'hand' in the way they more obviously do to the hand of painter or sculptor; certainly, in the behaviour of Bach's figuration something is brought forth,

> something is done, something is made, but this doing consists in thinking. This thinking is not that of a man who acts, this doing is not that of a man who thinks. Doing and thinking are wholly fused into one ... Not existence on the one hand and thinking about it on the other, but a thinking that by itself creates existence.

Something similar happens in a large-scale structure such as Mozart's G minor Symphony wherein—in contrast to the continuous extension of Bach's figurative polyphony—dynamic events occur. For the dramatic implications of the first movement are inherent in a small musical accident that transforms the initial rising arpeggio by a semi-tonic intrusion. 'Accident', if that is what it is, here equals inspiration, and Mozart's genius is to have revealed the accident's profound consequences. He helps the theme along, uncovers its destiny.

Like the mathematician, the musician deals in ratio and relation, for neither tones nor numbers exist independently of their construction into a system. But although the musician's thinking cannot be other than logical and rational, he does not think conceptually; and thinking about musicians' thinking may suggest a fresh approach to the general problem of thought. What, Zuckerkandl asks, is implied by Chopin's failure (reported to us by George Sand) to get 'right' a tiny passage in one of his Preludes? Clearly there can have been no question of deficient craftsmanship in connexion with a not particularly abstruse progression; how, then, did Chopin know that something was wrong?

This question is meaningless, since Chopin could not answer it himself; so Zuckerkandl proceeds to a similar case, which the composer succeeded in answering. The manuscript of Schubert's 'Wasserflut' proves that the wonderful ending was literally an afterthought. The first version which, though erased, is clearly visible in the manuscript was perfectly adequate to the tune's premises; but the second version is sublime, and is so because— as Schenkerean analysis can demonstrate—it is a fulfilment of the tones' struggle to reach and transcend the octave: a musical synonym for the controlled agony of the words. The emended version is demonstrably an afterthought: so what becomes of a dichotomy between inspiration and thought?

The most impressive demonstration of the interrelationship of musical thought and inspiration is, however, provided by Beethoven's sketch-books: from which Zuckerkandl chooses the A flat Adagio from opus 127 for detailed consideration. This celestial, apparently effortless, melody was evolved by Beethoven only after prodigies of mental labour; and the verb 'evolve' would seem to be no mere metaphor. The process seems to have taken place independently of the composer's will or imagination; or rather he assisted at the theme's birth with what Teilhard de Chardin, referring to biological process, called a *tâtonnement dirigé.** So,

the domain of music appears rather close to that of nature, where forms similarly germinate, grow and mature. The only difference is that plants and animals, upon reaching maturity, generate others of their kind and die, whereas works of art reproduce themselves by coming alive again each time we experience them . . . When the composer seeks guidance from the tones, he seeks guidance in his own thinking: he thinks not only in tones but out of tones. A tonal pattern, a work of music—they stand before us wholly the product of human thought . . . Conceptual thinking is cognitive, its purpose to add to our store of knowledge. Musical thinking is productive, its purpose to add to our store of reality.

It follows that the closest analogy to the functioning of a musical composition such as Beethoven's opus 127 is the functioning of an individual human life:

we act as we do because we are what we are; we become what we are because we act as we do. The process is a gradual one of progression from amorphous beginnings towards ever more sharply defined forms and is complete only when the last step has been taken. A man's death, then, might be compared to the birth of a melody— to the moment when it has ceased to 'grow' and enters actual existence . . . Musicality is not an individual gift, but one of man's basic attributes . . . In music, man does not give expression to something (his 'feelings', for example), nor does he build autonomous structures: he *invents himself*. In music, the law by which he knows himself to be alive is realized in its purest form.

Presumably it is to be inferred that some lives are 'better than' others, just as Schubert's song is more integrated and fulfilled than that of a hack. But questions of value are ultimately insoluble and irrelevant; one can demonstrate only degrees of 'livingness', and this Zuckerkandl does in masterly fashion. He provides musical evidence to back up insights that have previously come only from non-musicians such as Susanne Langer, the philosopher, and Lévi-Strauss, the anthropologist; and the most persuasive evidence to support his theories is that provided by practising musicians, whether they be composers or interpreters. A good string quartet, performing Beethoven's opus 127, will intuitively reveal the organic structure without need of Schenkerean demonstration; but that they know, in blood and bones, heart and mind, how music lives and breathes does not render Zuckerkandl's book redundant. Our post-Renaissance world demands to know *why*, as well as instinctively to know. That being so, it is important that theory should square with practice.

Zuckerkandl offers an account of music's meaning that—perhaps for the first time—makes sense in terms of our experience as music-making human creatures. This must be why his book is strangely moving, rather in the same way as is a work of art! All the more reason to be grateful to Norbert Guterman whose translation—as will be evident from this review's copious quotations—remains elegantly lucid even, or especially, when the argument is most tortuous.

TLS, MARCH 1974

MAKING SPIRITUAL CONTACT

Mark W Booth, *The Experience of Song*
(New Haven & London: Yale University Press, 1981)

I T WOULD SEEM THAT NO PEOPLE KNOWN TO HISTORY, NOT EVEN THE MOST
barbarous, has been without the satisfaction or solace of song: a form,
perhaps, of self-expression and/or communication that predates speech,
since it can exist without benefit of words. This being so, it is curious that the
phenomenon of song has been so little investigated. Why do we sing? What
kind of activity is it? Is it different in kind from anything that may be offered
by words or music *per se*? In this book Mark Booth bravely approaches these
questions head on. Though he produces no definitive answers to them, and
in some cases such answers may not be possible, he none the less uncovers
some of the deepest springs of human behaviour; and leads us to speculate
as to why such enquiry has been so long delayed. Perhaps literary folk have
been too doubtful of their proficiency to comment on musical matters,
while musicians have, as so often, been wary of a presumed threat to what
they erroneously consider the autonomy of their art.

Mark Booth doesn't approach his theme from the standpoint of a musician but proves that for the most part he has no need to. He opens with a
theoretical chapter which defines the fundamentals of song as oral communication, starting from the pioneer work on epic ballad by Milman Parry
and Albert Lord.* Folk and other types of primitive song offer a low density
of information, since that is not the main function of song. As soon as he
sings, man embarks on an activity that carries him beyond mere personal
expression; when his words become music—even in the most rudimentary
incanted and enchanted form of the reiteration of a single pitched tone, or
the alternation of two pitches—he enters a different dimension. His purpose is no longer only, or even mainly, to convey a message: on the contrary,
song tends to deny linear and temporal progression and to put the singer
into communion with something other than himself, whether it be called
God or the community or his immediate friends or his children. In primitive song, indeed, words are often replaced by magical or nonsensical voca-
bles, as is evident from such disparate folk as waulking women in the Outer
Hebrides or horse-breaking Amerindians on the Southern Plains. All forms
of oral song use repetition, refrains, hollers and borrowings from previously established songs in order to enforce a togetherness that to some
degree effaces self; all oral songs depend upon living within given assumptions, while being at the same time outside them. Different *données* are
evolved for different kinds of song, from ritual incantation to folk ballad,

from courtly song to art song, from country song to soul and gospel and glossy pop. All types operate by virtue of their conventionalism. When conventions have outworn their social or magical meaning we call them clichés, though they may still have a limited efficacy.

These considerations apply even to what appear to be, and in a sense are, 'protest' songs, which seem to oppose rather than to ballast conformity. Bob Dylan, castigating the social conditions that have produced the plight of suicidal Hollis Brown, invites us to join with him in pointing an accusing finger at the off-stage villains of the piece: "The more vigorously such songs declare lonely alienation, the better they function as rituals of solidarity in an accepted state of mind." Intelligently enough, Booth rounds off his preludial section by reference to Zuckerkandl's great book *Sound and Symbol*, which profoundly explores the nature of song as self-transcendence. "The singer who uses words wants more than just to be with the group: he also wants to be with things, those things to which the words of the song refer . . . Tones remove the barrier between person and thing, and clear the way for what might be called the singer's participation in that which he sings." Both singer and audience, if there is one, become the song; and the central substance of Booth's book demonstrates this by way of detailed analysis of songs of widely varied character and calibre. In the course of the analyses some important if speculative insights are revealed: notably the suggestion that whereas speech and, by corollary, written verse or prose are a linear process existing in time, song is not a process but a state, by its very nature circular and atemporal. This is patently the case with incantations, most folk songs and many pop songs of contemporary vintage, all of which either have no intelligible words or, even in telling stories, employ circular refrains and jumble temporal sequence, obliterating barriers between chronometric and mythological time. Booth suggests that this is true of the more efficacious art songs also.

His first subject for analysis is, appropriately, the most celebrated of medieval songs, 'Sumer is icumen in'. This combines a folk-like ditty in English with a learned commentary in Latin, musically complemented by a synthesis of monophonic artlessness with polyphonic artfulness which has commonly if inaccurately been considered unique. The mnemonic alliteration in the English verse has musical implications reflected in the guileless tune, on which some modest musical commentary would not have come amiss. One might say the same of the discussion of 'The holly and the ivy' as a game-and-dance song; Booth is on the mark in revealing the ambiguous social-sexual burden of the song, but might have demonstrated how the nature of the tune and the gestures of the dance (in so far as we can recreate them) palliate these ambiguities. Most revealing is the in-depth

analysis of 'The bitter withy', on the basis of which Booth reaches the conclusion that

the dependence of singing on right-hemisphere (brain) activity sheds light on the
nature of songs as marriages of music and words and also on the nature and function of the patterns in addition to music that have been discovered binding oral
compositions. 'Time-independent', 'appositional', and 'Gestalt' as characterizations
of the right hemisphere, the part of the brain on which song primarily depends,
indicate that the binding of song words into patterns above the flow of discursive
syntax is what distinguishes song and related phenomena from speech.

No less acute is the next chapter, on an art-song, Campion's 'I care not
for these ladies'. It has long been recognised that the richness of Elizabethan
culture involves an interrelationship of courtly grace with folksy virility, but
this is by far the most impressive demonstration of how the interrelationship works in the context of a specific sung poem. The account of the
delightful poem is totally persuasive—more so than John Irwin's recent,
admirable and far more exhaustive analysis of 'Now winter nights enlarge'.
Despite the artifice of the artefact, Booth convincingly relates the poem to
his central theme: wanton Amaryllis is always available and accommo-
dating, unlike the fine ladies who may be occupied with other men and
other events, at another place and time. They live in time, aware of "what is
past and passing and to come", whereas Amaryllis is song-like in living in
the existential moment. She is the folk element, they the literate; and this
links up with a discussion of songs as commodities and with the general
implications of commodity in Elizabethan literature. Such musical backing
as Booth gives to his argument is accurate, though more would have been
welcome. The relationship between Campion's highly 'conscious' artifice
both as poet and as composer and the 'instinctive' folk utterance here represented by Amaryllis is a fascinating subject, little explored but by no
means impervious to analysis.

The remaining chapters return to 'popular' as distinct from 'art' songs,
though their popularity is now inseparable from their status as commodities. The discussion of 'The Description of a Strange Fish', now a broadside
ballad, is a point where orality and literacy meet. "Defined as it is by bought
printed words to be processed by the left hemisphere and a familiar tune to
be recalled out of the right, it represents a long intermediate stage of mental
accommodation." The main purpose of a broadside is to sell itself, as a commodity; a subsidiary purpose, which renders the main purpose more effective, is to flatter the listener's (and potential purchaser's and singer's)
self-esteem—in this case in the form of a 'marvel' ballad of brashly phallic
import. To this end verbal niceties are unnecessary, even disadvantageous;

all that is called for is a thumping rhythm and a tune that may be inappropriate but has the virtue of familiarity. At a slightly more sophisticated level stands a theatre song like Polly's 'O ponder well', in *The Beggar's Opera*. This achieved a prodigious commercial success by adapting an old and well-loved tune to words of which the sentimental cynicism awoke echoes; as Booth puts it, "The song opens to its audience an exquisite moment of disinterested self-pity, an ecstasy above the self to savor its lovely sadness from not too close". Again, song is at once within and outside the temporal situation, and in this case Booth demonstrates precisely how the tune Gay selected contributes in musical terms to the equivocation. He might easily have done so in his account of Wesley's congregational hymn, 'Love divine, all loves excelling', though he could legitimately argue that in this instance comment is unnecessary since the squareness of the tune and the enveloping homophony work so crudely to promote, out of the *données* of biblical reference, "absolute ecstatic lostness in the divine presence". This is an overtly religious use of the basic condition of song: "liberation from the well-defined place and time of the self, into community, concert, communion". A work song such as 'Blow the man down' complementarily relates the primary 'uses' of song to practical exigencies. Several individual sailors synchronize their efforts through a co-ordination of consciousness, so that manual labour on ships becomes a manifestation of incipient industrial technology. Like prison songs, shanties promote labour which benefits the employer while at the same time releasing the aggression the sailors bear to their bosses. The gain is mutual, at once practical and psychological, and the qualities of the music—metrically corporeal, melodically reiterative, divided between leader-master and chorus-plebs—are equated with its functionalism.

The book ends with an analysis of four pop songs which have become overtly commercial while retaining the status myth. Booth is especially penetrating on the parlour-song 'After the ball', which, published in 1892, sold around ten million copies in sheet form. The appeal of the song, which was a harbinger of pop music as big business, must have been that it "lamented the loneliness of this world, as much of both the popular and the high art of the age did". The verses, presenting the lonesomeness of the uncle who had not trusted love, questioned by the flaxen-haired little girl who might have been his daughter, alternate with the insidiously lilting refrain, which evokes in waltz rhythm the social solidarities from which uncle is self-banished. We, lonely mortals one and all, identify with uncle who represents our lost opportunities, but at the same time enjoys a privileged position outside the hurly-burly of family relationships; the words hint that he lives in a grand mansion. What validates the mythic status of the situation is the

48

tune, which is extremely fetching, as Booth says, though he denies it the musical investigation it deserves. The song raises questions about the relationship between art and commerce, which Booth confronts in the penultimate chapter, linking the TV jingle 'Pepsi Cola hits the spot' to the time-effacing and self-transcending aspects of song defined in the previous chapters. Clearly the ritualistic aspect of advertising jingles, sung rather than spoken, works in much the same ways as do children's games and ditties, and has qualities in common with the patterns of repetition and allusion shared by folk ballads and modern pop songs.

Having progressed from oral to notated song, Booth takes a further step in his final chapter, which concerns a commercial recording of the apparently trite 'White Christmas'. The idea of a *record* is, as the term implies, to preserve something that might otherwise be swept away. The avowed purpose of 'White Christmas' is to obviate forgetfulness, to make time stop in an imagined Edenic past: an end to which the music contributes cannily. But of course time won't stop; even as perdurable a commodity as 'White Christmas', which in Bing Crosby's version sold more copies and was presumably heard by more people than any other single pop song, is subject to inevitable if not planned obsolescence; which is why the music industry cultivates "patterns of recurrence". The "staggering number" of new songs offered to the public makes it possible for us to find the closest equivalent to the songs that

worked best for us last week, last year, or long ago . . . As objects keeping the record of songs through time, [our new records] are the correlatives of what we hold out from time: intervals where we think we see that the isolating differences of the world of extension and duration are not the whole story.

Some may think that the examples Booth selects from our modern age are depressingly weighted, as contrasted with those he discusses from previous eras. He might have chosen 'mythic' songs—for instance by the Beatles or Dylan—which would have given a more favourable image of what makes us tick. On balance, however, Booth was probably right to analyse examples that spring or ooze from the grass roots of our industrial technocracy, and to demonstrate that their impact is less simple than it seems. In his epilogue he reminds us that we begin to experience song before we are born, since music is "the only form of art and perhaps the only expression of what is specifically human that can reach us in the womb". 'White Christmas' and 'Love Divine', like much eletrophonic tribal pop, returns us to the womb in a sense that is perhaps validated by our pre-natal experience, and is certainly relatable to the time-effacement and self-transcendence which occur in types of song we feel no need to apologise for. At the head of his Conclusions, Booth quotes Ruth Beebe Hill, reporting on the Lakotahs:

First Born, the grandfathers told, had emerged from quivering mud to the rhythm of his own heart and so man had known the true rhythm from the beginning. Soon afterwards man had learned to use this rhythm for making songs. And then certain ones had discovered the true power in song, the power for making spiritual contact.

This power offers "the experience of unity with what seems to lie apart from ourselves", so song is a human need as basic as bread, perhaps more basic, since without bread some people might die of starvation, but without song no one could, in Zuckerkandl's phrase, "invent himself". This brilliant book is worthy of its tremendous subject. It reveals new perspectives, which will be increasingly pertinent to the new-old world our technology is spawning.

TLS, NOVEMBER 1981

MAKING THE SPIRITS SPEAK

Stanley Sadie, ed., *The New Grove Dictionary of Musical Instruments*
(Oxford: Oxford University Press, 1985)

W HAT IS THE DIFFERENCE BETWEEN A *BANG*, THE THREE KINDS OF *banga*, a *bangali*, a *bang-co*, a *bangdi*, a *bangu*, a *bangia*, a *bangibang*, a *bangili*, a *bango*, a *bangsi*, a *bangwe* and a *bangzi*? Those who don't know may admit to their ignorance with small discredit, and may even be permitted to add that they don't greatly care. But this reviewer does know the difference, having bumped bang into the *bangs*—widely assorted, geographically dispersed instruments that don't necessarily have anything to do with English banging—when he first opened *The New Grove Dictionary of Musical Instruments*, in search of information about the relatively accessible *bandora*. It is a strength of this, as of all good dictionaries, that its incidental seductions should prove more potent than the user's self-discipline.

The example cited is by no means frivolous, for it reveals the most significant characteristic of this dictionary, mostly extracted from *The New Grove Dictionary of Music and Musicians* with the original articles so revised and expanded—sometimes rewritten or replaced —as virtually to amount to an independent compilation. In addition, many articles have been commissioned for the dictionary, most of them in ethnic categories. Mulling over the contents as a totality, one is inevitably struck by the fact that a very high proportion of the articles, although appearing in what is and must be a central achievement of the musical establishment, none the less deal with exotic material. Such an admission that Western values may not be the be-all and end-all in musical, as in other, matters would hardly have been feasible only a few generations back. Although Western man has been proud to be obsessed with his growth towards 'consciousness', his maturation may be really beginning in his belated recognition that he must learn to be conscious of unconsciousness. Our polyglot pluralism is forcing this upon us, perhaps for the good of our souls, certainly for our physical survival.

There are also intrinsic reasons why a dictionary of musical instruments should be weighted in the direction of non-Western and especially of so-called primitive cultures. In literate societies such as our own music has become composition, the placing together of musical 'events' in time, notated in abstract terms, however closely those abstractions may be related to extra-musical dimensions. When music is an artefact, individually composed, the sound-sources through which it is incarnate will be clearly defined and relatively few, developed, however, to extreme degrees of subtlety and refinement; one has only to think of the evolving story of *bel canto* singing, and of the complementary development and perfection of the violin during the seventeenth and eighteenth centuries. For primitive peoples, on the other hand, there is usually no artefact in the form of a score. The discovery of sound-sources in the world around, and their literal metamorphosis into 'instruments' through which both the human and the supernatural may speak, is itself a creative act; primitive people make 'music of necessity' because for them the medium is indeed the message. Hence the multiplicity of sound-sources described in these pages.

I was sorry to find no mention of a senior American radical, Conlon Nancarrow, whose extraordinary studies for player-piano have affinities with 'corporeal' barrelhouse piano as well as with guitar blues, flamenco guitar and Mexican marimba bands, while at the same time investigating, by means of the perforations in pianola rolls, miracles of polymetrical complexity far beyond the control of human fingers, however well tuned the nerves and agile the sinews, not to mention the mind directing them. In Nancarrow's later studies physical excitation and mathematical abstraction become one through the agency of partially mechanistic techniques. The player-piano is *instrumental* to a reunion of head and body; and that this matters acutely to our divided and distracted world can hardly be gainsaid. Nancarrow's more advanced mathematical studies have qualities in common with electrophonic musics, which are described in the dictionary in a substantial, remarkably cogent series of articles by Hugh Davies. One wonders, however, whether electrophonic instruments can ever become 'instrumental' to human bodies and spirits in the way that, for example, Partch's instruments are; not to mention those of the savages. It is noticeable that man has done so little with them over so relatively extended a period of time; they may be another form of Artificial Intelligence, controlling us, rather than we them.

Such speculations would be improper in *Grove*, for although a dictionary of instruments should not ignore the human impulses that govern the evolution of instrumental resources, its main function must be to purvey information: on that count *The New Grove Dictionary of Musical Instruments* unequivocally delights. Keeping to a personal level in the interests of honesty, I may report that I next turned to matters peripheral to Couperin. I came up with fascinating and illuminating information about musettes and hurdy-gurdies, bird instruments, musical snuff boxes and clocks. Looking up the flute and hurdy-gurdy man Hotteterre, I found that there were seven of him—a musical dynasty less distinguished than the Couperin family, or of course the Bachs, but one making a considerable stir in the windy corridors of Versailles. These are peripheral matters, though far from trivial. On central themes relevant to this area the dictionary proved thorough and reliable. The substantial pieces on harpsichords and their registration, to which most of the leading authorities have contributed, do all that can be expected, defining distinctions between Flemish, French and Italian traditions, leaving one to deduce the relevance of the instruments' physical structure to the musical effects different schools of composers called for. The exhaustive article on lutes presents them as the fundamental Orphic instrument whereby the divine spark could be ignited from the guts of beasts; it also makes clear how instruments of the harpsichord family began as mechanized lutes. There is a generic relation between the two, but harpsichords embrace more of man's canny intellectual contrivance. This reminds us that the simultaneously mythic and mechanical equation referred to in the player-piano music of Conlon Nancarrow is not new in principle. Throughout recorded time there has been recurrent interplay between instruments' God-given potentialities—the prime instance is the bell, reverberating to the overtones prompted by 'divine' mathematics: on which Percival Price's article is as entertainingly illuminating as it is factually informative—and what man has done to and with them through the exercise of 'techniques'.

One of the most curious of God's anomalies is that his absolute consonance of the perfect fifth won't fit exactly into the cycle that makes harmonic, modulatory music feasible: that troublesome 'comma of Didymus' continues to plague man's hopeful inventiveness. Pure intonation may be possible in the purely monophonic music of angels, savages, orientals, and Harry Partch in his somewhat arbitrary forty-three-toned octave; but in the harmonic systems of the Renaissance, and especially the Baroque and Classical eras, octaves, fifths and thirds are in many cases incommensurate in their pure forms. In harmonized music, therefore, especially that for keyboards, intervals need to be tampered with or 'tempered' in order to make God aurally amenable to our needs: which sounds as though temperament is a musical consequence of the theological Fall. Leaving God out of the matter, temperament remains a phenomenon which any European instrumentalist, and many non-Western ones, have to be aware of. Mark Lindley's masterly essay means that we have no excuse for evading it; it is hard going but intelligible even to a mere musician: some of whom, notably Bach, seem to have been higher mathematicians by instinct if not training.

Though temperament is not an instrument, its place in the dictionary is unassailable, since modern instrumentalists can't manage without it. Editorial policy seems to have been to allow into this compendium any topic which won't find its way into the studies of specific 'great composers' extrapolated from *New Grove*, to be published as separate volumes. This is fair enough, though some may think David Fallows's succinct translation of, and

53

comments on, Italian musical terminology a shade unnecessary. For the general reader the articles on related themes will probably prove more rewarding than those on instruments *per se*. This applies to the subject—closely related to temperament—of *musica ficta*, through the intricacies of which Margaret Bent treads a wary path, abetted in the later stretches by Lewis Lockwood and Robert Donington. The latter is also represented by his justly celebrated pieces on ornamentation, and on rhythm, tempo and *notes inégales* in French and other baroque music. The evidence remains as confusing, even as contradictory, as it always was, though Donington disarms by the lucidity, even the grace, of his prose. An honest musicologist can only present the documentation in all its contradictoriness, leaving the performer to sort it out according to his proclivities. In these matters ambiguity is not necessarily a liability, for it may induce a sense of spontaneity such as was, after all, the aim of ornamentation, and especially of *notes inégales*. Perhaps the early authorities disagreed with one another precisely because techniques of ornamentation reflected the vagaries of the human heart.

Articles on *musica ficta*, on tuning, and on ornamentation and tempo inevitably overlap with the substantial pieces on performance practice and improvisation, which may establish some claim to being the contributions of most outstanding general import. Not surprisingly, they call on a number of contributors, of whom Howard Mayer Brown is the most conspicuous; all display professional competence; some are brilliant. The two themes are difficult to disentangle, for both depend on extemporization which, given its evanescence and ephemerality, is resistant to historical research. In the Middle Ages notation was invented as an aid to memory, being adequate enough only to remind singers of the presumptively God-given *cantus firmus* from which their troping alleluias might (or might not) take wing. Secular music in the Middle Ages is even further removed from definitive form. We know more or less the pitches sung by troubadours and by the makers of lauds and cantigas, but the rhythmic interpretation of their music remains even more dubious than that of plainchant. Nor do we know what the singers did with the instruments they're pictured blowing, banging, scraping or plucking. We can only take pot luck in scoring for the lutes, flutes, shawms, rebecs, and assorted drums and bells that appear in visual iconography, creating sonorities such as may *perhaps* survive in some of the more exotic European folk cultures. Experience suggests that modern performers who, like Christopher Page and Thomas Binkeley, most chance their arms tend most to convince. To a degree similar conditions obtain in Renaissance music, which remained 'open' both in instrumentation and in the degree of licence permitted or encouraged in the interpretation of the written notes.

With the more autocratic baroque world coherent musical rules prove collateral to rules meant to govern human thought, feeling and behaviour; but improvisation remains essential since through it is effected the two-way traffic between the public and private life. Its interpretation is still highly problematical, but less so than in earlier periods since an age obsessively conscious of a need for humanly imposed law and order was prone literately to theorize about it. We have 'something to go on', even though contemporary authorities were outrageously disputatious. The guidebook to baroque practice in the article on improvisation is finely presented with well-chosen examples from contemporary sources. With the classical age, we find that research has demolished the former assumption that improvisation is no longer relevant, apart from the accepted licence of the cadenza wherein the soloist—who might well, as in the cases of Mozart and Beethoven, be himself the composer—momentarily asserts his identity, as distinct from the orchestral *hoi polloi*. One must start by recognizing that give and take between notated, socially sanctioned stylistic conventions (public assumptions) and *ad hoc* elements (private responses to them) remained paramount; but one must temper this knowledge with the probability that great composers—Haydn, Mozart, and Beethoven—wrote down more than did the average hack, presumably because they'd grown suspicious of the unmusical excesses with which inferior composers or non-composers might bedeck their work. The same applies to Bach, in an earlier generation.

In the nineteenth century, virtuoso composer-performers such as Chopin and Liszt didn't always play what they notated, the former out of sensibility, the latter out of rhetorical panache. Successive generations of pianists have made widely differing shots at interpretation, all convinced they were authentic to the spirit if not the letter, some in arrogant self-confidence, others with undue humility. It is interesting—though *Grove's* improvisation article doesn't mention this—that the last two great piano sonatas of the Romantic tradition, those of Charles Ives, hardly attempt definitive notation, since for Ives completion was an illusory virtue.

This is early evidence of the ways in which modern civilization may be reinstating some of the concepts of oral cultures. With these, about which Nazir A. Jaibasbhoy writes coherently, problems of interpretation are, though naturally more esoteric for us, easier for Asiatics since they have minimal notation, but a long established oral tradition offering 'sets' of interval relationships and metrical patterns, most of which have sacramentally or socially symbolic as well as musical connotations. To compose is to improvise, with a wealth of microtonal inflection and rhythmic nuance, on these unwritten assumptions, if not laws. Such articles demonstrate how, after all, the twain *may* meet; and had better, if our polymorphous world is to have a future. In this context it is regrettable that there is no adequate discussion of jazz improvisation, nor of the variety of timbres which jazz musicians, black and white, instrumental and vocal, habitually exploit. The brief article on the saxophone virtually ignores its jazz role, which has become its main aesthetic justification.

But it would be unfair to end on a quibble. These volumes are a superb achievement, which usually satisfies, often stimulates, and occasionally startles. Those verbs apply no less to the lavish, adequately though not always well-produced illustrations.

TLS, JULY 1985

MASTERS, ORIGINALS AND ALSO-RANS

Don Michael Randel, ed., *The Harvard Biographical Dictionary of Music*
(Cambridge, Mass: Harvard University Press, 1996)

D ICTIONARY-MAKERS ARE PLEDGED TO A MEASURE OF NEUTRALITY; their job is to record and inform, not to praise or blame. Any indication of value in their work must not be spelt out, but implicit; as is the case with this *Harvard Biographical Dictionary of Music*, edited by Don Michael Randel (who is Professor of Music at, and Provost of, Cornell University), and written under his direction by a team of between twenty and thirty research scholars—perhaps of graduate status? Quite properly, the writers evade idiosyncrasy, sound much alike, proffer information, but for the most part leave us to make of it what we will.

The dictionary restricts itself almost but not quite exclusively to Western traditions, thereby begging many questions, for, given the multi-ethnic pluralism of modern culture, the boundaries around and between the sundry kinds of musical activity are more hazily defined than they used to be. The categories known as 'classical', folk, jazz, pop, 'performance-art' and whatelse still exist, but bewilderingly overlap. If one prescribes them too strictly, one will give a misleading impression of what our culture is like; if, on the other hand, one admits every category equally, the sheer amount of material will be intractable, and perhaps self-defeatingly contradictory. As editor, Randel has had to make difficult decisions. He has done so creditably.

For him, criteria of value would seem, as usual, to be roughly inherent in the space allotted to each biographee. His entries for composers may be grouped under three headings: (i) the Master Musicians, who rate six to seven columns each; (ii) composers with distinctive originality enough to have made putatively indelible marks on history, who merit 1½ to 2½ columns; and (iii) the innumerable also-rans whose names, accorded five to fifteen lines, are dimly remembered or half-forgotten but who ought, 'for safety's sake', to be included in case they may one day matter more than we currently think; this applies both to composers of the past and to the burgeoning armies of the present. Each age has to make its own decisions as to the onset of *rigor mortis* in a dead or, for that matter, an ostensibly living composer. Indeed, it's in claiming to know who is dead and who is alive that we define ourselves, so it would be foolhardy to hope to make a dictionary foolproof enough to be valid for much more than our own time. Since most people who read it are likely to be our near-contemporaries, that doesn't greatly matter: so, recognizing that the amount of space we allot to Tom, Dick, or Harry, Jane or Joan, is an assessment of what we value now, we should, while trying to avoid the grosser prejudices, have the courage of our hazardous convictions.

On the evidence of the space allotted in this dictionary, the Big Names are Bach, Handel, Haydn (just), Mozart, Beethoven, Schubert, Brahms, Wagner, and Verdi. This is a straightforwardly conventional list, though I think Monteverdi should have been among the elect, not only because he is a great composer, but also because no one so clearly illuminates the crucial transition from the seventeenth century to our modern world. The writers of these main essays recount the events of the composers' lives chronologically and describe the conditions wherein—in great homes, civic halls, opera houses, salons and concert halls—they operated.

When we come to composers in my second class—those who have original distinction and by now established positions in the 'canon'—we are better rewarded, since merely in describing distinctiveness an author is obliged to offer more than factual information. Romantic composers lend themselves readily to this, the articles on Chopin (especially), Schumann, and Liszt effectively mating biographical facts with evidence of the spiritual pilgrimage audible in the music. Bellini, Berlioz and Bruckner also provoke more than factual accounts, whereas the more classical Gluck has to make do with a piece that has difficulty in distinguishing between his many conventionally baroque operas and the so-called Reform operas of his maturity; admittedly, the distinction is subtle, even intangible. Peripheral figures such as Chabrier, Satie, and Busoni of their nature call for distinctive characterization, and are accorded the right kind of regard.

They provide a transition to the Masters of Modern Music, who, in my distant youth, were considered to be Debussy, Stravinsky, Schoenberg, Bartók and perhaps Berg, Webern, and Hindemith. Sibelius was an ambiguous figure, since, while no one questioned his greatness, some argued that he belonged more to the nineteenth than to the twentieth century. On the evidence of this dictionary, Stravinsky and Schoenberg now reign supreme: Stravinsky because of his representative significance as a twice-deracinated global composer, Schoenberg because he invented a compositional technique which became widely influential, though it did not, as he had prophesied, settle the destiny of European music for the foreseeable future. On the evidence of this compilation, Hindemith's reputation has slipped; so, surprisingly, has that of Bartók, though both earn respect. Boulez and Stockhausen are handled with intelligent generosity, probably for polemical as well as musical reasons. Among the lesser, peripheral moderns, Frank Martin, Dallapiccola, Malipiero and Szymanowski are discussed with intelligence and aural sensitivity, at reasonable length, though some French composers—Fauré, Koechlin, even Poulenc—are inadequately, because blandly, treated. The British too have a rather distant presence. The status of Elgar and Delius between British and European (German) values is not clearly defined; Vaughan Williams is curiously said to have been influenced by Bax; Britten is given short shrift for a composer of his indubitable genius, while Tippett's crossover tendencies are rather crudely presented. Nor do Maxwell Davies and Birtwistle emerge, from short articles, with the plaudits we currently accord them, though it is possible we have been a shade over-indulgent. Brian Ferneyhough, whose New Complexity some have thought un-English, is considerately treated, but Howard Skempton, whose New Simplicity is Ferneyhough's polar opposite, unfairly fails to make the grade. Incidentally, one of the few serious omissions from this dictionary is that fine English composer Rebecca Clarke who, although long forgotten (she is barely in *New Grove*), has been partially rehabilitated with feminism's rise. A more surprising omission is Michael Nyman, a composer as currently fashionable and over-played as Rebecca Clarke was, until very recently, ignored and unperformed.

Two composers whose major status has been fairly recently established are Shostakovich and Charles Ives. Both are accorded substantial assessments that confront the psychological ambiguities and sociological complexities in their different but complementary positions as composers of democratic principle. In a Harvard dictionary, it is hardly surprising that American composers fare well. Along with Ives appear the other grand old American pioneers, Ruggles and Varèse, with, in a slightly later generation, John Cage as composer, 'inventor' and musical philosopher. The second rank of pioneers—Henry Cowell, Wallingford Riegger, Elliott Carter, Conlon Nancarrow and (the surprisingly still active) Henry Brant—get entries that tell us what we need to know. Even problematical figures like Milton Babbitt and Ernst Křenek are handled sympathetically enough to make one want to hear more of their music. The mainstream composers—Copland, Harris, Barber, Piston, perhaps Sessions, up to Lou Harrison as west coast East-West guru and Morton Feldman as near-static heir to Cagean silence—are assessed with kindly competence. A vast gallery of minor Americans, many of them no more than names to us and sometimes not even that, may or may not merit their entries; still, when I've looked up an obscure American with whom I was momentarily concerned, he has usually been present. As one would expect today, the crossover composers so significantly active in the States are all assessed, from Stephen Foster, Gottschalk and Scott Joplin, through Gershwin, Blitzstein, Bernstein and Sondheim, not forgetting the more commercial strata represented by the likes of Kern, Berlin, Porter and Rodgers, and so to the minimalists Reich, Glass and Adams. Discrimination in these fields might have been finer, but discrimination is not the main function of dictionaries. It is more serious that the folk-mongering sons of Ruth Crawford-Seeger—that adventurously innovative composer who would stand among the grand old pioneers, were she not a woman who died of cancer at the age of fifty—are given slightly more space than their mother.

All the entries so far referred to concern *bona fide* art composers in Western traditions. But the editor would have been off the mark as an American, had he not given comprehensive coverage to jazz, which embraces much of the finest music made by Americans. The choice of musicians represented—from country blues and barrelhouse piano, through New Orleans and Chicago jazz and the Big Band era to the sophistications of Bill Evans and Gil Evans, and to the (in some ways non-Western) avant-gardism of John Coltrane and Ornette Coleman—is exemplary. None of the articles is long, but most vividly catch the music's essence, since much of the music, having no score, exists in its moments of creation. Only in the case of Duke Ellington does the account seem inadequate, for he was halfway between an instinctual jazz artist and a literate art composer. The rock and roll and pop entries also cover the relevant names; and if they are less musically revealing, this may be because they have less to reveal. The long parade of Joneses includes Hank, Jonah, Philip, Philly-Jo, who overlap the categories of jazz and pop; but alas, the delectable Rickie-Lee is absent. Still, among the pop stars, the Beatles, Bob Dylan, Joni Mitchell and Jimi Hendrix deservedly have pride of place.

All this Americanism needs to be, and is, ballasted by backward glances into Europe, for Early Music is now not only a cult, but an industry. Some will feel that in the sight of God or any serious criterion of value, the greatest of 'early' composers—before as well as after Monteverdi—ought to make the first category; but it could also be argued that a dictionary for general use should emphasize composers whose works are likely to be frequently performed in our society. As it is, the panoply of 'early' names is exhaustive, but the entries tend not to involve one deeply. Medieval composers—Hildegard of Bingen, Pérotin, Machaut, Dunstable—are listed and dated, but we're offered no account of how their music functions. One doesn't ask for opinions as to how 'good' the music is, but one would like to know the kind of exercise it is. Similarly, it wouldn't have taken an inordinate amount of space to indicate how the musics of Renaissance composers such as Gesualdo, Ward, Wilbye and the Ferraboscos express their *Zeitgeist*; perhaps it's merely my British origins that make me think that the great William Byrd and his successors, Gibbons, Dowland and Bull, are meanly treated. The baroque classical composers, too, with the obvious exceptions of Bach and Handel, are not generously covered; the entries for Purcell,

Couperin and the two Scarlattis don't convey a sense of their indubitably major ranking, while the space accorded to Rameau is risibly demeaning. Of the two composers named Charpentier, the maker of *Louise* gets more space than his seventeenth-century namesake who, on a crudely quantitative basis, is now the more frequently performed and recorded.

Interpretative artists, including maestro conductors, are justifiably less generously treated than composers. Again, the entries are comprehensive, though most of us will cherish a pet conductor who has failed to make it. Among singers and instrumentalists I miss Alan Hacker and Frederick Fuller, a clarinettist and a singer important not only as performers, but also for their impact on the evolution of both Early and New music. Most of the entries on performers specify their fields of interest, properly regarding them as servants of music, rather than as audible circus acrobats. A few opera librettists who, like Metastasio and Chester Kallman, marry dedication to music with literary quality merit inclusion, though a real and great poet, W. H. Auden, who wrote at least two of the most brilliant opera books ever, is absent. General questions about the relation between words and music don't impinge on this volume, but on the companion work known simply as the *Harvard Dictionary of Music.* Together, the two books deserve a place in any educated person's library. Whatever the shortcomings of dictionaries *per se*, these will be frequently referred to, seldom in vain.

TLS, NOVEMBER 1996

THE BLUES IN HISTORY

Peter van der Merwe
Origins of the Popular Style: The Antecedents of Twentieth-Century Popular Music
(Oxford: The Clarendon Press, 1989)

I N HIS PREFACE, PETER VAN DER MERWE TELLS US THAT HE FOUND THIS book difficult to write. Since the subject is immensely complex, this is not surprising; and the reason for the difficulty is creditable to the author. For the substantial heart of the book is an account of what van der Merwe calls "the uniqueness of the blues"—its opposition to the norms of classical European music and its "tangled, complex and frequently obscure history". At a technical level he asks, and comes near to answering, some fundamental questions: what is 'mode' in the blues? What is the relation between melodic mode and tonal harmony? Why does the blues favour, if not exclusively, a twelve-bar structure? These and similar questions cannot be adequately confronted by way of the accredited techniques for the analysis of 'art' music: so van de Merwe offers a theoretical foundation—"an enlargement of musical theory to take care of the peculiarities of popular music". The concepts of the 'matrix', of flexible mode rather than of anchoring key, of the 'beat' in relation to rhythm and metre, and of 'wholeness' as a morphological rather than preordained notion of form, provide the tools with which the author operates. Using them adroitly, he approaches the ways in which the blues experience functions in the ever-changing contexts of time and place. In so doing he reveals that an account of what happens in music, here and now, is a gateway to more fundamental questions: the most crucial of which is why the blues—the music of an alien, dispossessed, black and often persecuted minority—became an urban folk music pertinent to most members of industrial cities, whatever the colour of their skin.

It would seem that—as D. H. Lawrence put it during the First World War—"humanity today is like a great uprooted tree". We are all, in our industrial technocracies, to a degree alienated and dispossessed, whether or not we are also persecuted and oppressed. The blues sprang from a dichotomy between two views of the world: Black and White, body and head, and—with the alignments reversed—materiality and spirituality. If the music spoke forcefully to us all, at levels we didn't need to be conscious of, this was because it made aurally incarnate a breach (far deeper than any sociological division between cultures*)within the human psyche. Black African rhythm and (monodic) melody came into contact, and then into conflict, with white American metre and (harmonically oriented) tune, particularly as manifested in the American march and hymn. Indeed hymn and march became a prison against whose bars the black African singer or instrumentalist beat: yet not in vain, for from tension was generated resilience. Against the military thump of the march the flexible rhythms of the African body pranced and danced; the rigidity of martial metre induced tension as Black and White rhythms interlocked. Similarly Black melody and White harmony interacted in a pain that at once disturbed and healed. The phenomenon of 'blue' notes epitomizes this because the 'natural' flat sevenths of modal melodies clash with the sharpened leading notes demanded by Western dominant-tonic harmony. This repeats a process that had happened in European history, when 'false relations' occurred between the vocal flat sevenths of medieval modality and the sharpened intervals called for by post-Renaissance harmony. Blue notes in Afro-American jazz are exactly comparable, likewise springing from a clash between worlds. They too imply false relations, which may prove symptomatic of a change no less crucial than that between the Middle Ages and the modern world.

If we consider the blues in the context of history the reasons for its crucial significance emerge. And in van der Merwe's book it is through particularities that general truths become manifest: as when, presenting detailed analyses of a few archetypal song-types, he demonstrates how inextricably mingled are the British, African and White American sources of the ballad of Frankie and Johnny and the related boll-weevil ballads. How long did it take for this British song-family to turn into Mississippi John Hurt's very Black variant? It would seem that 'Josie' and 'Tottie Jock' began in Britain, became White American mountain songs, and garnered Black inflexions around the time of the Civil War. "However far back the origins", van der Merwe adds, "there is no denying the wildfire rapidity with which it spread; and this has as much to do with the strength of the musical structure as with the squalid glamour of the theme."

The author's analysis reveals that many of the characteristics of the black-blue versions were already latent in the British prototypes, since the prototypes are also archetypes, valid over vast areas of time and space. Given this realization, we see the relevance of the first part of the book, headed 'The Historical Background', wherein van der Merwe defines "the Old High Culture" that links together "communities that existed some three thousand or four thousand years ago from the Nile to the Pacific, while northern Europe was still the domain of wandering and illiterate tribes". Many of the techniques of these ancient musics, despite their radical distinctions from Western music, continue to crop up in remote places—such as the Scottish Highlands and the Appalachian Mountains. In that context the time-and-place-travelling of the blues seems less inexplicable.

The blues looked to the future as well as to the past, as becomes evident in the book's third part. This concentrates on harmony, the element that is of its nature outside 'pure' folk tradition. Again, this is by a long way the most revealing account yet offered of the links between 'primitive harmony' as manifest in phenomena like community singing, and as evident in relatively sophisticated instances such as Elizabethan instrumental music, in which the concept of 'levels' is more applicable than the notion of chords, and in which modulation is a matter of 'shifts' rather than of 'changes'. If both the boogie bass and the so-called 'Gregory Walker' chord-progression are perceptible in sixteenth-century instrumental music, that is because they too are prototypical. To differentiate between art music and pop music in such contexts is obfuscatory, just as there is no need to cite arty Elizabethan parallels to the side-stepping mode-shifts or key-shifts in early Beatles songs. That they occur is interesting as archetypal musical mythology, but it is not explanatory. There are inescapable links between illiteracy and literacy, and if the blues is the most potent link, that's because it had "a fundamental coherence that could bear the burden of so many tunes, not to mention innumerable thousands of improvisations". This is also why it couldn't establish its primacy until the nineteenth century, when the crosscurrents of past and present in several disparate cultures—and technically of melody, organum heterophony, polyphony and homophony—had had time to become recognizable.

The 'late' manifestations of blues harmony led inevitably into parlour music and ragtime, which is the theme of Part Four of van der Merwe's book. By parlour music he means popular or 'light' musics not necessarily performed in parlours, but derived from classical-romantic models, the 'matrices' of which are distinct from those of (basically rural) folk music and of both the country and the urban blues. Van der Merwe's purpose is to demonstrate that 'conscious' sophistications of technique need not impair spontaneity. On the contrary, symbiosis was a natural function; artful types of popular music affiliated themselves to folk principles, while at the same time folkily oriented pop musics borrowed from art traditions with unabashed avidity. There was always a two-way traffic. The corniest pop song may exploit harmonic processes no less complex than, and sometimes identical with, those of a masterpiece like Schubert's String Quintet in C. This is not merely a triumph of cliché over invention, for "bad taste in the arts is always a sort of failed good taste, the result of the Barnbys of the world trying to be Schuberts". Even so, composers of the lighter styles of parlour music were not trying to produce the emotional effect of Schubert's progressions; they were merely changing—and, as they believed, enriching—the *lingua franca*, wherein new relationships between tune and harmony must be defined. So parlour music became an essential element of the blues, and therefore of jazz—in its sophisticated forms (Theolonius Monk, Miles Davis) as well as in its commercialization (Frank Sinatra, Glenn Miller). The thirty-two-bar ballad form, the white American march, and Black (and White) American rag fused with, rather than confronted, the blues, in ways perceptively outlined in the book's last section.

Peter van der Merwe's final paragraph is worth quoting, since it encapsulates his synthesis of intelligent insight with humility:

How is it that we find so many parallel lines of development between parlour music and the blues? . . . Recent research has shown that there was far more mutual influence between supposedly separate genres—particularly between country and town music, in both Britain and America—than used to be thought. But even allowing for all such possible influence it still remains a puzzle. The whole development of the popular style tempts one to invoke a mystical Spirit of History. Though we are entitled to feel awe at the processes of History, this temptation should be sternly resisted. But though history may not be mystical, it is undeniably mysterious. The hints thrown out above only begin to approach its complexity and subtlety. As J. B. Haldane said of the universe, it is not only queerer than we suppose, but queerer than we possibly could suppose.

The ripples this remarkable, perhaps great, book has left on the musicological pool will be spread wide and deep.

TLS, SEPTEMBER 1990

PART TWO

ANNIVERSARIES

I think continually of those who were truly great . . .
The names of those who in their lives fought for life,
Who wore at their hearts the fire's centre.
STEPHEN SPENDER, 'I THINK CONTINUALLY', c. 1933

The articulate audible voice of the past.
THOMAS CARLYLE, *HEROES AND HERO-WORSHIP*, 1841

Introduction

CLOCKS AND CALENDARS, AGENDAS AND ANNIVERSARIES GIVE STRUCTURE to life. We mark our special occasions and we remember important events in history, but we also celebrate men and women whose achievements have been influential. At the close of his book, *Caliban Reborn*, which examines the process of renewal in twentieth-century music, Wilfrid Mellers draws a 'chart of relationships' showing lines of influence from Beethoven, by way of Wagner, through Schoenberg on the one hand and Debussy on the other, to Berio and Cage respectively. It also reveals vital cross-influences; for instance, by various routes between Webern, Debussy, Messiaen, Satie and Stravinsky. Similarly significant (if sometimes indirect) links can be traced between those whose achievements are celebrated in the seven 'anniversary' essays that make up Part Two of this book—links which also have much to tell us about Wilfrid Mellers's own enthusiasms and influence as critic and teacher.

"What we call 'explanation'," wrote Wittgenstein, "is a form of connection", and one of Wilfrid Mellers's most obvious strengths is the range of reference which he brings to his thinking-through a topic and the connections he makes in his teasing out of *meaning*. From his Cambridge days, as a tutor in English during the 1940s and 1950s, his work in literature—on Shakespeare, Ben Jonson, Milton and Dryden, and on Congreve and other Restoration dramatists—has continued to illuminate his writing about seventeenth-century music, especially the music of Purcell. The same lines of thought connect us to English music and poetry of the first half of the twentieth century—for example, Housman and Warlock—while another route takes us from Warlock by way of Delius and Percy Grainger to Grieg, the last "a mini-master who acquired major status" such that his 'Jubileum' in 1993 was celebrated in every part of Norway. That celebration stood for not only Norway's but also all of Scandinavia's late-nineteenth-century and early twentieth-century flowering of professional music and drama. In much the same way, the Housman and Warlock centenaries refocused appreciation of words and music in the England of the immediate pre- and post-First World War years. Throughout that period, and beyond into the 1920s and 1930s, the kind of musical thought inherited from Haydn, Mozart and Beethoven was, understandably, pervasive (and is recognised here in an essay marking Mozart's bi-centenary). But the French connections in particular—the later legacy of Debussy, Satie, Stravinsky and Diaghilev—had possibly even more far-reaching influence, not least upon American composers such as Virgil Thomson.

And here there are also are some important 'Mellers connections'. Early in his career he played Debussy's Sonata for violin and piano with André Mangeot, "who had been taught it by Debussy"; and Mangeot had collaborated with Peter Warlock in editing little-known seventeenth-century English string music. Then again, there is Wilfrid Mellers's considerable involvement with American music (of which, more in Part Five), his friendship with Virgil Thomson, and his continuing friendship and correspondence with Lou Harrison. In their different ways, the compositions of Thomson and Harrison have drawn substance from the Old World and made it New with singular American viewpoints. Similarly, the depth of knowledge and experience which Wilfrid Mellers has gained in the twin worlds of music and literature is for him, as a critic and a teacher, akin to that "abundance of technical means" which, as Messiaen said, "allows the heart to expand".

JP

DIOCLESIAN RESTOR'D

Henry Purcell, 1995

Y ORK'S EARLY MUSIC FESTIVAL, GARNERING *ÉCLAT* WITH EACH SUCCESSIVE
year, unsurprisingly dedicates 1995 to Henry Purcell in his tercentenary
year. Characteristically, this is not a casual doffing of the hat to genius,
but a coherent, intelligent, imaginative collation of concerts, recitals and
'events', embracing lectures on music, theatre, poetry, architecture and
fashion, thereby setting Purcell in his environment. While this programme
is, in the psychological sense, an act of restitution, it also underlines how
closely Purcell's contemporaneity then is allied to ours now. Nothing could
better reveal this than the semi-performance of (what now seems to be
called) a semi-opera presented, if not staged, in the Sir Jack Lyons Concert
Hall at the university, as the first grand event on the first Sunday evening.

After the halcyon days of English theatre in the early seventeenth century, internecine strife followed by Puritan hegemony delivered a frontal
assault on our mimetic and terpsichorean arts, whether at court or in the
public theatre. Although in 1660, after the Civil War, the monarchy was
'restored', this apparent triumph was not a restoration of old values. Politically, the brilliant Halifax pointed out in his wry prose, that "when people
contend for Liberty, they seldom get anything by their Victory but new
Masters". Culturally, Bishop Spratt—in his history of the Royal Society of
Science which, founded in 1667, was the artificer of the scientifically orientated future—remarked that "if our Church should be enemy to Commerce, intelligence, discovery, Navigation, and any sort of Mechanicks, how
could it be fit for the present Genius of the Nation?" (The nouns rewarded
with capitals make their point.) Of course, it couldn't; the pristine world of
the first Caroline court was beyond recovery. Neither Court nor Country
won the war; if anyone did, it was the City, since with the growth of scientific enquiry, Britain was becoming 'a nation of shopkeepers'. By 1640 we
had produced three times as much coal as the rest of Europe combined;
thirty years later mercantile adventure and misadventure were unstoppable.
Standards, both cultural and moral, had much in common with our own,
being those of the smart alec.

It is not therefore surprising that Charles II was so different from his
father—even physically. Over six foot in height, compared with his minus-
cule father's less than five feet, he had a flamboyantly royal presence, while
being indifferent to the finer things, human and divine, to which the first
Charles had been addicted. Gregarious, voluble, affable, Charles II was a

Modern Man in being palpably democratic, eager to chat with Tom, Dick and Harry, and still more with Jane, June and Joan. After his exile during the wars (which Lucy Hutchinson called "the Dishonour of the Kingdom"), he understandably pursued *fun* in the form of women, wine and song, in that order; and his people, chuffed by his mateyness, on the whole approved. This fury for frivolity, of which the king was symbol not cause, ended by sapping the energy of the nation. Rochester is merely the most extreme example of a man of exceptional ability who in several senses dissipated his talents, while Buckingham—potentially a great man so placed socially that he might have been a healer of and mediator between rival factions—was likewise undone by what contemporary chroniclers accurately described as "lack of Principle". Dedicated to pleasure and frolic, Charles II himself preferred to avoid politicians, embarking on a grandiose project to build himself a Versailles in sight of Winchester Cathedral, remote enough from London but close enough to the coast, should escape become advisable.

In his years of exile, Charles had visited the French court, and it was on the French model, with Italianate trimmings, that he refurbished the secular rituals of his court. At his instigation, artists mimicked continental glamour, making Frenchified theatre music even for the Chapel Royal. Given the democratic hedonism of the prevailing English temper, our artists for the most part failed to discover grandeur of spirit beneath the grandiose façade. This is why even Dryden, the supreme Public Poet of that or any English time, was superb as a satirist and as translator and moderniser of ancient classical traditions, but could assay the heroic or tragic only with disillusioned wishful thinking. The tussle between the veracities of private passion and the necessities of public duty—the very heart of Corneille and Racine—was abandoned in favour of a display of simulated emotions such as the characters, faced with synthetic moral choices, might exhibit. A tragedy of simulation and dissimulation is a contradiction in terms. Since comedy flourished on deceit, it worked more efficaciously in the Restoration theatre, though only Congreve among the dramatists achieved anything comparable with Molière's comedy of manners *and* morals.

Our failure in tragic drama is complemented by our failure to create a tradition in heroic opera, comparable with that fashioned by Lully for his master, Le Roi Soleil. In London, Purcell, more generously endowed with genius that Lully in France, succeeded in making a theatre piece on the Heroic Theme only once, and that in a short work designed not for the court, but for a girl's school. True, *Dido and Aeneas*, though of modest dimensions, is a masterpiece that incorporates into authentic tragedy satirical, even farcical, elements that mirror a changing world. But *Dido* is a once-off, a creation of genius greater than its age warranted. We can understand, perhaps accept, the Restoration comedy of (mostly bad) manners, and even on occasion swallow Dryden's attempts to emulate Racine. More difficult to take is the Restoration's rehashing of Shakespeare in rhyming couplets, even running to a Happy Ending for *King Lear*, with Cordelia married off to her yuppie fairy prince. Purcell himself contributed to this tarting up of 'old' plays by out-of-date dramatists like Shakespeare; his *Fairy Queen* bears much the same relationship to Shakespeare's *A Midsummer Night's Dream* as does a twentieth-century movie musical to 'the book of the film', being a series of 'shows' introduced, with commercial expediency and mechanical ingenuity, at lavish expense, into a spoken play. The botched-up text makes virtually no reference to Shakespeare, though there's nothing especially heinous about Shakespeare's original serving as trigger to a different kind of experience. Certainly, Purcell's genius offers alternative delights, and one might make out a case that although Purcell's Fairy Queen is a candyfloss figure compared with Dido, his Carthiginian queen, her demotic spirit, allied with the fecundity of Purcell's invention, becomes a kind of virtue. The Purcellian confusion of values is a harbinger of the future, which is us. Purcell deserves credit for prescience, though this does not effect the problems inherent in his hybridisation.

These problems we may explore by way of this York Festival performance of the first of Purcell's semi-operas. Like all these pieces, *Dioclesian* is halfway between a masque and an opera proper. Masques had attained their heyday in the wake of Europe's Renaissance when proud man, drest in a little brief authority, believed or hoped that aristocratic rulers, being absolute, might, or even should, emulate God. Given the rebirth of classical antiquity that the renaissance in part was, these shows were rituals of humanism, wherein legendary nymphs and shepherds consorted in song, dance, mime and spectacle, with an exquisite elegance that claimed to be oblivious of Time. At the end the mythical protagonists proved to be not creatures from a Golden Age, but (literally) the current King and nobility, and by inference ourselves. In so far as negative forces are admitted into paradise (and often they aren't), they are laughed off or shrugged aside in an 'anti-masque' that renders devils farcically grotesque, rather than scary. Thus a masque was wish-fulfilment in ritual action; one might almost say that the maturing of a civilisation could occur only when the 'dark' forces facetiously dismissed in the anti-masque were allowed their rights, so that masque could grow up into opera, with tragic conflict between real human beings, and between reality and illusion. This is precisely what happens in Purcell's *Dido and Aeneas* as a mini, but fully heroic, baroque opera; and it is what cannot happen in his semi-operas which, of their nature, must remain semi-civilised.

Nowadays the cult of (inevitably unrealised) authenticity has led to a belief, or at least assertion, that any artistic convention, however apparently obsolete, will, if understood and interpreted on its own terms, prove both viable and valuable. This is a heresy, for only a little intelligence and good will are necessary to recognise that some conventions are 'better than' others. Let us consider *Dioclesian* in this context. The source of the piece is again an 'old' play, this time not by Shakespeare, but by his contemporaries Beaumont and Fletcher who, in being a 'team' who consistently worked in collaboration, are forebears of the factories of musicians, theatre people, and business tycoons who 'produce' musicals as part of our entertainment industry. Even in their own day Beaumont and Fletcher, in comparison with Shakespeare and 'rare' Ben Jonson, were prone to exploit 'strong' situations, startling reversals, and disguise as an obfuscation rather than exploration of ambiguous relations between illusion and reality; this may be why they retained their popularity longer than better dramatic poets, including Shakespeare, and were frequently revived and 'adapted' after the Restoration. The decision to refurbish this particular play—in which Massinger also contributed to the 'team'—was probably not arbitrary, for the story is pertinent to a monarchical society recently 'restored', albeit with a difference. Thomas Betterton, an actor-manager at Dorset Gardens Theatre where the piece was first produced in 1690, rehashed the original into commonsensical modern prose and verse, while Henry Purcell, brightest of our young composers, was brought in to furnish songs and dances, along with ceremonial numbers appropriate to the gorgeous spectacle and "Wondrous Machines" that would enrapture a demotic public not at court, but in a commercial theatre, wherein a product had to be marketable.

The situation behind the play has a modern ring in that it turns on a prophecy by a tabloid-Cassandra-figure called, after the Delphic oracles, Delphia. She asserts that in this New Age any man (or any woman?) may become president (or in Roman terms emperor) if he succeeds in slaying a rampant wild boar. Diocles, a common soldier, takes up the challenge: so a Hero still dominates the plot, though he is no longer a royal leader by inherited right. Democratic reward for this vengeful act will be half the kingdom, and the hand of the Princess Aurelia. But though the public or market value of this enterprise is patent and potent, its private implications are confused, since Diocles already has a girlfriend, who happens to be the prophetess's niece. So the inner conflict of a tragic heroine of Racine, or for that matter of Purcell's Dido, lapses into vacillation and confusion. Momently, Diocles is equally enchanted by both his women; first opting for the marketable goods and goodies, he is then persuaded by conscience, stimulated by a discarded lover more enraged than any boar, to renounce Glory altogether, and to retreat to romantic Lombardy and the Happy-Ever-After of an elaborately staged masque.

This farrago was fraught with contemporary social and political parallels. Diocles, the plain-man-heroic-soldier-emperor, has points in common with Charles II, and more directly with William III, who had recently been crowned after rescuing perfidious Albion from the still more perfidious Roman Catholics. Attempts have been made to unravel an intricate political allegory, with roles for Monmouth and Cromwell, along with the royals. Names and dates don't fit accurately, but hardly need to, since what matters is that such resonances were in the air, much as the escapism of modern musicals—not to mention the canniness of crossover musicals like those of Bernstein and Sondheim—mirrors the dreams we think we live by, even if we don't. But for Purcell's music—and this is a big But—*Dioclesian* remains a trivial experience because the traditional conflict between love and duty, the private and the public life, reality and illusion, proves to be no such thing. Instead of conflict, there is confusion which is not resolved but dismissed in the mindless hedonism cultivated by the Merry Monarch himself. Diocles's air in Act III propounds the piece's only positive value: an eternity of sensual pleasures that time cannot stale; a tumescence of ego that is an apotheosis of the seventeenth-century equation between sexual orgasm and dying. This makes a point, since it is through sexual orgasm that life is born! In this piece the consummatory masque itself, when the action is finished, climaxes in homage to Bacchus, invoking Charles II as "the mighty Jove" who

> ne'er troubled his head with much thinking
>> He took up his glass,
>> Was kind to his lass,
> And gain'd Heav'n by love and good drinking.

> The Chorus's addendum
> Begone, begone, importunate reason,
> Wisdom and counsel in now out of season

hits the nail smack on the head, serving too as an epitome and epiphany of post-Thatcherite Britain.

In *A Secular Masque*, an aptly titled poem written in the last year (1700) of Dryden's life, the laureate wrote off the Restoration with the words

> The Wars brought nothing about,
> The Lovers were all untrue;
> 'Tis well an Old Age is out,
> And time to begin a New.

When Sir Christopher Wren rebuilt St Paul's and much of the City after the Great Fire, he achieved a British compromise—between Court and Country, Church and Parliament, Religion and Science—such as the tormented century had been painfully seeking. He lived to establish a great, ongoing tradition in British architecture, as Purcell had not done for our music. Even so, the British compromise that Purcell effected is still the key to our future, should we have one. Non-racist, non-sexist democracy, though an unattainable ideal, remains the best we have.

And of course Purcell's genius, as distinct from his talents, is the reason why *Dioclesian* is worth reviving, though the major part of the masque has always been among the most popular of Purcell's ceremonial odes to the (materially) Good Life: in which Purcell, living like his contemporaries in the sensory moment, is apt to be a shade short-winded, unless buoyed on the continuity of a ground bass that represents at once the remorselessness of fate and the human capacity to endure it. Even so, his art, displaying exceptional genius, intermittently reveals the numinous world of spirit, opening magic casements that are not evasive since, being both perilous and forlorn, they embrace the anti-masque along with the masque. Purcell's frolicsomeness, unlike his monarch's, grew up.

To me, at least, the masque would have been more aesthetically satisfying than the whole concoction, though Peter Seymour's Baroque Soloists and Orchestra, in collaboration with Riding Lights Theatre Company, made a brave shot at effecting a willing suspension of disbelief. Inevitably, the actors had a hard time of it in a concert hall rather than theatre, with a less than inspiring text to utter, with no ostentatious costumes to lend lustre to the baroque façade, and with no hope of 'flying flutes', let alone a fire-snorting dragon, to render us goggle-eyed. The actors attempted to compensate by trying too hard, enunciating with too conscious rhetoric, though they got across the mildly funny jokes that, in the temporising temper of the Restoration, served as substitute for drama.

The music needs no apology, especially since the performance offered all we've come to expect from these mostly young but well-seasoned artists. Seymour's familiar team of soloists were in top form, interlacing English baroque swagger with the vulnerable pathos that must underlie it, since in this world self-confidence and cynicism are uneasy bedfellows, as are love and lunacy. It cannot be fortuitous that Purcell, the flower of his age, excelled in mad songs, "the last Song that Mr Purcell made" being that distraught *scena* 'From rosy bowers', contributed to a play rehashed from Cervantes's *Don Quixote*, itself a parable of lunacy and illusion.

The solo singers' contributions were ballasted by that of the chorus, as usual both youthfully enthusiastic and, when occasion demanded, maturely expressive; and by that of the orchestra, with wirily resilient strings, astringent oboes, and cooing recorders. Peter Seymour was the inspirational conductor, whose lively tempos never effaced the vulnerability inherent in the paradoxical pathos of Purcell's ebullience. We need the sane effervescence of this music to help us to counter the lunacy of our own world; the hedonism of which hardly encourages bodies to frisk and spirits to levitate, as did, three hundred years ago, that of Purcell in a world so like ours, but for its propensity to life-enhancing laughter and tears.

MT, SEPTEMBER 1995

LITTLE TIME TO SPARE
WHAT MORE COULD MOZART POSSIBLY HAVE ACCOMPLISHED?

Mozart, 1992

HAVING SPENT A YEAR CELEBRATING THE EVENT, WE CAN HARDLY avoid knowing that Mozart died 200 years ago this past December 5. We came near to sinking beneath the spate of words putatively in his honour; but it is possible that, in retrospect, there may be lessons to learn. In particular it may be rewarding to reflect on the difference between what his death meant in 1791 and what it meant to us in 1991, for the two meanings, though obviously related, are not identical.

Nobody denies that Mozart was the most phenomenal infant prodigy in the history of music; his musical life began early, as it was to end. Whereas Haydn seemed to know intuitively that he had time at his disposal, and composed at a fairly mature age most of the works for which we now revere him, Mozart seemed to know that he had little time to spare. He was technically proficient by the time he entered his teens; by the age of twenty-five he had written some of the masterpieces of European music; in another ten years, having created and perfected a new kind of tragi-comic opera and a new, quasi-dramatic instrumental form in his mature piano concertos, he was dead.

From Mozart's childhood pieces we would know that he was an unprecedented musical phenomenon but not that he was going to be one of the three supreme composers in European history. Indeed, a case can be made that the music Mendelssohn wrote before and during his teens is of greater intrinsic value than the music Mozart composed at the same age. But Mendelssohn, who didn't survive much longer than Mozart, relatively speaking declined, whereas Mozart fleshed out boyish miracles of technique (and, to a degree, of feeling) with artistic experience that in height and depth can only be described as Shakespearean. The parallel is apt not only in scales of value but also because Mozart was pre-eminently a dramatic and often explicitly theatrical composer. He and Handel were the supreme humanists of music, and his ambitious father had reared him in the Handelian traditions of heroic opera, the prime artistic convention of an age dedicated to the glory of man in the highest. A child of twelve producing operas about the triumphs and tribulations of kings and conquerors—men pretending to be gods, and usually discovering that they aren't—seems grotesque. Having grown up, at the age of twenty-five Mozart created in *Idomeneo* a heroic opera that effaces the conventional model precisely because it is aware of the tragic implications inherent in

78

any human pretension to divinity. By that time, however, Mozart had realized that the old Italianate *opera seria* was not for him. Heroic opera had dealt in closed musical forms with absolute ethical values, which claim that we know how people ought to behave even if they don't do so. But in a rapidly changing, increasingly democratized society such an approach, aiming with equivocal success at unity, was no longer pertinent. Nor was it adequate to substitute for the aristocratic-autocratic *opera seria* an *opera buffa, opéra comique,* or *Singspiel* dealing, in vernacular Italian, French or German, with the low life of common men and women. As a child, Mozart had explored these increasingly popular genres; grown up, he knew that the only musical-theatrical convention appropriate to the new, volatile world must be at once aristocratic and democratic, tragic and comic. If *opera seria* by its nature sought for unity, mature Mozartian opera was dualistic in its essence.

The very stories of Mozart's mature operas concern tensions between worlds old and new, and there are no unambiguous good and bad guys. *The Marriage of Figaro* is about the fight between a moribund aristocracy and the democratic world of common people. Figaro and Susanna, the young representatives of the new society, are lively and lovely but humanly fallible; the autocratic Count is a pathological case rather than a monster; and his aristocratic Countess, far from being a villainess, is a tragic victim. We can identify with all the protagonists, since the opera's moral standards are, like Mozart's society, in process of formulation. Similarly, there is a three-way relationship among the aristocratic but decadent Don Giovanni, the women (whether aristocrats, middle-class upwardly mobile types, or peasant-servants) who are his prey, and Leporello, the underdog who is also Giovanni's *alter ego,* in so far as he, rather than the Don, is the future. At the end the ambiguous hero is yanked down to hell, his crime having been his literal destruction of the old world, when he slaughtered the Commendatore in the opera's first scene. The descent to hell is so intensely dramatic that it is rightly regarded as a harbinger of Romanticism; but it is also comic, and is followed by full-scale *buffo* finale affirming society's return to its primrose path, now that the threat presented by uncontrolled libido seems, momentarily, to have passed. Civilization must be preserved, and cannot be unless at least lip service is paid to the status quo. None the less, some form of change seems to be both necessary and inevitable.

All this is inherent in the techniques of Mozart's music. He was the only composer of his age whose distinction came equally from operas and from instrumental works in sonata form—the new, dualistic compositional principle apposite to conflict, growth, and change. His mature operas fuse the 'closed' forms of *opera seria,* such as the *aria da capo,* with the 'open', evolutionary sonata. People grow while they sing Mozart's arias, and may not be the same at an aria's end as they were at the beginning. They are still more transformed as they interact with one another, democratically expressing different responses to the same situation, in the ensemble numbers that are the climax to each act. Social transformation implies a metamorphosis of individual identities, and *vice versa*. The vital music of the sonata era deals with the relationship between public and private life, in which respect Mozart is the most profound, as well as the liveliest, humanist in music.

But there is another dimension to art which Mozart—unlike Bach and, in his different way, Beethoven—did not for most of his life explore. This is the dimension usually called religious, concerned not so much with relationships between people as with the relationship between man and God. Although Mozart was as a very young man employed by the Catholic Church, and had naturally produced ecclesiastical music, this was—and was meant to be and was accepted as—rococo social music, secular in spirit, and in technique operatic in the old sense. But during the 1780s, the great years of his operatic creation, Mozart became fascinated by what one can only call religious experience, though it had little to do with his traditional Church and much to do with the fashionable religion of enlightenment, as promoted by Freemasonry.

Fundamentally, eighteenth-century Masons were opposed to what they considered the 'superstition' of revealed religion, and were in turn distrusted by the Catholic Church. The Premier Grand Lodge in England claimed in 1723 that "we ... are resolved against all Politicks", and defined its aim as the conciliation of "true friendship among persons who must otherwise have remained at a perpetual distance".* In France the Masonic programme paralleled the universal liberalism of the Encyclopaedists; in Germany it moralistically became "an exercise of Brotherly Love [whereby] we are taught to regard the whole human species as one family, the high and the low, the rich and the poor". Clearly, there were two interlaced strands to such concerns, one psychological and even mystical, the other political. Gradually the Masons bifurcated: one camp, the Rosicrucians, stressed the psychological aspects of the creed, while the other, the self-styled Illuminati, became politically subversive—at least in the frightened eyes of the ecclesiastical establishment. By the end of the century a hysterical establishment could even maintain that the Illuminati were directly responsible for the French Revolution. The charge was paranoid: even Franz Heinrich Ziegenhagen, who in 1792 boldly advocated a classless society, believed that it could be peacefully attained through education. In any case, not even the enlightened took any notice of him; the rich did not surrender their loot, let alone their inherited wealth, to the common weal. The starry-eyed Ziegen-hagen committed suicide in 1806.

Gluck and Haydn were both Masons, and it is obvious that the Mozart who, quoting the Latin tag, "deemed nothing human alien" to him,* would have relished the political aspects of Masonry. It is also unsurprising that Masonic creeds appealed to him at the deeper, Rosicrucian levels, as they did, still more, to the Beethoven of the *Missa Solemnis*. Shifts of emphasis in Mozart's music, after he formally became a Mason in 1784, are unmistak-able, if discreet; it cannot have been fortuitous that in these years he made an exhaustive study of the counterpoint of Bach, the greatest of all religious composers. Fugue, especially as practiced by Bach, is the fundamental prin-ciple of unity in European music, as opposed to the duality of sonata, the compositional principle that was the essence of Mozart's work. The some-what frenzied intensity of Mozart's conscious exercises in Bachian fugue—such as the C minor Adagio and Fugue for string quartet or two pianos—suggests that the idiom didn't come to him naturally. What mat-ters, however, is the effect his studies had on the general tenor of his cre-ation. In particular, the final trinity of symphonies, written over a remarkably short time span, embraces polyphony and counterpoint at once more complex and more lucid than was common in Mozart's earlier works. Together the three symphonies amount to a magnificent Masonic credo. No. 39 is in the Masonic-ritual key of E flat major, symbolizing the three knocks on the door to enlightenment; no. 40 is in Mozart's 'tragic' G minor, delineating a purgatorial progress; no. 41, in 'white' C major, represents the triumph of light, climaxing in a synthesis of opposites—of homophony with polyphony, of the dualistic principle of sonata with the monistic prin-ciple of fugue. The string quintets, perhaps the greatest of Mozart's chamber works, likewise reinterpret the social aspects of Masonry in psy-chological terms; the G minor, in particular, is an initiation, *agon*, and rebirth such as masonic ritual re-enacted, in emulation of the Eleusinian mysteries. Significantly, the tragic pain of this quintet dissolves in a major apotheosis that reminds us of Papageno.

And of course it is Mozart's *singspiel, The Magic Flute*, that, in directly invoking the Orpheus story, reveals how Masonic initiates hoped to rein-troduce transcendence into humanitarian ethics. Written in Mozart's last year, for a vaudeville theatre run by Emanuel Schikaneder (himself a Mason), it embraces a diversity of manners from grand opera to street song and an eighteenth-century equivalent of the TV jingle. It seems confused, as do we, because it deals with a world in transition, as is ours. We have noted that Mozart himself was profoundly ambivalent: a Roman Catholic who dispatched his lecherous Giovanni, tragi-comic symbol of modern libido, to hell; but also a Mason dedicated to enlightenment through reason, social benevolence, and a liberal education. He could not—his Shakespearean stature depends on this—passively accord with an either-or view of the human condition. Both rational thought and irrational belief had their own truths. Like Blake, his near-contemporary, Mozart knew that "without Contraries [there] is no Progression."*

So Mozart's Masonic opera proves to be not so much about the conflict between darkness and light as about the new man and woman who are born of it. When the Masonic vow of silence forbids Tamino, the hero on trial, to speak to his beloved Pamina, her anguish parallels that of Eurydice when Orpheus is forbidden to look back. But Pamina does not just 'fade away' of her sorrow, as does Gluck's Eurydice; she sings what is perhaps the most sublime aria even Mozart ever wrote—in G minor, of course, in a slow *siciliano* rhythm, as though the pulse is dying of inanition. The arching melody drops balm; the Neapolitan progressions and German sixths of the harmony at once hurt and heal. Spiritually, if not in the superficies of technique, the air, mating operatic aria, folk song and hymn, is the most Bach-like music Mozart ever wrote—certainly far more so than the self-conscious imitation of a Bach fugue he experimented with in that C minor Adagio and Fugue.

Pamina, saving herself from despairing suicide by her song, becomes the agent of redemption in presumptively eternal love between a man and a woman. In this sense she, not Tamino, is the central character, and the redemption she achieves is comically echoed in the sub-plot of Papageno and Papagena. He, a bird-man halfway between nature and us, is also saved from suicide (probably in his case a mock suicide), by the appearance of three magic boys, who advise him to resort to his musical bells—a demotic substitute for Orpheus's lyre. As he tinkles them, his bird-girl Papagena is restored to him 'alive and well'; and although these bird-innocents cannot graduate to light along with Tamino and Pamina (the new world's new man and woman), their smaller rebirth offers to the commonest common folk, including you and me, the possibility of at least a mini-redemption. It is Pamina, the catalyst between masculine intellect and feminine intuition, who makes this possible. In being herself restored to life, she, like Persephone, restores the world. Day and night, man and woman, reason and love, are mutually incarnate.

The orthodox morality of the Enlightenment adhered, of course, to the well-illuminated notion of God as Master Mechanic and First Architect and Mason. Even though the mystery latent in Masonic pilgrimage appealed to the Enlightenment cult of Hellenism and the Exotick, rational man could only blench at the irrationality (and still more the feminism!) thus revealed.

None the less, the truly great artists of the time were great precisely because they *didn't* blench. Mozart's last works, despite their light-shedding sociability, are profoundly death-haunted. One thinks not only of the irrational pluralism of *The Magic Flute*, with its descent into the dark labyrinth that the legendary Orpheus confronted, but also of the Concerto for Clarinet, a relatively new instrument much favoured by Masons for its mysterious tone colour—especially the concerto's slow movement, wherein the soloist chants a sublime melody that, like Pamina's G minor aria, is a hybrid of an operatic aria, an innocent folk song, and a wise Sarastro-like Masonic hymn. This is music of man-woman re-born, to make, it is hoped, a newly democratic world. There are hints of this hopefulness even in the explicitly death-dedicated *Requiem* that Mozart embarked on in response to a commission from a mysterious dark-liveried stranger. Although the man was in fact the harmless emissary of a count who wanted to pass off the piece as his own memorial tribute to a deceased wife, the incident seemed sinister to the ailing, overworked Mozart, who feared that the requiem might be for himself. Such it proved, in the sense that Mozart died before he could finish it; and there is an added irony in the fact that he had inadequate time for the task because of pressure to complete an old-fashioned *opera seria*, *La Clemenza di Tito*, designed to celebrate the coronation of Leopold II as King of Bohemia. A paradox remains, even though Leopold was a benevolent despot with Masonic inclinations.

Mozart survived for only half of his biblically allotted threescore years and ten, and living with such brief intensity, he seemed to have been more than normally death-conscious. On this subject he wrote a remarkable letter to his father:

I need not tell you with what anxiety I await better news from you. Since death (take my words literally) is the true goal of our lives, I have made myself so well acquainted with this true and best friend of man that the idea of it no longer has terrors for me, but rather much that is tranquil and comforting. And I thank God that he has granted me the good fortune to obtain the opportunity of regarding death as the key to our true happiness. I never lie down in bed without considering that, young as I am, perhaps on the morrow I may be no more. Yet not one of those who know me could say that I am morose or melancholy, and for this I thank my Creator daily and wish heartily that the same happiness may be given to my fellow men.*

Although Mozart remained formally a Catholic as well as a Mason, we cannot know whether he preserved a traditionally Catholic view of life after death. But we can say that such a belief is not necessarily latent in that extraordinary letter, nor in the consummate perfection of the music he wrote in his last year. This music leaves nothing to be said. Had Mozart lived longer, he would presumable have added something to a musical experience that seems already all-inclusive, but it is impossible to imagine what. In this he differs from Schubert, who died even younger, leaving us with a tragic sense of potentialities on the brink of fulfilment. We can speculate on the implications of the fact that Schubert could, indeed should, have survived well after the first performance of *Tristan*, but we cannot think of Mozart in those chronological terms. Even the slightest work of his final year seems to exist independent of time and place. In the little piece for glass harmonica, K617; in the cantata composed for Masonic rites, K619; and above all in the last of the string quintets, K614 (in the Masonic key of E flat major), we find a new idiom: luminously diaphanous, not so much seeking the light as letting light *through*, seemingly of childlike simplicity, yet fraught with *lacrimae rerum*. Such divertimenti diverted Mozart, no doubt, and they would divert a company of angels; but they are poles apart from the serenades and cassations of his boyhood, and are no longer music to eat or to chatter to. It almost seems as though Mozart had relinquished the task of writing music for a society that of its nature is as ephemeral as a dream. He now wrote in a celestial drawing room, where the only audience was himself and silence (and he, having fathered the music, did not need to listen): just as Bach in his last years, composing *The Art of Fugue* in an outmoded fashion, played to himself in an empty church.

AM, JANUARY 1992

INVADING NERVES, BLOOD AND BONES
EDVARD GRIEG AND THE TRIUMPH OF NORWEGIAN MUSIC

Nils Grinde, *A History of Norwegian Music*, translated by W. B. Halverson & L. B. Sateren
(Lincoln: University of Nebraska Press, 1991)
Einar Haugen & Camilla Cai, *Ole Bull: Norway's Romantic Musician and Cosmopolitan Patriot*
(Madison: University of Wisconsin Press, 1993)
Lionel Carley, *Grieg and Delius: A Chronicle of Their Friendship in Letters*
(London: Marion Boyars, 1993)
Finn Benestad & Dag Schjelderup-Ebbe, *Edvard Grieg: Chamber Music – Nationalism,*
Universality, Individuality (Oslo: Scandinavian University Press, 1993)

T HE CULT OF NATIONHOOD IN NINETEENTH-CENTURY MUSIC FOLLOWED
in the wake of the cult of Faustian will and ego: for when the 'I' dominated, the nation that 'I' belonged to received a boost, in a process at
once psychological and political. In particular, 'little' nations asserted their
authority in defiance of master-races: which is why nationalism grew
potent in the turbulent Central European and peripheral Scandinavian
countries. Norway, for instance, was out on a limb: an agrarian community
linked by way of cosmopolitan Denmark to Europe—which entailed the
overbearing German hegemony. Not fortuitously did 'little' Norway produce in Grieg a mini-master who acquired major status, proving that small
may be beautiful—Grieg was a mere 4 feet 8 inches in height, and he wrote
mainly in small forms.

The big *History of Norwegian Music* by Nils Grinde tends, as is usual with
such surveys, to cover the ground on plodding feet. Affinities with Danish
and German cultures are charted, and the roll-call of art composers is comprehensive. The book also embraces a pre-history of Viking culture, which
sports some handsome illustrations to little musical effect, since the music
does not survive except in what we may deduce from the putative resources
of obsolete instruments. More rewarding is the book's account of folk traditions, many of which are still extant. Herding songs, lullabies, mountain
calls and rowing chants are 'music of necessity' that may still be sampled in
the field; and such functional techniques are ballasted by music that is communal as well as practically communicative. People in Scandinavian cultures sing and dance together to pipe-and-tabor-like duos, to plucked
string instruments of great antiquity and, above all to fiddles. The music of
the peasant hardanger-fiddle culminated, in the eighteenth and nineteenth
centuries, in a tradition of dance music that was simultaneously function,
entertainment, and art. The *gangar, springar, halling* and *pols* are (usually
triple-rhythmed) dances that resound, on the open-stringed fiddle, with a
grandeur apt to vast spaces, and appropriate to heroic events as recounted
in ancient ballads. Not only sturdy peasants, but trolls also, are rampant in
this music, which is closely related to the fiddle music of the Shetland

Islands, since cultural cross-currents between Norway and Scotland prospered from the sixteenth to the nineteenth century. These countries were
cohesive enough to permit, even to promote, interfusions of rural with
urban culture, until in the late eighteenth century folk fiddlers attained a
high degree of virtuosity, relished as much in towns as in villages.

The near-legendary figure of Ole Bull—described by Einar Haugen and
Camilla Cai in their amiably written, well-produced book as "Norway's
Romantic musician and cosmopolitan patriot"—personifies this two-way
traffic between 'music of necessity' and art. The authors describe how as a
child Bull was familiar with, and contributed to, the work of folk fiddlers;
they proceed to explore the ways in which, being a prodigy of exceptional
talents and charisma, he went on to become a city man and itinerant pop
idol comparable with Paganini, whom he revered and emulated. He did
not create a distinctive if limited *oeuvre* to complement the usual
pyrotechnic pots-pourris of barnyard imitations and hits from Italian
operas, as did Paganini; certainly he never challenged Liszt as a showbiz
man who was also an intrinsically and historically significant composer.
Even so, Bull's celebrity as a 'performance artist' was internationally 'fabulous'; and if his music, as distinct from his legend, is now forgotten (he
seldom bothered to write down the show-pieces he had arrived at empirically), he slightly survives by way of a few published arrangements of folk-
fiddle tunes. In a rural community, folk traditions are less ephemeral than
artistic fashions.

Throughout the nineteenth century, these complementary strands—a
folk tradition still rurally operative and an art tradition stemming vocally
from romantic Italian opera and instrumentally from German-Austrian
sonata—slowly fused to make possible Norway's National Hero in the tiny
person of Grieg. A few art composers made a modest impact on him: such
as Kjerulf, a song writer of personal and national savour, and Lindeman,
who forged a link between peasant music and the 'ongoingness' of Bach
which, as Percy Grainger discovered, could serve as an alternative to the
"paradise of archetypes and repetition" in which folk musics habitually
operate. Encouraged by the prolific Dane, Niels Gade, Grieg followed in the
steps of most Norwegian music students in attending the Leipzig Conservatory of Music, where he claimed to have learned nothing. He must surely,
however, have fuelled his enthusiasm for Schumann's short piano pieces,
which, dealing in dreams, fairy-tales and childhood experiences, were prototypes for his own *Lyric Pieces* for piano, written intermittently
throughout his life; while technically he acquired the ability to compose, at
the age of twenty-two, a fugue for string quartet which is far too fierce to be
dismissed as academic. It is true that his approach in the same year (1865) to

the writing of a violin and piano sonata was a shade tentative, and that the work in question (in traditionally pastoral F major) displays little of the master Brahms's craft and cunning. But Finn Benestad and Dag Schjelderup-Ebbe, in their usefully thorough if unexhilarating book on Grieg's chamber music, defend the sonata on the grounds that craft and cunning would have been inapposite to a work whose virtues lie in spontaneity; whereby the sweet-flowing lyricism, absolved from Teutonic *Angst*, reveals depths within luminosity. Folky drones undermine academically functional harmony; genius flowers in the first movement's wide-eyed opening, and through the slow movement, pervaded by the motif of a descending second followed by a falling major or minor third. Benestad and Schjelderup-Ebbe call this "the Grieg formula", though it is pervasive in many folk-affiliated composers, notably Vaughan Williams.

Written two years later, in 1867, Grieg's Second Violin Sonata was described by its composer as "my national sonata": by which he presumably meant that he no longer needed to apologize for 'Grieg-formulae', peasant dance-rhythms, and 'gypsy' scales. A fervent slow introduction in G minor leads into a sonata allegro in *springar* triple time; the key is (frequently benedictory) G major, though the second subject is unorthodoxly in B minor. The slow movement is an exquisite lament in a modalized E minor, relative to G major; but the middle section of the ternary form is dichoto-mously a fiery dance in E major. The coda incorporates a hardanger-fiddle-style cadenza, preparing us for the drones and open fifths of the final rondo-sonata, which again lives between worlds in that it fuses folk virility with Neapolitan modulations and a twist, in the coda, into the remoteness of E flat major.

Twenty years later, at the age of forty-three, Grieg wrote a third violin and piano sonata in the traditionally dynamic key of C minor. Benestad and Schjeldrup-Ebbe have no difficulty in disposing of the once current view that this work is a Brahmsian exercise antipathetic to Grieg's native wood-notes wild. On their showing, the work emerges as a mysteriously romantic masterpiece, especially in its first movement's darkly passionate recapitula-tion, with its final, modally severe, cadence. The Romanza is remotely in E major—a relationship possibly borrowed from the slow movement of Beethoven's C minor Piano Concerto. Its bliss is not, however, unsullied, for the tenderly harmonized tune is rudely disrupted by a fierce folk dance in the modalized minor, returning to the A section by way of weird enhar-monic puns. Ambiguity between worlds peasant and polite is resolved in the finale's oddly truncated sonata structure, which ultimately transforms Aeolian G into a G major apotheosis. Grieg seems to have grown up in writing this sonata, both musically and in human terms. At the time, he was coping with marital problems that sprang more from his loving and loveable nature than from a lascivious eye or malicious heart. We learn something about this from the Greig-Delius letters intelligently compiled and meticulously edited by Lionel Carley, basically a Delius man, though here the maker of the most valuable of these Greig-affiliated books. Why the two composers loved one another is not far to seek. Both relished sensuous spontaneity, whether in music or in human relationships. Grieg admired the heroic span and sometimes tragic grandeur of Delius's nature-mysticism, while Delius savoured the intimacy of Grieg's. Both, in their *recherches du temps perdu*, countered nostalgia with strength; both were dedicated to mountains and to women. Delius, twenty years Grieg's junior, apparently talked more freely about his amours to Grieg's wife Nina than to the master himself; still, the elvish Norwegian and the hawkish Yorkshireman must have recognized a bond in their sexuality; and that both marriages did much more than survive is possibly a tribute to the men's humane empathy as well as (more patently) to their wives' forbearance.

The human turmoil latent in the C minor violin and piano sonata erupted in the major work that immediately succeeded it: a string quartet in G minor that belies the common account of Grieg as a miniaturist in being ambitious in scope and dense in texture. After a grand if short introduction, based on the 'Grieg formula', the first subject of the allegro is wild, carried through with flair, if with an excess of multiple stopping prophetic of the solitary quartet of César Franck. The second subject is, unsurprisingly, chromatically nostalgic, and the development has to be 'difficult' since the two subject-groups—surely reflecting Grieg's current nervous bifurcation—are so disparate. Extreme contrasts of tempo and mood culminate in fiery hardanger-fiddle rhythms and a microtonally gypsyish lament, rising to near-Bartókian vehemence.

The slow movement starts as though it will be as cosily Norwegian as the first movement had been 'beyond the pale', but it soon reveals the turbulence currently—and perhaps to a degree habitually—latent beneath the surface. For the lovely B flat major tune sung by solo cello in the domestic parlour is countered by fierce, gypsyish explosions in the tonic minor: a dichotomy that recalls the sublime slow movement of Schubert's C major string quintet. Grieg's Romanza, though not in that class, likewise teeters between dream and reality, and ends dramatically, in ghostly tremolandi. The scherzo similarly juxtaposes, rather than fuses, opposite poles, for it is lumpishly peasant-like, whereas its trio is quietly comic, tinged with chromatic nostalgia. The jollity of the coda is more alarming than funny; and the finale exaggerates all these contradictions, beginning with a 'heroic' introduction, followed by a folky sonata-rondo, again prophetic of Bartók in its veerings between anger, sentimentality, catastrophe and farce.

Although—as Benestad and Schjelderup-Ebbe ably demonstrate—the G minor quartet is a big work in more than one sense, it remained a one-off. Grieg started an F major quartet intended as a comic foil to the tragic G minor, but completed only two movements, no less richly written than the G minor, though their mood is spring-like, as is the early violin sonata in the same key. Grown to man's estate, Grieg can no longer be content with the mindless vivacity of that delightful work; dark undercurrents stir in the development of the quartet's first movement, hinting at threats inherent in envious and calumniating Time. It may be significant that Grieg resorts to self-quotation—not merely in the shape of generic relationship to the early violin sonata but in specific reference to his greatest public success, the Piano Concerto; the troll-haunted scherzo also borrows a theme from the Vinje songs of 1880. Such hopeful aphrodisiacs from vanished well-springs didn't enable Grieg to complete the quartet; and he composed no more works in fully fledged sonata form.

Grieg's health was never robust and we learn from these Grieg-Delius letters that his wife not only frequently acted as amanuensis but also as a lively surrogate correspondent. Even so, that Grieg concentrated in late years on short piano pieces and songs rather than on sonatas, let alone symphonies, may be mainly attributable to the fact that it was in small forms that his minor-major genius most flourished. They had the further advantage that they were the basic source of his comfortable income, from the time when, in 1867, he published the first volume of *Lyric Pieces*, just before the Piano Concerto. Between 1867 and 1901 Grieg issued ten volumes of *Lyric Pieces*, transporting hints of the lovely and lovable Concerto into the parlour. The concerto itself, though marvellously written for the instrument, is a very intimate display-piece; and intimacy is the heart of the *Lyric Pieces*, which are mostly recollections of boyhood experience in his agrarian native land, or revelations of the solitary heart. Often Grieg discovered the universal within the particular—occasionally in the early volumes, as in the radiant 'Arietta' from opus 12, commonly in the later volumes, whether in vividly descriptive pieces like 'Wedding-day at Troldhaugen' and the astonishing bell-piece 'Klokkeklang', or in indrawn mood-pieces like the breath-stopping 'Phantom', the near-immobile nature-mysticism of 'Evening in the Mountains', or in a moment of rapture outside time, like 'At Your Feet'. The titles of many of the pieces—'Homesickness', 'Once upon a Time', 'Gone', 'Remembrance'—indicate that nostalgia triggers the music; but they don't tell us how magically memory of things past leads into undiscovered futures—in terms of Debussyan impressionism, Ravelian polytonality, and Bartókian rhythmic audacity. When, in 1974, Emil Gilels made his famous recording of Grieg's *Lyric Pieces*, he praised the "depths of tenderness and mystery the music contains", as Grieg "formulated in musical terms the 'truth' of an ever-seeking solitary human being". Complementarily, in his opus 66 and opus 72, Grieg metamorphosed folk songs and hardanger-fiddle dances into piano pieces with a raucous immediacy challenging that of Bartók's refashioning of Magyar song and dance. Intimate personal identity and communal identification prove to be the opposite sides of the same (valuable) coin.

Grieg's songs, written throughout his life, parallel the evolution of his *Lyric Pieces*, and have patent links with his spiritual history in that many of them were written for, and more were sung by, his wife. The early songs, such as the familiar setting of Hans Andersen's 'Jeg elsker Dig', remain fresh as Norwegian daisies because of their instantly memorable, lastingly unforgettable, tunes. The settings of German romantic poets, especially Goethe and Heine, are scarcely less spontaneous; and when Grieg turned to Norwegian poets like Krag and Vinje, spontaneity was enhanced by a subtler sensitivity and more potent sensuality. The final song-cycle *Haugtussa*, written in 1895 to folk poems of Arne Garborg, is a masterpiece which inspires Nils Grinde's responsible but pedestrian account of Grieg's composing career to unbuttoned warmth. The cycle recounts an adolescent girl's thwarted love for a fickle swain. Even—or especially—in this 'late' work, Grieg responds to adolescent grief with tingling immediacy, while preserving the impersonality of folk art: for the tunes, always in simple strophic form, *persist*, while garnering new shifts of meaning through each stanza. Life hurts, but goes on, like the babbling brook, magically imitated in the luminously spaced piano part. Here is Grieg's ultimately healing synthesis of folk consciousness—or preconsciousness—with art.

This Norwegian 'premier matin du monde' is capped by one other work, Grieg's *opus ultimum*, the *Four Psalms*, opus 74, written in 1906–7. These *a cappella* choruses are religious music with only the remotest connection with a church—that of Norwegian Protestantism, which invigorated and irradiated German Lutheranism with Scandinavian air, light and water. Grieg seems to have been fairly indifferent to God, without hating him fanatically as did Delius and Grainger. Despite Delius's world-weary Nietzscheanism, Grieg's uncertain health and intermittent melancholia, and Grainger's sexual perversities, all three men were denizens of a lost Eden, and all accepted nature-worship as a viable alternative to godliness. Percy Grainger, most charismatic performer of the Grieg Concerto, translated the sixteenth-century hymns that Grieg used as texts for his Psalms into affectingly gauche English. The verses' open-eyed wonder is precisely caught in Grieg's open-eared music; we can believe that before Nature he "stood in silent veneration as before God himself". In the first Psalm, the harmony Grieg distils from radiant tune, gentle homophony, and lilting rhythm is at once suave and surprising. In the second psalm, hints of major-minor bitonality confess to inner unease: which is dispersed in the Easter hymn 'Jesus Kristus er opfaren', with its ecstatically 'out of this world' refrain on Kyrie Eleison, and in the heart-whole, carol-like tune of the final 'I Himmelen'. Both poetically and musically, these Psalms live simultaneously in "divided and distinguished worlds", old and new, religious and secular.

If, at the end of this 150th anniversary year [1993], we try to assess Grieg's place in Europe's story, we may say that his heart lies in his songs and in his *Lyric Pieces* and folk-song arrangements for piano, with a rare appendix in the *a cappella Psalms*. But the other Grieg, who stretched his wings towards 'Europe' to create the complex G minor quartet and the C minor violin and piano sonata, also has major status; and it was probably by way of a fusion between his intimacy and his intensity that Grieg attained to the third identity whereby he was, if not a popular entertainer comparable with Ole Bull, an instant international celebrity whose world-wide fame endures. His genius embraced a wonderful capacity for concentration and subtilization along with a command of the common touch. In a show-piece like the Piano Concerto, art and craft perpetuate the music's guileless *élan*; while in the *Peer Gynt* theatre music the tunes are so haunting that we feel we've known them all our lives, whether we're rehearing them in a theatre as intended, or more probably in a symphony concert, or tattily played in some Pump Room or on a seaside pier. After so many often indifferent performances, the music still invades nerves, blood and bones: because although Grieg grew up, as Grainger didn't, he remained also a *puer aeternatus* from whose truth we emerge refreshed, in a Thoreauesque "new world everlasting and unfallen, with dew on the grass".

TLS, DECEMBER 1993

REBEL WITHOUT APPLAUSE

Barry Smith, *Peter Warlock: The Life of Philip Heseltine*
(Oxford: Oxford University Press, 1994)

T HIS YEAR PETER WARLOCK, BORN PHILIP HESELTINE, CELEBRATES, IF that is the word, the centenary of his birth. I, having recently become an octogenarian, was a teenager when the Warlock legend was in its heyday: so this seems an occasion to recall what the legend meant to us then, and to consider what survives of the art, which justifies the legend, now. 'Sensitive', 'artistic', intellectual young people—the inverted commas are needed for the first two but not the third and fourth adjectives—found in him a slightly up-beat James Dean figure: a rebel addicted to powerful motorbikes and without a cause except the negative one of dislike of the society he and we lived in. We were all anti-Establishmentarians, though my own and my friends' link with Establishment was less direct than that of Philip Heseltine, whose family was well-connected as well as affluent, and who went to Eton and Oxford, hating both. Typically, his Mum and Dad "fucked him up"*—father by dying when Philip was two, mother by loving him, in her way, rather too much: though she staunchly supported Church, Army and Civil Service, at the expense of music, that frivolous adornment of society by which her son had been, from an early age, tiresomely seduced. Even so Philip, like many sensitive children, found hope of salvation in one man who saw what he was and might be: Colin Taylor, a master at Eton who had an enthusiasm for the kind of contemporary music that was anathema to Mother, and probably to her second husband also. Debussy, Ravel, Bartók, even Schoenberg, swam tantalisingly into Philip's orbit. So did Delius.

Delius, although an outsider in being of teutonic extraction, was born in the northern manufacturing city of Bradford, son of a wool-tycoon. Abominating everything Bradford stood for, the young Delius escaped when and where he could—to the Bohemian pleasures of *fin-de-siècle* Montmartre, to the mountainous solitudes of Scandinavia, to the grapefruit groves of Florida: for he was, as a direct consequence of the industrialism he despised, financially independent enough to pursue Nietzschean 'courage and self-reliance'. He hymned the twilight not merely of mercantile Britain, but also of Europe, employing to that end techniques basically German but stemming, not from 'academic' Brahms, but from that climacteric egotist of European culture, Wagner. Living in and for the self, Wagner's quasi-autobiographical Tristan found that he had ultimately no choice but to surrender that self to nirvana. Delius did the same, his nirvana being Nature's infinitudes of wind and sea that are antipodes to Bradford City. In his *Song of the*

High Hills—scored for an immense orchestra such as was paradoxically made feasible only by industrial technology—impetus may spring from the fluctuating tensions of Wagnerian chromatic harmony, but the individual lines—in the orchestral as well as choral parts—recurrently seek the pentatonic innocence of folk song. In discovering Delius, during the 'death of Europe' initiated by the First World War, Heseltine also discovered too his smaller self. Perhaps he suspected, even at the start, that his whole life would be a quest for nirvana, ultimately attained in an act of self-immolation.

Philip was not only sensitive, he was also clever; but he was not academically a high-flyer, at least when cramming Latin and Greek as steps towards a socially respectable career. For formal music education he had little or no time, though, encouraged by Colin Taylor, he turned out a few deft songs in the manner of Roger Quilter. These might have purred in his mother's elegant drawing-room: which Delius's music would have assaulted. To Philip, that music was a blast of air and a shaft of light, and although he had neither the confidence nor the skill to emulate its grandeur, he could be ecstatically levitated by it at second hand. Evidence of his fine ear and intuitive musicianship is proffered in the fact that experience of Delius's music had to come through score-reading, by eye and ear or at the piano, for he had few opportunities to attend orchestral concerts, while the recording industry was still embryonic. On the basis of enthusiasm and knowledge he penned reams of dionysian letters to Delius, who relished his own music to the exclusion of almost anyone else's, but looked kindly on young composers who paid him the sincerest form of flattery. If Philip's Delius-imitation couldn't be direct, it was evident in the chromatic flexibility that insinuated itself into what might have been parlour songs. Complementarily, his literary sources were increasingly drawn from 'old', especially medieval and Elizabethan, sources, thereby effecting another, probably unconscious, retreat from modern materialism.

Philip's literary range was wide and deep, as a consequence of native wit and sensibility and perhaps because of his abortive years at Eton and Oxford. If he couldn't, like Delius, be an ecstatic if nostalgic visionary, he could wear the mask of medieval peasant or priest, or of Elizabethan gallant or malcontent (but not merchant). Similarly, if he was incompetent at living in the nasty present, he could make congenial pasts momently present to himself and us. This he did while, having abandoned Eton and Oxford geographically as well as imaginatively, he bummed around, waiting for something to turn up. It did, in wild Ireland, in the last year of the war that was the beginning of the end of Old England. Acutely aware of failure in his own identity, he dispatched a small sheaf of songs to a publisher, Winthrop Rogers, under the pseudonym of Peter Warlock: names that toughen his wavery incertitudes with a hint of Peter's Rock, and sharpen them with Mer-linesque wizardry. In a few of these songs his small flame of genius, as dis-tinct from talent, first glows: for instance in neo-Elizabethan settings of Peele's 'Whenas the rye' and of Dekker's 'Golden slumbers' and 'Sweet con-tent', wherein vocal rhythms spring vernally from poetic scansion, while the keyboard textures irradiate parlour-conventions with a linearity embracing Renaissance modality and falsely related harmonies. Still more affecting are songs that hark back to the Middle Ages in spirit if not in strict chronology. 'My ghostly Fader', for instance, re-animates medieval incantation, with key-words expressively 'pointed' by the subtlest harmonic shift, and with a refrain that insidiously haunts. Yet more magical is 'The bayley bereth the bell away', in which the lilting 6/8 tune, tremulously harmonised, renders audible the enigmatic promise of sun, lily and rose.

At this point Philip Heseltine became, for both professional and personal purposes, Peter Warlock: a composer who, admitting that he could not com-pete with Delius in large-scale works, was grateful for small mercies. He had learned that "it is impossible for utterance to be impeded by lack of tech-nique", and that if he couldn't make Delian music, that was because he was a lesser man. (Reading the correspondence of the two, one finds 'Fred' Delius's tough Yorkshire common sense a relief after the adolescent Heseltine's self-communings.) But if Philip's intelligence recognised that when once one knows what one wants to say, the technique will be forthcoming—indeed the technique *is* the self-knowledge—he also knew that one artist may some-times learn from another: not by formal instruction, but through commu-nion of thought and feeling. Certainly in these crucial years Warlock's self-discovery was abetted by his friendship with Bernard van Dieren, a Dutch composer who, having settled in London, was intimate with a distin-guished galaxy of musicians, writers, painters and sculptors (including Epstein, about whom van Dieren wrote a pioneering book).

Warlock, living in London, gravitated into the van Dieren circle, with no 'career' but with a small private income, supplemented by occasional largesse from his loving if emotionally estranged mother; by pickings from his published songs; by work for publishers making piano arrangements, mostly of the music of Delius; by miscellaneous musical journalism in which he wielded a lively if sometimes reckless pen; and by acting as general factotum to Sir Thomas Beecham, the conductor who was Delius's main advocate. Van Dieren did not supplant Delius as role model and idol; but Warlock—dazzled by van Dieren's 'foreignness' and esotericism, by his physical beauty, and by his varied talents as musician, philosopher, linguist, bookbinder, gunsmith, antiquarian, and researcher into occult lore—increasingly thought of him as the Master. In duo with Cecil Gray, critic and composer, Warlock laboured to persuade the musical establishment that van Dieren was among the supreme composers of our century: efforts that met with scant success and not a little contempt. Yet van Dieren's weirdly introverted music, as chromatic as Delius himself and rather more atonal, may still exert a spell—perhaps related to the fact that he was, as victim of a rare, excruciatingly painful liver complaint, frequently drugged. His music's harmonic sophistication and rhythmic freedom, accruing from fine-spun polyphonies, offered Warlock what he needed: as is patent in the lovely 'Along the stream' (from *Saudades*, 1916), a song dedicated to van Dieren. But the Dutchman's influence is latent too in the early but vintage songs mentioned above, in the heart-rending setting of Shakespeare's 'Take, O take, those lips away', and in the setting of 'Mourn no Moe', from a play of Beaumont and Fletcher. These songs were later arranged for voice with string quartet, in which form the linearity of the concept is palpable. More-over, the 'presence' of van Dieren informs Warlock's peerless setting of Fletcher's 'Sleep', in which a vocal line "framed to the life of the words" in the manner of Dowland is mated with a keyboard texture that, being poly-phonically harmonic and modally chromatic, transmutes Dowland's lute idiom into entrancingly pianistic terms. This may be the most consummate of Warlock's fusions of past with present; and its technique has points in common with the work usually considered his masterpiece—*The Curlew*, a song cycle to poems of Yeats for voice, flute, cor anglais and string quartet. By this date (1922) the style is parasitic on no one, and the intensity of both vocal and instrumental lines is such that we're almost tempted to say that *The Curlew* makes van Dieren unnecessary, though the part he played in the work's genesis cannot be gainsaid.

During the middle years of his short life Warlock not only brought his creative talents to fruition; he also turned to literary account his interests in the past, for his writings (especially for his predictably short-lived critical journal, *The Sackbut*) combined strong scholarship with entertaining if rather juvenile vituperation of the musical establishment, especially as rep-resented by Percy Scholes and Ernest Newman. As a by-product of his scholarly preoccupations, he turned to the editing of 'early' music from the English lutenists to Purcell, carrying through the task with native musical instinct and high intelligence, long before editing had become an industry.

Yet whatever modest fulfilment he found in his composition and editorial work, his life remained a shambles. He never acquired a home but lived peri-patetically in and around London, Oxford, his mother's house in the Welsh border-country to which he was addicted, and in a cottage at Eynsford, Kent, the closest he came to a 'centre'. His role as a rebel was inseparable from his appetite for sex and alcohol. Women found his priapism irresistible and he even, in a thoughtless moment, garnered a wife, intriguingly known as Puma, who came and went among his female menagerie and the often drunk cronies who haunted his Eynsford years, and who spawned a son, called Nigel, whom Warlock handed over to his mother and never attempted to nurture. Moreover he was accused, not altogether unfairly, of destroying the composer 'Jack' Moeran, who couldn't carry his liquor to Warlockian standard, during the time they shared the Eynsford house; though it would seem that Warlock himself managed to cram an impressive quota of composing and editing between the gaudy weekends. On the whole, his life-story, as recounted in Barry Smith's well documented biography, comes over as at once pitiful and shameful. Peter Pans whom mothers won't allow to grow up may be at once blithely carefree and criminally careless. Warlock was a typecase. He was beastly to his women yet famous for generosity of spirit and even of purse—and that at times when he was himself nearly destitute. Many of his relationships were indeed mysterious. His maltreated women remained willing servants: including the apparently plain, unprepossessing woman to whom he wrote oddly touching (possibly unposted) letters during the last few days, and to whom he bequeathed, in a last-minute will, what little remained of his worldly estate.

Forces of light and dark, good and evil, coexisted in Warlock; but they do in all of us, and we shouldn't countenance Cecil Gray's view of him as a Jekyll and Hyde split personality. His addiction to practical jokes and his expertise in devising obscene limericks may have been playfully Machiavelian, intended to shock; but such adolescent antics are hardly diabolical, and the nervy youth of the medieval-Elizabethan love songs and the boozy extrovert of the pub songs are opposite sides of the same coin, validified in the former by sensibility, in the latter by the momentum of the tunes and the hilarity of the keyboard frolics. Warlock accepted the vulnerabilities of his inner self and the bluff façade he presented to the world not as contrarieties but as complementary truths. Delius could find momentary release in a visionary transcendence and, with the help of Eric Fenby, continued to compose long after his syphilitic paralysis—a consequence after all of a corporeally dedicated youth—had threatened to destroy him. But Warlock, a quintessential manic depressive, was left with no alternative to opting out—into the nirvana of his close-shuttered, gas-filled London flat, from which he'd characteristically remembered to put out, with meat and drink, his little cat, last survivor of a feline tribe as numerous as his women, and comparable with them and him in dedication to sensuous delight.

Reading Barry Smith's book, so many years after the events, I find the tale of Warlock's life and death almost too painful to be borne. Yet pain was not what his friends and lovers, or even the enemies he made through his irrationally bellicose writings, remembered of him: at least on the testimony of the singer John Goss, the only member of the Warlock entourage I knew well. Moreover, although his greatest piece is the blackly melancholic *Curlew*, there is evidence of some spiritual amelioration in the exiguous music of his final years. Especially moving are the three Belloc songs of 1927: among which 'Ha'nacker Mill' is an elegy on Old England Lost that exactly catches the verse's fine equilibrium between nostalgia and austerity, for the arching tune is as assuaging as a folk song, while the harmony is as 'Desolate' as is our 'fallen nation'. In 'The night' Warlock encapsulates his mode of ecclesiastical intonation within his 'antique' lullaby rhythm, evoking 'false delight' in an ironic recognition of "other modes of experience that may be possible".

The very last songs—a projected but unfinished cycle to verses by Bruce Blunt, a minor poet and drinking companion of Warlock, salvaged from oblivion by these settings—are small miracles. 'Bethlehem Down' started as a choral carol, but was transformed into a solo song with modal melody, linearly harmonised for organ rather than piano. Although Warlock was, like Delius, a fanatical non-believer and, indeed, anti-Christian, he was obsessed with the Christmas story, which stands for a *potential* birth at the dead time of the year; this serene song evades nostalgia in a spiritual radiance that has no need of a church. Complementing it is the most famous of the Blunt songs, 'The Fox', which offers *no* palliative for death. It was inspired by a real if stuffed fox-head in a real rural pub where Blunt and Warlock caroused. Barry Smith acutely comments that,

the fox's grin mocks his [Warlock's] own dead, wasted years; yet at the same time he *is* the fox, the mask, the warlock who would have the last laugh. For the supreme irony of this sardonic poem is that, long after huntsmen, horses and hounds are dead and forgotten, the fox lives on: "High on the wall/Above the cask/Laughs at you all/The fox's mask".

Distant horn-calls shiver the silence; the piano's harmonies grind ungrammatically.

Excelling even 'The Fox' in emotional charge is another Blunt song wherein Mary the Mother confronts her dead son in 'The Frostbound Wood'—another merely potential rebirth. A single monotone piano line winds around the voice part, often in semitonal dissonance. This is an *opus* even more *ultimum* than 'The Fox' in that its death-in-life, or life-in-death, is beyond irony, let alone the melodrama that intrudes into the fox-song—justifiably, since both Fox and Warlock are masks, and both are dead.

Although he is no longer a fashionable composer, Peter Warlock created a few timeless masterpieces, notably *The Curlew* and the *Corpus Christi*

Carol for solo voice and chorus (which he himself believed to be, with *The Curlew*, his finest work), plus a handful of solo songs with piano, among them 'Sleep', the Bruce Blunt songs, and perhaps the late Belloc numbers. There's a larger group of songs and a couple of instrumental works which, if not 'timeless masterpieces', have passed the test of survival in the repertory. The *Capriol Suite* for strings (or piano duet, or full orchestra) was a by-product of Warlock's editorial work, combining respect for and love of its source with a re-creative faculty whereby Renaissance dances occasionally blossom into newly invented Warlock, and no seams show. The *Serenade* for strings, made for Delius's sixtieth birthday, hasn't the ubiquity of *Capriol*, but is still a repertory piece that at its climax catches—it is intentionally parasitic on its revered model—the authentic Delian ecstacy. Among his literary efforts, Warlock's book on Delius preserves documentary interest, though its sycophancy was ultimately rejected by its author, as well as by critical opinion. The little book on the lute ayre, superseded by bigger books, perpetuates the excitement of a voyage of discovery for which scholarly meticulousness can, of itself, be no substitute. The book on Gesualdo as Musician and Murderer,* written in collaboration with Cecil Grey, still fascinates with its biographical sleaze, while Warlock's typically vivacious account of the evolution of 16th and 17th century chromaticism is still as good an introduction to the subject as one could hope for.

Yet in the long run what matters is that Warlock, knowing that value is not commensurate with size, wrote a small song like 'The frostbound wood' which achieves a tragic objectivity comparable with that of the final number of Schubert's *Winterreise*. Warlock's frozen Mother has the eternal validity of Schubert's frozen organ grinder; that alone should suffice for a modest immortality.

MT, APRIL 1994

BLUE REMEMBERED HILLS

A. E. Housman: the complete *A Shropshire Lad* in poems and song-settings by
Samuel Barber, George Butterworth, Mervyn Horder, John Ireland,
E. J. Moeran, C. W. Orr and Lennox Berkeley.
Alan Bates (reader), Anthony Rolfe Johnson (tenor), Graham Johnson (piano)
Hyperion CDA 66471/2 (1995)

ANNIVERSARIES COME ON APACE: AFTER MOZART'S BICENTENARY IN 1991
came Purcell's tricentenary this year; while next year [1996] will bring
a more specific, less grand but still potent celebration: the centenary
of the publication of Housman's *A Shropshire Lad*, a 'slim volume' of verse
that made, and still makes, an impact incommensurate with its unpreten-
tiousness. A. E. Housman was a Worcestershire, not Shropshire, lad, and
was only a part-time poet. By training he was a classical scholar of exceptional brilliance who, for obscure but interesting reasons, fluffed his finals
at Oxford, only to become internationally famous for the razor-edged
acumen of his editing of Latin texts, in the process of which he annihilated
a Popean Dunciad of scholars variously obtuse or otiose. Eventually he
spent many years as Professor of Latin in Cambridge—a legendary figure in
Trinity Great Court, visited, admired and feared by scholars world-wide.

Yet this crusty academic and Latin disputant, "masochistically practising
heroics in the last ditch" (as Auden put it), now owes his fame not so much
to his impeccable scholarship as to his poetry: which he did not begin to
write until he was thirty-five; which is exiguous in quantity; and which he
regarded not as his 'life's work' but as therapy, something he had to do, usually provoked by ill health, in the form of a sore throat. Yet although his
verse was a private matter, he did try to get *A Shropshire Lad* published, even
to the extent of helping to finance it himself. When issued, the little book
was little noticed; the prevalent belief that it was an instant success is
untrue. Imperceptibly, however, it 'caught on', enjoying enormous popularity over a surprisingly wide cross-section of the British public. This popularity endures: *A Shropshire Lad* is one of the few books of poetry one can
count on finding even in a provincial bookshop. Housman refused to profit
from the accruing substantial royalties, the book being his heart's blood.
That it meant so much to him may bear on why it meant so much to other
people. What is the secret of its appeal?

1896, when the volume appeared, heralded the end of the nineteenth
century and the beginning of the end of the Imperial Dream—itself fostered by rampant Victorian industrialisation. In this context Housman created, from the depths of his mind and senses, pseudo-folk ballads making a
highly artificial deployment of simple metrical forms to deal with universal
themes of death, mutability and a world lost. The verses brought home to
the guts the loss of the old rural England such as Hardy mourned; but they

also revealed, beneath nostalgia, a bleak awareness of impermanence in a post-Darwinian, incipiently Freudian, godless and faithless world. 'Tommies' in the trenches of the Somme stuffed copies of *A Shropshire Lad* into their pockets, perhaps finding in the stoicism of Housman's negations a paradoxical affirmation, helping them to get by without self-deception. Housman described himself not as a pessimist but as a pejorist, convinced that everything was bound to get worse;* if one could admit that, there was hope that, against the odds, one might survive. These haunting poems awoke inner disturbances that people were racked by, yet not fully conscious of. War and death pervade the verses—both the imperial wars that culminated in the Boer War, and the Great War still to come, in which Shropshire (and other) lads were indiscriminately slaughtered in "the twilight of Europe".

The weird fascination of Housman's verse comes, perhaps, from its equivocal nature. Lovely lyric stanzas as apparently artless as a folk song or an aubade or threnody of Shakespeare or Heine (debts that Housman admitted to) at the same time reveal that the nineteenth century had ravaged the heart's truth once and for all. Yeats's "ceremony of innocence" was indeed 'drowned'; and Housman's 'beautiful' verse is often rent by savagery and sometimes carries, despite frequent biblical overtones and undertones, a burden of blasphemy. This safeguards Housman against self-indulgence, and may give an edge of macabre farce to the war- and self-slaughtered lads of a rurally mythical Shropshire that Housman seldom visited, though he recognised, in the "blue remembered hills" he could glimpse from his native Bromsgrove, the irretrievable Land of Lost Content. Three small poems may be cited as evidence of Housman's magical best: 'Loveliest of trees, the cherry now', a lyric of mutability timelessly perfect in cadence; 'From far, from eve and morning', a tiny lyric wherein Housman's apparent impersonality touches a private nerve in each of us ("Take my hand *quick* and tell me,/What have you in your heart"—my italic*); and 'Is my team ploughing?', a dialogue in the style of a narrative folk ballad between a dead lad and his erstwhile friend who cheers a dead man's sweetheart, "Never ask me whose"—a poem that gives a grimly comic twist to the irony typical of many folk songs.

In homage to *A Shropshire Lad's* centenary the always-enterprising Hyperion have issued these two CDs. That Housman's verses appealed strongly to British composers is unsurprising, both for reasons of 'content' and for technical reasons, since his forms, related to those of folk songs and of Renaissance lyrics, are of their nature halfway to music. Housman himself preferred music hall to music, but didn't object to composers setting his verse, so long as they didn't cut or tamper with it, as they sometimes did.

Wryly, he said that he allowed composers to use his verses in the hope of attaining a vicarious immortality. Of course, he didn't need anyone's assistance to that end; and perhaps, among the scores of composers who set his verse, only Vaughan Williams, in his *On Wenlock Edge* cycle, made an indubitable masterpiece. That work doesn't feature on these CDs, since it is scored for tenor solo with piano and string quartet. But we are offered settings by the best Housman composer after VW—his pupil and disciple George Butterworth who, killed on the Somme, himself became an honorary Shropshire Lad. That Butterworth's settings are the most moving on these discs is related to their pristine nature. After a reading of the invocatory poem, the first song is Butterworth's version of 'Loveliest of trees', in which the pentatonic line, dropping like the cherry blossom, flowers as though spontaneously from the spoken inflexions of the words, the modal harmony being diaphanous. Butterworth's 'When I was one and twenty' is almost indistinguishable from a real folk song, except when it cannily points the little joke about the transition from innocence to experience. 'In summertime on Bredon', given the verse's narrative content, is longer and pianistically more illustrative, or at least impressionistic, in dealing with larks and bells, summer and winter, life and death. Textures are luminously spaced, and the song holds its own against Vaughan Williams's setting, to which Butterworth paid the sincerest form of flattery. This is the piece of Vaughan Williams that most betrays the effect of his then recent studies with Ravel, thereby countering the Englishman's straw-booted image; and there's a comparably refined art in both Vaughan Williams's and Butterworth's settings of the balladic dialogue in 'Is my team ploughing?' The young man's version, though close to the older man's, has independence enough, without being as palpably 'Butterworthian' as 'On the idle hill of summer', which renders summer and idleness incarnate in an undulating vocal line veiled in hazy piano sonorities, out of which the bugles of war summon nightmare to rout dream.

These profoundly simple settings could hardly be 'rendered' more consummately than they are by Anthony Rolfe Johnson (equally sensitive to verbal nuance and linear contour) and by Graham Johnson (magically evocative of Butterworth's tenuous keyboard sonorities). In 'Is my team ploughing?' I've never heard the dead (head) voice of the ghost and the living (chest) voice of the surviving lad more mysteriously realised, in chilled and chilling wonderment, nor have I heard a domestic piano more evocative of the potentially spectral. The two Johnsons are hardly less adept in the other settings, which are less good in proportion to their portentousness. Closest to Butterworth (and to Vaughan Williams) are the two E. J. Moeran settings ('Oh fair enough' and 'Far in a western brookland') which have tunes as guileless as a real folk song and elusive piano parts that neither expatiate on nor intrude into the verses. John Ireland's settings predictably do expatiate and intrude, but they are expertly written, and beautiful if one takes them as art songs that are sophisticatedly nostalgic, as Housman wasn't. 'The heart's desire' mates a haunting tune to Ireland's typically bittersweet chromatic harmonies, impeccably laid out on the keyboard, but becomes a shade melodramatic in the final stanza. Ireland's setting of 'The Lent Lily'—the poem about the Land of Lost Content—evades such rhetoric, and is almost worthy of the *discreetly* heart-rending verses. Ireland is also responsive to Housman's rougher and tougher aspects, rigorously and vigorously tackling one of his football songs and a red-coat soldier ballad wherein the music matches the gritty verse.

C. W. Orr's settings resemble Ireland's, while carrying the inflationary process a bit further. They too are beautifully written, but the piano parts—out of Delius by way of Warlock—wring the withers in a way that Housman would have deprecated. One might argue that this is valid, in the same way as Bax's opulent harmonisation of quasi-Celtic tunes works as a 'modern' commentary on a mode of life long lost. This is not, however, what Housman—or what Vaughan Williams or Butterworth in setting him—does; and the only Orr song that approaches the authentic manner is 'This time of year', which juxtaposes dead Fred and living Rose and Me as facts of nature, without ethical, let alone religious, implication. Compared with this directness, 'Oh see how thick the goldcup flowers' seems overwrought and even, in the rhodomontade of its end, faintly silly.

Butterworth's settings come from the First World War or just before it; Moeran's, Ireland's, and Orr's are of the late 1920s and 30s. A song from Samuel Barber's opus 2, written in 1928 when he was a mere eighteen, tells us that 'With rue my heart is laden' in wide-eyed, open-eared music that demonstrates again how this American composer is always happiest when dealing with adolescence. A charming setting of 'White in the moon the long road lies' by the octogenarian Mervyn Horder proves that the old manners and modes are still valid, if not 'going strong', and makes an extra-musical point in that Horder was a Classics scholar at Housman's Trinity College, Cambridge. Two youthful songs by Lennox Berkeley, from the early 1940s, touch obliquely on Berkeley's and Housman's homosexuality: which in the latter's case 'dare not speak its name'. Significantly, these two poems do not come from *A Shropshire Lad*, which Housman considered his essential testament, preferably to be kept separate from his later verses. It's a slight cheat to violate the autonomy of *A Shropshire Lad*, but a case might be made that nowadays a rounded portrait must make reference and pay deference to Housman's ambiguous sexuality, patent in the poems sparked by the death of Moses Jackson, the Oxford friend for whom Housman nursed a probably unrequited passion over many years. Housman's sexuality, then considered 'sinful', now underlines his outsider status, linking his personal story to the mythical legend of the Shropshire Lad.

On these CDs the poems that aren't sung are read, or spoken, by Alan Bates, an intelligent as well as charismatic actor. I'm not sure how I rate his readings, probably because with poems one has known intimately over sixty years one evolves a reading in the mind's ear that comes to seem right, or at least right enough to make other people's spoken versions sound wrong. Perhaps the trouble is Bates seldom misses a trick, but knows that he doesn't: whereas the verse read plainly, with respect for the stresses and syntax that Housman laboured on so assiduously, creates its own sound and sense. Still, I'm grateful for these discs, which allow us to adjudicate between Housman spoken and sung; and I'm entranced with the singer and pianist, especially in the Butterworth numbers. Housman knew that, since art may efface time, *his* cherry tree outlasts the perennially falling blossoms, and that this is a simple fact that is no cause for self-congratulation. I'll hazard that, if civilisation survives, this cherry tree will still, a hundred years from now, be "hung with snow".

MT, DECEMBER 1995

VIRGIL THOMSON A HUNDRED YEARS ON

*This centennial tribute to Virgil Thomson was given first as an address
at the Dartington Summer School of Music in 1996, and subsequently
in the Music Department of Exeter University.*

W HEN HE DIED IN 1989, AT THE AGE OF NINETY-THREE, VIRGIL THOMSON
had been living in, or centred on, his top-floor apartment in New
York's famous-infamous Chelsea Hotel for around half a century.
The place owes its fame and infamy to the gallery of celebrated or notorious
people associated with it, from most of the leading American abstract
painters and sculptors to Arthur Miller and Dylan Thomas, who began to die
there, and the Sex Pistol who murdered his girl-friend in a tatty bedroom.
Virgil's elegant suite of rooms managed to reconcile Kansas City, whence he
came, with Harvard intellect, Boston respectability, New York energy, and a
Parisian chic redolent of the twenties. A bright boy from Kansas whose
musical legacy included the bric-à-brac that was also Ives's birthright,
Thomson was academically and musically precocious, finding his juvenile
way to Harvard and thence to Paris where, as an American cosmopolitan, he
was a poor student who, as he put it, "might as well starve where the food is
good". He also became an intimate of the circle of the American ex-patriate
Gertrude Stein and, like her, made wildly experimental, impudently
debunking works in (partly homosexual) protest against a post-war world
that had had its day. The protest was that of a child; in returning to diatonic
fundamentals while at the same time deconstructing musical grammar and
the logic of connection, Thomson arrived at an American permutation of
the music of Parisian Erik Satie, who deflated Europe's post-Wagnerian egomania, and even Debussy's narcissistic dedication to the moment of sensation. There's a clear relation between Thomson's collocation of emotionally
disparate elements—plainchant and café-concert ditty, Handelian fugue and
Middle-West hymn, barrelhouse honky-tonk and Mendelssohnic Song
without Words—and Satie's surrealistic unsentimentality. There's an American insouciance in Thomson's bizarre juxtapositions that we don't find in
Satie's chaste art but, given the distinction between an old world and a new,
the technical methods and the sophisticated naivety are the same. The best of
Thomson's music may have a modest durability comparable with that he so
admired in the work of the Parisian mini-master.

By far the most celebrated work of this American *puer aeternatus* and
enfant terrible is *Four Saints in Three Acts*, the opera on which he collaborated, in 1927, during his Parisian years, with Gertrude Stein, though it
wasn't produced (in America) until 1934. The libretto, defining a New
World by refurbishing language, syntax, and grammar, presents 'moments'

in unchanging 'landscapes' in the lives of saints who are child-like holy ones. Thomson's music—originally improvised in pristine immediacy, at a piano—also evades chronology, auralizing visual moments in a fabric of memory and dream. The ragbag of musical clichés amounts, in Thomson's words, to "a virtual total recall of my Southern Baptist childhood". Fragments of kiddies' runes, idiot scale and arpeggio practice in rising sequences (overhead on a Sunday morning), bugle-calls in the park or buskers in the busy street, snatches of urban parlour ballads and showbiz tunes, rural hoe-downs and hill-billy waltzes, sleazy Tex-Mex tangos and shanty-bar rags, meld with State parade marches and Gospel musics black and white. A similar demotic permissiveness typifies the music of Ives; only, whereas Ives identifies himself with his world, Thomson (from remotely sophisticated Paris) is always artful in his artlessness. His Americanism lies in his detachment, as the child's listening ear and watching eye.

In 1926, in Paris, just before he embarked on his Stein opera, Thomson had composed a *Symphony on a Hymn Tune* which explores his basic experience in overtly American terms. Indeed, the improvisation, if not the writing of *Four Saints* came in between the composition of the first three movements of the symphony and its last: so the interrelation of the two works could hardly be more intimate. The Southern Baptist hymn tune referred to is Scottish in origin, sung in the Southern States to several texts of which the commonest is 'How firm a foundation'. A second hymn, 'Yes, Jesus loves me', appears as a counter-theme; but both tunes are presented not in argumentative sonata-style, but with a simplicity enhanced, rather than debunked, by the wrong-note harmonization, the dislocations of rhythm and pitch, the often out-of-focus tonality. These reflect the innocence of a child and of the hymn's original makers, reseen and reheard through the prism of Thomson's wide-eyed, open-eared canniness. In the final cadenzas to the first movement—for the bizarre concatenation of piccolo, trombone, cello and violin—Thomson 'frees' each soloist into a childhood reborn, momently sufficient unto the moment. The slow movement, which is not very slow, is a lyrical variation-set on the hymn, again diatonic if sometimes out of focus. There's a weird coda based on the hooting of a railway train: a deeply American aural image of the emptiness of vast plains and prairies, within which, always in transit, we vulnerable mortals precariously exist. The scherzo uses the tune as bass for a passacaglia more dance-like than hymnic—a social rather than religious get-together. The finale, a contrapuntal canzona in the seventeenth century sense, reintroduces most of the material of the symphony, culminating in a coda based on the introduction.

Ten years later, Thomson adapted this finale to the music he wrote for a New Deal documentary film, *The River*. The latent political implications of this film (as of all Thomson's movie music) bear on the paradoxical but significant relationship between his rediscovery of an agrarian 'old' America and the search for an urban New Society; and it is no accident that the collage technique explored in the *Symphony on a Hymn Tune*, as in the opera *Four Saints in Three Acts*, was readily adaptable to the technique of the cinematic cut or clip; we may recall, too, that Satie was an adventurous pioneer—in the cinematic interlude in his ballet *Relâche* (1925)—of musical techniques that, being based on collage and patterned repetition, were appropriate to film. Another ten years on, Thomson produced a film score that proved to be not only a landmark in the history of movie music, but also one his most satisfying works in purely musical terms. Robert Flaherty's *Louisiana Story* was a semi-documentary film that saw the clash between man and nature through the eyes of a child, opposing the Acadian and Arcadian existence of a boy's life in the Louisianan bayous, with loving family and faithful hound, to the impact of the encroaching oil-prospectors. This contrast, rather than conflict, is not an excuse for moral comment: the meeting of disparate ways of life is simply accepted by the boy with Satie-like impartiality. We see-hear him frolicking with his dog in the sunny-watery meadows, this vernal Eden being musically incarnate in a real Acadian folk tune indicative both of his boyish nature and of the rural values that had gone to make him. Against this, the oil-derrick's imperial floating on the vast Mississippi is evoked by Satiean unrelated diatonic concords harmonizing a twelve-note row! This music is in part visually descriptive (following the derrick's almost-motionless drifting), and in part psychological (reflecting the wonder and scared bemusement which the river-boat—not a creature of Nature but a mechanical contraption—excites in the boy's mind). The mating of plain diatonic concords in almost static rhythm with chromatic serialism generates a *serene instability* which is perhaps the deepest, and certainly the most disturbing, feature of Thomson's music. Significantly, it has much in common with the technique of Satie's *Messe des Pauvres*—a 'poor man's mass' written as long ago as 1895. One can understand why Thomson categorized his derrick-music as a 'Chorale', for it evokes a quasi-religious fusion of humility and awe, with a slight spicing of terror. The same ambivalence surfaces in *Symphony on a Hymn Tune* and in *Four Saints in Three Acts*: not to mention more patent instances in Thomson's *Missa pro Defunctis* and *A Solemn Music* for wind band, written in 1949 for the obsequies of Gertrude Stein and, like the derrick-music from *Louisiana Story,* involving a twelve-note row harmonized exclusively in diatonic concords.

But if I had to choose one work that may count as quintessential Virgil Thomson, I'd opt for his setting of *Five Songs of William Blake* of 1951. As one would expect, they celebrate Blakean Innocence rather than Experience, bringing the British Bard to rebirth in an American township, in the context of the emergent Industrial Revolution in the Old World's eighteenth and early nineteenth century and in the New World's New Deal. The first song, 'The Divine Mercy', is in the spirit of eighteenth-century evangelical hymondy, and was probably sung by Blake to his own improvised tune. For Thomson, it becomes an American parlour song with devotional overtones. The tune is deeply affecting because it springs from affection for its models; and the religious if not orthodox Christian implications of the words, which prophetically abolish distinctions between race and creed, are not belied by the music's apparent commonplaceness. On the contrary, the music reveals "the heart of common humanity" no less profoundly than does the Allcotts movement of Ives's great *Concord Sonata*. The second number, 'Tyger, tyger', is no less simple in means but very different in mood; for the creature's savagery, which is also his innocence, is manifest in broken bugle-call arpeggios over bare fifths and a sinister, because remorseless, march beat. The impervious rhythm hints at an Asian immobility beneath the brash here-and-now of Kansas City: against which the magical stanza about the Lamb who is the dark Tyger's light complement shines in diatonic radiance.

'The Land of Dreams' is technically more complicated, for here Thomsonian bugle-calls awaken a little boy in wonderment at the disparity between reality and dream, or between earth and heaven, where his dead mother may putatively be. The music meanders into grammatically unrelated triads, major-minor bitonality, parallel scales in chromatics, and abstruse modulations engendered by whole-tone non-progressions that leave us in limbo on a high F sharp in B major, at the furthest possible remove from the initial C. Thomson's American empiricism comes near to equating the child's vision with a *pre*-conscious state such as Blake sometimes hints at in his Prophetic Books.

'The Little Black Boy' returns to the small-town parlour, with a Stephen Foster-like tune at once touching and unparodistic. The 'false' relations of the blues are banished from this plain diatonic presentation of an American black-white theme as pertinent today as when Blake penned the words. But false relations appear in the middle section which, shifting from pastoral F major to A flat major, envisages a New Eden precisely *by way of* (not by evasion of) those 'falsely' or 'bluely' related triads—which must learn to cohabit, if the New World is to be truly new and newly true.

In the final number, 'And did those feet', Thomson's music is more apt to the words than is Parry's famously stirring, but most un-Blakean, patriotic hymn. At first, pentatonic arabesques on violin and harp over a bagpipe drone sound exotic, even oriental: as is apposite since barriers of race and class dissolve in Blake's New Found Land. Yet these exotic elements prove to be also local as imitated Kentucky fiddle, mountain dulcimer, chapel harmonium, and village hall squeeze box evoke (even in the piano version) an American country-music gamelan, while the baritone's bugle calls equivocate between Eastern incantation and American Gospel shout. Throughout, the meticulous prosody, springing from Thomson's Stein-like dedication to the word-in-itself, gives the music an immediate truthfulness, like that of a Shakespearean Clown or a Steinian Saint. Virgil Thomson, in the guise of clown, saint, or child, glimpses the New Jerusalem with rare clarity.

The collocation of Virgil Thomson with William Blake—with a little help from the likes of Stephen Foster—made it possible for him to create this mini-masterpiece, one of the 'seminal' works of America's twentieth century. More commonly, however, Thomson's literary mentor was Gertrude Stein, whose texts spontaneously triggered his unexpected, at times alarming, juxtapositions of corny melodic clichés, as-though-preordained metrical patterns, common chords, and plain diatonic keys. Another Stein setting written in Paris in 1927—the year of *Four Saints*—is a delightfully zany, pseudo-baroque cantata called *Preciosilla*, the words of which are uncompromisingly hermetic, though the piece ends on one of Stein's most deservedly famous lines: "Toasted Susie in my ice-cream". A song-cycle, *Mostly About Love,* sets words by Kenneth Koch, which though not exactly Stein-imitations display her New World inconsequentiality, as though language were in process of being born. The first number, basically called 'Love song', exploits Thomson's grammatically unrelated common chords to express not so much a 'serene insecurity' as the surreal (and therefore intangible) joy evoked by the beloved ("I am crazier than shirttails in the wind . . . I am bicycling across an Africa of green and white fields"). 'Down at the docks' goes slumming in a fast hill-billy waltz, accompanied by rudimentary guitar-style arpeggios, the poem turning on the relation between Nature (a maple tree) and Art (a mandolin that is fashioned from it). "Jealous gentlemen" are encouraged to "devise" love with a comparably cunning innocence: thereby leading into the next song, 'Let's take a walk', which is specifically about redemption as the lovers walk, or rather waltz, into a city purged by rain, moon, and river in which, "bathed in a light white light", they are baptized. In the final song, 'A Prayer for Saint Catherine', a teenage girl crucified by "heartache and shyness" prays in an E flat major recitative as guileless as Stein's saints, addressing St Catherine because she, unlike most Saints, wouldn't harp on self-help, sin or guilt, and might even "answer the prayer this song contains", and "so make that person that sings this song less shy than that person is, and give that person some joy in that person's heart". This number almost attains the visionary candour of the Blake songs, reminding us that it's a miracle—a small one, maybe, but a miracle—when an artist can answer a prayer.

While Thomson set mainly American texts, he didn't restrict his English commitment to bardic Blake. He musicked a few older English poets, notably Campion (who, like Thomson, was interested in prosody) and the supreme Shakespeare. The Shakespeare songs reveal Thomson's appreciation of the Elizabethan-Jacobean equation between voice and verse whether in the weirdly witty syncopations of 'Sigh no more, ladies' or in the corny Country-Western ballad the composer makes of the sublime 'Take, O take, those lips away'—while at the same time telling us how to read a Shakespeare lyric aloud. But the authentic Thomson derives not so much from 'old' English song as from English Puritan hymnody as reborn in American Southern Baptist soil, and mutated through the alembic of Gertrude Stein's vast novel, *The Making of Americans* and of her early novellas called *Three Lives*, possibly the first, and certainly the most acutely poignant, attempt to make 'literature' from within minds and senses so embryonic as to be barely conscious of being conscious. In his purely pentatonic setting of Isaac Watts's hymn 'My Shepherd will supply my needs', and in the wide-eyed child's blessing 'Before sleep', Thomson finds, like Stein, a juvenile self-sufficiency that may serve in lieu of a faith. Again, there's a link with the Blake songs: and it's fascinating to note that a similar motif survives in Thomson's third and last opera, *Lord Byron* (1966). Byron—being a sexually and emotionally ambivalent character whose apostrophe to the bedlam city of London, spectrally sung to the tombs of the Poets in Westminster Abbey where his own commemorative statue has just been erected—debunks the past and accepts the however hazardous future. He sings his aria "masked, and carrying a beribboned mandolin": a clown, a singer-actor, and a Hero, if not a Saint.

Whether Virgil Thomson is making music as disturbingly personal as this, or whether he's concocting a chain or 'continuum' of *Synthetic Waltzes* for the domestic medium of piano duet, he creates music that is fun to play and difficult to fall asleep to. His tribute to his main musical mentor, Erik Satie, applies also to himself, for his aesthetic too has

eschewed the impressive, the heroic, the oratorical, everything that is aimed at moving mass audiences. It has directed its communication to the individual. It has valued in consequence quietude, precision, acuteness of auditory observation, gentleness, sincerity, and directness of sentiment.

In Thomson's case, as in Satie's, a demotic music "directed to the individual" is a paradox which, if mysterious, is also, on further reflection, profound; for an ideal democracy would honour each person *per se*.

MT, APRIL 1997

LOU HARRISON AT EIGHTY
A BIRTHDAY TRIBUTE

L OU HARRISON WAS BORN IN OREGON IN MAY 1917, AND IS THEREFORE ON
the verge of becoming an octogenarian. When he was a child, the Har-
risons moved south to California: where in the course of time Lou became a composer living between worlds and times. This is the measure of his
importance, in terms of what he means to his own society and to the world
at large: especially since he assumed the mantle of East-West guru on the
death of Harry Partch in 1974.

As a San Franciscan, Harrison was remote from 'old' Europe, in a world
cobbled together from the detritus of several cultures: sometimes literally
so, since he followed the precepts of his first teacher Henry Cowell, that
archetypal American Boy in the Woods who, reared by his hippy parents as
a child of Nature with minimal formal education, picked up orts and fragments from his environment while indulging in acoustic experiments on a
battered upright piano stored in a shed in the wilderness. Not for nothing
was Harrison also a friend of the young John Cage, the ultimate aboriginal
composer whose work was founded on and in silence and chance rather
than on humanly contrived sounds. In their teens and early twenties Cage
and Harrison made percussion musics from 'found objects' garnered on
beaches and parking lots.

From such *ad hoc* music-making Harrison gravitated towards what we
now call 'world music', in which Cowell himself became expert. The three of
them—Cowell, Cage, and Harrison—explored, from the South Bay area of
San Francisco, their pristine New World, looking, from the Pacific Coast,
towards Asia rather than Europe. In childhood and youth Harrison was
'exposed' to Cantonese opera and to Spanish, Mexican, and Indonesian folk
musics before he'd become familiar with the rich variety of Western concert
music, though he accepted Christian plainchant as a monody complementary to those of the East. His oriental orientation implied a philosophy of
music's nature and purpose: about which he learned much from Harry
Partch, a guide and mentor sixteen years senior to him. Partch evolved a
theory of music based 'corporeally' on Just Intonation which, in his view,
represented a purity of heart, as well as of the ears, such as harmonically
functional Western music had forfeited in the interests of materiality and
greed. Indeed this is what the Californian Beat Generation, at its noble best,
was about: a new-old art, liberated from the tattered rags of the past, was to
be our only salvation from the oppression of industrialism and technology.

In its most extreme form Harry Partch's making of a theatre-music from wayside graffiti and the babble of transitory radios picked up while riding the rails as a hobo, was a more radical version of Cage's and Harrison's scavenging on beaches and derelict lots.

Much of the music Harrison made in the thirties and forties, in the company and sometimes with the collaboration of John Cage, eschews Western harmony and even melody in being purely percussive: closer in sonority, as well as in formal conception, to Eastern than to Western musics. The *Double Music* of 1941 (so called because it was devised pragmatically by Harrison and Cage in duo), and the lovely *Canticle III* of 1943 have attained the status of minor classics: the latter piece, in particular, combines unpitched percussion instruments with pitched instruments tuned in just intonation, both haloed by ethnic pipes tootling pentatonic runes recalling the musics of 'primitive' savages, and of children of any time and place. This is 'New World' music in an affectingly literal sense: as are, in less extreme form, several early works that employ instruments soloistically, chanting melody in some kind of non-Western, fairly just intonation, usually accompanied by quasi-ethnic percussion in pre-ordained metrical patterns. In the *Concerto* for flute and percussion of 1939 the wind instrument is literally a pipe 'inspired' with the breath of life, while the patterned percussion provides a continuum to live in. The music, still fresh as a daisy or the day's eye, evades psychological trauma in living in the moment, with a radiance springing from body and spirit simultaneously. Such music, merging into dance and ritual, evokes the Child in a shining New World, linking him with the Californian Indians and the related Asiatic, Indian, and Chinese people with whom Harrison consorted in early youth. This music comes out as oddly liberated from any specific time or place, as though the world itself were reborn. It is significant that similar music has remained a constant throughout Harrison's long career. *Ariadne*, a flute and percussion piece written almost half a century later, for Harrison's seventieth birthday in 1987, is similar to the early concerto in both technique and intention, though the danced ritual for which it was conceived was that of a sophisticated *faux-naif* Dance Group.

Yet, although the sources of Harrison's music had no truck with the Beethovenian ('Faustian') notion of growth-through-conflict but were rooted in non-Western musics both primitive and cultivated, he is none the less a white, educated American who inevitably inherited the legacy of Western consciousness, conscience, and choice— a legacy that is at once the white man's burden and his privilege. This may be why he preferred, as solo melodic instrument, the 'expressive' violin to the 'pure' flute, and composed, in his *Concerto* for violin and percussion, one of the most beautiful and moving of his many works: a piece of melismatic line, supple rhythm and varied colour devised for Western instruments yet sounding, simultaneously and unselfconsciously, both Western and Eastern. Solo violin features, too, in later works composed in the early sixties, during the years in which he often substituted for orthodox Western instruments his invented Javanese-American gamelan. In any case, although Harrison was more aware of the evils accruing from Western heritage than of its outstanding achievements (including Shakespeare and Beethoven), he did not deliberately *ban* that heritage, as Harry Partch tried to. Indeed, Harrison's significance lies precisely in the compromises he effected *between* worlds: as was already patent, in his early years, in what he called his 'Californian Mission' music, most exhaustively explored in the forties and fifties, though the strands are still active. 'Europe' had made a specific impact on California when Spanish colonists tried to Christianize the Amerindians: as a consequence of which Christian ecclesiastical music of the sixteenth and seventeenth centuries became a quasi-indigenous tradition. A few Amerindians proved surprisingly responsive to the alien idiom, making reasonably competent, sometimes innocently touching, Christian masses in what, during my student days at Cambridge, used to be called 'Palestrina style', the 'rules' of which provided effective, if not very inspiring, guide-lines. Harrison's Mission music is neither parasitic nor passively imitative. His American-aboriginal temperament embraces Renaissance and Baroque Europe more readily—for obvious reasons—than did his remote Amerindian ancestors; and the modal linear purity of the mass he wrote in 1939, when he was twenty-two, creates a *pristine* feeling that accords aurally with the visually simple lines and proportions of Californian Mission churches, sparkling in the lucid morning sun. The effect is less 'new-born' than that of the early flute or violin and percussion pieces because centuries of European craft and care had gone to mould the counterpoint of the Roman Church; even so, a strangely wistful radiance seems to be distilled from the collocation of old and new. The flavour of this music is rare, perhaps unique, as is most evident in the Agnus Dei's fusion of symmetrically patterned rhythms with ostinato figures in purely modal linearity.

Nor is Harrison's Mission vein restricted to Renaissance revocation. His set of *Sonatas* for cembalo, written in the same year as the mass, combine Renaissance modal textures with Baroque dance rhythms, rather as though Domenico Scarlatti has been transported from a 'decadent' eighteenth-century Spanish palace to the empty Californian desert. The effect is the more touching because Scarlatti's own keyboard music, notwithstanding the moribund society wherein it was fashioned, bubbles and glints with hopeful dawns. It may be pertinent that Harrison's pieces were composed in 1939, when the second of the Wars that were physically 'the Death of Europe' was about to explode. Nor is it fortuitous that most of the small instrumental works that Harrison wrote around these years are not public pieces associated with Church or State, but private pieces dedicated to friends, for 'use' in their domestic lives, often celebrating birth, marriage, or death. Harrison is not a 'religious' man in espousing a creed, but his music might be called religious in that it is hybrid between art and the folk's 'music of necessity', evoking a *premier matin du monde*, with dew on the grass. His Mission mass may owe part of its appeal to wish-fulfilment.

By this date we all know that Western civilization is threatened with self-destruction, if not directly by way of what Lou in the sixties called "the Hateful Bomb", then indirectly by way of our pollution of the environment we live in. Paradoxically, *at the same time* as Harrison was a disciple of Henry Cowell, wild boy of the American woods, he also studied with Schoenberg, exiled from the Old World in the New World's Hollywooden Los Angeles. As heir to anti-Semitic Wagner, Schoenberg was a Jewish outsider who hymned the twilight of Europe, resisting the disintegration of our harmonically functional tonality by way of the linear principle of chromatic serialism. Since Harrison's music has no affinities with German expressionism, one suspects that he saw Schoenberg as a liberator from, rather than a perpetuator of, European tradition, welcoming serialism as a formal principle unconcerned with the evolution of consciousness through Time. He therefore aligned Schoenberg with the grand old American Pioneers, Ives, Ruggles and Varèse, on whose behalf he had laboured energetically as promotion agent and, in Ives's case, as patiently meticulous editor. For a while Harrison moved to New York the better to foster the cause of what he considered to be the *real* American tradition, at the same time seeking support for his own work from progressive Modern Dance groups empathetic to its nature. In New York City he became friendly with the key figures in American music and theatre—not only renewing acquaintance with Cowell and Cage, then resident in the City, but also joining the circles of Aaron Copland (revered Dean of American composers), of Virgil Thomson (who offered Lou journalistic work on the *New York Herald Tribune*), of Paul Bowles (soon to be self-exiled to a European desert), and of Mexican Carlos Chávez (who veered between the rocky deserts of 'real' Mexico and the Asphalt Jungle of New York City). In his San Francisco adolescence Harrison had lived on the fringe of the beatnik life, working as florist, horticulturalist, and oddjob man as well as a composer, dancer, poet, journalist, and nurturer of Peace movements and of the universal language of Esperanto, regarded as a philosophy, not a gimmick. Even so, urban sophistication was essential if he were to effect a 'fusion of the genres'.

Through contact with the leaders of American music and theatre this proved feasible; opportunities to work in dance were plentiful; scholarships made it possible for him to study at first hand exotic musics to which he had responded intuitively from his earliest years.

Yet Harrison didn't *stay* in New York; having found there what he needed he returned to California, and not to San Francisco, but to 'the country' where, at Aptos, he still lives. Here, over the years, he has continued to make music which, as he beautifully puts it, serves to "Cherish, Conserve, Consider, and Create", in the process nurturing "love, plant-growth, peace, and concerted enjoyment on the journey to death".* This music, like that of most primitive and some oriental cultures, helps us to live in the present moment, in Blake's phrase "kissing the joy as it flies", and leaving us, in "Eternity's sun rise", stronger, more at peace with ourselves, the world, and whatever one calls the Absolute.

Harrison's finest music betrays, as one might expect, an interfusion of the Californian rudiments he started from with aspects of Western heritage, mostly medieval, Renaissance, and early Baroque. These European elements fuse spontaneously with his garnerings from Eastern cultures, especially from Java, Bali, Korea, Japan, and India. Like his early friend John Cage, Harrison is not strenuously concerned with beginnings, middles, and ends, nor with the notion of art as a pilgrimage. The European sonata principle, at least in its Beethovenian apotheosis, is thus not powerfully evident, though it is not entirely eschewed; and Harrison's music does not conspicuously 'develop', either within single movements, or from work to work. He seldom calls his works sonatas, except in the basic sense of something instrumentally sounded rather than vocally sung; and the word 'sym-phony' implies for him the notion of voices sounding in togetherness, but without any undercurrent of progressive evolution. Significantly, his favourite term for an extended piece of orchestral or chamber music is Set or Suite, implying a collocation or convocation of movements, or a sequence of them. This we may observe in the lovely *Set* for string quartet, some of the material of which derives from the forties, though the piece has become famous because in 1978 Harrison refashioned it as a tribute to the Kronos Quartet, who have so radically remodelled the classical string quartet's image. The first movement is purely linear in modal, often pentatonic heterophony, being a variation-set on a melody of the medieval minnesinger, Walther von der Vogelweide, significantly absorbing Arabian traces into its Europeanism. The second movement, *Plainte*, has no specifically medieval root, though it has a generic relationship to the age-old Laments that pervade both occidental and oriental monody, enhancing potency by its flexibility of both rhythm and microtonal pitch. The scherzo is an *estampie*, a

Breughel-like medieval peasant dance to which Harrison is partial: athletically air-borne in monodic line for a single instrument, percussively supported by the other strings. The *Rondeaux* was described by Harrison as "my only piece in fully harmonic European style": a somewhat extravagant account, though its rhythm, structure, and even harmony accord with French baroque precedents, making specific reference to a piece by Dandrieu. Even so, the music preserves the 'cool' detachment typical of Harrison, and is very beautiful, as sustained in invention as Vaughan Williams's modal cantillations. The final movement reaffirms ongoing routine, as is so often the case with Harrison's finales. It purrs in contented monody for solo violin over a percussive string continuum, and is consistently in a Turkish *Usul* (rhythmic mode). Compared with the previous *Rondeaux*, this music sounds as though it has been going on 'since time was'; but in imitating a Turkish court music Harrison is not indulging in "the old exoticism trip", as was Mozart in making 'Turkish' marches in imitation of Janissary bands. Harrison's 'ethnic' piece reflects, in universalized camaraderie, the plurality of the world we inhabit. As Auden put it in one of his finest poems (which he later renounced): "We must love one another or die."*

Synthesis of East and West functions at a more complex level in the *Suite* for violin, tack piano and small orchestra of 1951: a tack piano being an ordinary instrument with tintacks inserted, on very simple analogy with the 'prepared piano' of early John Cage. The first movement, 'Elegy', explores the truth of the Interval in Just Intonation, while the Westernized harmony of the 'Chorale' attains, through its pure modality, a serenity beyond personal accident or distress. The Javanese-style gamelan movements that separate the Western-style pieces inevitably affect the way we listen to the work as a whole. Indeed in later years Harrison, espousing what he calls an 'American Gamelan' constructed by himself and his partner Bill Colvig out of local materials, has explored what amounts to a technique of social therapy. The crucial dividing date seems to be 1960: only by the presence or absence of a gamelan can we differentiate Harrison's early from his late works, since the idiom does not notably change. It was in 1960 that Harrison made his first extended visit to Java, sketching out on the boat the score of a *Concerto in Slendro* for solo violin, two tack pianos, celesta and percussion, in which the three movements are strictly tuned to Javanese *slendro* modes—the Prime Pentatonic ("the most common and generally lovely of all man's modes—practically the Human Song") and its associated Minor Pentatonic.* Sweetness and light are distilled from melodic formulae that are almost as natural as breathing. It's pertinent to note that Harrison, having evolved his 'American gamelan', came to understand the educational as well as the amicably domestic implications of his East-West music. The young in schools and colleges now participate nation-wide in Harrison's gamelans; innumerable educational institutions own a gamelan at some level of sophistication, and the vogue is by now wide-spread in Europe. The effect of such music on the minds and senses of the young (and for that matter the old) must surely alleviate the dehumanization inherent in our technocracies.

While Harrison's 'house' and 'school' musics are mostly brief, devised for some specific social occasion, his large-scale works imply a similar philosophy. Although their "going-onness" and "long flow form" (to use Percy Grainger's terms*) are more likely to be presented in concert-halls or perhaps churches than in homes or schools, their function might be described as communal ritual. Three among these works are of exceptional power and beauty, the earliest being the *Suite for Symphonic Strings*, which contains material harking back to 1936, though it was finished only in 1960. I have written about this, in reviewing a new recording of the piece, in the issue of *Musical Times* for April 1996. The *Third Symphony* was also started a long time ago, in 1937 when Lou was just on twenty, but it wasn't finished until 1982, on commission from the Cabrillo Festival, with which Harrison has been associated since its inception. In its definitive form the *Third Symphony* is scored for a large orchestra, and its first movement is grand in scale, sweeping onwards in vocally conceived, freely modal, seldom modulatory lines, with a Bachian openendedness that reminds us of what Percy Grainger said about the improvising Polynesian polyphonists, encountered on his travels, in relation to the music of Bach. Harrison's flowing linearity contains no whiff of the Protestant Christian *angst* that Grainger abominated; its total effect is of grandeur and energy. The movement is symphonic in being a concourse of independent voices that 'go on', chary of Western *leading* notes and *dominant* sevenths, while springing and singing across the *bar*-lines that imprison, even as they measure, Time. Melody endures, in evolution, but without conflict. Given the fragmented state of the modern world these simultaneously Bachian and Polynesian qualities are the more significant.

After the first movement's grand communality comes the personal music for friends: a real reel for Irish Henry Cowell, evading beginning, middle, and end; a modal waltz for Evelyn Hinrichsen, content to swing in the movement's passing moments; and another medieval Estampie for Susan Summerfield, exuberant in polymetres over eternity's unbroken drone. All these short pieces affirm life while the music lasts, and are dedicated to friends who are also professional colleagues. After friendship, the slow movement, 'largo ostinato', sings in hymnic serenity over a quasi-oriental ground. That the social and religious aspects of this music are interdependent is suggested by the finale which, in returning to communal togetherness, sounds like Californian-Mission-style Vaughan Williams—he, after all, being a 'Christian agnostic' who also sought release from Western will and consciousness, and occasionally compromised (in *Flos Campi*, for instance) with oriental idioms.

Harrison's *Third Symphony* is not a world masterpiece, as is Bach's B minor Mass, but it is pertinent to point out that both works embrace material garnered over a longish lifetime. Harrison's *Piano Concerto*, on the other hand, is unusual in his output in that it seems to have been composed in one long sweep between 1983 and 1985. It is dedicated to Keith Jarrett, significantly both a straight keyboard player and a jazz pianist-composer responsive to non-European musics and, of course, partial to free improvisation. Here the solo piano itself becomes a kind of American gamelan, retuned in compromise between Eastern and Western traditions.* The first movement, like that of the *Third Symphony*, is long and celebratory, and is such because it is spiritually liberated. Not needing to 'go anywhere', there is no reason why it should stop, unless it ceases to enliven and stimulate: which it never—well, hardly ever—does. The difference between this piece and conventionally minimalist music of the twentieth century lies in its long attention-span; only the magnificent *Piano Concerto* of the Mexican Carlos Chávez can rival it on this count, both pieces sweeping us triumphantly into timeless *fiesta*. The second movement has *in toto* a comparable effect, though it would seem to be unambiguously corporeal. This is the biggest of all Harrison's *estampie* movements, the term being here Americanized into *Stampede* and therefore, in equine terms, celebrating sheer animal vitality, corybantic with no before or after.

The piece, though superabundantly *vigorous*, with note-clusters hammered by fists and fore-arms, sometimes at hair-raising speed, is never violent: so that it may prove a complementary foil to the almost immobile slow movement, which is Californian Mission music floating into a dimension beyond time and place. In the piano introduction the luminosity of the retuned keyboard glows and glimmers, magically serene and perhaps healingly holy. Yet after the two vast allegro movements and the monumentally slow largo the finale, reasserting the present of fiesta, is brief, though sustained enough to affirm "concerted enjoyment on the journey to death". Again, Harrison's music is not concerned with peril and progress, but with affirmation in the face of whatever momentary deaths of the spirit we're afflicted with. Moreover, Harrison does not need large forces to attain such monumental effects; the scoring of the concerto is for strings and three trombones, ballasted by percussion and two plangent harps. In this context it's worth mentioning that a work scored merely for violin and piano, written for the Cabrillo Festival of 1988, justifies its title of *Grand Duo*, for it is genuinely grand in the scope of its long-flowing 'Prelude', the energy of its 'Stampede' (again with ferocious note-clusters), and the majestic gravity of its slow movement. Characteristically, it also incorporates a graceful Round addressed to personal friends and concludes with an unpretentious Polka, perky in melodic insouciance, if with percussive note-clusters that recall, in a domestic parlour, the wildly Polish antecedents of the dance.

California is geographically a long way from us, but its Global Village is now dispersed over the wide world. Being a crossover between modern American and ancient Asiatic cultures, Harrison has been little concerned with the painful precipitation of mind-boggling masterpieces from the womb of Time, but has rather—like most primitive and some oriental peoples—offered an ongoing therapy to the world at large. If this therapy evolved from the Beat Generation and from Californian hippy-culture—stressing its alienation in being in more than one sense gay—it also suggests that the most dangerous kind of alienation may be inherent in industrial technology itself. The plurality of the world today gives validity to many different, even contradictory, kinds of music acceptable and sometimes valuable to many different groups of people: some of whom probably consider that what Harrison does is infantile—as, in the profound sense defined by Gertude Stein in the passage quoted below, it occasionally is. But we cannot, certainly should not, deny that the causes Harrison's music espouses—peace, the rights of all creatures and forms of Nature to respectful coexistence, the need simultaneously to foster life and to accept death—are causes that ought to prevail. The forthcoming celebrations for this celebratory composer's eightieth birthday should encourage people to be born again—not in the often sinister Christian Evangelical sense, but "out of the mouths of babes and sucklings", as described in a passage from Gertrude Stein's *A Long, Gay Book* of 1909–12:

there are some who when they feel it inside them that there was once so little of them, that they were a baby, helpless and no conscious feeling in them, that they knew nothing then when they were kissed and fixed and dandled by others who knew them when they could know nothing inside and around them, some get from all this that once surely happened to them to that which was then every bit that was them then, there are some when they feel it later inside them that they were such once and that was all there was of them then, there are some who from such a knowing have an uncertain curious kind of feeling in them that they having been so little once and knowing nothing makes it all a broken world for them that they have made inside them, kills for them that everlasting feeling; and they spend their lives in many ways, and always they are trying to make for themselves a new everlasting feeling.

On his eightieth birthday, let us honour Lou Harrison whose music manages to be both *new* and *everlasting*. It is encouraging to note that a work originally announced as *Last Symphony* has been retitled *Fourth Symphony*; that it seems to be still ecstatic in its ongoing polyphonies and exuberant in its corporeal stampedes; and that it offers the bonus of a startling verbal epilogue.

MT, MAY 1997

PART THREE

MUSIC THEATRE:
AN IMITATION OF HUMAN ACTIONS

Opera, next to Gothic architecture, is one of the strangest inventions of western man. It could not have been foreseen by any logical process . . . opera provides a real extension of the human faculties.

KENNETH CLARK, *CIVILISATION: A PERSONAL VIEW*, 1969

Opera in English is just about as sensible as baseball in Italian.

ATTRIBUTED TO H. L. MENCKEN.

I sometimes wonder which would be nicer—
an opera without an interval, or an interval without an opera.

ERNEST NEWMAN

Introduction

O PERA HAS PROBABLY ATTRACTED MORE RIDICULE THAN ANY OTHER art form. Dr Johnson is credited with having called it "an Exotick and Irrational Entertainment", and plenty of others have enjoyed poking fun at its seemingly unnecessary extravagances. In our modern scientific and—as probably most people would like to think of it—pragmatic world, we may easily overlook the continuing importance of ritual and symbolism; allied to which, extravagant spectacle, permanent or ephemeral, does seem to be almost a necessity. We are impressed by symbols of power, the exotic and the lavish in architecture of all kinds—medieval castles and baroque palaces; the modernism of London's Lloyds Building or Paris's Pompidou Centre; and even the bizarre post-modernism of almost every out-of-town hypermarket (representing the *power* to purchase). Each of these spectacular settings creates a certain atmosphere and provides a theatrical backdrop for the action of the imagination. Perhaps, then, opera's increasing popularity in Britain during recent years should not surprise us.

Beginning in the 1950s, first in London, with English National Opera building upon the success of Sadler's Wells as the alternative to Covent Garden, and then elsewhere through the enterprise of Opera North, Scottish Opera and Welsh National Opera alongside festival productions at Glynde-bourne and Aldeburgh, the developing enthusiasm for opera blossomed into a more noticeable expansion in the 1980s and seems set to continue in that way. Every company is now mounting its 'workshops' for schools and other outreach activities, and the Royal Opera House is "proposing to transmit its opera and ballet productions on giant screens in parks and stately homes throughout Britain in an attempt to increase public access and dispel the house's elitist image."* Will these transmissions meet people's expectations? True, the spread of interest has resulted in more opera and ballet on television, but opinion is divided about the suitability of that medium. Aside from technical considerations—such as the spatial linking of sound and image so that we are not *seeing* singers in close-up while *hearing* them at a distance—the most obvious problem is the screen itself: not merely because it is small, unavoidably diminishing the larger-than-life quality which is, after all, what we expect from music theatre, but because, quite literally, it comes between the performers and us, the viewers. Even if what we are witnessing is live, the effect is indistinguishable from a recording.

Music's most compelling attribute is its immediacy: its 'presence' or what Scholastic philosophy defined as 'haecceity'.* By its very nature, every musical work is an 'event' which we apprehend through participation; and possibly nothing is more event-like and totally absorbing than the integration of music, words and movement experienced *in the theatre*. Here performers and audience are conjoined in much more than a glorious make-believe fairy-tale existence: this is an imitation of both the glory and the limitations of human actions writ large, uniting on a grand scale the worlds of illusion and reality, action and meaning, sentiment and understanding, experience and revelation.

JP

OUT OF ARCADIA

Silke Leopold, *Monteverdi: Music in Transition*, translated by Anne Smith
(Oxford: The Clarendon Press, 1990)

C LAUDIO MONTEVERDI WAS BORN IN THE MID-SIXTEENTH CENTURY (1567) and, having enjoyed a long if intermittently troubled life, died in the mid-seventeenth century (1643). He remained vigorously creative until his last days and was, indeed, unexpectedly struck down by a 'malignant fever', shortly after the first production of his last, possibly best, and certainly most prophetic opera, *L'Incoronazione di Poppea*. He had survived plague and the harassments of a busy professional life in the service of sometimes peevish and cantankerous autocrats in Mantua and Venice; and both his longevity and his energy contributed to his recognition as the supreme composer of Europe's most turbulent century, crucial to us in that in its course the modern world was born.

Monteverdi lived through, and mirrored in his musical-theatrical artefacts, the breakdown of the old, presumptively God-given values, and seems to have been stimulated to creation by the desperate knowledge that " 'Tis all in Peaces, All Coherence gone". Embracing the Renaissance's hope that man, emulating Orpheus, might arrogate to himself properties and powers traditionally assigned to God, he remained undaunted when such hopes proved to be, however courageous, not so much glory as vainglory. For his *Poppea*, the ultimate seventeenth-century opera, remains strangely affirmative in its inventive plenitude, even though in its mundane world God seems to be obscurely (if at all) operative, while people, motivated by greed, malice and self-interest, are at worst chaotic, at best directionless.

In a sense, the positive qualities of Monteverdi's art, when it appears to be most disintegrative, are the strongest evidence of his genius: for, as Wyndham Lewis pointed out, a great artist is "always engaged in writing a detailed history of the future because he is the only person aware of the nature of the present". Monteverdi was a seer. His music shows, though he himself cannot have guessed, that there is logic in the apparently arbitrary fact that in the year Monteverdi died, Isaac Newton was born. To us, a pattern is perceptible: which must be why it is only in our century, perhaps in the past fifty years, that Monteverdi has been accepted not only as the supreme composer of his own age, but also as one of the master composers of European history. Since our world in so many ways parallels his, with our electronic revolution superseding his scientific one, we may even find that Monteverdi speaks to us with peculiar urgency; certainly the title of this book suggests that its author holds such a view, and has planned his book accordingly.

The 'chronology' that precedes the book proper records the events of the composer's life within the social, religious, and political turmoils he lived through. A few years after Monteverdi was born, Kepler too entered the world and the Turkish fleet was destroyed in the Battle of Lepanto; in the year in which Monteverdi published his *First Book of Madrigals*, the English fleet obliterated the Spanish Armada. Such collocations need no comment; God works in his usual mysterious way, in the process throwing up the wonder that was Monteverdi. So the body of Leopold's book, which concerns not Monteverdi the man but the music he created, unfolds in relation to the story of his life and of his tumultuous century, notwithstanding the fact that the author doesn't deal with the music chronologically, except in so far as he tends to discuss each genre of Monteverdi's work at the time when he was most preoccupied with it. Inevitably, he starts with the madrigal, wherein violent disruption in the world 'out there' became incarnate in the forging of new vocal styles.

The Renaissance madrigal adapted the conventions of ecclesiastical polyphony to secular ends: understandably, since man heroically hoped to take over from God. Monteverdi himself—"a man who was about the same age as Kepler and Galilei, and who studied Plato and alchemy"—began with madrigals conceived in the 'First Practice' of polyphony* as used by the Church, and ended with vocal concerti that were, in the spirit of the monodic Second Practice, incipient opera. The heart of the Monteverdian matter is contained in the detailed comparison, with which Leopold launches his book, of the words and music of two madrigals about man and nature, one ('Ecco mormorar l'onde') from the *First Book* of 1590, the other ('Hor che'l ciel e la terra') from the *Fourth Book* of 1638. Leopold's analysis, as sensitive as it is acute, demonstrates how Monteverdi's techniques shift from Renaissance description and illustration within a scheme which was preordained and philosophically if not religiously coherent, to Baroque re-enactment, whereby music becomes *process*: aural synonyms for the ways in which people, here and now, feel, think and act.

The transition is subtle yet also spontaneous: for Renaissance schematization was mythologized as Arcadia, the Golden Age wherein always elegant, always young men and women consort in a pretend eternity of sensuous indulgence, only to discover that, though no serpents, dragons, or things that go bump in the night affright them, they are pierced by darts of their own devising. Sex, as distinct from love, proves stronger than decorum; and although in a piece like 'Si ch'io vorrei morire' (which deliciously puns on the literal and sexual meanings of dying), sensual pleasure may seem only a game, Monteverdi knew that, even for *homo ludens* and the Arcadian poets of *Il Pastor Fido*,* the game was for real. This was why he had to develop the madrigal towards theatrical projection, in which other people, outside the charmed and charming circle, might participate. By the time of his *Fifth Book*, published when he was thirty-eight, instruments—lutes, theorbos, harps, keyboards, bowed strings—have become habitual, and madrigalian convention has been transmuted into a ritual of humanism, with implicit and sometimes explicit stage action, hopefully civilized by the *cortesía* of communal dance.

Leopold is illuminating both on Arcadian stylization, and on the transition from vocal polyphony to incipient theatre; and he devotes a separate chapter to madrigals that have evolved into a cross between masques and mini-operas. Especially apt are his comments on the near-miraculous 'Lamento della ninfa' from the *Eighth Book*, published in 1638, when Monteverdi had turned seventy. This nymph grieves not merely because she's conventionally lovelorn, but also for the sorrow inherent in the human condition, irremediably subject to Time. The poet, Ricuccini, produces strophic verses similar to those he had devised, early in the century, for overt monodic recitative in Peri's first operatic experiments; but he allows for theatrical antiphony between the lamenting soloist and three choric male voices whose harmonies, though often painfully dissonant, prove consolatory in relating the girl's plight to that of every woman. Meanwhile, the most rudimentary form of the ostinato bass—the descent through a tetrachord down a diatonic scale—continues unbroken, at once measuring time and effacing it. Since the pulse is unruffled, we became habituated to it; since we can't resist it, it becomes a release that itself makes feasible the lyrical grace of the girl's lament.

Leopold is perhaps less persuasive in theoretical speculation than in specific analysis: he barely touches, for instance, on the reasons why ground basses were so pervasive in seventeenth-century music, fulfilling a dual, almost punning, function as representations simultaneously of the inexorability of fate and of mankind's potentially heroic capacity to endure. Similarly, his analysis of *Orfeo*, the central credo in the Monteverdian canon, fails to explore why the fable of Orpheus so obsessed the post-Renaissance imagination; nor does he investigate very deeply why *Poppea*, notwithstanding its apparent abandonment of Orphic heroism and pretension, still leaves us not only with a sense of the vanity of human wishes, but also of the heartrending pathos of human failure, and especially of the vulnerability of love, to which valets and serving maids are no less susceptible than are emperors and empresses. But any theoretical shortcomings are not serious, since Leopold's strength, like that of Monteverdi, is in his specificity.

Monteverdi remarked that his Orfeo moved people so much because he was a man, his Eurydice because she was a woman: truth lies in faith to the human heart, as is even more potently evident in another lament of the heroine of a lost opera of his middle years—Arianna, whose *Lasciatemi morire* became the ultimate best-seller of the seventeenth century. Originally cast in the form of monodic recitative of astonishing lyrical intensity, it was rearranged in every conceivable format, even being retranslated back into the kind of chromatic madrigal from the disintegration of which operatic recitative had evolved. Leopold's exhaustive account of both versions contains the finest writing in his book.

Late in life, Monteverdi transmuted his famous lament for the suffering Arianna into a lament of the Virgin Mary over her slain son: and if one considers that version in the context of the church music that Monteverdi produced in furtherance of his duties at ducal chapels, one will understand why, for Monteverdi, barriers between the first and the second *prattica* seemed ultimately illusory. Leopold is impressive on the fusion between genres in Monteverdi's greatest and now widely celebrated church work, the *Vespers and Magnificat* of 1610: about which, significantly enough, scholarly disputation still rages as to the degree, if any, to which it was liturgically conceived. In any case, it effects an Orphic equation between the Word and the Flesh no less potent than Monteverdi's direct musical dramatization of Orpheus's story in 1607. Indeed, the composer freely exchanged material between the two works, just as he had identified wailing Arianna with the Virgin Mary. Perhaps man, having once fallen, had no choice but to find metaphysical solace, as well as physical succour, in his humanity: in which case there may be point in the fact that *Orfeo* and the *Vespers* coincide in date with the greatest and latest plays of Shakespeare.

Leopold's book is not new, having been first published in German in 1982. It does not claim to make substantial contributions to Monteverdi scholarship, of which there has, over the last few decades, been a great deal. It does claim to be a "comprehensive monograph directed chiefly towards a lay audience but also in part towards specialists", and this claim it fulfils, perhaps more ably than any other book. Given its appeal to the still growing audience for Monteverdi's music, a cheap, or at least cheaper, edition is surely called for. This edition is, however, as handsome, as well-designed and as impeccably printed as one expects of the Clarendon Press's musicological monographs.

TLS, JANUARY 1992

A PRETEND PARADISE

W. A. Mozart, *La Finta Giadiniera* (Theatre Royal, York, 1989)

S A CHILD OF TWELVE MOZART COMPOSED A STOCK *OPERA BUFFA* WHICH, though jolly and expert, only slightly ruffled the surface. Three years later he returned to old-fashioned *opera seria* but illuminated conventionality with incipient passion—especially when dealing with woman as victim rather than with the tragic hero himself. Having attained the advanced age of eighteen, however, he produced a comic opera in which turbulent changes in his own psyche enabled him to understand social reality in depth. The libretto of *La Finta Giadiniera* had been set previously by Pasquale Anfossi, an able professional without the boy Mozart's genius. Given that genius, however, the preposterous plot, rampant with multiple disguises, mistaken identities and reversals, reveals both wittily and pathetically how flimsy was the façade of decorum with which eighteenth-century civilisation attempted to disguise chaos. Adolescent Mozart knew this at first hand; his opera was composed in 1774, early in his 'storm and stress' phase, just after the celebrated-notorious 'Little' G minor symphony. So his music, though often funny, like the libretto, is never insouciant; symphonic drama informs the convolutions of the plot and the all too human dubieties of the characters, and stock *buffo* types become human beings credible in their own contradictoriness. Love, hate, jealousy, fright, murder stalk in the undergrowth of the mayoral garden, and the young Mozart embraces them all, especially in the sustained sonata-style ensembles that conclude the first two Acts.

Opera North has had the bright idea of presenting *La Finta Giadiniera* in tandem and alternation with their justly esteemed production of *The Marriage of Figaro*. The early opera does not, of course, attain the Shakespearean plenitude and the consummate resolution of the later piece, but in this brilliant production it establishes its right to enter the Mozartian canon. Its strength is its truth both to the adolescent Mozart's inner turmoil and to the incipiently revolutionary forces that were changing his world. Tim Albery's production brings this out intelligently, establishing the Mayor's garden as a pretend paradise undermined by the pretend gardener-aristocrat and her redeemably murderous lover; transforming the dream into nightmare when anarchic human passions literally drive the noble lovers mad as they wander through Milton's "blind mazes of this tangled wood"; and restoring the dark forest to the civilized garden in the last act when the pairs of lovers comically and pathetically pretend that all is as it was. In fact, since everyone has been changed by shifty experience in a shifting world, the restoration of the *status quo* is a cheat sweetly admitted to. What's to come is still unsure.

The details of the production are, as is now almost habitual, extravagantly fussy: too many predatory women asserting their feminist rights, too much perilous scampering up ladders to indicate an ecstasy adequately provided for by Mozart's music. This one accepts, however, if not for its intrinsic liveliness, then for the genuine insights of the whole conception. And musically the production, under Alan Hacker, catches exactly the right tension between decay and germination: civilized grace is charged with electrical energy, the woodwind sounding paradoxically seedy yet pristine.

The singing, in an ensemble opera that offers seven rewarding parts but no star role, is responsive to Mozart's youthful vehemence and, where necessary, to his physical and spiritual grace. Nigel Robson, as so often, acts as well as sings with heartfelt intelligence as the Mayor who is a far from masterful master of ceremonies, since although he's the official representative of social conformity, he disarmingly blunders in trying to sort out the lovers' ambivalences. Nardo, the male pretend gardener, is imbued by the towering Peter Savidge with an authority apposite to a servant of Violante-Sandrina, while Linda Kitchen finds in the soubrette role of Serpetta a pertly subversive feminism as well as the young Mozart's dangerous sexuality. Paul Nilon, as the 'real' lover of the pretend gardener, is most hampered by production gimmicks. We aren't allowed to take him seriously, which is a pity, since the moral dubiety is the hub on which the action turns.

Typically, Mozart neither blames nor praises. Man's or woman's unpredictability is his or her truth and the Count, like all of us, may be noble in intent, ridiculous in execution. The Mayor, being outside the action, though far from a *deus ex machina*, alone recognizes that *his* truth, when he has lost the dream-woman he had idealized and idolized, must be to accept man's solitariness, hoping that it is not irremediable.

TLS, DECEMBER 1989

FIDELIO AND LEONORA
THE DEMOCRATIC HERO AND THE FEMALE PRINCIPLE

This paper was given at a conference on 'The Eighteenth Century'
at the University of Calgary in October 1995

W E LIVE IN THE MIDST OF MOMENTOUS EVENTS THAT ENTAIL PERHAPS
insoluble problems, hingeing on the relationship between freedom
and social responsibility. Reflecting on them, it occurred to me that
one of the greatest of composers—certainly the supreme composer most
pertinent to our troubled times—had, in a masterwork central in his career,
faced up to these issues with unflinching courage. He, of course, is
Beethoven; and the crucial work is his only completed opera *Fidelio*.

The heyday of classical opera was, logically enough, the High Baroque—
stretching from the mid-seventeenth to the mid-eighteenth century. *Opera
seria* or Heroic opera was a highly stylized musical-theatrical art designed,
at the height of post-Renaissance man's self-glorification, to embody his
pretence that he was heroic (or monstrous) enough to play God. The
formal codes—recitative, arioso, ternary aria, binary dance, rondo and cha-
conne—had to be rigorously defined because they were man-made artefacts governing human behaviour by laws within which civilized man was
expected, even required, to act. Of course his attempt at self-deification
must inevitably fail since, being human not divine, the best his vainglory
can ultimately hope for is to grow old and die. For this reason baroque
operas at their supreme point—those of Handel, including his oratorios,
which are operas on Old Testament rather than classically mythological or
historical subjects— are prodigious acts of courage. Handel's Julius Caesar
is a Ruler of the World undermined by sexual befuddlement; his Saul is a
biblical Leader who betrays both himself and his people by the unreason of
a jealousy violent enough to turn lunatic. The happy endings tacked on to
these tragedies of human fallibility are what we would call wish-fulfilment.
Such games of let's pretend could be played only within a self-enclosed
social hierarchy that knew, or thought it knew, what its values were.

Self-confidence wavered as society loosened the trammels of aristocratic
autocracy; and that Mozart is the greatest of opera composers is inseparable
from the fact that his genius knew the right time and place to be born. He
inherited enough of the old order to exploit aristocratic conventions, ballasted by their implicit laws; he was also sufficiently within the aegis of
newly-emergent democracy to be passionately concerned about people as
they are in themselves, overriding barriers of class and social distinction.
Dramatically, his operas are about this duality. *Figaro* turns on tensions
between the old world of Count and Countess and the new world of barber

and serving-maid, without weighting the scales either way; *Don Giovanni* is about the cataclysmic impact of newly-released libido on an established order—indeed it opens with the literal murder of the old order (the Commendatore) by the new (the Don). And to this dichotomy of experience there is a technical complement: for Mozart fuses the 'closed' conventions of *opera seria*, such as aria da capo, with the 'open' idiom of sonata, which was concerned with *growth* through conflict, within the mind as well as in the world outside. Vocal lyricism and instrumental drama attain perfect equilibrium in Mozart's mature operas: which are significantly at once tragic and comic, implying—as Heroic opera could seldom allow itself to— a democratically ironic recognition of "other modes of experience that may be possible".

In the generation after Mozart, opera—originally an imitation of human action indulged in because human actions, being those of presumptive gods, were considered worth imitating—was no longer the main outlet for man's creative energy. Democratic man, hoping to find his law within himself, not imposed from 'above', whether by Church or State, tackled this inner drama of conflict and resolution by way of the instrumental drama of sonata: of which Mozart's successor Beethoven became the supreme exemplar. This may be why it is sometimes said that the core of the conflict in *Fidelio* is contained in its four alternative overtures, especially *Leonora no. 3*, an exhaustively worked-out sonata movement about imprisonment, freedom, and enlightenment within the psyche. It doesn't follow that Beethoven's attempt to relate this inner drama to the external world by way of operatic projection was redundant, for at that stage of his life Beethoven was convinced that the spiritual revolution of his music could and should have practical consequences. Nor was his path solitary, for he could profit from the example of French Revolutionary opera as practised by Cherubini—whom Beethoven admired above all living composers—and Méhul. Indeed, Beethoven took over a libretto by Bouilly, one of Cherubini's collaborators, because he knew that his music could reveal the human truths behind the political façade, and could do so with an intensity far beyond that of the several composers who had already musicked it.

He didn't, however, find the task easy: partly because of the nature of the stock 'torment and rescue' text, which he radically changed or had changed between the first version of 1805 and the final version of 1814; but also because the demotic musical conventions of French *opéra comique* and German *singspiel* were themselves problematical. High baroque opera was a convention wherein drama was absolved in music for the very reason that human beings who claim superhuman powers might be expected to sing.

Mozart's tragi-comic operas achieved the perfect democratic balance between the demands of humanly expressive spoken theatre and of sung music precisely because they were poised between the real and the ideal. But in the next generation, when democratic man aimed to emulate common life in the common raw, opera tended to be degraded into a spoken play, into which songs and dances might be interpolated as occasion offered—or didn't offer. Although the convention was supposed to reflect, in dialogue mostly in vernacular prose, the world as it is, the introduction of songs and dances counteracted the attempt at realism since it involved another, irreconcilable level of reality. The democratic world's opera was thus a hybrid doomed to defeat its ostensible ends. *Opéra comique* and *singspiel* were the ancestors of what we call musical comedy: an entertainment dedicated not to reality but to escape from it by way of euphoria and nostalgia, which together become barely distinguishable from amnesia. Only comparatively recently—with pieces like Gershwin's *Porgy and Bess*, Bernstein's *West Side Story*, Sondheim's *Sweeney Todd*, and, today, *Miss Saigon*—has the musical 'show' begun to hit back.

But Beethoven had hit back the best part of two hundred years ago—by way of a cunning paradox which gave meaning to everyday routine and imbued common men, and still more common women, with uncommon grandeur. He made the conventionally operatic features of his score conformable with the minds and gestures of relatively low types who might be expected to speak rather than sing; taking their spoken converse as the norm, we are able to accept their occasional shifts of gear to their own rudimentary kinds of music, whether it be a rustic folk song or an urban, bourgeois pop tune. Marzelline's lyrical amiability at first sounds nearly as arch as that of her bumpkin lover Jaquino; her father Rocco's buffo bluffness tends to be bovine because that is what, in his conforming commonness, he is. But this doesn't mean that these basic offspring of democracy are puppets; they are human beings moulded, and also limited as are we all, by the prejudices that dog them. This is literally symbolized by the fact that Rocco is the gaoler of a prison in or near which they all live. We have met many Roccos, havering between timidity, stupidity, cupidity and a dimly-stirring conscience; it is probable that at some point in our lives we will ourselves be guilty of Rocco-like prevarication. Nor have we the right to condescend to Jaquino because he is unimaginative and inarticulate in his self-conceit. Beethoven—like Mozart, and Terence of classical antiquity—deemed nothing human alien to him,* and knew that human beings are seldom what they seem. Very early in the opera it becomes clear that Marzelline, at least, is intuitively aware of a world beyond her social conditioning, as well as beyond the prison walls.

One might make out of a case that Marzelline is the second most important character in the opera—the first being the other woman in the cast. The action opens with Marzelline singing a duet with her 'steady' boyfriend: music in a low-class, post-Mozart buffo style, in the youthfully innocent key of A major, for she is not yet fully aware of herself, while Jaquino—a representative of the tabloid-skimming, bingo-playing multitude—is aware of almost nothing. It is clear that Marzelline, being more intelligent and sensitive than he, has little time for his bullying bounce and crass machismo. In the context of the opera this has much to do with her being a woman and, indeed, with her mistaking a woman for a man. In the course of the duet and her subsequent solo—no longer in A major but in C minor and major, veering between darkness and light—she reveals that she is impatient with Jaquino not only because she finds his boorishness tiresome, but also because she's in love with someone else. The object of her devotion is the beautiful and conspicuously unloutish Fidelio, who is helping her father with his prison duties. Now Fidelio is, of course, really Leonora: a woman in disguise, who has insinuated herself into the prison in the hope of effecting the release of her husband, politically victimized by and incarcerated in a totalitarian state along, it seems, with most other 'men of good will'. So Marzelline falls genuinely in love with an illusion: which in a sense is not an illusion because it is an ideal. Her intuitive awareness of human potential beyond the blinkered world she lives in is not a Hollywooden dream, but a painful path to self-knowledge. Fidelio is not what she thinks he is; but in loving him-her she shares in her-his heroism. She *grows into* love and truth—like a sonata movement, a technique which modestly informs her idiom, at least as compared with Jaquino's perkily self-enclosed tunes. She teeters between the roles she is expected, and she herself expects, to play and the mysteries released by her dream of love, which is also truth.

So it is not fortuitous that the opening scene should climax in one of the sublime wonders of music: the quartet wherein Marzelline, her father, her everyday lover, and her ideal lover sing in mutual incomprehension *and* in togetherness. The acts of Rossini's comic operas often climax in an Ensemble of Perplexity wherein the protagonists sing simultaneously of their risibly different responses to a situation. But the perplexity in the *Fidelio* quartet is far from risible; and that the music is freely canonic indicates how, from within their perplexity, four people are seeking understanding and unity. Canon is a technical device effecting many-in-oneness: a number of voices or instruments make harmonic congruence by singing or playing the same, or nearly the same, theme at different points in time. In this case it is significantly Marzelline who initiates the canon in a tentative, hesitantly broken arpeggio of G major, traditionally a key of benediction.

The softly padding gait of the pizzicato bass, the dovetailed perfection of the counterpoint as each character enters with a slightly different version of the theme, induce a trance that, carrying the protagonists outside Time, discloses realms of truth beyond the masks they comically or pathetically or tragically present to the world. Rocco can see no further than potential material advancement if his daughter were to 'make a good match' with the elegant and presumptively rich outsider; Jaquino cannot see beyond the self-interest of his pride's and lust's need for Marzelline; but Marzelline and Leonora-Fidelio sing of their and humankind's deepest hopes and fears. We must remember that at this stage Leonora is literally masked: neither Marzelline nor we the audience know who she really is (except that we may have seen the opera before, or read the programme book). None the less, although Leonora is an X in the cypher, it is her truth that is creating, through Beethoven's music, a world fit for men and women—not heroes or presumptive gods—to live in.

Before we consider how Leonora's truth operates, we must ask what it is that frustrates the burgeoning of love in Marzelline's heart, preventing the translation of dreams into ideals. It would seem that the body and spirit of heroism are locked in a state corrupted by tyrannical power: a negative climax to the self-deification post-Renaissance man had once bravely sought after. That power corrupts and absolute power corrupts absolutely is a perversion apparent at the first entry of Pizarro, governor of the state prison of which Rocco is humble custodian. For it turns out that although Pizarro's victims, including Leonora's husband Florestan, are political, the impetus behind his paranoid fury is neither political nor even public; Florestan has caught him out in nefarious double-dealing as a step towards self-promotion, and he cannot face the pricking of the bubble of his self-conceit and self-deceit. Beethoven, however, faces it for him, since his entry is preceded by a footling, tootling little march—ironically in Beethoven's 'power' key of B flat major—in which the accents are oddly displaced, inducing a bizarre glee, perhaps, on Pizarro's part, but certainly a sense of the ridiculous on ours. He is cut down to size, yet not deflated: which is on the mark since destruction, though unheroic, may be and in this case is awe-ful. Significantly, while the inane march is rococo music in current fashion, the spitting virtuosity of Pizarro's frenzy is disciplined in the old-fashioned baroque convention of an Aria of Rage—though not quite in closed da capo form, but in the sonata-style modification of it that Mozart created, especially for the use of (mostly mad) tyrants; the key, too, is Mozart's 'demonic' D minor. Fanatically obsessed with his public image, Pizarro makes a fallacious pretence of heroism, wherein formal aria becomes an ironic gloss on the venom of his spoken words. We recognize the nasty veracity of his pyrotechnics, which sound like human attributes mildewed into kinky sadism by the jittery rhythms and serpentinely flickering diminished fourths.

If Pizarro's grandeur is cankered, what is the nature of true heroism in the newly democratic world? Leonora and Florestan—the positive heroic beings who counter Pizarro's negation—are common only in being without hereditary rights, uncommon in their ability to love and suffer, and to triumph through suffering. They are passionately human representatives of the Age of Enlightenment and of the spirit of the Fifth Symphony; for them Beethoven, taking a hint from Gluck and Mozart, evolved a new kind of dramatic arioso, incorporating what might have been 'closed' aria into large-scale 'open' tonal organization. We are first aware of this when Leonora draws aside from the action to reveal the truth of her heart in a dramatic soliloquy, the structure of which is symphonic. In the first section she *acts out* in physical gestures and turbulent modulations the distress of her body and spirit, given the situation she and her husband are placed in. In the second section she sings a *developing* aria, like a slow sonata movement, lyrically affirming hope from the heart of darkness. The words involve images of rainbow, rising star and snowdrop; the key is E major which, being in the baroque period the sharpest major key in common use, was traditionally associated with heaven; and she sings in duo with an obbligato horn—a royal instrument—standing in as a disembodiedly romantic lover-husband. Rising scales suggest prayer and aspiration: which in the third section becomes a sonata-style allegro, since light may triumph only through strife. In this symphonic sequence Leonora, through faith and love, wins freedom for Florestan, for herself, and for mankind—then as now an Endangered Species. The relation between this wife and husband is prefigured by that between Pamina and Tamino in Mozart's *Magic Flute*, another allegorical torment-and-rescue opera which Beethoven admired above all Mozart's works—interestingly enough, Schikeneder, Masonic part-librettist of the *Flute*, had a hand in the commissioning of *Fidelio*. Like Pamina, Leonora, being a woman, is blessed with the heavenly gift of intuition, as against the patriarchally dominating Will which Beethoven himself supremely represents, but which also fashioned the social masks by which we've been perverted as well as protected. Leonora's truth becomes an agent of redemption: as she demonstrates in this purgatorial scena, ending in thrillingly upsurging scales.

Through the potency of Leonora's love and Fidelio's faith renaissance has already occurred in this light-generating scene; so Florestan's complementary scena, at the dark beginning of the second act, can have practical consequences. We meet him in the depths of his dank dungeon, where he is chained and pinioned, like Prometheus on his rock—a mythological hero germane to most of Beethoven's middle-period music. The act starts from the heroic convention of the French operatic overture, harking back to the worldly glory of the Sun King Louis XIV. But pride and presumption are darkly shadowed, for the key is F minor, traditional key of *chants lugubres* and of the infernal regions: so even tonally, the wife (with her four major sharps) and the husband (with his four minor flats) form a unity in duality. This is musically incarnate when Florestan's anguished, corporeal arioso touches mysteriously (because enharmonically) on Leonora's E major bliss. Florestan's arioso dissolves into chromatics reminiscent of Bach's Passion music—reminding us that we may think of Bach's Passions as the greatest of all heroic operas, differing from the norm in that their hero not only pretends to be, but presumptively is, God! The words of the libretto hint at an affinity between Florestan and the crucified Christ: in which case the relation between Florestan and Pizarro may form a Jungian *conjunctio oppositorum* between victim and persecutor.

Some such religious, if not explicitly Christian, dimension emerges in the middle section of Florestan's scena—an aria tentatively echoing Leonora's hopeful rainbow. The key is not heavenly E major but its upper mediant A flat, which is balanced by *its* submediant F when the music swings into fast, sonata-style psychological action. F major is also, of course, the major of Florestan's originally tenebrous F minor, to which it traditionally formed an open-air, pastoral complement. Here it is resurrection music achieved from symphonic evolution: a vision of a *world* restored.

But before his physical resurrection into the 'real' world, Florestan has to undergo a mock burial—a magnificent duet sung by metaphysically aware Leonora and physically unaware Rocco as they dig his grave—and to confront the opera's ultimate climax, his attempted murder. For Pizarro, having heard rumours that the Minister of State is coming to inspect the prison, armed with evidence of the tyrant's duplicitous practices, decides that Rocco is too craven to act as hit-man on his behalf: so he, Pizarro, must himself liquidate Florestan, before he reveals all. The situation is all too familiar to us from cinematic and televisual drama, and nowadays theatrical producers draw parallels with Nazi Germany and Stalinist Russia, as though tyranny had only recently been invented. Such literalism can only denature the force of the quartet scene in the dungeon, perhaps the most explosively and intensely concentrated scene in all opera. It climaxes in a tonal no-man's-land when Leonora, interposing her body between the murderous tyrant and her husband, reveals her *true* identity. Her arpeggiated figures, ringing with high B flats, axe through the D major tonality in

music which may well be the most demanding—physically and psychologically if not technically—in the entire operatic repertory. Coincidentally,
the trumpet of the Day of Judgement sounds, at first from afar, as the Minister arrives to right old wrong. This is of course a symbolic event: the pragmatic enactment of the freedom Leonora has already won through her
truth. Her intimately fraught speech inflection (even her spoken words are
music), her resounding bel canto and whirling cantilena carry her and us
through arioso of despair into aria of liberated joy; and so into the ecstatic
jubilation (in blessed G major) of the famous duet, in the wondrous tipsi-
ness of which the lovers are reborn. Pizarro's private spleen has been the
driving force behind his public oppression; complementarily, in another
conjunctio oppositorum, the fulfilment of Leonora's and Florestan's private
love transfigures and validates the public world. A commonweal and a com-
monwealth are attained, within the mind and potentially within the body
politic, of which the chorus, and you and I, are a part.

Leonora's vocal quality in the dungeon quartet and in the 'Namenlose'
duet should sound superhuman in its very assertion of humanity, for that is
what the opera is about. The plot—like those of many operas, and not
merely those, such as Wagner's *Ring*, which are overtly mythological—has
many subterranean links with the archetypal life of the psyche; one may
even construe it as a version of the fable of the ego-conscious Hero who
fights and slays the preconscious uroboic dragon in order to win 'the pearl
without price', 'the treasure hard to get', or the captive princess. Only the
roles are reversed: at this juncture in history it is male Florestan who is
imprisoned in the cavern of the urobos or 'unconscious night', female
Leonora who heroically effects his release. It is she who, in the duet, makes
Florestan *flower*, as befits his name; and while this is fundamentally a psychological event, it is manifest too in the world out there, for Beethoven's
equilibrium between psychological truth and material circumstance is
exact. It is hardly surprising that in the dungeon scene Florestan's *heldentenor* often finds it hard to compete with Leonora; we would hardly expect
him, for all his nobility, to emerge after months of near-starvation in a fetid
dungeon with Leonora's pristine fervour.

The same balance between physical and metaphysical truth is manifest
when, after the private liberation of the duet and the public liberation of
the chorus as the gates are opening, the Minister becomes a naturalistic
deus ex machina who announces the dawn of a new era. His music is grand
enough to make him a supernatural angel as well as a political agent, but
not so grand as to sully the lustre of Leonora, whose transcendent majesty
is the crown of her humanity, as Pizarro's virulent violence is the paradoxical apex of his. Though Leonora's voice is not quite the Voice of God that

Beethoven is to hear in his *Missa Solemnis* and in his last sonatas and quartets, it is prophetic of that voice. We may recall that Beethoven originally named his opera after Leonora and always objected to its renaming—insisted on by his publisher and impresario—after pseudo-male Fidelio.

In Leonora's music the divided self is healed: a psychological process that makes the opera a religious experience. It is also a social event, since the prisoners, We the People, are released not into a metaphysical heaven, but into a real if Enlightened world in 'white' C major. In this brave new world, as delineated in the final choruses, there can be no place for a Pizarro's neurotic self-love, nor even for the relatively harmless self-conceit of a Jaquino or for a Rocco's bumblingly self-regarding greed: hence the appeals, from the private fulfilment of Leonora and Florestan, for the Revolutionary ideals of liberty, equality and fraternity, whereby *all* common people might hopefully become uncommon. The electrically-charged homophony of the choric jubilation is now scored for mixed chorus, women as well as men, presumably because the chorus has come to represent humankind, liberated by Leonora's female principle. Since the public triumph depends on the private apotheosis of the hero and heroine, we recognize that the opera is asking a question pertinent to our foundering, and Russia's precariously emergent, democracy: one day, may *hoi polloi*, even the commonest man or woman, storm the heights?

About this the ultimate triumph-songs are, not surprisingly, somewhat ambivalent. In a democratic act rare in the world of professional music-making, all the soloists join in the choric ensembles, a manifestation of at least potential equality. But Jaquino and Rocco tag along with the rest while seeming unchanged by the world-shattering events they have lived through; Jaquino even twines in parallel thirds and tenths with Marzelline, though if that means she will accept convention and settle for her 'steady', one cannot rate her chances of happiness highly, for it seems improbable that she could teach Jaquino how to grow up with her. That Beethoven thought she deserved a better fate may be implicit in the fact that her relation with Leonora remains crucial; in the F major Hymn to Light she sings the same music as Leonora, *on equal terms*. I think this suggests that Beethoven, when composing his opera, believed that a positive answer to our question about the destiny of the common man—and still more woman—was at least feasible. I doubt whether he still thought so during the last years of his life; and I am certain that his positive answer was not the same as Mrs Thatcher's.

MM, APRIL 1990

PERPLEXED ENSEMBLES

Gioachino Rossini, *The Thieving Magpie* (Grand Theatre, Leeds, 1992)

ORN 200 YEARS AGO IN 1792, ROSSINI ENTERED THE WORLD THE YEAR
after Mozart left it. This makes sense, for although he is in many ways
Mozart's successor, there's a kind of death in the difference between
them. Mozart, like many geniuses, managed to be born at the right time and
place, in a transitional world wherein his operas could be simultaneously
aristocratic and democratic, tragic and comic. The process of history is
incarnate in the sounds and sights he created, for people change in Mozart's
operas, and we change with them. This is not true of Rossini, who also
teetered between inherited privilege and revolution.

Although his fabulous popularity in both his own country and in
Mozart's Italianate Vienna was deserved, Rossini tended—writing for a
more culturally amorphous public than Mozart—to expatiate on his jokes,
'presenting' his characters theatrically, rather than persuading them to
create themselves. This is why he abandoned Mozart's psychologically dramatic sonata-aria in favour of the audience-directed rondo-aria in which a
symmetrical tune is stated several times, interspersed with episodes and
rounded off by a stretto-coda, garlanded with vocal pyrotechnics to work
up the applause. Rossini's partiality for the Crowd Scene, culminating in a
notorious Rossini Crescendo, makes a complementary point; and the
planes of private and public experience seldom cross, since comedy lies in
the very failure of human communication. Whereas the ensembles that
conclude the acts of Mozart's mature tragi-comedies concern the (admittedly bewildering) reconciliation of different responses to the same situation, Rossini was most adept at what came to be called an Ensemble of
Perplexity, which may be momentarily pathetic but is commonly both farcical and scary.

But if there is a streak of sadism in Rossini's comic art, this is not because
he was oblivious to the terrors and traumas that may afflict us when we
drop our social masks. His 'serious' operas, on dubious heroes such as Oth-
ello and Moses, contain powerful music, while at the height of his career he
created, in *Guillaume Tell*, a new kind of opera that found its theme not in
a glorification of monarchy, nor in the traditional conflict between love and
duty, but in historical events and national aspirations. The significance of
Tell in relation to romanticism and revolution can hardly be over-esti-
mated. Yet it would seem that the gulf between Rossini's habitual hedonism
and his attempt to evolve an opera of social and political commitment was

too wide to be bridged. *Guillaume Tell*, which brought him legendary success throughout Europe, led only to his retirement from professional life, at the age of thirty-seven.

How the 'Mozartian equilibrium' between the aristocratic and the demotic, the tragic and the comic, was undermined in Rossini's work is demonstrated by the piece which Opera North is presenting for his duo-centenary. For *The Thieving Magpie*, first produced in 1817, the year after *The Barber of Seville*, the most popular and perhaps the best of his operas, is neither a comic nor a tragic piece, nor is it quite an Italian *opera-semi-seria*, nor a Frenchified *comédie larmoyante*. It's rather an opera based on divisions of social class and of ranges of experience appropriate to them, literally bifurcated into two acts, the first of which is conventional rococo *opera buffa*, while the second is tragic in implication though not in the event.

Act One generates the routine complications of *opera buffa* plot. Fabrizio, a successful farmer, and his shrewish wife Lucia await the return of their soldier-son Giannetto from the wars. Their serving-maid Ninetta is secretly in love with Giannetto, and since he (as revealed by a pet magpie) apparently loves her, all seems set for a merry marriage. Yet even in this conventional set-up shadows may be cast in sunshine: class-conscious Lucia is dubious about the social acceptability of the liaison, while Ninetta's father, also returning from the wars, is in disguise, unjustly charged with treason and sentenced to death. To help her father escape, Ninetta has to raise money; and several plots thicken as, furthering this end, she is involved with an itinerant pedlar and the local mayor, who offers assistance in return for clearly specified favours. The sequence of these machinations is obscure; but the act climaxes when Lucia, noticing that a treasured household spoon and fork are missing, enquires who the thief might be. The caged magpie briskly chirps "Ninetta", confirming Lucia's snobbish suspicions; the Mayor makes a formal report of the incident, reminding everyone that according to law the penalty for domestic larceny is death. Ninetta is arrested to the dismay of all except the frustrated Mayor, who sees in the situation renewed hope for his libidinous intentions.

The second act—with Ninetta in prison, visited by the rape-intent Mayor, by her disguised father, and by a childhood playmate, Pippo, who is involved in the devious financial transactions—is potential catastrophe. The action moves inexorably towards death and the scaffold, propelled by a grandly sustained funeral march, interspersed with ensembles by the protagonists, culminating in a genuinely noble quintet. Even so, the beauty of these ensembles, being skin-deep and formulaic, never approaches Mozart's assuagement of human differentiations; nor could one expect it to when action is precipitated by a humanly unpredictable magpie, a notoriously tricksy bird. Significantly, the most deeply felt if not the most beautiful music in the score is the all-male chorus of hate and destruction when the law delivers judgement.

But Rossini was too amiable a man to accept such dire reality as the last word on the human condition: so in the nick of time, guilelessly rustic Pippo discovers the missing fork and spoon in the magpie's nest, thereby proving Ninetta's innocence. The opera can then end with a reversal of the second act's reversal, though this is only another arbitrarily cynical trick of fate. This must be why we're not deeply moved by Ninetta's predicament, though we're momentarily entranced by the music's wish-fulfilment.

Opera North's production does all that is possible for a piece that suffers rather than—like Mozart's operas—profits from its ambivalence. Ninetta's role, though demanding in endurance as well as agility, is basically a soubrette part, as Anne Dawson demonstrates in preserving bucolic simplicity in a wily world; she almost deserves the saintly canonization which the production seems oddly to reward her with, leaving her epiphanized on an altar of trees. Andrew Shore's Mayor tempers villainy with charm. Barry Banks as Ninetta's soldier-lover is a lightly tuneful Italian tenor who lacks charisma in comparison with the ebullient Mayor; but Matthew Best, as Ninetta's father, has an unportentous gravity that provides a centre for so much magpie-induced irresponsibility. Elizabeth McCoarmack is affecting as Pippo, a role that, being transvestite, may hint that illusion is kinder than, even preferable to, reality; certainly the men of the chorus make reality grim enough in the trial scene. Ivor Bolton as conductor summons precise vivacity from the woodwind of the orchestra. He encourages vocal cantilena to flower over the simplest arpeggiated 'guitar bass', and pointedly characterizes whirligig scale-figures to express public unease.

Martin Duncan's production and Sue Blaine's designs are imaginative but practical, which Rossini would have approved of. Perhaps the magpie (vocally impersonated with relish by Pauline Thulborn) is the star of the evening, in his various metamorphoses debunking pretension while admitting to human vulnerability. He makes us laugh, in the right way, at the right times. It seems sad, if also funny, that we should be at the mercy of his caprice; and since self-deceit may apparently sometimes make us more rather than less human, we are grateful for the wish-fulfilment of the conclusion. In the true story on which the libretto was based, both the girl and her father end up hanged—which leaves even less than Rossini suggests to be said on behalf of our magpieishly inhumane race.

TLS, MAY 1992

AN ARBITRARY MALIGNANCY

Giacomo Puccini, *La Bohème* (Grand Theatre, Leeds, 1993)

W HEN 'NESSUN DORMA' WOWED VAST CONGREGATIONS AT FOOTBALL stadia throughout Europe, Puccini became Top of the Pops in a sense previously inconceivable. At the start of his career, his ambition had been to follow in the footsteps of his hero, Verdi, though he lacked both Verdi's ability to engender people utterly different from himself, and Wagner's compensatory egomania that rendered objectivity unnecessary. Puccini knew that to make living music he had to identify with his creatures; and recognized that, since the range of experience that moved him was limited, he must contrive the situations that turned him on. He became an artist who, like Tchaikovsky and Rachmaninov, owes his immense popular appeal to his being psychologically odd. This shouldn't surprise us, since we, unable to compete with a Wagner or Beethoven, both suffer and savour the common maladjustments.

In his mature work, Puccini's nervously wrought melodies, obsessionally non-directed harmonies, and fanatical rhythmic ostinatos lend themselves to the expression of suffering, whether sadistic or masochistic. While such experience was the reality from which he evolved so potent a language, it was also the source of a quality inherently synthetic: for, having so narrow an emotional range, he was tempted to resort to any expedient to stimulate it; and stimulation may become simulation, self-induced. This is why Puccini's art, though validly heir to Verdi, also anticipates twentieth-century musical comedy, and the media rampant today.

If *Madam Butterfly* is Puccini's finest opera, the reason is that at the beginning of this century it powerfully fused the old type of musical theatre with the new. Its very story is about a clash between an Old World (religious, magical, ancestor-ridden, butterfly-impaling) and a New World (mercantile, mercenary, militaristic, butterfly-bashing). Given this social-political context, Puccini holds the scales evenly, wringing the last ounce of pathos and potential tragedy out of a situation wherein people are victimized by forces they are half-aware of, but can't control. In *La Bohème*, however, he opts for something simpler, though no less heart-rending: for in this piece his creatures, being 'bohemians', are victims mainly of their own self-delighting irresponsibility. The villain is neither moribundly old Japan nor brashly new America, but God, who allows young artists starving in garrets to swim or sink in euphoric amnesia. Half a century later, at the period in which this production is set, Bohemians have ceased to be a picturesque minority and have become a majority of young folk, especially those of the less privileged classes. What destroys poor Butterfly we observe, and revile; what destroys poor Mimi is neither timidity nor folly but simply and irremediably her consuming consumption. There but for the grace of God might go we, lopped off by AIDS or whatever *our* scourge may be. Puccini proffers no evidence of the efficacy of God's grace, in the unlikely event of his displaying it.

Mimi, as Puccini conceived her, is the pivotal character because she is the only one with the potential to scale heights and plumb depths. Playing her, Jane Leslie Mackenzie, a delightfully strapping Canadian, doesn't remotely look eighteen, or *petite*, or frail, as Puccini wanted her to be, nor even wantonly vacuous, as she was in the original book and play; what matters is that she has the voice to cope with the glorious tunes, and acts intelligently. William Burden, her Rodolfo, doesn't produce the scalp-prickling buzz of the Loud Italian Tenor, but looks and sounds convincing in well-meaning, if feckless, exuberance; while Juliet Booth and Robert Hayward, as the initially irrepressible Bohemians, Musetta and Marcello, beautifully negotiate their transition from jolly folly to stunned bemusement at the final catastrophe. The scene of Mimi's death, as here enacted, reveals why *La Bohème*, often condescended to as a tear-jerker, owes its durable power to its alarming truth. Rodolfo's final caterwauling over the dead girl freezes the marrow—as, we are told, it froze the marrow of Puccini himself, who bellowed uncontrollably over his Mimi's fate. This production makes one admit that his emotion, like his music, was not 'in excess of the object', since that object is the arbitrary malignancy of God.

Puccini managed the musical comedy and television aspects of his entertainment no less adroitly than he coped with his verismo opera's appalling verisimilitude. Phyllida Lloyd's vivacious direction serves him well here, though the rotating stage gets a trifle tiresome. Anthony Ward's designs reanimate 1950s Abstraction and 1960s Pop Art neatly; Roy Laughlin as conductor keeps the music moving in two senses, though the decibel level of the band might, on occasion, have been advantageously restrained. On the whole, this production balances professionalism with an *ad hoc* inventiveness appropriate to the theme: which teeters between the illusory heavens of television and the baying of the hounds of hell.

TLS, APRIL 1993

THAT MIXED UP KID

Ambroise Thomas, *Hamlet* (Grand Theatre, Leeds, 1995)

UROPEAN OPERA BEGAN AS A LARGER-THAN-LIFE CELEBRATION OF Man in the Highest, elevating his achievements in military conquest and empire-building to quasi-divine status. When, with the thud of the years, this optimistic schedule proved untenable, operatic heroes, and still more heroines, tended to become more credible because more vulnerable. Prophetically, Shakespeare's Hamlet was a prototype of these modern heroes. Although supremely articulate, he is also Everyman, whose mystery is his normalcy; we all recognise bits of ourselves in him even if we cannot expatiate on them as he does.

That *Hamlet* has not often served as an operatic subject is in part a consequence of Shakespeare's genius; for if Hamlet is a mixed-up kid and/or ageing intellectual like many of us, his subtlety and complexity are beyond the range of operatic stereotypes. He enthrals us because he seems to contain most of the paradoxes of human nature. Humphrey Searle, in his 1968 opera on the Hamlet theme, used Schoenbergian expressionism in an attempt to reveal the up-to-the-minute significance of the hero's tangled psyche. Understandably Searle, though a talented composer, didn't get much further in this enterprise than had Shakespeare's Players, who bootlessly tried to sound Hamlet's 'stops' on their tootling recorders. Understandably again, most operatic Hamlets have sidetracked Shakespeare, or concentrated on the tough counterplots and strong situations of the primitive Revenge play that was Shakespeare's source.

There was a classical baroque *Hamlet*, by Gasparini, as early as 1705. He came more into his own in nineteenth-century France, whose composers, having a long theatrical tradition and a classical opera akin to Racinian tragedy, occasionally tackled Shakespeare. Berlioz came within measurable distance of Shakespeare in his *Romeo and Juliet* choral symphony, in his 'Ophelia' compositions, inspired by the Irish actress, Harriet Smithson, whom he eventually (if unpropitiously) married, and, closest of all, in the nobly tragic Funeral March for Hamlet's final scene. Ambroise Thomas, like Berlioz, was taught by Jean François Lesueur (from whom Berlioz inherited his veneration for classical French theatre and his linear approach to composition), but was a cosier composer than his teacher, let alone Berlioz. Born in 1811, he won the Prix de Rome (which for so long eluded Berlioz) at a remarkably early age, succeeded the fashionable Daniel-François-Esprit Auber as director of the Paris Conservatoire, and was esteemed as a composer of lyric or comic light operas, among which *Mignon* is still a repertory piece. Even so, he wanted to prove himself in a more substantial undertaking, and the Paris Opéra encouraged him to capitalize on his success by making a big, 'serious' opera. Hamlet's story fitted this, or any, bill, and Thomas embarked on the project, with a libretto by Michel Carné and Jules Barbier, with due gravity, devoting six years to the task.

He didn't produce a piece that is Shakespearean in Shakespeare's, or even in Berlioz's sense, but he did make a splendidly professional opera that offered his public something of everything they relished: twinkle-toed ballet dancers for businessmen relaxing at the close of day; mellifluous choruses, often genuinely assuaging, for well-heeled courtiers and fashionable opera buffs; vaudeville turns and comic acts in the spirit of *opéra bouffe*, usually lively and often brilliantly scored; a 'pathetic' part, with Mad Scene, for Ophelia as a coloratura lyric soprano; strong dramatic, or melodramatic, parts for the King and Queen; a plethora of neutral minor roles; and, as go-between, a Hamlet who, like Shakespeare's hero, flits in and out of different social contexts. Such pluralism no doubt accords with our own, as well as that of France's Second Empire, and Thomas adroitly handles the shifts between disparate worlds.

So does this production, as it ingeniously exploits the 'play within the play'. A nineteenth-century French vaudeville troupe validly deputizes for Shakespeare's *commedia* players; the 'low' acts are often very funny and manage not to repudiate the pathos of Ophelia's lunacy, the slightly rancid libidinousness of the ageing King and Queen, or Hamlet's role as paradoxical negotiator. Anthony Michaels-Moore has the energy and intelligence necessary for his part (I particularly liked the quaint charm of his 'antic disposition' in the midst of blood and thunder). Rebecca Caine as Ophelia attained, in her frenzied coloratura, just the right dangerous equilibrium between virginal grace and covert rakishness, sustaining tone and line until her watery death, accompanied by a seductively lovely off-stage chorus. John Rath made a hellish yet affecting Ghost, now pallidly beyond the pale, now a wrathful father; John Galla as Claudius looked every inch a King, and, if he didn't quite sound it, that may have been appropriate for such a seedy monarch. Linda Finnie as Gertrude looked a shade Widow-Twankyish, but that, too, may have been appropriate, and she was superb in her powerful bedroom scene with Hamlet and Ophelia. The minor characters, perhaps inevitably in so populous a play, tended to be phased out. Rosencrantz and Guildenstern are simply effaced, Polonius is a cypher instead of a funny-sad father who is out of his emotional depth, while his son Laertes, though sweetly sung by Alan Oke, surrenders the subtle ambiguities of his Shakespearean role.

The orchestra and chorus, under Oliver von Dohnányi, seemed to enjoy responding to Thomas's many-faceted and always well crafted music, savouring limpid lyricisms along with unabashed vulgarities. The total effect, by Shakespearean standards, is inevitably anodyne—only the wicked stepfather gets his just deserts, for the Queen, Polonius, Laertes, and Hamlet himself all escape the mayhem that the tragic hero unleashes in Denmark. Still, if we can forget Shakespeare, Thomas's opera is one that usually entertains and sometimes moves and excites us, here directed by David McVicar, with designs by Michael Vale and lighting by Paul Sharman. The dancers, at least by the standards of the Paris Opéra in 1868, lack ostentation, but mingle frailty and comicality in ways that bear on the piece's essential confusions of reality and illusion. Pointedly, the main set of the Danish court was also a Stage—which, according to the bard, all the world is.

TLS, OCTOBER 1995

ONE DAMNED THING AFTER ANOTHER

EMMANUEL CHABRIER'S CORNY BUT BRILLIANT OPERAS OF MODERN LIFE

L'Étoile and *Le Roi Malgré Lui* (King's Theatre, Edinburgh, 1994)

THIS YEAR'S EDINBURGH FESTIVAL HONOURED THE CENTENARY OF Emmanuel Chabrier's death by presenting two of his operas—one of them in the triumphant 1991 resuscitation made by Opera North, the other currently re-created, by the same adventurous company, after years of banishment consequent on an even more than usually inept libretto. Libretto problems are seldom fortuitous; they reflect confusions and incertitudes within society; and Chabrier was himself an equivocal character. A stocky peasant type from the Auvergne, he displayed "une rondeur joyeuse" while being at the same time an *habitué* of the salons and a fairly affluent civil servant who hobnobbed with the high and mighty and was friend of musicians, poets and painters. He embarked on operatic projects with Verlaine, though they proved abortive; he was drawn or painted by the likes of Manet and Fantin-Latour, and owned a collection of Impressionist paintings that would today be worth a fabulous fortune.

Everyone seems to have loved him as much for his affability and wit as for his talents as pianist and composer; today, we find him congenial because his position between worlds and times, between amateurism and professionalism, and between populism and élitism accords with our volatilities. In his own day, he for a while enjoyed pop-star celebrity as composer of his orchestral *España*, a piece of entertainment-music equally at home in concert hall or in a park or on a pier: proletarian in rhythmic zest, melodic allure and colouristic glamour, yet sophisticated in its ironical stance, since its Spanishness is a game and a mask rather than for real. When Chabrier tells us that the music makes him "rebondir comme un jeune jaguar" we can hardly resist capering with him; then we remember that some such balance between earthy immediacy and playfulness characterizes most of Chabrier's music and was, indeed, the essence of the conventions of *opéra bouffe* and *opéra comique*, which technically compromised between 'real' speech and 'pretend' song-and-dance. Bizet's *Carmen*, the most successful of French nineteenth-century operas both artistically and commercially, raised this ambivalence between verisimilitude and dream to tragic heights and depths. While Chabrier's incursions into music theatre never attained the probity that Bizet, with Prosper Merimée's help, uniquely achieved in *Carmen*, they are musically no less distinguished, and perhaps even more innovative.

Chabrier's bifurcation is overt in the fact that despite his relish for the

148

low life of Parisian theatre, he was knocked for six by Wagner's *Tristan*, which provoked him to delusions of grandeur. His Wagnerian tragic opera *Gwendoline* (1885) had some success in Germany, and is still accorded an occasional revival there. But it never caught on in France, or elsewhere, and by hindsight, with knowledge of Chabrier's later work, his Wagnerism now seems an aspect of his exquisite French sensuality rather a portentous cultivation of Teutonicism. There is some evidence of this in the more substantial of the two operas which were presented at Edinburgh.

The earlier piece, *L'Étoile* (1877), is revived in the acclaimed Opera North production by Phyllida Lloyd, still succoured by Anthony Ward's designs, Rick Fisher's lighting and Quinny Sacks' choreography. This brilliant team added lustre to what had been Chabrier's first manifestation of genius as distinct from talent; with the help of Jeremy Sams's new translation, rivalling Ira Gershwin and Cole Porter in adroit versification, it revealed the cynicism of a hedonistic society comparable with, if more amiable than, our own, while at the same time it debunked that and our society's duplicities. One suspects that the original fashionable audience for *L'Étoile* was more tickled than shocked by its latent subversiveness: whereby the tiny Ruritanian King Ouff is bested by a "marchand ambulant" who eventually runs off with the mini-king's fairy princess. Trade gets the better of privilege: which may have pleased the newly wealthy, if not the Old Guard. In this Edinburgh revival Paul Nilon was not a 'natural' for the role of the kinglet, as Anthony Mee had been in the Leeds production, while the charismatic Pamela Helen Stephen, who had played the transvestite part of the gamin commercial traveller, didn't make it to Edinburgh, being indisposed. (Her understudy proved vocally unequal to the part, though she acted intelligently.) The other main roles were uproariously realized by the original cast, with Clive Bayley balefully idiotic as the Court Astrologer, Alan Okie and Kate Flowers smoothly vivacious as the Ambassador and his wife, and Mary Hegerty prettily pert as the candyfloss Princess. The Opera North orchestra, directed by Valentine Raymond, a Frenchman indigenous to the tradition, released bubbles in the aural champagne of Chabrier's tunes, rhythms, and pellucid sonorities.

L'Étoile offered a retaste of delights many of us had already savoured. The more significant Edinburgh event was the restitution of the *opéra comique*, *Le Roi Malgré Lui* (1885), perhaps the apex to Chabrier's musical inventiveness; Ravel remarked that modern French music, including his own, dated from this piece, and more extravagantly hazarded that he would rather have written this single score than the entire cycle of Wagner's *Ring*! Yet as an opera in performance *Le Roi* has fared less well than a *jeu d'esprit* like *L'Étoile*, for the more there is at stake in human terms, the more damaging is the disability of an inconsequential libretto. Even by current French standards, the book of *Le Roi* was grossly incompetent, being cobbled together, admittedly at Chabrier's instigation, by no fewer than three musically recalcitrant and mutually incompatible hacks, on a theme itself involving disguise, illusion, and mistaken identity. Yet despite his impatience with the dithering text-mongers, he was carried along on a flood of musical invention, overriding his collaborators' stupidity. When Jeremy Sams was invited to follow up his now-famous version of *L'Étoile* with an Englished *Le Roi Malgré Lui*, he decided that the original libretto was irredeemable. He would have to invert normal process and to concoct, for Chabrier's already existing music, a comparable set of characters and a story that might validly have inspired such music. On the whole, this bold undertaking came off: perhaps because the theme of a tussle between 'established' social values and the chance gambles and gambols inherent in a market economy itself involves shiftiness between different, even contradictory, artistic conventions.

If subversion is latent in the plot of *L'Étoile*, it is patent in that of *Le Roi*: which happens in another Ruritanian community wherein a Dying King is likely to be succeeded by a Black Bastard with the makings of a dire Hitlerian tyrant. But the King also has a legitimate son who, despising the panoply of power politics, has taken to the mountains to become an outlaw and a revolutionary harbouring egalitarian ideals. Jeremy Sams, here his own producer, makes discreet references to the Russian Revolution, with a playful parade of hammers and sickles, though the action remains legendary rather than historically political. Cunningly, Sams runs the 'public' events alongside the 'private' unfolding of the characters' destinies: which is exactly what Chabrier does in his music, though the original libretto disguised this parallelism. Here rebel-king Henri—sung by Russell Smyth in a manly baritone that sounds noble without embarrassing either him or us— is counterpointed against his committed revolutionary lover, sung by Juliet Booth with (after an unfocused start) an appropriately naive fervour. Complementarily, the Beautiful Spy Minka, consorting in male disguise with the rebels but in the pay of the Master of the Old King's Household, is paired with Nangis, "a dissolute nobleman with republican sympathies". Her virtuosic coloratura role, superbly negotiated by Rosa Mannion, twines with the heroic tenor of Justin Lavender, who reveals, in love, the true heart of a character prone to self-deceit. Nothing is what it seems, given the conditions of a changing world; if the Beautiful Spy and the Doubtful Revolutionary encapsulate the ambiguous truths of human experience in the present and a possible future, the King who Ran Away and his new-style Political Woman batten on truths revealed retrospectively, as they nostalgically recall, in a ravishing barcarolle, the love of their Venetian youth.

The plurality of moods and manners in this score reflects the half-articulate action in which past, present and future overlap. Modern life is one damn thing, and one pose or posture, after another, from the corny verismo of the first act's rebel music (with briskly martial choruses and comic turns from minor characters such as an Italian partisan who, fetchingly sung by Geoffrey Dolton, has a knack with mechanical gadgets, including bombs) to the passionate exploration, throughout the second act, of the relation between the public forces manifest in the stunning Waltz Scene and the private loves of forward-looking Minka and Nangis and of backward-looking Henri and Alexina. The third act demonstrates that the Established Past and potentially Political Present are mutually interdependent, as the public world climaxes in the magnificently effervescent *Fête Polonaise* to welcome the new Republican King, and the tangled fates of the lovers are unravelled in music of *Carmen*-like and Verdian potency, if hardly of Wagnerian mythic grandeur. Though Chabrier is never pretentious, there is point in the fact that the final chorus of reconciliation between (embarrassed) Monarch and (nervous) Hammer-and-Sickle-ites is not merely muscular, as the initial workers' choruses had been, but also deeply moving. Reconciliation was an ideal endemic to Chabrier's warmly hopeful heart, however improbable its fulfilment.

This hopefulness bears too on Chabrier's orchestral *trouvailles*, as resonantly interpreted by the orchestra under their fine house conductor, Paul Daniel. Recurrently, we are entranced, or startled, by Chabrier's metrical subtleties and by chromatic and enharmonic ambiguities prophetic of Satie, Ravel, and Poulenc (who wrote an endearing small book about his predecessor). Since we need such recharging of our sensual and spiritual batteries to confront the future, we should be grateful to Jeremy Sams for rendering *Le Roi Malgré Lui* stageworthy. Though he doesn't totally convince in the difficult task he set himself, one has no doubt that his version deserves to enter the repertory, for Chabrier's sake, and for yours and mine.

TLS, SEPTEMBER 1994

NEW LIFE IN A NEW WORLD?

Ernst Křenek , *Johnny Strikes Up* (The Grand Theatre, Leeds, 1984)

IRST PRODUCED IN LEIPZIG IN 1927, KŘENEK'S *JONNY SPIELT AUF* ENJOYED a fabulous *succès de scandale,* being presented in more than fifty opera houses during its first year.* After that it sank stonily if not without trace; the contrast with Weill's roughly contemporary music-theatre pieces is striking. Both Křenek and Weill were Teutonically trained professional composers who youthfully attained fame and fortune by flirting with (in the strict sense) vulgar musics appropriate to the 'decadence' of the Weimar Republic; both were exiled from Nazified Germany to America. The difference between them is the disparity between the chalk of Křenek's talent and the whiffy cheese of Weill's genius, wherein maggots mutate into germs of new life.

New life in a new world is the overt theme of *Johnny Strikes Up,* although unlike Weill's pieces it has no overt politics. That the opera should surface in 1984 is presumably attributable to current nostalgias for the era of the First World War and its aftermath. A more interesting question is whether we may detect, from this revival by Opera North, any explanation of its initially 'prodigious' success. An obvious reason is that its theme was live on the mark, revelling in past excesses while offering illusorily hopeful panaceas. The old world is represented by frigidly glacial mountains and by Max, an 'intellectual' German composer of grandly European operas who is in part, Křenek confesses, a self-portrait. The new world is personified by Johnny, a Black musician-entertainer whose music rekindles defunct but still smouldering fires in Anita, an opera singer whom Max loves rather less than his ice-bound mountain peaks. She also has an affair with Daniello, an effete Italian violin virtuoso whose instrument Johnny lusts after rather more than he lusts after Anita. The plot of the composer's idiotically corny libretto hinges on hanky-panky with Daniello's 'old' violin and Anita's 'new' banjo. After elaborately symbolic misadventures, the new wins out. Johnny jazzes on the priceless ancient fiddle, musically reanimating 'Europe'; the moribund composer, nervously negotiating a Charleston, is presumptively but improbably renewed, in the New World, with his glamorous girl.

Another reason for the piece's 1920s triumph was its eclecticism.* Theatrically, it veers between grand opera, musical comedy, and cinematic slapstick; musically, Křenek responds with facility, melling Puccinian lyrical panache with music-hall-minstrel effervescence, Ravelian (or Massenet-like?) Sensuousness with arid Hindemithian bustle. This eclecticism is not in itself to be deplored since it is what the opera is about: the new world is fashioned from a rag-bag of cultures as German expressionism, Parisian Dada and American movie collage coexist with the realism of the newspapers—as they still do in the world around us. Contemporary opinion found this deliciously shocking, both morally and technically. It no longer shocks us, since Křenek's talent was not potent enough to fuse the elements, as does Janáček in *Osud*, a far more highly charged, partly autobiographical, opera about a composer. In comparison, Křenek's theatrical expertise, dazzling at Leipzig in 1927, is a damp squib at Leeds in 1984, notwithstanding an inventive production. What makes the production fall flat in more than one sense is Křenek's feeble music: in which the promise of a Puccinian Big Tune fails to materialize; in which the musical comedy numbers don't echo in mind and senses, as do those of Kern or Berlin, not to mention Gershwin; and in which the ragtime cavortings lack the tension between line and beat which is the heart of jazz—though there were intermittently enlivening burps from trumpet and trombone. At best, we're borne along on the production's romping ebullience; at worst corn non-satirically comes into its own, with comic policemen and with celestial chorus in the mountains as the despairful composer threatens suicide but tiresomely changes his mind. This very German composer suffices to explain the young's disaffection with the Old World.

Křenek, however, was not thus disenchanted. Geographically, both he and Weill landed up in the New World. Weill, whose German music-theatre had been at once an end and a beginning, worked effectively on Broadway and in Hollywood; Křenek, during his forty American years, has produced post-Schoenbergian, well-crafted, rigorously serial music untainted by his environment—even when setting a catalogue of place-names of railway stations on the Santa Fe Trail. Serialism, however—abominated by Hitler for its formalistic decadence—proved for Křenek not an aspiration towards freedom but an imposed European Law analogous to the Roman Catholicism he also espoused. Yet although Křenek didn't practise what his Johnny preached, he had a right to his defences and, ballasted by a small if ardent following, has preserved in his American music an integrity which *Johnny* didn't need. Even so, I'll hazard that Weill's American musicals will outlast Křenek's American string quartets; and I'm certain that there is more musical substance in Weill's *Alabama Song* than in the whole of Křenek's opera.

TLS, OCTOBER 1984

INNOCENCE DROWNED

Benjamin Britten, *Billy Budd* (Grand Theatre, Leeds, 1992)

W HEN THE YOUNG AUDEN WROTE HIS NOW CELEBRATED LETTER TO Benjamin Britten,* benevolently reproving him for stifling the dark side of his nature in his need to be loved, he was on the mark in psychological acumen—except for the crucial fact that he ignored what was already happening in Britten's music. For, if not an intellectual in Auden's sense, Britten had his own intuitive intelligence, and those who think he remained cosseted in conformity cannot have really listened to his music, nor fully experienced his theatre. His habitual theme was the scapegoat; and his 'success' is inherent in the fact that people came to accept him as surrogate for us all. There is no dearth of suffering in Britten's art.

The opera that made Britten internationally famous, *Peter Grimes*, dealt (in the wake of the Second World War) with the necessity of the scapegoat to our tortured times; we are obsessed with innocence because we have lost it, and we have lost it because we hate and persecute those who preserve it. The opera's unheroic hero is the Savage Man who, in different circumstances, might have grown to civilized consciousness. Deprived of Ellen's love, Grimes destroys the boy who is his own soul, and is hounded to death by an inimical world. True, the opera ends, as does Crabbe's poem, with the re-establishment of bourgeois convention in the diurnal life of the village. Even so, in the course of the opera, Britten has confessed, with Shakespeare's Prospero, that "this Thing of Darknesse I / Acknowledge mine". In so doing, he countered Auden's reprimand.

Britten's second 'grand' opera, *Billy Budd*, first produced in 1951, gives a more personal slant to the same theme. The text, based on Melville's probingly ambiguous tale, was written by E. M. Forster, master of psychological insight, and another homosexual artist. The parable is about the agony, and the tragedy, of growing up: for which reason, perhaps, the positive and negative forces within the psyche are objectified in characters 'out there' in the world. The young sailor, Billy Budd, is not a Savage Man but a prelapsarian Adam, a budding Beautiful Boy, victimized by his own childishness, manifest in the *mea culpa* of his stammer. If, except for that stammer, Billy is beauty unsullied, Claggart—appropriately the master-at-*Arms*—is a Cainlike force of destruction; while Captain Vere is the potential reconciler of opposites, which we call civilization. Being able to focus on the womanless world of an eighteenth-century man-of-war enabled Forster and Britten to confront the homosexual implications of the story without endangering its universal validity. The power and terror of the piece—which tells us that we cannot dispose of evil by a blind blow, provoked by the inarticulacy of the good within us—have intensified with the passage of the years: nothing could be further from upper-middle-class cosiness.

Initial evidence for this is the sheer sound of the score—the realism with which the orchestra evokes the salt savour of sea, the tang of wind, the hard, harsh sonorities of nautical labour. If, from one point of view, we think of the ship as a synonym for a social world, we vividly live in it while the music lasts. The tootling of fifes and bugles, at once grimly martial and inanely ludic, the battering of drums, at once assertive and destructive, epitomize the savagely lunatic games we live by, while Britten's orchestral seagulls are more uncannily actualized than they would be on tape. The response of the orchestra, under Elgar Howarth, to this dazzling score is the first tribute to be paid to this Opera North production, for the orchestra creates the world in which the dire events unfold. That Britten could now objectify the contrary poles of his psyche while preserving their subjectivity testifies to inner growth. Through this he was able—climatically in *The Turn of the Screw*—to confront the ghastly, ghostly, yet all too human, machinations wherein "the ceremony of innocence is drowned". John Tomlinson, as Claggart, was as usual dynamic in presence, magnificent in voice, and wondrous in articulation, notwithstanding the ferocity of the (cunningly deployed) brass that supports him. Jason Howard's Billy Budd was said to be labouring under a throat infection. If this was a vocal complement to his stammer, its effects were not comparably catastrophic, for the radiance of his cantilena was still audible, and he looked as beautiful, and moved as athletically, as he needed to.

By far the most difficult role in the central trinity of bass, baritone and tenor is that of Captain Vere, within whose memory the action is recapitulated; for to arbitrate between moral contradictions is even trickier than to steer a vessel though the mists of war. Nigel Robson added cubits to his ever-increasing artistic stature in presenting Vere (whose name embraces both *vir* and *veritas*) as a rigorous representative of aristocratic authority, who is also humanely compassionate, irrespective of social convention. Hints of overt sexuality, in both the Budd-Vere and the Budd-Claggart relationship, were strong enough to convince, but not so potent as to undermine the moral obliquities that are the opera's main theme. Ultimately, *Billy Budd* is a parable of redemption through the agency of a Parsifal-like Holy Fool, whose final words are a benediction: "Starry Vere, God bless you!". This is why the opera proved a turning-point in Britten's progress, leading to the purgatorial *Curlew River* and the near-autobiographical *Death in Venice*.

There were no weak links in the minor characters, either among the well-meaning but bewildered officer-class, or within the brutal or craven ranks. The Chorus, in this case all male, was superb in the wild music that made seafaring actively present, not something happening on stage. Graham Vick's direction was adept at creating visual images apposite to Britten's stunning sound-metaphors; such as the B minor/B flat major dubiety of the opening, the weird enharmonies for the error-inducing sea-mist (invented by Forster) and the famous, almost-immobile procession of unrelated concords before the final moments of truth. Chris Dyer's design, at once realistic and abstract, abetted by Nick Shelton's lighting, worked in creative harmony with production, singing, acting, and orchestral playing. All were worthy of Britten's abrasive, tender, tragic, great music.

TLS, DECEMBER 1992

Benjamin Britten, *Gloriana* (Grand Theatre, Leeds, 1994)

LTHOUGH THE FAILURE OF BRITTEN'S ONLY 'OCCASIONAL' OPERA, devised for the very grand occasion of the coronation of Elizabeth II, has been overplayed,* there can be no doubt that the relative incompr-hension on the part of public and critics caused the sensitive (but suc-cessful) composer deep distress. Britten's genius entailed an acute intelli-gence that saw how any theme or occasion might be pertinent to him and us; and he must surely have hoped that people would realise that the point about *Gloriana* was that it dealt not only with the fact of monarchy but also with the issues of human vainglory that underlie it. If God invented man, man certainly invented Him; and as we aspire towards divinity, we're increasingly assailed by the disparity between His omnipotence and our impotence. In a general sense, this disparity is that between illusion and reality: as is manfiest when, in telling the tale of Elizabeth I and the Earl of Essex, William Plomer and Britten, starting from Lytton Strachey's famous-infamous account, reveal both its tragic and its ironic implications.

The first Elizabeth was a Virgin Queen and a kingly Monarch—a species of divinity in her own and her people's estimation. Larger than life as a cross between an Earth Goddess and the Virgin Mary, she was none the less subject to human passions, and loved Robert Devereux, the noble Earl of Essex, to her own distraction, though not to his. If she was a goddess betrayed into humanity, he was a volatile, quixotic Renaissance man called upon to dispatch grand, even godly, affairs of state on behalf of his Queen. To this task he proved, perhaps because he was so spontaneously human, unequal. In their mutual dichotomy between duty and passion Elizabeth and Essex each failed, for opposite reasons. The failure was a tragedy for them personally, and also for England, and it may have been Britten's honest acceptance of this that the Coronation public couldn't stomach. Yet, of course, Britten was right. With Plomer he had made an opera that was at one level a celebration of a national ideal, glorious in pomp and circum-stance, while at another level it was high tragedy not only about an indi-vidual man and woman, but also about men and women, in so far as human creatures, pretending to be divine, must in fact grow old and die. "You grow old while I tell you this", as Ben Jonson put it.

In its hybrid genre as a festive masque, a public ritual, and a personal drama, *Gloriana* manages to be an old-fashioned 'numbers' opera and a psychological drama at one and the same time. In this new production by

Opera North it takes its place amongst Britten's masterpieces, since the music's by now irresistible quality is abetted by a production that overcomes any pitfalls the enterprise might offer. The director is Phyllida Lloyd (who was responsible for the brilliant rehabilitation of Chabrier's *L'Étoile*, now being revived by Opera North), working with Anthony Ward as designer and Rick Fisher as lighting-man. The startling illusion of limitless height the stage presents fosters the dreams of divinity on which the opera turns; yet sets are so constructed that they can shift in a twinkling from starry heights to mundane depths. The orchestra, under Paul Daniel, negotiates Britten's score—dazzling in public panache, intimate in private sensibility—with the expertise we've come to expect of it; the chorus, whether as hyper-sophisticated courtiers or as ravenous rabble, is equal to all occasions, while the choreographed set-pieces (devised by Kate Flatt) are exactly appropriate to Britten's ceremonial music which, if Elizabethan pastiche, in also new-born. One suspects that the dancing bears much the same relation to genuine terpsichorean revelry of Elizabeth's age as does Britten's music to current dance-forms.

All these elements are incidental to the human drama, and wouldn't count for much were not the lead singers up to their task. In particular, this means Josephine Barstow, who persuades us that Britten's Elizabeth is one of the great operatic roles of the twentieth century, and certainly his own most formidable part for a woman. First gazed at wonderingly as she is poised on her dais-throne, she seems a glittering goddess a mile high; come down to earth, divested of her more superhuman finery, she converses with politicians and even people, a formidable woman, toughly truculent, teasingly waggish, and at moments girlishly coy—perhaps it was intentional that she looked, in these early scenes, remarkably like Margaret Thatcher.

But her congress with the Earl of Essex displayed other, un-Thatcherite dimensions, whether in the direction of tenderness or passion, admiration, solicitude, or uncondescending reproof. And when, in the Dressing Room scene, the Queen, trinketless, wigless, unpainted, garbed in something like a shroud, confronts herself as 'unaccommodated (wo)man', we recognize that to this favour we must all come; and that this is the fact that all works about monarchy must ultimately confront, however much monarchial institutions may be designed to pretend that the King's Real Body and his stone-or-wood-imaged Body are the same. The point is explicit in the epilogic scene wherein the Queen speaks, not sings, words of the real Elizabeth I, admitting, in prose of pellucid grace, that in material terms she has failed. Yet though she relinquishes song, which is her and our ideality, she knows in her heart that this song (Britten's opera) justifies her. Josephine Barstow responds to the tiniest spoken nuance of her part as magnificently as she rises to the wide-spun cantilena of her imperious poise and potentially destructive passion.

Thomas Randle's task, as the Earl of Essex, is less daunting, since he is no surrogate of God but a mere man, vaulting in ambition, yet so confused as to aims that, having bungled his public duty, he betrays his private passion and traitorously threatens his Queen. Wrong but Wromantick, he cultivates his Renaissance wilfulness in defiance of reason, let alone truth. Yet if he is a victim of his moral insufficiency, he arouses, in Randle's performance, our admiration, as well as our dismay. There, but for the grace of God, might go we, for his fall is the Christian Fall writ large. The ebullience of his vocal line and the swagger of his movements *exhibit* his basic humanity, and maybe we love ourselves in loving him. Certainly he's a very modern type, whose dreams complement his braggadocio. Like most of the nobility, Essex was a minor poet of whose verse Plomer makes exquisite use in his libretto. Since the second lute song ('Happy, happy we') that Essex sings to the Queen is about the Forgotten Garden (Eden), it is hardly surprising that it should have inspired Britten to such ravishing music. This lute song to Essex's verse becomes a leitmotif throughout the opera, and the reminiscence of it in the Dressing Room scene, when the disgraced Essex confronts the balding and dying Queen, is surely one of the most heart-rending moments in twentieth-century opera.

Illusion and reality are not only interlaced in the story of Elizabeth and Essex, but also throughout the strands of intrigue and counter-intrigue. Distinctions of gender parallel disparities between illusion and reality, though we should be wary of associating the former with the female, the latter with the male. (The Queen, being both a Virgin and a King, is androgynous, as she herself points out.) Clive Bayley and Eric Roberts as the men of state, Raleigh and Cecil, convincingly balance public will against Elizabethan craft and irony; Yvonne Blunt lends dignity as well as grace to Essex's long-suffering Countess, while Susan Chilcott's Lady Rich (Essex's sister and the lover of his rival Mountjoy) shines in the Garden Scene— another glimpse of Eden, bird-haunted, fairy-entranced, prophetic of *A Midsummer Night's Dream*. David Gwynne's Blind Ballad Singer brings bardic inspiration into the purlieus of Low Life, proving that levels of reality are independent of class and social context. This may be why the opera functions so potently, because, rather than in spite of, its confusion of genres. The Queen's Divine Image and her shrouded unaccommodated self are opposite sides of the same coin: the extravagant, even grotesque, costumes sported by Elizabethan courtiers cannot efface the skinny bodies glimpsed through the rags of the poor, and all our clothes, rich or poor, only temporarily cover the skeleton; as Raleigh put it, "Our mothers'

wombs the tyring houses be / Where we are drest for this short Comedy".
Even so, Britten's *Gloriana* leaves us glad to be alive, for it reminds us that
though the masquerades and the frou-frou are pathetic, they are also courageous and beautiful.

TLS, JANUARY 1994

RESTORED BY INNOCENCE

Benjamin Britten, *The Prince of the Pagodas* (Royal Opera House, Covent Garden, 1989)

T HE ORIGINAL 1957 PRODUCTION OF *THE PRINCE OF THE PAGODAS*—
Britten's only ballet—was not greatly esteemed.* Indeed, it proved so
traumatic an experience for the composer that he later dismissed the
piece as "that beastly work" and for many years refused to sanction its publication. One would expect Britten to be more at home with opera, battening
on specific human beings in specific social contexts, than with so-called classical ballet which, being in fact the ultimate testament of romanticism, deals
in mute myth, seeking exorcism through dream. Yet from the start the score's
prodigality of invention must have been self-evident. As dramatic music for
dancing it rivals Tchaikovsky, whose ballets absolve intense personal neu-
rosis in the ordered grace of mime, taking their themes from those mythic
fairy tales that plumb the often horrendous depths of childhood fantasy.
Having studied Tchaikovsky's ballets, Britten recaptured the lucid *élan* of
their gestural music in terms unambiguously his own. The story too emu-
lates Tchaikovsky in being a mishmash of fairy tales; the Frog Prince, Beauty
and the Beast, the Sleeping Beauty and Cinderella all contribute to the saga,
reinforced by overtones from the Eurydice story and from Lear, a dying king
who, unable to distinguish between right and wrong in the forms of his good
and bad daughters, senselessly surrenders his kingdom.

In the 1957 version by John Cranko, so many tangled strands of myth
confounded confusion. In this new production, Kenneth MacMillan, with
Colin Thubron's help, has recast the narrative, thereby revealing its psychological scheme. The ballet's seminal theme now proves central to Britten's
life-long preoccupation: for it is about a girl's growth through adolescence
to sexual (and other) maturation, aided by a holy fool who safeguards her
as she confronts the evils of the world, the flesh, and the devil. The interde-
pendence of good and evil is implicit in La Belle Rose's having a wicked
sister who is the Rose's *Epine*. The World is figured in four Kings of North,
South, East and West, each representing a kind of material potentiality
and/or illusion. The Emperor is sick because of the evil rampant in the
world, abetted by his own errors of judgement; his courtiers are transformed into simian bestiality, while the Prince, the Kingdom's hopeful
future, is reduced, cursed by the envious Wicked Sister, to reptilian state. La
Belle Rose's spiritual journey—during which she faces instinctual dream
and nightmare as well as threats posed by the world—is at once a voyage of
self-discovery and the world's redemption. Both the Prince and the

Kingdom are (momentarily) restored by her innocence and love: though one has to admit that the courtiers, having reassumed their human shapes, are less attractive than they were in their monkeydom—just as princes in fairy tales are often less fetching than the beasts they change into.

In Britten's score, character and psychological motivation *are* musical and corporeal gestures, existing in the present moment, yet capable of perpetual metamorphosis. The oboe melody to which Princess Rose first appears creates, in its virginal vernality, her quintessence; it is many times transformed, most wonderfully in the violin cadenza to which she enters the dream-world of the pagodas, evoked by Britten's ingenious orchestral simulation of Balinese gamelan, and is resolved in her final solo, wherein innocence and experience are one. Similarly, the ailing Emperor's music preserves regality even as it grotesquely totters; while the Wicked Sister mells her serpentine lines and jagged rhythms with the deceitful corporeality of the suitor-kings. The dazzling instrumentation is itself characterization; the entangling of thematic motives is the psychological process of the myths.

Given musical mastery at this level, all a choreographer need do is what the music tells him. At this MacMillan succeeds (as the talented Cranko apparently didn't), selecting his two alternative castes with uncanny prescience. Darcey Bussell, as the Rose, is so tenderly graceful that the salamander's re-metamorphosis into the Prince brings tears to the eyes. Deborah Bull, as her dark opposite, is less charismatic than evil often is, though spikey enough; Anthony Dowell, as the Emperor, deals adroitly with his ambivalence: while the four Kings—especially Ashley Page as a lubriciously vibrant monarch of the South—prove equal to the dauntingly impulsive music Britten offers them. Simon Race's Fool is a catalyst who reminds us both of the tragic pathos of Lear's Fool and of the witty malice of Britten's Puck in his *Midsummer Night's Dream*. All the set pieces succeed, climaxing in a final fight between goodies and baddies that caps the tipsy bravura of the music.

The ultimate accolade must go to the orchestra which, under Ashley Lawrence, negotiates Britten's stunning score with the panache and sensitivity that are alike essential to it. Nicholas Georgiardis's designs, intelligently fusing orientalism with Brittenesque Elizabethanism, provide visual magic to match the aural dimension. In the performance I witnessed, MacMillan, whose sixtieth birthday this production celebrates, received a standing ovation. It is pleasant to hope, if not believe, that Britten, among the Immortals, relished this belated tribute to a neglected work of genius.

TLS, DECEMBER 1989

YONGE FRESSHE FOLKES, HE AND SHE
THE INHERITANCE AND BELATED TRIUMPH OF WILLIAM WALTON'S
TROILUS AND CRESSIDA

William Walton, *Troilus and Cressida*
(Grand Theatre, Leeds, and Royal Opera House, London, 1995)

THE TALE OF THE STAR-CROSSED LOVERS, TROILUS AND CRESSIDA, IS ONE of the great, originally orally transmitted legends from classical antiquity, for the potent reason that it embraces the basics of human experience: sex and war, love and death, loyalty and betrayal, presented against a backcloth of anthropomorphic gods and goddesses who are ourselves writ large. The story submerged somewhat during the mystical heyday of medieval Christianity, but surfaced again in the early Renaissance, which by definition was in a part a rebirth of classical (Greek and Latin) mythology. The first literate version of the story seems to have been made by Benoît de Sainte-Maure, dated around 1160, and widely distributed, a century or more later, in a Latin prose version by Guido delle Colonne. Boccaccio made a typical lively, sensuously secular version of the story, which English Chaucer substantially drew on for his longest and greatest poem. He incorporated a dose of Boethian philosophizing about fate, such as had been appropriated by the Christian Church, and appended a sublime epilogue exhorting "yonge fresshe folkes, he or she" to set their minds (and senses) on matters more durable than this world "that passeth soon as floures faire". Yet what makes *Troilus and Cressida* one of the great—and most singularly 'modern'—poems ever created is the degree to which it empathizes with the chaos released by human fallibility which, in the absence of a Law or a God, may be not far from imbecility.

It is hard to credit that, as far back as the 1380s, Chaucer recognized that it was women who paid the price. Criseyde is Chaucer's central character, despite the conventional stress he gives to Troilus as a man of destiny. Trying to submit to the social and religious hierarchy imposed on her by patriarchal decree, Criseyde searches for identity, yearning to be, even from within her aura of privileged persiflage, her own woman. No wonder she is momently "slyding of corage"; no wonder she is one of the most deeply felt characters in English literature. Clearly, Chaucer's (frequently noted) partiality for women was not that of the low womanizer! Criseyde makes the 'wrong' choice because she can see no solution to her predicament; and neither, if we are honest, can we.

Chaucer's impartiality was exceptional; his Scottish successor, Robert Henryson, in adding a sixth book to Chaucer's five, saw to it that his dour Scottish god afflicted the girl with leprosy, and then sang on her behalf a "testament" of contrition. Shakespeare, the only English writer to equal Chaucer in compassion and excel him in psychological acumen, took up the tale around two hundred years later but produced from it, in the wake of *Hamlet* and *Measure for Measure*, his most desperately nihilistic play, in which the Young Hero fights for an Honour as incomprehensible to him as it is to us, while Cressida becomes an anti-heroic wanton and Pandarus, who brings them together in the spirit of a japing ringmaster, is given the last, syphilitically deranged word. Love and Death are outflanked by War and Lechery, as Troilus expires raging against the irresistible because unmotivated odds. The Greek-Trojan entanglement becomes an engine of self-destruction.

In the 1950s occurred the justly lauded renaissance of English opera, out of which were spawned Tippett's *Midsummer Marriage* and Britten's *Billy Budd, Gloriana, The Turn of the Screw*, and *A Midsummer Night's Dream*: all pieces that manifested the mysterious dimension of genius over and above talent. This fact was not unconnected with the archetypically Jungian, and often childlike, visions they embraced, partly as a residue of their creators' homosexuality. Unambiguously straight, William Walton could not enjoy this 'advantage' when he decided—encouraged by the fabulous success of Britten's *Peter Grimes* in 1945 and succoured by a BBC commission—to embark on a fully fledged opera. Whether the subject of Troilus and Cressida was Walton's idea is uncertain; but he accepted as librettist Christopher Hassall, a poet who had no operatic experience, though he had worked in the theatre as a (skilful) lyricist for Ivor Novello. In cultural circles this probably told against rather than for him, and Hassall's 'hammy' libretto was proffered as a reason for the opera's failure on its first performance in 1954. Other reasons were said to be an unsympathetic if not incompetent conductor, and difficulties over casting, after Elizabeth Schwarzkopf had turned down the part of Cressida. But the main reason for the failure was surely that the piece, unlike the above-mentioned operas of Tippett and Britten, was not concerned with "moving into Aquarius", but was an old-fashioned love-story triggered by Walton's passion for his belatedly acquired wife, who had also inspired the heartfelt lyricism of his Cello Concerto. All this predisposed him to Italianate *bel canto* relatable to the tradition of Verdi and Puccini, itself a stylistic liability in the climate of the 1950s. In our pluralistic present, however, anything goes, providing it is good enough—and sometimes, of course, even if it isn't.

This performance by the indefatigable Opera North leaves us in no doubt that the opera is good enough, at least to the degree that it is at all levels professional. In this we should include Hassall's libretto, for he was canny enough to see that Chaucer's ironic compassion, functioning through the mediacy of a narrator, wouldn't work in the immediacy of Grand Opera. So he turned Cressida into a love-goddess and tragic victim who, having religiously retired from a war-weary world that had slaughtered her first husband, suffers like a Puccini heroine while being mettlesome enough to act out an agon. He gives her credibility by inventing a serving-maid called Evadne who, by intercepting Troilus's letters to his beloved, gives Cressida some excuse for disaffection. This comes near to equating the Greek Parcae with human cussedness, for although Evadne claims to be acting humanely in that for Cressida to have thrown in her lot with Diomede would have been plain common sense (the more so because her father had already absconded to the Greek cause), Evadne's real, self-interested motive is that she herself has a yen for Cressida's handsome boyfriend. Hassall further absolves Cressida in making her father villainous, as no one is in Chaucer's version but as almost everyone is in Shakespeare's. Calchas stabs Troilus (in the back) as he duels with his legitimate adversary Diomode. Perhaps this Cressida needed to "strike the father dead" and to throw in the envious girl soul-mate for good measure. Certainly she doesn't take her troubles supinely, for Walton and Hassall give her a part "to tear a cat in", with powerful psychological motivation ballasted by dignity, if not by Chaucer's embryonic humanity. At a more routine level, Hassall offers 'strong situations' with a professionalism that Walton brilliantly caps, embracing seething crown scenes, cunningly placed ensembled numbers, interior soliloquies, and lone voices and solo trumpets off-stage.

The first act begins riotously in the public world, with crowd-music of Verdian trenchancy, yet none the less rooted in the savagely personal choral writing of *Belshazzar's Feast* and the sadistic brass of the First Symphony, both dating from 1930–31. The lyrical writing for solo voices, though fluent and grateful, at first seems more anodyne, sub-Puccini without the scalp-prickling tunes. Yet as Cressida's interior drama heats up, Walton responds to challenge. The love-scene of the second act begins with Puccinian exoticized sociabilities; mounts to personal passion; and climaxes in a thunderstorm-tormented sexual orgasm rivalling Tristan's in physical impact, if not in transcendence. The third act, faced with the chaos that seems to be the human lot, ultimately reveals the higher and deeper verities of Love and Death; and it cannot be fortuitous that Cressida's most ravishing music evokes a childhood vision wherein she has an intuition of the relevance to herself of her father's treachery. There may be an unconscious link with the Aquarian operas of Tippett and Britten, so that Walton's opera, even in the distant 1950s, was not altogether the outmoded oddity it was mistaken for. It is worth mentioning that *Gloriana*, the most overtly 'public' of Britten's operas, also got a bad press initially, occasioning distress for its composer hardly less extreme than that suffered by Walton.

If Walton's grand opera is rehabilitated, as on balance it ought to be, it will owe much to Opera North's stirring production, in which the direction, design and lighting of Matthew Warchus, Neill Warmington and Nick Chelton display exceptional intelligence in responding to the interlinked demands of music and theatre. The orchestra is steered by Richard Hickox with a fervour apposite to the lovelorn and tempest-tossed music, and the chorus are 'naturals' in rediscovering the edgy blaze of the young Walton of *Belshazzar's Feast*. Ultimately, however, the performance depends on its soloists, especially its Cressida, to the extravagant demands of whose role Judith Howarth proves—as the great Schwarzkopf couldn't or wouldn't— more than equal. This should launch a distinguished career; and although one can't say as much of Arthur Davies's Troilus, he too doesn't wilt under a scarcely less demanding part and looks reasonably heroic without sounding like a genuine Heldentenor. This may suit Hassall's intent, for his Troilus is only a foil for Cressida's anguish; certainly Alan Opie as Diomede has so much more vocal and visual charisma than this Troilus that one almost wishes that Cressida would seek an alternative destiny in another country. Clive Bayley sings Calchas with his usual firmness of line, making him not only baleful but also brave in getting right his own priorities, which he believes to be also those of his country. Nigel Robson, as Pandarus, offers another of the masterly character studies with which he has enriched twentieth-century British opera; lucent of voice and impeccable in diction, he also acts with a Chaucerian equilibrium between playfulness and passion— which is more in tune with our temper than Hassall's romanticism, if less so than the savage cynicism displayed, in his Troilus play, by Shakespeare. In any case, this Pandarus's good humour offers necessary release from purple-dyed tension; one suspects that the Brittenesque chains of thirds that pervade his music may have been Walton's softly sly dig at Peter Pears, the Pandarus of the ill-fated first performance.

Ivonne Howard, as the Hassall-invented Evadne, has vocal and visual presence enough to support her cruelly crucial role in the plot; and the opera's belated triumph is encapsulated in the fact that this tale of human brutality, muddlement, and sheer ineptitude climaxes in a final sextet almost worthy of Puccini himself, or even of Verdi. As the main characters sing together of their inextricably painful destinies, confusion becomes genuinely tragic catharsis: the point of which is underlined in the only music to succeed the sextet—Cressida's lovely threnody, to which she stabs herself with Troilus's sword. If this is an act inconceivable in relation to either Chaucer's or Shakespeare's Cressida, it has a relevance to us all, in that it leaves us with the most basic of basics—the ultimate solitariness of the human condition.

TLS, FEBRUARY 1995

MUSIC FOR EVERYMAN
THE MODERN TRIALS OF GAWAIN

Harrison Birtwistle, *Gawain* (Royal Opera House, London, 1991)

THE SOURCE FOR HARRISON BIRTWISTLE'S EAGERLY AWAITED NEW OPERA is a late medieval poem of unknown authorship. Like much medieval literature, it embraces a core of archetypal material stemming from oral folk traditions, while being a highly sophisticated artefact created by and for an upper-class court culture. Both in its archaic and contemporary manifestations, *Sir Gawain and the Green Knight* is a text congenial to Birtwistle: a modern ritualist who seeks—as was miraculously evident in his operatic 'mystery' on the theme of Orpheus (1986)—the wellsprings of renewal for a world foundering on inflated ego and will, while also being an artist aware (given the legacy of Frazer and Jung) that his and our world is sick, if not necessarily unto death. Attending the new opera, we go on a pilgrimage with the hero, discovering with him that the word 'experience'— deriving from *ex periculo*—means from or out of trial or peril. This process is neither a revelation nor a vision of faith, but is an *act* of which the outcome is uncertain and the moral issues obscure. To a degree this was true of the late medieval poem itself: so the librettist, David Harsent, had merely to remould its ambiguities in terms applicable to us.

The original poem, dating from the late fourteenth century, incorporates into the background of medieval chivalry a traditional quest into unknown wildernesses, and a trial of courage, centred on human fear of death, and on no less human vulnerability to sexual temptation. The action is triggered by Morgan le Fay, an enchantress who, in the Arthurian cycle, is racked by jealousy of the 'ideal' love of Arthur and Guinevere, and by envy of the idealized court in which it flourishes. Harsent stresses the psychological motivation, making supernatural Morgan the mainspring of the action, but twinning her with a natural woman, Lady de Hautdesert, whose husband is a 'real' knight, Bertilak de Hautdesert, who also has a supernatural *alter ego* in the mythical Green Man of folklore.

Of the basic medieval virtues—courage, courtesy, chastity, loyalty and truth—perhaps only the first is still alive and well. The poet seems to be exploring the contradictory variety of virtues revealed through the two Beheading Games, the three Temptations, and the three Hunting Games, with exchange of winnings; all of which parallel the difficulties that beset moral choice in real life, then and now. Indeed, the curiously modern tone of the poem springs from the irreconcilability of its proffered choices. Harsent's new verse-play needs merely to exploit this ambivalence, veering

167

between the seriously sacral and the ludic and satiric, and using traditional devices of incantatory repetition while keeping the language clear, at once colloquial and hieratic.

In Harsent's interpretation, Morgan le Fay is both the honey of corruption and the debunker of chivalric myth. Superficially a villainess, she is also a liberator, with whose help a true Hero might hope to break from the traditional "paradise of archetypes and repetition", so that he might himself decide on the choices he cannot or should not avoid making. Arthur's court is an idealized paradise degenerating—as, in terrestrial contexts, paradises always must. Morgan le Fay offers escape from paradisal Eternal Returns through the agency of her human *alter ego*, and of Bertilak, who, as Green Man, is a mythical figure of seasonal renewal. Gawain is the 'chosen' hero who doesn't in the course of the opera achieve self-fulfilment to become the arbiter of his destiny, though he does attain a point at which he learns that self-realization is a consummation devoutly to be wished.

This approximates to the position occupied by 'modern man', for whom Birtwistle has stood surrogate throughout his life's work, repeatedly drawing on folk myth to make the human predicament incarnate in music and action. Even purely musical pieces like *Secret Parade* turn out to be ritual action—even a quest or pilgrimage—relatable to the legendary cycles of his theatre pieces, from *Punch and Judy* to *Bow Down*, to the climactic *Masks of Orpheus*, and to *Yan Tan Tethera*. *Gawain* is the latest step in this pilgrimage. If it doesn't presume to the apocalyptic grandeur of *Orpheus* it confronts its elemental theme with no less shattering intensity. As usual, Birtwistle functions with no holds barred; a very large orchestra (rooted on nine double basses, three tubas and euphonium) is inexorably active, while the vocal parts, often soaringly lyrical, make near-superhuman demands. Under Elgar Howarth, that most committed disciple of Birtwistle's muse, the orchestra plays as though possessed, while the singers give of their utmost, both vocally and mimetically, even terpsichoreanly. For *Gawain*, like *Orpheus*, is not so much opera as renovated masque, enacting a rite, rather than telling a story, by way of choreographed mime as well as song.

Morgan and her *alter ego* Lady de Hautdesert have parts of phenomenally strenuous audacity, to which Marie Angel and Elizabeth Laurence prove more than equal. Compared with them, Arthur and Guinevere, chivalric idols in decline, seem fallible humans whose roles, though demanding by normal standards, are relatable to normal operatic exigencies. If Richard Graeger and Penelope Walmsley-Clark are less impressive in these parts than are the two enchantresses, so they ought to be, given their place in the opera's mythic pattern. There is a similar duality between the natural and supernatural males. John Tomlinson, doubling as the human

knight Bertilak and the legendary Green Knight, has a presence as magnificent as his voice, which is always firmly on the note. He is unique in being
verbally intelligible through the hurly-burly of Birtwistle's orchestra; and
although one wishes that the other singers, especially the crucial
enchantresses, were equally audible, one may generously say that this makes
a point, since we need to understand the Green Man above any character,
for he is our chance of survival.

Gawain, for all his courage in submitting to the tests, is no more than a
semi-hero, with a role somewhere between the renovative Green Knight
and the failing King Arthur, who cannot admit to the possibility of miracle.
His desperately reiterated assertions that the fabulous events are "nothing,
nothing but a raree-show" are balanced at the end by Gawain's no less frequently reiterated denials that he is the redeemer the court is looking for ("I
am *not* that hero"). The part Birtwistle gives Gawain thus lacks the charisma of the Green Knight's music, while being even more strenuous.
François le Roux tackles it heroically, as is necessary, but without totally riv-
etting the attention, as is perhaps inevitable, given that he's a mere human
and not a presumptive god. It may not be fortuitous that the most
enthralling performances among the lesser characters come from people
affiliated to, through not a part of, the supernatural world. Kevin Smith as
Bishop Baldwin, Arthur's confessor and spiritual adviser, exultantly
exploits the mystery of his counter-tenor tessitura, while Omar Ebrahim
displays his habitual vocal assurance and mimetic grace and wit in playing
the court Fool who, like King Lear's, speaks in riddles that momentarily
turn contrarieties into unities.

While the singers and orchestra bear the brutal brunt of this enterprise,
it inevitably presents problems in the theatre. Di Trevis as director and
Alison Chitty as designer cope wondrously, bringing modern technology to
the aid of primitive magic. The severed head of the Green Knight that,
echoing the Orpheus story, miraculously sings on is a brilliant *coup*; while
the immense masque of the Seasons, measuring time between the first
Beheading and Gawain's journey to the second, is so entrancing that one
welcomes its four-fold repetitiveness. Static music collaborates with visual
effect here, since Gawain's purification and garbing in the armour of
knighthood are accompanied by the chanting of Latin motets, written in a
potent mutation of medieval polyphony, and superbly sung by The Sixteen.
Something similar happens in the three seduction scenes, counterpointed
with the three Hunts related to the sexual motif.

In such scenic contexts any *longueurs* in the exuberant score must be dismissed as irrelevant, since the piece's obsessive recurrences, and consequent
timeless length, are its basic theme. It is true that, compared with *Orpheus*,

Gawain seems claustrophobic, for the fierce orchestral textures allow for no blissful catharsis such as occurs at *Orpheus's* sublime end; and even Morgan's three-fold lullabies, though ravishingly beautiful and ravishingly sung, sound more desperate than assuaging.

Still, the claustrophobia makes a point, for the text depends on contrast between the world within and the world 'out there'. Birtwistle's sound-world, both within and without, continues to astonish and remains unique. For although parallels may justifiably be drawn with the 'static' ritualism of Messiaen, Birtwistle is not, in Messiaen's terms, a religious (Christian) nor even a sensual composer. His archetypes plumb more deeply the perilous experience of a twentieth-century Everyman; and at this date the only composer who seems to offer a valid analogy with him is Varèse; whose epochal creations of the 1920s discovered magical, arcane and alchemical sound-renewal in such natural processes as crystal- and rock-formation, allied with industrialized principles of mechanical engineering and architecture (appropriate to his new home in New York). Sixty or seventy years later, Birtwistle mates a venerably Old World to a technological New World, making magic at the heart of a metropolis. Going through this elemental rite of passage in the slightly tatty luxuriance of the Royal Opera House feels both anachronistic and disorientating. Still, at the end Morgan le Fay leads Gawain out into the wide world, if not in catharsis, at least to begin his and our cycle again, a shade wiser as well as older.

TLS, JUNE 1991

MONOTONOUSLY MINIMAL

Philip Glass, *Opera on the Beach* (London: Faber and Faber, 1988)

WITH SEVERAL OPERAS BEING PRODUCED SIMULTANEOUSLY IN SUNDRY cities of the Old and New Worlds—on one occasion with two premières in different countries on the same night—Philip Glass is, perhaps, the most commercially successful opera composer since Richard Strauss. Strauss was an Old World maximalist whose ripely complex musical-theatrical techniques sang at once an epiphany and an elegy on 'Europe'. Glass is a New World minimalist whose beginning-again throws out the European baby along with the, by now, murky bath-water. The operas of Strauss are still about human heroes (and villainous monsters) whose psychological evolution complements ours. Glass's operas are not about people but about abstracted archetypes: Einstein as the (Jewish Outsider) Man of Science whose name is a household word to millions who can't hope to understand him; Gandhi as the (non-Western) Political Man who is unconsciously part of everyone's consciousness and conscience; the pharaoh Akhnaten as the Religious Man who, though living in a world temporally and spiritually remote from us, 'invented' a monotheistic religion prophetic of the Judaic Christianity that is out birthright. Appropriately enough, Ahknaten appears to us, after so many thousand years, mummified. Though he sired offspring, he looks like a hermaphrodite; and prompts from Glass music which, in hypnotic repetitiousness, becomes a potent auralization of impotency, as befits the death-haunted ancient Egyptians and, it would seem, us. His part is given to a countertenor, perhaps deputizing for a castrato; throughout, the opera is sung in a dead language (Egyptian, Coptic, an archaic Hebrew), except for Ahknaten's Hymn to the Sun which his One God is associated with but abstracted from. This moment is in the language of the audience: as, of course, are the narrative links and momentary shifts to the tourist-infested modern world.

In his account of himself in this engagingly naive, understandably self-congratulatory, rather breathless book, Glass stresses that his operas are a radical departure from traditional humanistic operas, which told stories unfolding in time. He doesn't mention that there is, in the Gertrude Stein-Virgil Thomson *Four Saints in Three Acts*, a nearly sixty-year-old precedent for what he does: which is to highlight 'moments' in a legendary life by way of techniques that, far from defining a developing musical psychology, create a continuum in which, extrapolated from history, we exist. The texts, when in English, are usually a collage of quotations from people famous and infamous and from press reports and documentary sources; if original, they may be distinctly Steinian. The music serves the same function as the ritual music of 'savages', as well as that of some of the great oriental civilizations. There are parallels, in our own culture, verbally with the fashionable 'libidinal' philosophy of Derrida and Lyotard, and musically with tribal pop, which uses the machinery of advanced technology to obliterate the mind that created it. In all these phenomena—so-called primitive musics, some oriental musics, tribal pop, and Glass-music—the sound-dimension functions in collusion with runic words, dance, mime, and visual spectacle. Glass has been fortunate—no, clever—enough to find brilliant collaborators in all these fields. In the Western sense he is hardly a composer but rather a 'maker' of pseudo-ritual—pseudo because we, unlike primitive peoples, don't know what it 'means' until it happens, if then; with the assistance of singing and dancing priests and priestesses, and of magician-scientists in the control room, he creates a world we may enter vicariously. It follows that his music as such does not need to be very 'good' (interesting, stimulating); it might work less efficaciously if it called more attention to itself.

Even so, the question of value cannot be thus lightly disposed of, for the continuum a minimalist offers may vary in the degree of involvement it asks for and gets. The Estonian Arvo Pärt is sometimes claimed for minimalism because he uses few notes, often repetitively; but since his minimal formulae are themselves highly expressive, the effect of his music is not minimal at all. Though this may have something to do with Pärt's being a man of profound religious conviction, this does not apply in the case of Steve Reich, whose 'process' music—evolved somewhat earlier than Glass's and partly as a consequence of actually living and studying in Africa and Bali—calls for considerable skill, thereby enlivening, rather than *mortifying*, the human spirit. In comparison with two such dissimilar composers—and one might add Carl Orff, a now unfashionable pre-minimal minimalist who wrote tunes more memorable than Glass's—the effect of Glass's spell-weaving dismays. Clearly, on the evidence of this book, he has worked and even thought hard about the potential significance of his mythic archetypes; why, therefore, do the formulae in which he musics them have to be so banal? The 'themes' (his word) here quoted in music type amount to little more than an interval (usually a rudimentary fourth or third) or an arpeggio: a minimalism so minimal that there is less in it than meets the eye, let along the ear. Consider, in comparison, the acoustical subtlety of the apparently child-like formulae of Balinese music, not to mention the tonal and metrical sophistications of the real Indian music Glass says he studied with Ravi Shanker.

This question breeds another: why has Glass's music, rather than Reich's or Pärt's, made so fanatic an appeal to thousands—by now it must be millions—of people, especially young people, in our industrialized conurbations? It is possible that the two questions are really one: to which the cynical answer is that Glass's music appeals at the same level and for the same reasons as that of the most mechanistically contrived tribal pop composer, or even an Andrew Lloyd Webber. We relish his mindlessness because we have become, or are in the process of becoming, a society of lemmings whose disaffection with post-Renaissance consciousness has reached a point of no return. By now queasy about the prospect of self-annihilation in our mechanized wars, we may at least efface consciousness in relatively painless amnesia—not *entirely* painless, since the electrophonics of tribal pop and of Glass's music for electric keyboards may threaten both eardrums and nerves. Perhaps that is a risk worth taking, since relinquishing Western materiality may paradoxically bring immense material rewards.

This is not to suggest that Glass was initially other than disinterested; and if we believe that he is not hoodwinking anyone, even himself, another explanation of the Glass furore becomes feasible. For mindlessness, after many centuries of mind-obsession, may be momentarily a positive need. The wisely child-like G. K. Chesterton once remarked:

Children always say "Do it again"; and the adult person does it again, until he is nearly dead. For grown-up persons are not strong enough to exult in monotony. But perhaps God is. It is possible that God says every morning "Do it again" to the sun. It may be that he has the eternal appetite for infancy, for we have soured and grown old, and our Father is younger than we.*

Glass's next opera, due soon in Houston and at the English National Opera, is a collaboration with Doris Lessing, a formidable author who is unlikely to suffer fools gladly unless they be of the holy kind. Could it be that Philip Glass is our Heavenly Father? Only God knows, and he won't tell.

TLS, OCTOBER 1988

PART FOUR

INSTINCT AND SENSITIVITY: COMPOSERS NEW AND OLD

Poetry is the transmutation of reality into art.
CLEMENS PETERSEN, 1867

Music is a strange thing . . . it stands half way between thought and phenomenon, between spirit and matter . . . like and unlike each of the things it mediates— spirit that requires manifestation in time, and matter than can do without space.
HEINRICH HEINE

All art is an effort to make a *mould* in which to imprison, for a moment, the shining elusive element that is life itself.
WILLA CATHER, *THE SONG OF THE LARK*

The composer is not an 'apostle' who clings to formulae, but an artist who 'shapes his own ideas' independently and takes risks by entering unknown territory.
RICHARD HOFFMANN

Introduction

ARTISTS AND SCIENTISTS ALIKE ARE SEEKERS AFTER TRUTH. BUT WHEREAS, in the sciences, this consists in being able to demonstrate, by detached observation and testing, the universality of phenomena, the artist's 'truth' is established and re-established, over and over, in the essential unity of independent works—each one its own 'universe', literally *creating* the self (equally of composer, performer, and listener) in its carefully structured wholeness. And while new scientific discoveries can radically revise earlier convictions about the way in which existence *functions*—so that it may be said that, of necessity, science is continually changing its mind—at the heart of all artistic endeavour is the quest for integration which, because it is central to the human condition, remains constant.

What, then, are we to make of differences of style and procedure in the arts? Are some of these changes of direction false trails and dead-ends? Is there, for example, a 'right' and a 'wrong' way of making music? The fierce single-mindedness of certain composers and critics might persuade us that there are such distinctions to be made. Yet, it's reasonable to ask, as we did in Part One, 'What is music for?', and from there, perhaps, to reflect upon ways in which composers have sought 'certainty' through the music they have created and believed in. For, the claim of a musical work to be art (and thereby to be a window upon some kind of truth) rests not on the historical facts of its techniques but upon our taking possession of the music itself.

The articles in Part Four are concerned with some instances of this search for 'forms of finality' in the work of European composers from the late eighteenth century to the early twentieth century. Alongside such familiar names as Haydn, Schumann, Chopin, Berlioz, Brahms and Wagner, are four whose influence during the latter part of the period was significant, although (perhaps because of the sometimes 'oddball' character of their work) not always widely acknowledged: Alkan, Satie, Nielsen and Lambert.

As it happens, this chance grouping of ten composers points up some crucial factors in matters of musical style. Popular 'appreciation' tends to compartmentalize style features; for example, between music from different periods in history or between one composer and another—broad generalizations which may easily harden into prejudice, with "I know what I like" coming to mean "I am very sure of what I shall never try to like!" But the musical evidence will not support such hard and fast boundaries. As Heine pointed out, "Music is a strange thing". In strictly logical terms, the qualities which command our attention in any piece are *immanent* and unique. That is to say, they pervade that particular 'universe of sound' and no other. Yet, at the same time features of style and technique are both historically and contemporaneously *transeunt.** Thus, the process of composing is informed both by nurtured musical instincts and immediate, lively sensitivity.

Wilfrid Mellers's approach to this duality, for example in his 'analysis and comment' lectures, is characterized, first by his insistence upon the primary 'evidence' of a piece of music—What is happening here? What are the composer's intentions? What do we know of the circumstances of its composition?—and secondly by a broader historical, literary and musical context which he draws around the work and from which he can survey deeper undercurrents of human creativity. In effect, this practice acknowledges that, while a piece of music can only be discussed sensibly as an 'occurrence', it also has some kind of 'continuant' existence as part of the flow of human experience and expression. Thornton Wilder explains the same process from the playwright's point of view. Describing his aims in writing *Our Town*, he speaks of, first, giving dramatic energy to "the smallest events in our daily lives" in order that "something way down deep that's eternal about every human being" shall be understood; and at the same time of trying to present "illustrations of harmony and law . . . [which are] affirmations about mankind and his ends".

JP

A SINGLE-MINDED PURSUIT

Hans Keller, *The Great Haydn Quartets: Their Interpretation*
(London: Dent, 1986)

ANYONE WHO WAS FORTUNATE ENOUGH TO SIT IN ON, LET ALONE PARTIC-
ipate in, one of Hans Keller's masterclasses for talented young string
players (at the Menuhin School, Dartington, or the Guildhall), or one
of his coaching sessions with a well-known, even internationally celebrated,
quartet will think that he or she knows what to expect of this remarkable
book. To a degree he or she will be disappointed: not because the book isn't
good as well as remarkable, but because one recognizes, on reflection, that
Keller's classes were themselves acts of performance. Understandably, he
distrusted words about music, carrying his suspicion as far as to invent
what he called 'wordless analysis': which aimed to demonstrate, by way of
selective musical quotation and permutation, the relationship of parts to
the whole.* This exercise was of course valuable, for few have musical intelligence acute enough *fully* to sense what is happening in a piece of music: to
perceive where it is going, let alone why. Yet Keller himself never believed
that wordless analysis sufficed; if he had, he would hardly have used so
many penetratively accurate words in his classes. Although, when teaching,
he didn't often, at least directly, 'interpret' music verbally, everything he said
was concerned with the why as well as the how. His comments on shifting
relationships between predictability and surprise—acceptance of and reaction to or against musically and socially accepted norms—were always
implicitly evaluative. Though he thought one should try to 'speak' in
musical terms, he had no doubt that music was a language—the most
probing one we have.

Talking, acting, walking, miming, playing, Keller made this manifest in
class. But it can be trapped only intermittently, and fleetingly, on a printed
page. Knowing this, Keller doesn't attempt the impossible. Instead, he offers
a handbook for performing students. Kept literally to hand, it may offer
advice on tricky passages in his forty-five selected "great Haydn quartets":
the trickiness being hardly ever in a specific technical problem, but rather in
a musical problem of the relation of part to whole. For a mere listener, of
course, the book makes hard going: the more depressingly so since Keller
recurrently asserts that no one can 'really' understand a quartet who hasn't
played it. Even so, the mere listener, opening this book at random, may find
instant illumination—though he needs to have the score of the quartet he
lights on available. My (strictly) random sample is the account, on page 166,
of Haydn's multifunctional monothematicism in opus 64, no. 5. Talk about

the balance between first and second violin in a passage from the first movement broadens into the statement that,

it isn't only the spicey, scherzoid, essentially instrumental character of the original theme that changes into its opposite, a lyrical, essentially song-like flow: another aspect of the theme, too, is replaced with its opposite and thus paradoxically aims at extreme relaxation at the high point of tension—the theme's relation to what was its polyrhythmic partner.

That's enough to indicate how Keller's analysis is at once critical and inter-pretative. On the opposite page (167) I randomly alight on a no less experi-entially revealing comment on the difference between two ostensibly similar upbeats in the minuet. As Keller knew, the very brightest students sense these things by the grace of God, or whatever one calls it. Scores of students, however, will be grateful throughout their playing lives for the revelation afforded by this (not very) mere man.

For readers, as distinct from reader-players, there are in this book as many typically Kellerian *aperçus* as one expects; they always enliven, usually enlighten, occasionally enrage. Keller knew Haydn's quartets so well that one hesitates to question his findings. But did Haydn really 'innovate' *every-thing* in the story of (what Keller regarded as) 'grown-up' European music, and how much does it matter if he did? True, Haydn—in, for instance, the polarity of C major and A major in the minuet and trio of opus 74, no. 1—explored the potential of mediant relationships no less profoundly than did Beethoven, with whom they are commonly associated. But isn't this polarity a physiological-acoustical fact which was in the air, and which many, even minor, composers lighted on without fully realizing its implica-tions? It is odd to find so hyper-subtle an intelligence acting in a manner too simplistic. On the other hand, subtlety proves slightly obfuscating when Keller defines distinctions between Haydn's and Beethoven's wit (the "recognition of other modes of experience that may be possible") and Mozart's humour, for the distinctions become so fine as to be self-contra-dictory.

Similarly, Keller is intransigent in putting down the excesses of 'authen-ticity'. The difference between Haydn and Boccherini or Dittersdorf is,

not only world-shaking, but we actually understand it better, hear it more clearly, than did the ears of Haydn's time, Mozart's apart. In this all-important sense our approach to his [Haydn's] style . . . is actually more direct, more knowing, quicker of hearing, than was his contemporaries'.

Fair enough: though how can Keller *know* that *only* Mozart heard Haydn as Keller did? Another passage aphoristically asserts that "a historically authentic style can murder the music of a great composer: it's the small composers that should be played authentically—or better still, not at all: they represent, rather than oppose, their age, which is why they die with it". Brilliant—yet on reflection is it true, or at least more than part of the truth? I can think offhand of a dozen 'small' composers of whom authenticity has made sense, meaningful to us now: as it has, indeed, of a handful of great composers, most notably the now much performed and recorded Marc-Antoine Charpentier.

Keller wouldn't, of course, have accepted Charpentier's greatness: which brings us to the limitations which Keller (not Charpentier) shares with commoner humanity. As is often the case, his limitations are inseparable from his strengths. He came here as a war-exile from his native Austria where he had had, in childhood and youth, a musical education of exceptional intensity. He frequently—after a while slightly tiresomely—tells us how he knew this or the other Haydn quartet 'inside out' from the age of four or whenever. When he reached these shores, his playing knowledge of, and intellectual insight into, this music were unrivalled, and were to remain so. Given his up-bringing, he was convinced that 'evolutionary' sonata style, as practised pre-eminently by Haydn and Beethoven, was the highest point of European musical consciousness thus far. He may have been right: I go along with his typically dogmatic statement that "Beethoven was the greatest man who ever lived"—except that I would bracket Beethoven with Shakespeare, which Keller, in conversation, would not allow, I suspect because he regarded words as a *less* precise language than music. None the less, the 'Faustian', Haydn-Beethoven notion of music, however centrally progressive, is not the only one; and in this context it is pertinent to note Keller's slightly equivocal attitude, in this book, to Mozart. No one who heard him talk about Mozart's quartets, quintets, piano concertos and operas could doubt that he was a great and committed Mozartian: so it is surprising to find here a passage hazarding that Mozart's quartets and quintets are "more popular" than any of Haydn's great Forty-five, and that "there is little doubt that Mozart's wealth of melodic invention has a wider appeal than Haydn's wealth of harmonic invention; don't even serious music lovers consider Mozart a greater composer than Haydn, a more inventive, more moving one?" That sounds like a mild reprimand: to which the simple answer is, Yes they do, and he is. This is not to belittle Haydn's supreme talents.

This playing down of Mozart's melodic genius, if that's what it is, bears on Keller's relative lack of interest in classical baroque music, even at the level of Bach, Handel, Couperin and Rameau, never mind the Telemanns and Vivaldis. It would be unfair to say that he misunderstood this music since he didn't talk or write about it enough to provide a basis for discussion. One can say, however, that he was comfortably oblivious of Renaissance music; my efforts to communicate to him my enthusiasm for Byrd, Dowland, even the transcendent Monteverdi, were unavailing. Medieval music he regarded as totally irrelevant to modern man. On the whole he refused to look backwards; forwards he did look, mostly to composers who have roots in the 'innovations' Haydn effected. Among his later heroes Mendelssohn, Franz Schmidt (a chamber-music player like Keller himself), and Schoenberg were palpable heirs to Viennese classical tradition. Shostakovich made the grade because he was a composer of symphonies, and still more of string quartets, 'morphologically' Beethovenian in concept. He was also a composer of genius, for which Keller had a (nearly) unerring ear. I suspect that the unBeethovenian—even anti-Beethovenian—Britten entered the canon by a similar route. Few if any composers of our time can match the purity with which Britten's genius explored the "blind mazes of this tangled wood", wherein we are all, in our battered age, psychologically enmeshed. Britten transmutes an obsession with the outsider and scapegoat into a vision of a Boy who was, or might be, reborn: a motif which chimed with Keller's Jewish alienation. This bears too on Keller's superficially unexpected profound appreciation of the music of George Gershwin—another innate genius whose parable of the (Negro-Jewish) outsider and scapegoat is currently enjoying a triumphant revival at Glyndebourne.

Keller's knowledge of (Viennese-orientated) psychology was, of course, scarcely less wide and deep than his knowledge of music, though he had no need of psychology to bolster his recognition of genius. His pantheon of heroes—Haydn, Mozart, Beethoven, Mendelssohn, Schoenberg, Shostakovich, Britten and Gershwin—is too eclectic for us to accuse him of narrow-mindedness. I go along with all of them; but will never be able to swallow the bracketing of Schoenberg with Haydn and Beethoven as "the only composers capable of playful complexity on the very highest level of inspiration". The genius of *Erwartung* shines through the darkly complex forest; Schoenberg's approaches to playfulness sound to my English ears elephantine. This is a cultural distinction, which is trivial. To me it does matter, however, that Keller, living willy-nilly in our global village and pluralistic society, wilfully shut out so much musical experience that I consider not only valid, but essential. Only his single-mindedness made his depth and intensity feasible; but there are reasons, not all of them discreditable, why string quartet playing can no longer be the synonym for the musical good life.

Retrospectively, I think of Hans as a devastating opponent at table tennis, at which, in Hollywood, Schoenberg and Gershwin are said to have battled (I often wonder who won). At our more modest level Keller and

Mellers confronted one another, so many years back, across summer-school tables; my English caution, usually worsted, found uncanny stimulation in defeat. The image of the small, glittering-eyed, flashing, dashing, slashing man hasn't faded with the years: nor will his literate memorial, though he left and could leave no book adequate to his creatively critical genius. In paying this posthumous tribute I recognize the word genius as appropriate, though of course Hans would have insisted that no critic could be a Haydn, Mozart, Beethoven or Britten.

TLS, SEPTEMBER 1986

THE COMPOSER AS WOUNDED BIRD

SCHUMANN'S PASSAGE FROM ROMANTIC DREAMS AND JESTS TO THE PITY AND TERROR OF THE ASYLUM

R. Larry Todd, ed., *Schumann and His World*. Princeton: Princeton University Press, 1994)

W ITH CHOPIN, SCHUMANN IS THE SUPREME REPRESENTATIVE OF THE first flush of musical romanticism. Whereas Chopin's romanticism was to a degree exotic in that he came from a remote country, Poland, of high-born stock, and was reared on French literature and Italian opera, Schumann belonged to the respectable German middle class, was nurtured on the Viennese classics and on German literature, and embarked on (but abandoned) university training for the law. This volume dedicated to *Schumann and His World*, edited by the American scholar R. Larry Todd, contains a substantial essay on the composer's cultural background by Leon Botstein; a comparably comprehensive piece by Michael P. Steinberg, linking sociological to psychological motives under the title of 'Schumann's Homelessness'; and a fascinating account by the editor of Schumann's use of quotation and self-quotation. Smaller essays deal with Schumann's symphonic finales, his search for a new musical-theatrical genre in *Das Paradies und die Peri*, and with romantic irony in the Eichendorff songs. Bernhard Appel provides a rigorously scholarly examination of the 'sources' for the *Album für die Jugend*, which is informative rather than inspirational. Parts 2 and 3 of the book reprint letters, memoirs and critical commentaries by Schumann's contemporaries and successors.

Botstein's essay presents its sociological and cultural evidence with a sensitivity that illuminates the music, explaining how, as an adolescent with manic-depressive tendencies, Robert was swept off his feet by the (now much dimmed) writings of Jean Paul: a tissue of whims, dreams, and conceits of palpable appeal to romantic teenagers.* For Jean Paul music was "the language of the heart" because it could parallel "the sorrow (twilight) and desire (sunrise) that emerged in the conduct of everyday life". Jean Paul's narrative technique, if it can be called such, was often compared with that of Laurence Sterne; dreams and 'jests' jostle in whimsical caprice and in contradiction of the stable values that had defined eighteenth-century Reason, Truth and Nature. In his youthful music, Schumann was just such a dreamer and jester, who composed his discomposing music for his own instrument, the piano, and played it himself. His first representative piano work was called *Papillons* in reference to the social frivolity of the masked ball it depicted, but also to the fragility and impermanence characteristic of butterflies, both inhuman and human. The relation between illusion and reality remained a constant theme throughout Schumann's art; and his

romantic paradox involved too the psychological concept of a split personality; which Schumann was from early adolescence and which, in later
years, became a clinically certifiable condition. In the wondrous outpouring
of piano music over the third decade of his life, romantic paradox and
bifurcated personality are inseparable from original genius.

Schumann's musical model for *Papillons* (1829) was the chains of salon-
waltzes of Schubert; and we may recall that Schumann said that when he
played Schubert, he thought of the dances as musical settings of Jean Paul.
Commotion beneath the music's surface sometimes turns the butterfly into
a caged bird, beating his wings against a prison: an image more potent in
Schumann's first indubitable masterpiece, *Carnaval* (1834). Here, Schumann's contradictory masks of (extrovert) Florestan and (introvert) Euse-
bius mingle with Pierrot-figures from the *commedia dell'arte* who are not
easily separable from the girls he loved and the very select friends and
artists (such as Chopin and Paganini) with whom he identified. In *Davids-
bündlertänze* (1837) this coterie of special people takes up arms against the
sea of mindless and heartless Philistines; while in the following year Schumann withdrew from the salon into the parlour or nursery, creating a cycle
of small piano pieces called *Kinderszenen*, not because they were intended
for performance by *kinder*, but because they were images of childhood's
'pre-conscious' states, offered to Clara because she had said that Robert
reminded her of a child. The startlements of enharmony, the ambiguities of
polymetre, and the abrupt shifts of key and tempo that typify all Schumann's youthful piano music are incised in miniature; yet these tonal and
metrical puns ('jests') have a crazy Alice-in-Wonderland-like logic, since
each moment of truth is an aspect of a single, if kaleidoscopic, self.
Although each of the *Kinderszenen* is self-contained, all are unified by
motovic recurrences, so that the cycle approximates to a small variation-set.

The positive and negative poles of Schumann's first phase are encapsulated in the accurately titled *Phantasiestücke* (1837). The first movement, 'Des
Abends', reveals how Schumann, who loved to play to his friends at the twilight hour sacred to Jean Paul, lived in half-lights and shadows; for its time
signature is 2/8, while the figuration is in 6/16, and what we hear melodically
is a tune in 3/8, with an imitative inner voice metrically dislocated by a semi-
quaver. Tonal ambivalence between D flat major and E major (standing for
F flat, the upper mediant) renders dream yet more elusive. With *In der
Nacht*, on the other hand, dream becomes nightmare; whirligig arpeggios
(in traditionally 'lugubrious' F minor) tempestuously harry a melody that
strives to soar but is tugged down—another wounded bird or pinioned butterfly—by naggingly dissonant appoggiaturas in an inner part. Pieces like
this, irresistible in momentum and frenetic in figuration, hint at the only

means whereby the young Schumann might tackle works on a more extended scale; as he did in the three major piano pieces in which his first phase culminates.

The earliest is, indeed, a sonata such as any responsible German composer was expected to essay, though Beethovenian argument was hardly apposite to a composer dedicated to fleeting fancies and 'moments' of truth; this may be why Schumann started his G minor sonata when he was only twenty-three, but did not finish it until five years later. Even so, the work thrives, in romantic paradox, on its contrariety; a certain lunatic intensity was necessary to create, in the first movement, a nightmare overriding formality and generating, from a tug-of-war between classical orthodoxy and teeming invention, an awareness of peril reminding us of the derivation of the word 'experience', from the Latin *ex periculo*. Clara, superb pianist though she was, must have found the sonata terrifying; and its incipient lunacy may have threatened Schumann himself, if one accepts the theory that this piece ended his career as a virtuoso, since in trying to cope with its horrendous difficulty he resorted to a mechanical gadget that stretched his hand-span all too efficaciously.

The other two major piano works that set the seal on Schumann's youth were, however, neither overtly sonatas nor self-destructive. The *Études Symphoniques* of 1834 adapt and expand the variation technique typical of his cycles of small pieces into a grandiloquence at once classical and romantic; and this piece, inspired by Schumann's passion for Ernestine von Fricken, has a still grander sequel two years later in the *Phantasie* in C, for which the trigger was Robert's ultimate love (and wife) Clara. The dedication was, however, to the ultimate piano virtuoso, Liszt, and the piece was also a tribute to Beethoven, the ultimate German Master, since it was associated with the unveiling of a monument in his honour. The concatenation of classical tradition, romantic virtuosity, and sexual love results in an explosion of passion that doesn't quite burst the dykes, though it comes closer to it than any piano sonata apart from Beethoven's Moonlight and Appassionata. All three movements, resonantly entitled 'Ruins', 'Triumphal Arches' and 'Starry Crowns', embrace elements of sonata-structure, characteristically fantasized and fanaticized. This apex to Schumann's work offered a peculiarly potent synthesis of life and art, since its date coincided with the belated union of Robert and Clara, whose father at last withdrew his ban on their marriage.

After the marriage, 1840 proved to be Schumann's Year of Song: for song may effect a transition from the inner life of dreams at least into a domestic circle, if not into the world. The piano parts of Schumann's songs, still intimately personal, are as subtly crafted as his early piano pieces; but the presence of a poetic text and a human voice to enunciate it introduces another dimension, the more so because the literary Schumann chose his texts with reference both to poetic quality and to putative autobiographical import. Schumann's two great song cycles, the (male-orientated) *Dichterliebe* and the (female-orientated) *Frauenliebe und Leben* transport him from a hermetic inner life to bisexual relationship, specifically with Clara, but also with 'other people' in a social situation. And the cycles reveal that domestic bliss is a far from facile ideal, since any two-way relationship calls for self-awareness. Romantic paradox is often inseparable from dualistic irony, as John W. Finson demonstrates in his essay on the *Liederkreis* cycle.

As one might expect, Schumann's year of song led to attempts to expand his range towards opera and oratorio. Although the failure of his opera *Geneveva* distressed him, he had the compensation of a near-fabulous success with his hybrid opera-oratorio, *Das Paradies und die Peri*, written in 1843. John Daverio's account of this work in the context of Schumann's life is perhaps the most intriguing paper in the book; and the Peri's significance in Schumann's story is underlined by its relationship to one of the most extraordinary of his early piano works, *Kreisleriana*, which was prompted by an autobiographical story of the necromantic E. T. A. Hoffmann, wherein he described his traumas through the mask of an imaginary Kapellmeister. Robert, obsessed by Hoffmann's scary tale 'The Sandman',* rather alarmingly told Clara that his haunted and haunting piano pieces described himself, in relation to her: a case further ballasted by Steinberg's brilliant discussion of the relationship between the piano work and the oratorio. Schegel's "secret listening"—first referred to by Robert in reference to the Clara-inspired Fantasie in C—merges with Hoffmann's androgynous myth and is literally projected, in the opera-oratorio, from the private into the public sphere. Schumann's text fuses Orientalism from Tom Moore's *Lalla Rookh** with (quasi-Jungian) symbolism from *The Magic Flute* to make a witches' brew of hermeticism, alchemy, androgyn, and pietism that not only inflamed Robert and Clara but also awoke responsive chords in a national and even international context. Apparently Schumann's marriage was a personal fulfilment that was also a cultural event, in which a union of "independent femininity and gentle masculinity" made for "completed humanity". It cannot be fortuitous that Schumann in this work achieved an orchestral radiance not usually typical of him.

Despite the initial furore, the romantic paradox of the piece's androgyny wasn't fulfilled in social and political terms, and still hasn't been, though it is now much talked of. Presumably for this reason, *Die Peri* didn't maintain a place in the repertory; and Schumann's growing-up didn't follow his idealized relationship with Clara, but shifted ground towards his German-

Jewish friend Mendelssohn—quasi-androgynous in being 'feminine' in sensibility, 'masculine' in intellectual acumen. Born under a lucky star, Mendelssohn was reared in the civilized tradition of Haydn and Mozart, and handled the conventions of Viennese and German classical music always with technical facility, and often with imaginative power. Though he also relished romantic vistas, whether in Italy or the Hebrides, his romanticism was an adornment of, rather than a threat to, civilized values; in his exquisite scherzi he fostered fairies at the bottom of his (*heimlich*) garden, which couldn't or wouldn't accommodate elves and hobgoblins such as were the (*unheimlich*) familiars of Schumann.

Mendelssohn's rediscovery of Bach complemented his civilized sociability, for counterpoint and canon could stand for stability and in lieu of a faith. In his early works, Schumann, less concerned with Christian sanctity of either Bachian or Mendelssohnic vintage than with eldritch wizardry, had none the less used Bachian counterpoint to keep nightmares at bay. Now, in his *Rhenish Symphony*, the baroque and Protestant-liturgical elements make more overt gestures in the same direction; as do the compulsive rhythms, symmetrical canons and thick scoring in all the symphonies, including the forceful D minor, originally sketched in the early 1840s as homage to Clara.

The conventional view used to be that Schumann's attempts to turn himself into a 'public' symphonist were misguided, and that his orchestral writing sounds pianistic because it was written at the piano. (Like Wagner's and Stravinsky's, we might add!) In the first years of this century, Weingartner made a notorious attack (reprinted in this book) on the scoring of Schumann's symphonies; which Mahler implicitly condoned in rescoring them with his own impeccably sonorous lucidity. Current opinion, perhaps influenced by the cult of authenticity, seems to mistrust this mistrust of Schumann's abilities; more than one writer in this compilation hazards that, given Schumann's original resources, problems of orchestral balance evaporate. This argument is not entirely convincing, since a fair number of Schumann's contemporaries wrote symphonies without incurring comparable opprobrium. Authenticity may sometimes reinforce today's craven suspicion of value-judgements: it may be true, as several contributors point out, that Schumann's evolution from private to (more) public composer was 'logical', but it does not necessarily follow that logic guarantees quality. Surely the latish *Album für die Jugend*, though it contains beautiful music and has valuable pedagogic purpose, lacks the electrical charge of the early *Kinderszenen*; and surely the late piano pieces seldom recapture the youthful magic, except in that hauntingly pitiful 'Bird as Prophet'.

Is it fanciful to suggest that what that solitary bird—survivor from the fluttering butterflies and pinioned birds of Schumann's twenties—prophe-sies is the darkness which finally overwhelmed him, the silent melancholy that proved too much even for Clara's love? In the asylum, Schumann, who had lived for feeling and communion with the beloved, was caged in what Steinberg calls his "homelessness". Schubert dictated to him sublime melodies which, gone with the wind, he could not remember; his obsessive rhythms became a single hammered note, pounding in his head. It is diffi-cult to imagine anything more appalling than the letter Robert wrote to Clara, asking her to send to the asylum the "little tune" he had written for her, "long ago, when we were in love." He was forty-two. Not even modern scholarship should, or can, deprive Schumann of the pity and terror of his end.

TLS, JANUARY 1995

CHOPIN'S MELANCHOLY SPELL

THE COMPOSER AS SPIRITUAL EXILE AND UNCONSCIOUS RHAPSODIST

Jim Samson, ed., *The Cambridge Companion to Chopin*
(Cambridge: Cambridge University Press, 1992)

CHOPIN WAS BORN IN 1810, IN THE FULL FLUSH OF ROMANTICISM, AND in Poland—a country in his time, and still to a degree in ours, considered remote, romantic, and politically turbulent. Yet his affluent, near-aristocratic family was cultivated and French-speaking; and at the age of twenty he left his native land for the centres of European civilization. After a brief spell in Vienna, where Italian opera was rife, he settled in 1831 in Paris, where he became, as a piano prodigy, an idol of aristocratic salons and a friend not only of composers such as Liszt, Berlioz, Rossini, and Bellini, but also of fashionable poets and painters. Only against the backcloth of this glamorous social and intellectual life can we understand the loneliness of his heart. His spiritual exile had little to do with his physical exile; although he identified his emotional turmoils with those of aristocratic Poland, he was more at home in the artistic milieu of Paris than he would have been elsewhere. Poland became a symbol not of a native land, but of a mythical dream-world: a haven of human solidarity expressed through the medium of his own instrument, for which he created a new idiom and a new performing technique. All his contemporaries were impressed even more by his artistic originality than by his personal charm; it is significant that although, early in his Paris years, he composed salon music in the fashionable 'brilliant style', the work in which his genius was decisively established was his opus 10, a set of twelve piano études begun in his twentieth year. In these dazzling pieces, pedagogic exercises exploring pianistic sonorities by way of the behaviour of the hands on a keyboard become an act of self-discovery. Often a single figuration suffices to generate the thematic and harmonic substance of an entire piece, which may or may not be contained within a simple binary or ternary song or dance form.

The originality of Chopin's invention means that he is not a ready candidate for the attentions of musicology, which is concerned with the relation of one thing to another, in historical context, rather than with intrinsic identity and value. Jim Samson, himself the author of a fine book on Chopin, has assembled for this Companion a team of able writers who do not entirely discount Chopin's reluctance to submit to scholarship. Janet Ritterman's preludial survey of 'Piano Music and the Public Concert 1800–1850' provides a setting for Chopin's Parisian career, with a descriptive account of the work of sundry composers who cultivated 'the brilliant style'. This affords tepid interest and occasionally mild surprise, but sheds little light on the miracle whereby salon-titivated Mozart is transformed, in the 'La ci darem' Variations, into authentic Chopin. Nor does David Rowland's study of the origins of the piano nocturne illuminate the magic whereby the slow movements of Chopin's two youthful concertos become nocturnal elegies on the butterfly impermanence of the concerto's allegros. The historical information here proffered is worth the carrying; we need to know that John Field was not a solitary precursor of Chopin the nocturnist. Even so, no gates into secret gardens are unlocked by these historical parallels; nor are they by Adrian Thomas's piece 'Beyond the Dance', which deals with forgotten composers who exploited indigenous Polish dance—a main source of inspiration, along with Italian operatic *bel canto*.

Simon Finlow's chapter on the crucial *études* suffers to a lesser degree from the same disability. We learn much about other contemporary composers of *études*, and some of the material is fascinating. But the citation of parallels is no substitute for analysis, from bar to bar, of what makes Chopin's studies unique; and that such analysis is feasible and rewarding has been demonstrated in Gerald Abraham's small but great book on *Chopin's Musical Style* (1939). Finlow repeats, but doesn't follow through, Abraham's comparison of the economy and consistency of Chopin's figurations with those of Bach in the Preludes of his 'Forty-eight': works which Chopin regularly played to himself. The point is critical in that it establishes the fundamental classicality of Chopin's approach; no composer was ever less the unconscious rhapsodist.

This applies not only to Chopin's relatively small-scale pieces that spring, *as though* spontaneously, from his keyboard technique, but also to his larger structures: which Professor Samson discusses in the volume's most helpful analytical chapter. The four *Scherzi* start from the traditional notion of the form, and offer startlements that are more expansive, though no less cogent, than Beethoven's; they relate 'closed' *da capo* form to the 'open' processes of sonata, and no more than Beethoven's *scherzi* are they jokes. Complementarily, the four *Ballades* effect highly original permutations of the sonata principle itself. The first *Ballade*, in G minor, opens with a slow introduction, as did some classical precedents, and moves into an allegro with two subject-groups, one in the tonic minor, the other in the flat submediant major, both lyrical and in dance rhythm. Instead of orthodox thematic development, however, Chopin builds climax by what might have been (but isn't) harmonic improvisation, flitting through a kaleidoscope of keys. This leads, in mirror-structure, to a restatement of the second group modified, and to a curtailed recapitulation of the first group, rounded off by a coda that wildly, but with tragic inevitability, counterbalances the introduction. This evolving and resolving psychological drama, if not Beethovenian, proves deeply satisfying: the difference lying in the degree to which the interacting subject-groups are absorbed *within* figuration which, compared with Beethoven's, is more 'finger-directed', and collaterally more introverted. This process is still more subtly evident in the late fourth Ballade in traditionally infernal F minor, wherein Bachian counterpoint lends intensity to romantic afflatus. Samson is disappointingly skimpy on this wonderful piece, though he admits it to be "one of Chopin's mightiest achievements and one of the unchallenged masterpieces of nineteenth century music".

Chopin's probity in dealing with these forms compromising between classical precedent and high romanticism has always been admired; only over the past fifty years, however, has deeper study revealed him as a master of sonata form also. Admittedly, his initial experiment (the C minor sonata) was both uncharacteristic and unconvincing; but his second sonata, the famous B flat minor, offered a new concept—a big piano composition wherein unity is virtually derived from keyboard figuration such as is the essence of his *études*. The 'motto' stated in long, tonally ambiguous note-values at the opening expands into different but related figurations in all four movements, effecting what amounts to an inversion of traditional sonata principle, which creates unity from diversity. Chopin's first movement is closest to orthodox sonata form, being balanced between quasi-operatic song (the second subject) and the disintegrative force of piano-figuration (the nightmare-ride of the first subject). Both subjects are assailed by the cataclysm of the sequentially chromatic codetta theme, but song is heroically salvaged in the curtailed recapitulation. In the scherzo, classical European tonality and nationally Polish dance are more directly assaulted by disintegrative harmony and figuration, with self-contained song rendered retrospective in the trio. In the funeral march—the first movement to be composed—the motif of undulating minor thirds is unchanged as the death of the hero (the self) is ritually celebrated; song appears, in the trio, not as a dream, but as a ghost. Thus the fourth movement, which seems so insubstantial as finale to a large-scale sonata, proves inevitable: here line itself becomes harmonic disintegration, since the movement is in unison throughout, yet is in effect harmonic. Tonality, in some sections, virtually disappears, as the music becomes a fluttering of the nerves that tells us, in an intimate whisper, what *Tristan* proclaims in its grandly impassioned lament: the Faustian battle between Man and the World has been absorbed into the inner life of a single, hypersensitive soul.

The stunning originality of this sonata was first demonstrated in a masterly analysis by Rudolf Reti, published in *The Thematic Process in Music* (1951). Anatole Leiken's account of it in this *Companion* is thus not definitive, though it offers incidental stimulations, and links the B flat minor sonata to the magnificent B minor sonata, a work which, if structurally less audacious than the second sonata, is no less renovative in its linear transformations of sonata principle. In a fine piece of analysis, Leiken traces the process whereby Bachian polyphony and counterpoint prove regenerative throughout the four thematically interlinked movements. It is praise-worthy, too, that Leiken pays homage, if without detailed analysis, to Chopin's still critically neglected cello sonata, his last major work.

Perhaps it is not accidental that some of the most rewarding essays in this Companion are peripheral to Chopin's composition. James Methuen-Campbell is characteristically lively on traditions of Chopin performance; Derek Carew is instructive as well as entertaining on Victorian attitudes to Chopin; Zofia Chehlinska more soberly traces Chopin's reception in his native land. This Polish material illuminates the link between Chopin and his greatest successor, Szymanowski, who wrote mazurkas almost as melancholic as those of Chopin himself. Whereas the world of Parisian vivacity existed, or had existed, Chopin's Poland was 'real' only in the sense that such nostalgia haunts everyone, to the measure of his or her nervous capacity. The strength of Chopin's last works—whether in the sublimated operatic vein of the *Barcarole*, his sumptuous evocation of Venetian water and light, or in the last 'Polish' mazurkas and the mysterious, post-Wagnerian enharmony of the *Polonaise-Fantaisie*—lies in their crystallization of subjective melancholy into the timelessness of art. This is why his highly personal idiom foreshadows not only so much nineteenth-century music, but also the disintegrations and reintegrations of our century: as is demonstrated in Roy Howart's copiously illustrated essay charting Chopin's legacy to Chabrier, Fauré, Debussy, Ravel and even Bartók. It is also why his spell, having survived excessive and often incompetent performance, and having weathered commercialization, is as potent today as ever.

TLS, JUNE 1993

THE GREAT AND THE SMALL

Hugh Macdonald, ed., *Selected Letters of Berlioz*, translated by Roger Nichols
(London: Faber and Faber, 1995)
Robert Orledge, *Satie Remembered*. French translations by Roger Nichols
(London: Faber and Faber, 1995)

O F THE MAJOR EUROPEAN COMPOSERS BERLIOZ WAS THE MOST LITERATE, probably because he was generally intelligent; even if he'd never written a note of music he would still occupy, for his autobiographical writings, criticism and journalism, an honourable place in French letters. His intelligence bears on his musical reputation: which was sometimes problematical because he did not follow paths identical with those of nineteenth-century Teutonic tradition. True, the idols of his youth were Gluck, a German or at least Central European heir to classical French tragedy and *tragédie lyrique*, who "dramatised with the orchestra"; and Beethoven, who as symphonist incarnated drama in purely musical terms, remaking it 'organically'. For Berlioz as a nineteenth-century humanist, the aristocratic opera house was to be reborn in the democratic (post-Revolutionary) concert hall, since the purpose of music was not to titillate the senses, as did the pap of nineteenth-century French theatre music, but to communicate feeling and to define an implicit morality. He followed classical precedents in wanting to be "expressive and truthful, without ceasing to be a musician"; and although he admired Wagner's cataclysmic genius, he suspected that it might also prove catastrophic, since Wagner tended to "dethrone music and reduce it to expressive accents"; all those Tristanesque chromatics might, he feared, creep insidiously into his drawing-room and nibble the furniture!

Such verbal articulacy typifies Berlioz as both man and artist, as is patent in the letters he wrote from his early years. Nowadays people don't write letters, and so deprive themselves of the most immediate form of self-expression. Berlioz wrote letters voluminously, with a flair that matches the electrical magnetism of his music. This selection, made by Hugh Macdonald who as a scholar and editor has done much for Berlioz's cause, is therefore doubly valuable: as a human document, and for what it reveals about Berlioz's musical creation. Berlioz's intimate letters, to family and friends, reveal simultaneously the exuberance of his passions and the frustrations that, in all aspects of his life, tended to curb them. His father was a man of considerable intellectual distinction who favoured medicine or the law, rather than music, as a profession for his son. Hector respected his father, but was not cowed by him. The father's courtly prose finds echoes in the son's; and ultimately *père* Berlioz bowed to Hector's sense of personal vocation, albeit with a *triste* resignation. The elder of Berlioz's sisters seems to have been stiff-lipped like her father, but the younger sister Adèle, being lovable and loved, elicited from her brother letters tenderly teasing as well as witty. He opened his heart more to male friends like Humbert Ferrand, and he possibly sought a father-figure in Jean-François LeSueur, the one mentor who was, for Berlioz, beyond the constrictiveness of the establishment, encouraging his fascination with polymodality and 'non-western' techniques. For the most part, however, Berlioz was, in the eyes and ears of family and teachers, a congenital outsider whose originality disturbed more that it impressed.

The people involved even more intimately in Berlioz's life, his wives and lovers, brought him more pain than pleasure. Despite his reputation as a romantic icon, with hawkish profile, immense mop of hair, and piercing eyes, Berlioz was no womaniser. His ravaged appearance testified to a ravaged spirit, and his tumultuous life was not conventionally 'happy'. It may be that his failures in personal life were necessary to his artistic fulfilment; certainly his childhood passion for starry Estelle Fornier [Duboeuf], renewed when the composer was in his sixties and the little girl past seventy, fuses outrageous passion with grotesquerie in a manner familiar from his music. Significantly, his first consummated love-affair teetered between tragedy and farce. Repulsed by the Irish actress Harriet Smithson, for whom (or at least for whose Ophelia) Berlioz nursed a passion literally beyond words (though not ultimately beyond his music), he found refuge in the arms of the beautiful eighteen-year-old pianist Camille Moke: only to be betrayed by her—in favour of a piano-maker of the Pleyel clan!—whilst Hector was in Italy enjoying the fruits of his belatedly awarded Prix de Rome. Armed with a pistol to exact revenge on the minx and her lover, and a phial of poison for subsequent self-destruction, Berlioz rushed post-haste back to Paris. As a Frenchman, he did not forget to pack the stomach pump; and in any case his frenzy abated on the road: for although an arch-romantic in posture and gesture, Berlioz was a classicist in the icy performance of his role. Throughout his life he followed his own advice that "in music we must do coolly the things that are most fiery".

In a sadder sense, this is manifest in Berlioz's longer relationship with Harriet Smithson, as well as with the glamorous Camille. Unsurprisingly, Harriet's stoniness melted when Hector not only composed the *Symphonie Fantastique* about her, but also dedicated it to her. Although she succumbed to his assaults, and even married him without blessing from Hector's parents, bliss and triumph ended in lament. Harriet's career, at first luxurious, declined into Ophelia-like instability, and was not aided by her lack of expertise in the French language. Incipiently alcoholic, she was a long time dying; and through her declension Hector preserved an icy dignity, if little more. Even Marie Recio, the mistress Berlioz acquired to relieve his melancholy, wasn't very good at the task. Compared with his fevered transports over Harriet and Camille, Hector was mum about Marie, an indifferent singer whom the eager-eared musician found tiresome, though he waxed fulsome in (guilty?) grief when she too died prematurely. Even Berlioz's only son (by Harriet) rewarded his father's extravagantly professed love inadequately. A 'difficult' child, less bright than his father expected or needed, he went, in default of conspicuous talents, to sea, and died of a foreign fever at the age of thirty-two. The climacteric letter from Hector to the son Louis is a formidable dressing-down lacking in the humour that usually ameliorated his anger or distress.

Berlioz's failures in personal life were reflected in his relationships with the musical establishment. One cannot say that he lacked recognition, for his incandescent genius ignited sparks everywhere, and honours were showered on him throughout Europe and especially in Russia, whose inhabitants, being barbaric outsiders from the consort of European nations, perhaps spontaneously recognised in Berlioz's polymodal and polyrhythmic new horizons qualities relatable to those they themselves would later bequeath to Debussy, Ravel and Stravinsky. Yet despite Berlioz's international celebrity, the Parisian establishment did what it could to thwart him. The Paris Opera rejected the first masterpiece of this congenitally theatrical composer, being unable to swallow, in *Benvenuto Cellini*, a score of such melodic fecundity, rhythmic alacrity, and vocal and orchestral virtuosity, dedicated moreover to a notorious Outsider; even when Berlioz tried to present the piece in London it was hissed off the stage by a Paris-promoted claque. Berlioz's diatribes in his letters about the malice, effrontery, and crass stupidity of the opposition make lively reading, his fury always being countered by his sense of the ridiculous. Nor was he finally broken by the obtuse refusal of French academia to appreciate the sense in which his compromises between symphony, oratorio, and opera in *Roméo et Juliet* and *La Damnation de Faust* were a valid, profound and unique extension from the techniques of Beethoven's last quartets and piano sonatas.

For Berlioz knew, as Beethoven had known, that his 'originality' was a consequence of the relationship between his private and the public life. His initial work of genius, the *Symphonie Fantastique* (1830), "came to me in my manhood, a voice out of the burning bush", proffered by Shakespeare in the guise of Harriet Smithson, and the personal revelation couldn't have occurred without the literary one. Complementarily, public and historical circumstance led to the creation of his supreme public work, the *Grande Messe des Morts* (1840). In the *Symphonie Fantastique* autobiography becomes a testament of classicised romanticism; in the *Messes des Morts* external events provide a frame for inner verities. Both works tore Berlioz to tatters; he was always threatening to faint over the kettledrums, and was delighted by the visceral effects his music occasioned in the audiences ("a reasonable degree of weeping and trembling", as he put it in a letter). The private and the public dimensions of Berlioz's work are thus inseparable: an artist's autobiographical story becomes a generalised myth, while the cult of the colossal, product of the age's science and technology, reveals new potential for the human spirit, as well as for material progress. And despite the mean machinations of Berlioz's enemies, his triumphal progress was ultimately irresistible. Although he did not live to hear his immense legendary-historical opera, *Les Troyens*, performed in its entirety, he was well aware that his Virgilian vision of post-Napoleonic glory revealed a potential Good Life more real than 'reality'. Today, notwithstanding its agonies of parturition, *Les Troyens* stands as a work so massive, so rich in invention, so electrically charged in rhythm, so rapid (especially by nineteenth-century standards) in harmonic pacing, that it justifies its composer's belief that it coexists not merely with Gluck (its closest historical analogue), but also with the transcendent genius of Virgil, Shakespeare and Beethoven. In this sense art has replaced religion.

To follow—through these letters, vividly translated by Roger Nichols and meticulously edited by Hugh Macdonald—the evolution of Berlioz's works is an excitation and a privilege: which prompt us to reflect anew on the meanings of failure and success. The judges of the Prix de Rome objected to the wild extravagance of Berlioz's student cantata on the theme of Cleopatra, even suggesting that he'd done it deliberately to spite them, and must learn that, although undoubtedly "a volcanic being, you must not write for yourself alone". To this Berlioz retorted that "if you want me to write gentle music, you shouldn't give us a subject like Cleopatra: a queen in despair, who makes an asp bite her, and dies in convulsions". Of course the academicians are forgotten and Berlioz's vision still shines: a beacon not only against the professors' complacency, but also against the spiritual tawdriness of an age "seared with trade, bleared, smeared with toil", as Hopkins put it. That Berlioz's vision has survived to the present day is the more important because the folk for whom it was originally intended proved incapable of recognising its power and glory. The rule of the people came to mean not the rebirth of heroism, as Berlioz hoped, but lack of thought, absence of discipline, want of skill—the reverse of the artistic virtues. Perhaps Berlioz realised that the new world that was supposed to symbolise the artist's apotheosis would instead destroy all that he held most dear. He ceased composing when he was sixty, and gave up the ghost at the age of sixty-five.

Comparison between the posthumous destinies of Berlioz and Wagner offers pause for thought. Wagner became part of Europe's history: because his music happened, we will never be the same again. We will return to him because we are all preoccupied with ourselves, and are wedded to love and death. But it may be that—as Jacques Barzun proclaimed more than forty years ago—Berlioz, a romantic rooted in French classicism who anticipated our fumbling attempts to rescue civilisation from chaos, expressed the nineteenth-century more comprehensively and more deeply. To him we will return because we are fascinated by the (Shakespearean) diversity of human nature, and by the imagined prospect of a world in which we might more humanely exist. Wagner's success fills us with regret for the life we ourselves have not the talent to live; Berlioz's disillusion fills us with hope for the unborn lives that make our personal passions seem petty. The woof of hope and regret is the heart of our being; Berlioz and Wagner are necessary opposites, for each other and for us all.

Berlioz is a major master, the grandest, probably the greatest, of French composers, whereas Satie is a very minor master who eschewed even the notions of grandeur and greatness. None the less, they have qualities in common: both were highly intelligent and had memorably eccentric characters that people didn't forget; both had a linear approach to their art, however flamboyant were Berlioz's gestures, in contrast with Satie's discretion. If Berlioz ended up in the opposite camp to Wagner, one might say that Satie, who had revered Debussy in youth, came to represent ideals antipathetic to Debussy's. In this delightful book, Robert Orledge, author of the definitive big book on Satie, does not offer a mini-biography or a critical assessment of him or his music, but collates opinions of friends, colleagues and acquaintances about a man whose extraordinary human qualities accord with the durable qualities of his art. The contributors make an imposing gallery of twentieth-century musicians, painters, poets, novelists and film-makers; 'everyone' in Paris during the years of the First World War and the giddy 1920s knew Satie, and most people loved him. The integrity of his being comes across in the fact that so many disparate characters concur in their descriptions of his qualities and estimates of his worth. This is surprising in view of what are usually considered his surreal attributes. To browse in this book is to experience, in rapid sequence, pleasure, surprise, shock, and something rather like awe. I begin to understand why I, who have played Satie's chaste music on and off for more than sixty years, still find satisfaction in so doing. One can't say as much of some 'great' composers, and of no 'grand' ones. Roger Nichols's translations are again live on the mark; and the quotation from Satie chosen as epigraph to the book is a small perfection: "Although our information is false, we do not vouch for it".

MT, MARCH 1996

FORTITUDE WITHOUT FAITH

Malcolm MacDonald, *Brahms* (London: Dent, 1990)
Ivor Keys, *Johannes Brahms* (Bromley: Helm, 1989)

WHEN I WAS A STUDENT AT CAMBRIDGE MORE THAN HALF A CENTURY ago, we (fairly) bright young things tended to be condescending about, even downright hostile to, Brahms, whom we associated with the stuffier aspects of teutonicized British academicism which was said to have a 'stranglehold' on our native woodnotes wild. Of course our view was short-sighted as well as cloth-eared; Brahms wasn't and isn't a has-been, as these two substantial new books about him demonstrate. We forgot that, even on his own terms, Brahms was in youth wedded to Romanticism, itself an avant-garde movement. Schumann, whose disciple Brahms was proud to be, called Brahms the Young Eagle, and it was hardly surprising that Clara Schumann fell, however discreetly, for the eagle's exceptional physical beauty, and probably loved him for years, while his charm became sullied by grumpy self-assertiveness.

Musically, Brahms's adolescent enthusiasm for the presumed spontaneity of folk-song and of gypsy music didn't desert him. Never mind that, according to the later ethnic purism of a Kodály or Bartók, Brahms couldn't recognize a folk-song when he heard one; the spirit, as usual, mattered more than the letter, as it had done when Ossian's forgeries swept Europe, carrying the distracted Brahms with them. One might say that Brahms's trigger to creation was precisely the duality between such Romantic spontaneity and a rage for order. In this he was a more self-conscious successor to his god Beethoven, who came near to breakdown both mental and musical around the time of the Moonlight Sonata, and devoted the rest of his life to recovery and reconstruction. Beethoven's pilgrimage was an ultimately triumphant search for and discovery of faith. Brahms made do without a faith; if this makes him a lesser figure than Beethoven, it also explains his immense popularity throughout the later nineteenth century and his durability today. In an age of unfaith he speaks for mankind's courage and endurance, and also for its recurrent sensibility and joy.

Despite his agnosticism, Brahms was reared in, and deeply respected, Protestant tradition as well as bourgeois sociability. Protestantism entailed reverence for the German master Bach, whose baroque techniques offered Brahms a haven in a sea of chaos. This is most patent in the *Requiem*—setting biblical texts concerned with comfort for the bereaved rather than metaphysical sanctions of the dead—which he wrote in memory of his mother. But Bachian counterpoint recurs throughout his music, most directly in sundry vocal motets and instrumentally in the remarkable organ Prelude and Fugue in tenebrous A flat minor, and in a late set of chorale preludes. Baroque fugal and variation techniques are also manifest in works inspired not so much by Bach as by Handel. The large-scale Handel Variations for piano are only the most obvious instance; such music given the vigour and probity of its technique, asserts superabundant life in the present, whatever may be in store for us in a presumptive hereafter.

But Brahms's central affirmation was not in remaking the past but in the continuity he manifests with his immediate predecessors. As a professional composer, he made chamber music in all the genres practised by Haydn, Mozart, Beethoven and Schubert, dedicated to a public that in Germany—and later over most of the 'civilised' world—was avid for it, both as listeners and as performers. The appeal of this music lay in its encompassing so wide a variety of experience, veering between aggression and nostalgia, bounding exuberance and tricksy humour, even subtle wit. Brahms had an informed and musically educated public who knew the rules and relished both his accommodation to them and his intermittent rebelliousness. His contrapuntal skills honed his passionate fecundity, and in particular abetted the techniques of motivic metamorphosis which he took over from Beethoven. The ultimate climax to his career was his belated approach to the symphony which, after Beethoven's Ninth, was obliged to storm the heights and plumb the depths. If the fourth and last symphony seems Brahms's greatest work, the reason may be that it is a post-Beethovenian symphony that has the courage to admit that for modern man no transcendental resolution is possible. For its finale it adapts the old-fashioned form of passacaglia, which in its baroque heyday had imposed unalterable law on transience and change. For Brahms it does that with inexorable severity; and not only is the Fourth his most powerful use of an inherited classical form, it is also the most densely motivic of all his instrumental works. The contrapuntal intricacy of its textures effects a bridge between traditional symphonic thinking and the inner necessities of thematic serialism, whether it be chromatic or not.

This is why Schoenberg hailed "Brahms the Progressive", and wrote with such perspicuity of his last major work, the *Vier ernste Gesänge* which, setting biblical words affirming but not transcending mortality, may be said to celebrate the negation of his impending death. Malcolm MacDonald and Ivor Keys follow Schoenberg in tracing the relation between these wonderful songs and the Fourth Symphony. In both, chains of descending thirds root us to the earth we came from; while in the final song the immense Mahlerian expansion of the vocal line gives humanity wings. This is not merely a dying man's solace for the follies of the past; it hints that human love may regenerate a world.

200

Brahms does not need to be grand to be great. The tiny B minor Intermezzo from the last cycle of piano pieces, opus 119, is built from the same chain of falling thirds that we find in the *Vier ernste Gesänge* and the Fourth Symphony; in the suspended polytonality the interlaced thirds create, it is as though human dust were dissolving into air and rain; Brahms's pantheism is as natural as it is beautiful. This should remind us not only that Brahms the Conservative is Brahms the Progressive, but also that he is our representative, even at a time when composers no longer have a public who can understand the premises they start from.

Both these books revolve around this central hub. MacDonald's is the more substantial, offering all the documentary material that the Master Musician's series now rewards us with, and interweaving a thorough survey of the life with commentary on, and sometimes analysis of, the music. The portrait of the man has immediacy and vivacity, and MacDonald says all that may legitimately be said about the mysteries of Brahms's love-life: which may not be so mysterious after all. It is feasible that his boyhood experience playing the piano in a near-bordello may have been traumatic; it is certain that both his and Clara's dedication to art would have been a serious barrier, even without the disparity in their ages and Brahms's veneration for her mad husband. For the intelligent lucidity of MacDonald's discussion of the music one example must suffice. Speaking of Brahms and Bruckner as church or churchy composers he writes:

Whereas Bruckner's Latin motets are among the most wholly integrated expressions of mystical belief since the Renaissance itself, Brahms's German ones—though clearly alluding to the forms, idioms and thought of Lutheran sacred music tradition—are instinct with a detached agnosticism even while fervently expressing need for submission and consolation. They are not so much personal acts of faith as moving symbols of his admiration for the musical spirituality of Bach and Schütz, to whom his heart went out even as his intellect refused to accept it.

That helps us to understand a great deal about the nineteenth century, as well as about Brahms and Bruckner; and MacDonald's concluding chapter is no less illuminating with reference to Brahms and the present and future. His relation to Schoenberg and Berg has, of course, been much discussed; parallels with such diverse composers as Eisler, Ruggles, and Carter are unexpected, yet persuasive. Live on the mark is a comparison between the meticulous clarity with which half-lights and shadows are defined in the late piano pieces and similar effects in the piano music of Fauré. Malcolm MacDonald is rare among music journalists—he offers information, but also provokes thought.

Professor Keys's book is much shorter and at first seems less substantial.

Its stance is intentionally modest, for it restricts its main text to an elegantly written account of the life (again without psychological speculation) and includes no musical criticism. Instead Keys offers as Part Two of the book a catalogue listing each work in chronological order, with a commentary on points of interest mostly, though not exclusively, informative rather than interpretative or evaluative. This is a legitimate approach which in some moods one is grateful for; anyone who has tried to write about music will sympathize with Keys when, after giving an intelligent description of what happens in a passage from Brahms's opus 36 quintet, he remarks, "Here is the familiar Brahmsian paradox: one describes a piece of sheer poetry, and it sounds like a knitting pattern!"

The more one lingers over Keys's book the more rewarding it grows. His analytical comments enable one to enter Brahms's workshop, confronting his compositional problems as though one were his apprentice. Precision and authority are combined with informality and with a wry wit and cool appraisal that frequently remind one of Tovey—there could be no higher praise. This is particularly evident in an appendix-like chapter on 'finger-prints' manifest in the opus 117 piano pieces: a masterly piece of criticism that refutes the blanket judgement that Brahms was a cul-de-sac, the 'end of a line'. In fact 'old Brahms'—as we're apt to think of him, though he stopped composing at the age of sixty and died at sixty-four—showed Bartók "that there were still quartets to write", and demonstrated to Shostakovich that the symphony was "still a living form". "Composers", Keys adds, "are opportunists, though many are not fraudulent." That is an 'allegro ma non troppo' judgement that Brahms, in his modesty, would have relished.

TLS, MARCH 1990

RECLUSIVE REVOLUTIONARY

Ronald Smith, *Alkan. Volume Two: The Music*.
(London: Kahn and Averill, 1987)

S A MUSICAL PRODIGY AT THE PARIS CONSERVATOIRE CHARLES VALENTIN
Morhange ("dit Alkan") won first prize for *solfège* at the age of seven, first
prize for piano at the age of ten, and first prize for harmony at thirteen.
While still in his teens he was recognized as one of the supreme piano vir-
tuosi of his time—the only one, indeed, whom Liszt confessed to being
scared of. At the onset of what could have been legendary fame, however,
Alkan withdrew from public life. Though he continued to compose prolifically for his instrument music daunting alike in technical difficulty and
imaginative rebarbativeness, his hermeticism not surprisingly led to
neglect. But then and later he did not lack disciples and acolytes: Liszt
found in him a genius akin to his own, if tougher and pricklier; Berlioz
would probably have agreed with von Bülow's assessment of Alkan as "the
Berlioz of the piano". Later, Busoni and his pupil Petri promoted Alkan's
cause in the most effective way—by playing his music; while the eccentri-
cally formidable van Dieren and Sorabji championed him as a technically
and intellectually dazzling outsider congenial to their abstruse minds and
luxuriant imaginations. Today, Alkan's main advocates are the pianists Raymond Lewenthal and Ronald Smith, both of whom have the necessary
prodigious technique, allied to the equally necessary intellectual stamina
and emotional adventurousness. They have kept Alkan's flag vigorously
waving, abetted by the composer-pianist Roger Smalley, and a few more
professional academics such as Hugh Macdonald and the present reviewer.

On the whole, however, the academic fraternity has treated Alkan with
frosty disdain spawned of fear and ignorance. Familiarity with the music is
now inducing a thaw, for the work is substantially recorded, if still inadequately available in published score. We must hope that the flourishing Alkan
Society will promote a complete authoritative edition. Meanwhile, Ronald
Smith has beaten Raymond Lewenthal to the post by completing his book on
Alkan, the first biographical volume of which came out as long ago as 1976. It
tackled the enigma of the composer's life, wherein he was metamorphosed
from Morhange into the legendarily reclusive Alkan. Since the composer's
psychological abnormalities are interesting mostly for their bearing on the
music, it is regrettable that the second volume has been so long delayed. Even
so, it is enthusiastically to be welcomed, for it is well written, well produced
and, with the help of nearly three hundred music type examples, offers technical analysis of the kind that promotes experiential understanding.

Ronald Smith discusses Alkan's *oeuvre* by category rather than chronology; and doesn't evade the problems created by Alkan's being musically as well as psychologically enigmatic. He composed with immense fecundity, and some of his music looks, and even sounds, banal. All of it, however, is tinged with sudden startlements that make the scalp prickle; and with the major works one accepts Smith's case that Alkan—a "subversive conservationist"—is at once the most wildly revolutionary and the most traditional of the great romantic piano composers. For Alkan is no feather-brained keyboard exhibitionist, but a powerfully professional composer of formidable skills. He is a superb contrapuntist in baroque tradition, and is an heir to Haydn in his classical command of 'symphonic' argument; more directly, he shares Beethoven's large-scale, 'morphological' approach to form—as well as his partiality for gritty textures and for the abrupt punch-line or sudden reversal. Among his immediate contemporaries he is closest to Berlioz, who also "does coolly the things that are most fiery"; it may be the fusion of this aristocratic French poise with Jewish cabbalistic fervour that defines Alkan's unique savour—simultaneously wry and visionary, acrid and sumptuous, religious and mephistophelean. Berlioz described his own large-scale works as 'Babylonian', and one could say as much of Alkan's *Grande Sonate* describing the four ages of man, which he wrote in his thirty-fourth year, predating the Liszt Sonata by four years. The scherzo comes first, in D major, followed by a vastly intricate sonata allegro in D sharp minor; the third movement is in G major, the finale in G sharp minor, 'extrèmement lent'. The implications of this weird key scheme are profoundly explored, as are the Lisztian metamorphoses of themes between Faust and the Devil. The gigantic sonata movement climaxes in what Smith calls "exorcism by fugue", involving "six parts in invertible counterpoint plus three extra voices and three doublings—eleven parts in all!" Throughout, the music justifies its Beethovenian references to Faust, Atlas and Prometheus, for it exists at a level of apocalyptic imagination—and technical control—compared with which Liszt seems a pygmy. Nor does Alkan necessarily require vast dimensions to achieve such effects, which characterize, hardly less tellingly, the later and deceptively titled *Sonatine*, which lasts a mere twenty minutes, and is electrical in agility yet classically taut in texture—at least until the final cataclysm, which Smith likens, in one of his precisely revelatory metaphors, to a mass-precipitation of lemmings over a cliff.

Alkan's best-known work is the immense set of *Études* in all the minor keys, by now established as a masterpiece, even within the conservatory curriculum. They incorporate a 'Symphonie' in four movements in 'progressive' tonality, declining down the cycle of fifths: wherein authentic piano writing sounds convincingly orchestral. The even vaster three-move-ment 'Concerto' for solo piano manages to differentiate between solo and tutti, and even illusorily to suggest their interlacing. Smith demonstrates that what is most remarkable about these literally breath-taking works is not the originality of the conception, but the irresistible momentum with which the material is deployed over vast spans—especially in the first movement of the 'Concerto' . They demand more of the listener, as well as the performer, than does the dazzling variation-set, 'Le Festin d'Ésope', with which Alkan's opus 39 ends; yet that immediately 'effective' work proves, especially in the context of the complete set, to have its own tragic monu-mentality, for its veerings and tacking between crazy comedy and fearful frenzy climax in a coda which Alkan justly labels 'granitic'. Perhaps these almost surreal oscillations of mood and manner are related to the imperial glamour of the Parisian world outside the recluse's study; that royal fanfares should be metrically (and hilariously) punctured by barking dogs antici-pates Mahler's parodies of militarism.

But the great *Études* are fairly well known; the most useful part of Smith's book may be his charting of the paths through the jungle of short pieces, some of which don't claim to do more than charm, though many are fraught, lyrically, harmonically and of course pianistically, with Alkan's necromancy. They may be strikingly prophetic of Bartók, whose famous 'Allegro Barbaro' is both less barbarous and less disciplined than Alkan's Lydian mode piece with the same title; of Fauré, in the modal linearity and dreamy figurations of the Barcarolles and Nocturnes; of Debussy, in the sensuously static harmonies of 'Les Soupirs'; of Prokofiev, in the metallic, march-like 'Märchen' of the *Trois Petites Fantaisies*, which are fantastic cer-tainly, but rigorously controlled and not at all *petites*; of Mahler and Shostakovich in the sinister nightmare of a small tone-poem like *Le Tam-bour bat aux champs*; of Ives or Henry Cowell in the savage-ludicrous tone clusters of 'Les Diablotins' (which Alkan possibly adapted from Scarlatti's 'Spanish' acciaccaturas). The 'futurism' of these pieces is indeed remark-able; yet what, really, do they anticipate but themselves? They are "news that *stays* news"—most of all the wondrous 'Chanson de la folle au bord de la mer', wherein the mad woman wails her disconsolate folk-like lament high in soprano register, while the ocean sighs surlily in the bottom range of the keyboard.

Smith's comments on these pieces are unerringly perspicacious, the more so because he is not uncritical. When he finds a piece tiresome even in its adventurousness, he is not afraid to say so; occasionally he even admits that a possibly parodistic 'banal' piece may be simply banal. With Alkan, it is difficult to be sure; and in the last phase of his life another problem intrudes since Alkan, as his hermeticism increased, relinquished the grandiose grand in favour of an instrument virtually obsolete—Erard's pedal-piano. Smith hazards that the compositions Alkan wrote for this instrument contain "some of the profoundest music" for the medium since Bach; and adds that "if such a claim should strike the reader as wildly improbable and wilfully irresponsible . . . I can only say to my organ colleagues, 'Search and ye shall find' ". From all I know of Alkan's music and Smith's integrity I go along with that, and hope that the Alkan Society may find funds to salvage the music, even if only in compromising versions for piano or organ.

Smith's epilogue is a masterly summary which indicates how Alkan's ambiguities make sense in relation to the 'pluralistic' society he lived in but was not of. At once aloof and fierily passionate, Alkan will never be a member of the Establishment, though Ronald Smith has demonstrated that he cannot again be dislodged from his established position as (in Busoni's phrase) "one of the five greatest writers for the piano since Beethoven". He also composed an aborted symphony and a little chamber music, including a magnificent *Grande Sonate de Concert* for cello and (diabolically virtuosic) piano, the adagio of which—a sublimely strange meditation on a passage from the Book of Micah—seems to me one of the greatest, not merely most extraordinary, movements in nineteenth-century chamber music. Alongside such a tragic fresco we find a mordant *jeu d'esprit* like the *Marcia funebre sulla morte d'un papagallo*, brilliantly scored for four voices, three oboes and bassoon: music that looks parodistic but sounds, with its squawks and wails embraced within the most ingenious chromatic counterpoint, frightening as well as funny. Clearly this music came from the same "obsessional" mind (Smith's word) that created the adagio of the Cello Sonata and the more cabbalistic of the pieces for the pedal-piano. This reminds us that Alkan's life and death are themselves a cat's-cradle of tragedy and farce; the story that he was killed by pulling a bookcase on top of his then frail body, while stretching to reach the Talmud, bible of Hasidic occult lore, ought to be true but isn't.

TLS, OCTOBER 1987

THE WAGNER PHENOMENON

Stewart Spencer and Barry Millington, eds, *Selected Letters of Richard Wagner*
(London: Dent, 1987)

O VER THE LAST MONTH I'VE HAD A MUSICAL EXPERIENCE THAT TRAN-
scends music: I've been reading a fat volume of Wagner's letters and
interludially listening again to his music, In his case the fusion of Life
and Art is peculiarly pregnant, for more unabashedly than any previous
artist he created a mythology that directly reveals the splendours and miseries of his and our condition. His art is still dangerous, because terribly
near the bone; if it is stylized in being mythological, it is scarily naturalistic
in that its mythology is a direct projection of the inner life. He couldn't have
so powerfully embraced the depths as well as the heights of his humanity
had he not contained a dog to mirror the god within him.

Though we are nowadays very knowing about the workings of the
psyche and may even be better equipped to understand Wagner's intentions
than he was, this is because he himself lived through and helped to formulate the revolutions we associate with Freud, Jung and Marx; never was an
artist more conspicuously a "point at which the growth of the mind shows
itself". Yet if we recognize the extent to which the Wagner phenomenon
made us, we suffer from one immense disadvantage: for although we are all
too well aware of doggy corruption, we have lost the sense of the heroically
godly. Wagner can begin *The Ring* with the birth of consciousness from the
waters of creation; can portray the separate yet identical dwarfs, ogres,
heroes, sprites, and fairy princesses who are warring elements within his
and our minds; and can end with the death of the psyche, which is also a
cosmic new birth. The Pinter unhero, locked in his inarticulateness, the
Beckett antihero, crawling back to aboriginal slime, are valid descendants of
god-dogs Wotan-Alberich and Siegfried-Hagen; but they could hardly
evoke Wagner's music. Yet the pettier we become the more we are fascinated
by Wagner's grandeur—which is honestly the inverse of his pettiness. This
god-like prideful man had all the human weaknesses.

This comes home forcefully as we mull through the *Selected Letters*,
which have been translated—with a vivacity that makes Wagner momentarily a living presence—and scrupulously edited by Stewart Spencer and
Barry Millington. It would seem that in sheer physical and intellectual
potency Wagner was a Nietzschean superman. The selection covers a thousand pages; the 'complete' letters will run to thirty no less massive volumes—and this discounts the letters, probably equal in numbers, that
failed to survive. Wagner's psychological and spiritual stamina measures up

to this mind-boggling energy. A sickly child of provincial if intellectually well-honed stock, with some dubiety about his parentage, he knew at an early age what he had to do. Although he thought of himself, to a degree justifiably, as successor to the symphonic Beethoven he differed from Beethoven in that he had to create operas, rather than 'absolute' instrumental music, since operas told stories: his story, and by inference that of the human race, for which he stood surrogate. These operas could have little (he thought no) connection with Gluckian or Mozartian prototypes because they had to tell the tale of the New Man (himself), who alone could forge a new world, displacing current religious, social and political moribundidities. This is why the youthful Wagner flirted with revolutionary movements, and found himself threatened with imprisonment and for many years exiled. The courage of the young man's confidence takes the breath away; especially when he defines his position with atypical sobriety, as in a letter to Franz Hauser, written when he was only twenty-one, explaining why his operas could neither be amenable to traditional precedents nor could court the new sensationalism of Meyerbeer—from whom, none the less, Wagner solicited (and obtained) help in the promotion of his art. He lusted after Meyerbeer's international celebrity while despising what he considered to be his meretriciousness and the anti-human values it promulgated.

Although Meyerbeer was a Jew, one cannot merely ascribe Wagner's notorious anti-Semitism to personally motivated jealously. He was cross that Meyerbeer was internationally famous (he sycophantically addressed him in a letter as a "demigod") when he himself (who knew he was a god with no diminutive qualification) as yet was not. But the really important issue was that the Jews in general, those age-old usurers and manipulators of high finance, were in being hostile or indifferent to Wagner, also inimical to civilization, since he was the life-blood of civilization's future, should it have one. Years later, after the realization of his dreams in the opera-house-temple of Bayreuth, he thanked Ludwig II for having made it possible for him to fulfill "the destiny I had planned for myself and humanity". "Big of you", we're inclined to mutter—before being forced to admit that, in the light of Freud, Jung and Marx, Wagner's grandiose sentence was truth.

Wagner's hatred of Jewry grew rampant in his late years. In 1881 he writes to Ludwig that "the Jew is the born enemy of pure humanity and all that is noble in man. There is no doubt that we Germans especially will be destroyed by them". Even so, there is a dimension to Wagner's view beyond this dire, oft-quoted premonition of Nazidom. A few years previously he had told Ludwig that "we *want* to be worthless; this has been our motto ever since the Jesuits handed over this world to the Jews"; and he goes on, in a

letter of 1879 to foresee Europe's relapse, "about the middle of the next millennium", into a state of barbarism wherein inquisitions will "wipe out the
most talented and capable individuals". On that count he may have been
alarmingly prescient; and, as one reads this volume, what most impresses,
over and above Wagner's paranoia, is his formidable intelligence which
seems to have been at once conscious and intuitive. He surmounted the
herculean struggles of his youth because he was one of those rare beings
who, as Yeats puts it, feel deeply enough to *know* what the feelings are. Even
an apprentice work like *Die Hochzeit*, written when he was nineteen, lights
on his essential theme, for it is about a woman who kills a man because he
had threatened her honour and then, knowing she passionately loves him,
dies of grief by his grave. The first truly Wagnerian Hero, Rienzi, is
described by the composer in a letter of 1841, as "a visionary dreamer who
has appeared like a beacon of light among a depraved and degenerate
nation". That self-portrait doesn't in this early opera find an authentic
musical correlative, though something approaching one emerges in *The
Flying Dutchman*, wrung out of Wagner's story during the years 1839–41. He
too had been driven into exile, and from place to place; had been harried by
indefinable longings; and was recurrently on the point of being redeemed
by a woman prepared to sacrifice all for him. Other young men have had
similar experiences without feeling the need to elevate them into a programme of universal regeneration. But Wagner is explicit: "My course was
new", he announces, "it was hidden by my inner mood and forced on me by
the pressing need to impart this mood to others. In order to enfranchise
myself from within outwards, I was driven to strike out for myself a path
not pointed me by any outward experience".

Although the *Dutchman* still has contacts with traditional German
opera and is overtly indebted to Weber and even Meyerbeer, it is a new
music, informed by the punch and panache of Wagner's genius: which
becomes irresistible when he transmutes the Faustian motifs of the
Dutchman into more spiritualized concepts derived from medieval Germanic legends. Tannhäuser, like the Dutchman, is alone, fleeing from a
basely materialistic world. Again the "longed-for, dreamed of, utterly wom-
anly woman, the Woman of the Future" leads him from the sensual orgies
of Venusberg to paradisal purgation. Even at this early date we have a relatively crude statement of the inescapable link, in a humanistically rather
than religiously orientated society, between eroticism and renunciation. It
crops up more richly in *Lohengrin*, in whom Wagner becomes not only the
lonely hero in an alien world but also the god-messiah who, in being superhuman, is bound to be misunderstood. At face value *Lohengrin* is a silly
story about a pompous young man who refuses to tell his name to a girl

only too eager to love him. For Wagner, it was "the type of the only absolute tragedy, of the tragic element in modern life, and that of just as great significance for the Present as was Antigone for the life of the Hellenic state". Elsa is "the Unconscious, the Undeliberate, into which Lohengrin's conscious, deliberate being yearns to be redeemed. Through the capability of this 'unconscious consciousness' the nature of Woman came to ever clearer understanding in my mind." Woman is thus the arbiter of the future, 'unconsciously' liberating us from patriarchal law and will. Today, this feminism may even seem the most potent of Wagner's several prophetic strains, though one wonders how far the women in Wagner's life saw it in such terms. Certainly his indomitable will was modified by a deeply feminine streak, manifest even in his addiction to silks and satins.

The descent of the Grail in the Prelude to *Lohengrin* is the first consummate incarnation of the aspiration to godhead that became the lodestar of Wagner's life; it is also his first moment of transcendent orchestral virtuosity—a new sound for a new experience. Having achieved it, this extraordinary man relinquished composition for a period of six years: during which he wrote, in addition to those multitudinous letters, thousands of words in pamphlets that grew into tracts, tracts that evolved into books, books that were swollen to elephantine tomes. The purpose of these words was to explain Wagner to himself and us; but he was probably right in saying, years later, that the words were a rationalization of the unconscious processes whereby the music was already being created. Rationalization was necessary because of the unprecedented nature of Wagner's course: before the new world could be presented—made present—Wagner had to believe in himself to the exclusion of obsolete values like the eighteenth century's Reason, Truth and Nature. It was unreasonable to suppose that his emotional life was "the only modern tragedy". It was going rather far to maintain that his persecution and "sacrifice" could, like Christ's—the analogy is his—provide the theme for a ritualistic union of music, poetry and visual spectacle parallel to Greek religious drama, but in every aspect devised and controlled not by 'society', but by himself. It was not only unnatural but well-nigh lunatic to believe that because Wagner suffered from digestive troubles the "nobler nations" of Europe could be induced to adopt vegetarianism, and might even consider mass-migration to warmer climes where meat-eating would be less of a temptation. Yet even the lunacy is sublime.

When in youth Wagner wrote "We two, the world and I, are stubborn fellows at loggerheads, and naturally whichever has the thinner skull will get it broken", he was the heir to (symphonic) Beethoven. But one cannot imagine Beethoven saying, with the later Wagner (in a letter to Eliza Wille in 1864):

I'm not made like other people. I have finer nerves. I must have brilliance and beauty and light. The world owes me what I need. I cannot live on a miserable organist's post, like your master Bach. Mine is a highly susceptible, intense, voracious sensuality which must somehow or other be flattered if my mind is to accomplish the agonizing labour of calling a non-existent world into being.

Wagner meant this quite literally. The world owed him what he needed because the realization of his dream was synonymous with a future for the human race. And the miracle is that he brought it off; after turmoil and hardship that would have destroyed a 'mere' man, the Wagnerian myth became reality, if only through the agency of a young, immensely rich, possibly mad, king.

This archetypal world of the psyche was to be projected through the old Germanic sagas of the Nibelungen; and reading Wagner's letters as well as his polemical writings, we recognize how startlingly *aware* he was of the contemporary relevance—philosophical, psychological, sociological, and political—of the ancient legends. No wonder it was an "agonizing labour" to discover genuinely revolutionary musical and theatrical techniques to tell his story, while in the process offering regeneration for the despoiled human race. Brünnhilde is the White Dove, the troubadour's Eternal Beloved to be won or lost, and the light and dark forces that contend for her are inextricably tangled. This is why the villainous Hagen has no less uncanny presence than Wotan—Wagner as penitent sinner and scapegoat; and is why Siegfried—Wagner as knight-errant and dragon-slayer— becomes his own betrayer, as did Wagner in his life story. Reduced to despair by his frustrated attempts to get his vision theatrically produced, Wagner temporarily abandoned *The Ring*, somewhat more than halfway through. Turning from it, he created *Tristan*, his most directly autobiographical work; which marks the beginning of the end of the phase of consciousness that had evolved with the European Renaissance; and which is often referred to as the beginning of modern music.

Wagner took the Tristan theme not from the antiquity of the human race but from the theocratic Middle Ages, when the old Europe was dying and the modern world was in labour. After so many hundred years' burden of consciousness, aspiration, frustrated sexuality, guilt, and despair, Wagner starts from the weight of human passion: which proves too great to be borne. Harmonic chromaticism splinters into what he called a new polyphony, and ultimately seems to be seeking the monody of the old troubadours. At the beginning of the third act Tristan-Wagner has drunk the love-death potion and has failed to fulfil his passion in the conditions of the material world. Lying prone in his gangrened, cobwebby castle, he is (in our terminology) going through a nervous breakdown: from which he is awakened by the *monody* of a primitive Shepherd's pipe. The monody undulates between the god-like perfect fourths and fifths and the devilish imperfect fourths and fifths of the famous Tristan chord which, in the very first bars of the opera, has made Tristan's yearning aurally incarnate. It sounds at once Christian and pre-Christian; occidental and oriental. Simultaneously celebrating a light goddess and a dark, Tristan's animus, in Jungian terms, dies into life, leaving Isolde, his anima, to regenerate the fallen world.

Now, this experience Wagner was undergoing not only symbolically but physically, in the relationship currently existing between Mathilde and Otto Wesendonck and himself. Tristan (whose name makes him *triste*), Isolde and King Mark were real people, living through their *agon* here and now: at the same time they were archetypes in the Jungian collective unconscious, and therefore a part of us. Mathilde Wesendonck was undoubtedly the supreme love of Wagner's tempestuous erotic life. His letters to her and her husband are crucial, since they plumb to the heart of Wagner's equivocation between reality and dream. He knew that in *Tristan* he had made music unprecedented because transcendent. Writing to Mathilde in mid-April 1859, he babbled in near-incoherence:

This *Tristan* is turning into something *terrible*! This final act!!! . . . I fear the opera will be banned—unless the whole thing is parodied in a bad performance; only mediocre performances can save me! Perfectly good performances will drive people *mad*—I cannot imagine it otherwise—This is how far I have gone!! Oh dear!!!

Nor was he completely beside the mark. We know of the alarming psychological effects *Tristan* can have on an audience; several singers have been mentally unhinged by it; a few Tristans have died of their frenetic physical and emotional exertions. The violence of the effect must be in part attributable to the fact that these transcendent musical-theatrical events were so immediately triggered by the composer's relationship to a flesh and blood woman alive and (if the indelicacy be permitted) kicking in his arms; and hardly less out of his need to relinquish her to her also flesh and blood husband, who was Richard's patron and friend. We'll probably never know the exact truth of the matter. Wagner consistently maintained, at least in public contexts, that *this* fervent love, given the ideality of his aspiration, was never consummated. This is difficult to swallow from a man of Wagner's exceptionally demanding virility, and for that matter from Mathilde, on the evidence of her orgiastic outpourings to her beloved. There are passages in the letters that hardly make sense unless they imply sexual fulfilment, and it is generally accepted that the love music offers the most vivid simulation of copulation in any art. Even so it is just feasible that in this case Wagner told the unsober truth; that *this* dream was truer than truth itself. Mathilde was no ordinary woman, as was Jessie Laussot, Wagner's first serious (conveniently rich) extra-marital infidelity: not to mention the ships that passed in his years of exile and the nubilely adolescent housekeepers encouraged to have the house warm against his return ("I hope the pink drawers are ready too"). In comparison with such frolics Mathilde literally *embodied* Brünnhilde and Isolde. A yearning that fierce can be appeased only in its cessation, when love and death are identified in nirvana. Wagner's 'renunciation' of Mathilde thus acts out his 'philosophy', which turns out to be affiliated, by way of Schopenhauer, to Buddhism. Even so, he characteristically managed to have his cake and eat it by implying that Mathilde somehow betrayed him—as had Jessie Laussot, despicable because she eventually acceded to the 'sensible' advice of her husband and mother rather than lover.

As might be expected, a teetering between eroticism and renunciation pervades the heart of Wagner's technique: his chromatic sequences, obsessively repeated, aspire to movement (modulation), but recurrently subside to their source, to try again, usually a bit higher. If *Tristan* presents the apotheosis of the Wagnerian sequence, the device is scarcely less potent in his next-planned opera, which was to be the last to be completed. With his habitual awareness, Wagner knew that *Parsifal* was a sequel to *Tristan*, and in 1860 spelt the matter out in a brilliant letter to Mathilde—capped by an even vaster letter to the long-suffering Ludwig. The dark brother—the Hagen figure—is virtually abandoned or reduced, in Klingsor, to the level of a seaside-pier magician. But this does not mean that 'darkness' is inoperative, for the ambiguous figure of Kundry telescopes Isolde with Melot the betrayer. She is an Edenic serpent-siren, the carnality of whose kiss redeems Parsifal, the Holy Fool who, substituting for heroic Siegfried, pities "the wound of the world", Tristan's (probably sexual) wound having been transferred from Tristan to Amfortas, the Dying King. While this couldn't have happened outside a Christian heritage it is not necessarily a Christian theme, and Nietzsche, rounding on Wagner in reaction against his early idolatry, was unjust to denounce Wagner's 'hypocrisy'. It is rather that the burden of Tristan-Isolde's consciousness is released, along with the fervid chromaticism; and in the immensely slow exfoliation of harmonic polyphony, time, as Gurnemanz puts it, "is one with space". The slowness of the harmonic pulse in *Parsifal* may be an even more prophetic achievement than the chromaticism of *Tristan*. It is an ultimate relinquishment of the will's dominance, from which the principles of European opera—an imitation of human action—had painfully evolved. *Parsifal* uncovers a path through the Dark Forest which Debussy (in *Pelléas et Mélisande*) and

Schoenberg (in *Verklärte Nacht* and *Erwartung*) had to take. The degree to which Wagner *knew* what he had done seems incredible—until the letters reveal that for him art and life were not parallel but identical.

Just as *Tristan* and *Parsifal* carry us on their flood 'regardless', so these letters sweep us off our feet not merely by their phenomenal energy, but also by their affirmation of life and love. Wagner is, though self-obsessed, not self-regarding; he offers so much that we can understand why men and women gave him their all, notwithstanding the 'caddish' behaviour for which he could always find moral self-justification. The only acquaintance-friend-lover who was relatively impervious was his long-time wife Minna: a provincial girl who would have liked a settled income, a home and children, and didn't comprehend Richard's genius enough to consider it an adequate substitute. Yet he needed her for his home-comforts, tried not to be *crudely* brutal in his infidelities, and bumblingly attempted to care for her during the many years she lived, unsurprisingly in indefinable ill-health, not only apart but in another country. He wrote to her regularly and of course volu-minously, though she can hardly have relished his addressing her as "dear old", "poor old", or even "poor dear old Minna". Still, that is what she was in the context of his imaginative life, which was light-years away from her. He wasn't so much being condescending as viewing Minna's sufferings in terms that seemed to him appropriate—much as he wept at the sufferings of sick or maltreated beasts, which he thought more ghastly than human suffering precisely because animals are inarticulate, and cannot know what is hap-pening to them. Wagner's blessing and curse was that he indeed did know: *The Ring* must end with the gods' twilight, and man must have the courage of his illusion, as well as the illusion of his courage. In more than the obvious sense *Götterdammerung*, wherein 'consciousness' returns to ele-mental fire and water, is Wagner's most overwhelming work.

Götterdammerung, the fourth opera of the *Ring* cycle, and part of the third opera *Siegfried*, were completed before Wagner had fully composed *Parsifal*, though not before it was conceived. And *Parsifal*, the opus ultimum, was further delayed because, as an alleviation of *Tristan*'s anguish, Wagner returned to another project, *The Mastersingers*, first toyed with as early as 1845. Twenty years on, Wagner still intended it to be a comic opera, and in the Greek sense it is such. It takes place in a real city, medieval Nuremburg; it embraces many of the elements Wagner had jettisoned from conventional opera, for it contains, if not formal arias, at least a Prize Song, and is full of the 'togetherness' of jolly fugato and of dances of social soli-darity. Yet Wagner was right in insisting on the originality of his concept. For the heart of the music belies the everyday reality in which it seems to exist, and would do so even if Wagner hadn't told correspondents and the general public that the action really takes place in the minds of Walther and Sachs. Walther is Siegfried-Wagner the Artist-Hero, Sachs is Wotan-Wagner the Great Renunciator who loves and loses. The cantankerous contentions of the guilds and the rancorous tyrannies of academia are to be annealed by perfect love; and the eternal beloved is called Eva because she is Edenic and a mate for the New Adam. Like Elsa, that earlier Eve from *Lohengrin*, Eva is also the German Folk, so private myth becomes public, and personal regeneration racial. This is why *The Mastersingers* veers and tacks between naturalistic presentation, as in the discomfiture of Beckmesser, and dreamy extravaganza, as in the fertility rite for the German People at the end. Again, Wagner says quite explicitly, in a letter to Constantin Franz of 1864, that his relationship with Ludwig II would change the world; his art would be not only a "new religion", but a religion that implied new social and political formulation: "my artistic ideal stands or falls with the salvation of Germany. If this dream is to find fulfilment, Germany must attain to her preordained greatness". It is the more remarkable, therefore, that amid the junketings of *The Mastersingers*' third act, the true music of the New Age turns out to sound, in Walther's oration, as overripely chromatic as Tristan's dying fall, while Sachs's heart-rending monologue confesses that "all poetry is but the truth of dreams made manifest".

Intuitively, Wagner knew that his prescription for the solidarity of the blond Aryan race, hymned in the final chorus, was a cheat; after all, the Prize Song itself, like Elgar's 'Land of Hope and Glory', might be described, though not dismissed, as codswallop of genius. Certainly it has little in common with a Nazi triumph-march; the essence of Wagner's art, at least from *Tristan* onwards, gives primacy to the dreamer rather than to the man of practical affairs. By this time he saw himself as Hans Sachs, the divinely inspired poet who cobbled folks' shoes so that they might tread life's stoniest paths. Sachs was John the Baptist to Wagner's dream-world, of which Cosima von Bülow was patron saint. On becoming lovers, Richard and Cosima showed scant respect for the susceptibilities of her father Franz Liszt, to whom Wagner had owed so much, and even less for those of her husband, who was Richard's professional colleague and friend. But as usual other people played their allotted roles in Wagner's drama; von Bülow continued to conduct his operas, while Cosima, if not a *Grande Amoureuse* like Mathilde Wesendonck, was devoted to his emotional needs and a capable administrative assistant. She did not need to be swept off her feet and could, when necessary, be formidable: Richard's affair with Judith Gautier, the pretty young woman who fashioned his frills and furbelows, was abruptly nipped in the bud.

Most important of all Cosima, after Minna's death, married Wagner and gave him the son, of course christened Siegfried, about whose beauty, strength, intelligence, and virtue the doting father prattled tipsily to any correspondent who would listen, and perhaps to many who tossed the epistles into the trash-can. According to Richard, Siegfried was the living spit of the infant Jesus in the Sistine Madonna; he had a family portrait painted wherein Siegfried-Jesus is indulging in childish carpentry, while the adult members of the Holy Family smirk at his "witty and inspired remarks". One blenches to think what might have happened had Siegfried died young or taken to petty crime, for the son was Wagner's survival-kit in a world of strangers: the *only* human creature which could carry the flag into the New World which, given the illusory nature of human aspiration, can never *materialize.*

It may be significant that Wagner's charisma dissipates only when he is tackling problems of artistic materialization. I do not refer to his correspondence with performers, for in advising them how to approach the formidable because unprecedented problems his music presents them with he displays imaginative insight, sharp intelligence, hard-headed practicality, and surprising tact: as is evident in his correspondence with his favourite singer Franz Betz, and in his advice to Rudolf Freny as to how to negotiate the idiot high notes in the part of Beckmesser. He is meticulous too in his directions to producers, even proffering instructions as to the precise shade or dimensions required of Brünnhilde's horse—a beast hardly less hazardous than the Master himself! In such matters Wagner was a severe taskmaster whom no-one—well, hardly anyone—resented. The rub comes in the vast acres of his converse with the young king who was the fount of his material realization. Although sycophantic gush to patrons, especially royal patrons, was expected of artists in feudally derived societies, this doesn't render it less cringe-making from Wagner, who knew he was a god rather than a mere monarch. Again life and art are inextricable; at the time of *Parsifal* Ludwig is Wagner's "merciful Redeemer"; "thus may my gratitude mingle with my pain, that it may be dedicated to my reverend Lord as a tragic bloom from the garden of the Holy Grail, and thus may I perish at your feet in undying love". And this was at a time when Bayreuth was riven by political machinations even more squalid than those that had lacerated the youthful Wagner in commercial opera houses. One can take it once or twice, but not fifty or sixty times: though it seems that Ludwig could, for Wagner's justification must be that he won.

Still, one cannot imagine Beethoven penning these sickening letters, however deeply revelatory of aims and intentions some of them may be. And this may indicate why Wagner, though a superman, was in the last resort a lesser hero than Beethoven. Beethoven was, of course, a colossal egoist who could say, truly enough, that whereas 'they' thought that the destiny of Europe was being decided on the battlefields of Waterloo, it was really taking place in his mind. But he also said, of his own works, that "he who truly understands this music will be freed thereby from all the miseries of the world". He did not command us to *submit* to his willful will-lessness in order to be saved; he created artefacts which, if we have ears to hear, afford redemption. The difference, if subtle, is sublime.

MT, OCTOBER 1989

WHAT'S TO COME

Mina Miller, ed., *The Nielsen Companion*
(London: Faber & Faber, 1995)

ARL NIELSEN OWES HIS UNIQUE STATUS TO HIS BEING A MEMBER OF A relatively small, pervasively rural community (Denmark) that also has a long history and internationally sophisticated affiliations. This means that he is peculiarly sensitive to modern man's transitional position in time and place: he belongs to our post-renaissance attempt to master and even mould 'consciousness', while also being hazily aware that other, possibly 'preconscious', alternatives may be available, and are perhaps even essential to our survival. We honour him as a symphonist whose roots are local, topical, and agrarian; who is a direct heir to Beethoven; and who looks towards an unknown future.

Appropriately enough, this volume has a New World orientation, having been compiled by Mina Miller, an American musicologist who is also a pianist, and who, in accord with current fashion, has edited and recorded Nielsen's 'complete' works for her instrument. For this *Companion* she has commissioned essays from American, British and Danish musicologists, covering most, though not all, aspects of Nielsen's work, and has linked them with brief interludes of her own, establishing interconnections between the themes. Her choice of contributors is catholic, ranging from the formidably analytical to the quasi-biographical and even the impressionistic. Since her own interludial comments warn us of what to expect, we may chart our own way through Nielsen's Danishly civilised forest, or alternatively through his forest-inflected civilisation. Readers may find, as did I, that it's profitable to begin with the aspect of Nielsen's music that is most rudimentary yet also least known to us: his apparently simple songs for voice and piano, which surprisingly run to more than two hundred.

Nielsen himself had a way with words as well as with musical tones: his two small books, one on his childhood on the island of Funen, the other dealing, under the English title of *Living Music*, with his unpretentiously humane aesthetic, are small masterpieces. The autobiographical book is, even in English, both beautiful and moving, and is said to be even more so in its original Danish. Nielsen's childhood years seem to have been idyllic, and one cannot doubt that such bliss nurtured his courage in confronting, in maturity, our fall from grace to disgrace, and the perils endemic to experience. Tom Kristensen, Lewis Rowe II, and Jorgen Jensen write affectingly of Nielsen's formative years as revealed in his own writings. Especially interesting is his relationship to his father, a house-painter and country fiddler living in a community of farmers, school teachers and pastors. Denizens of an agrarian society who also enjoyed more than a modicum of 'educated' as well as ethnic culture, they played classical and romantic string quartets as well as, maybe in preference to, folk fiddle. It's not therefore surprising that although the adolescent Nielsen had the normal academic training available to a boy of exceptional talent, he found his earliest creative fulfilment in domestic parlour songs for voice and piano, the most directly 'functional' medium available to him. Anne-Marie Reynolds's survey of the early song collections proffers the unexpected information that more than half of Nielsen's total output is vocal, and directs us what to look and listen for in these early songs. They are already a hybrid music, for the Scandinavian and German poets Nielsen set were those favoured by Grieg and Delius: a fact that bears on their musical idiom, wherein romantic harmonies and textures are accommodated to vocal lines that are folkily polymodal, rather than academically diatonic, let alone chromatic. The often nostalgic late-19th-century romanticism of the verses is reflected in the illustrative immediacy of the piano parts, but is countered by the probably unconscious archaism of the vocal lines. Already, musical idiom is identified with the temperament of the embryonic man; and it's interesting that the later songs increasingly purge folk-like polymodality of sophisticated accretions. Although Reynolds's account of the songs doesn't offer enough musical illustration for us to find our bearings amid so much unfamiliar material, she sends us to the (now published) scores, and gives us the bonus of four beautifully printed songs, complete as to words and music.

The songs were mostly written in the 1890s, beginning collaterally with the First Symphony of 1892. While this symphony is in Brahmsian tradition, with a few Scandinavian inflections from the likes of Berwald, Svendsen and Nielsen's teacher Niels Gade, it further explores the evolutionary notion of symphonic form that Brahms inherited from Beethoven. Already in this first symphony Nielsen embraces tonality within symphonic evolution: for although the work begins in traditionally passionate and strenuous G minor, its goal is the potently resolutory subdominant of C major. David Fanning (a British contributor, one is pleased to note) impressively charts this process through the sequence of Nielsen's symphonies, but does not fail to indicate how progressive tonality is only one aspect of the motivic evolution first adumbrated by Beethoven.

A turning-point in Nielsen's creativity occurred with his Third Symphony, on which Mina Miller herself writes persuasively, being confirmed in her findings by Fanning's survey, and by Harald Krebs's retrospective comments on Robert Simpson's earlier account of Nielsen as symphonist, in the first book in English on this composer. The Third Symphony, written in 1910–11, may have been entitled *Sinfonia Espansiva* not merely in tribute to its optimistic expansiveness, but in reference too to its technique, whereby tonal, motivic and rhythmic permutations have become 'expansively' inseparable. Moreover, process can no longer be considered merely in the context of the Viennese classics from Haydn and Mozart to Beethoven, Schubert and Brahms. Relations between the private and the public dimensions of musical form are not absolutes but are, like life itself, always in permutation, so that there is no break between Beethoven's and Schubert's long-range approach to tonality and form and Wagner's still longer-ranged evolutions. Although the Nordic masters Sibelius and Nielsen (both born in 1865) affected to mistrust Wagner's egomania, it was inevitable that, once Wagner had revolutionised concepts of musical growth by 'interiorizing' them, his discoveries could be ignored by no composer who tackled large-scale instrumental structures. Whatever Sibelius thought he thought, there are passages in his Seventh (and last) Symphony, and still more in *Tapiola*, his final large-scale work, that *sound* irresistibly late Wagnerian; and although Nielsen's symphonic sounds seldom recall Wagner, he revered him only just this side of idolatry. If both Sibelius and Nielsen regarded with dubiety the quasi-Christian mysticism of *Parsifal*, they intuitively recognised that their Nature-worship also involved a mysticism to which they could not be immune.

In Nielsen's symphonies, however, mystery and transcendence usually remain humane: as becomes patent in his Fourth and Fifth Symphonies, now his most widely esteemed and frequently performed works. In these pieces Nielsen slimmed down and linearized his textures, probably in accord with his rediscovery of the interval *per se*. For him a second, third, fourth, fifth, sixth or seventh—not to mention the more ambiguous, chromatically inflected tritone—were 'signifiers', each with a human content potent enough to withstand whatever threats an inimical destiny might confront us with. Traditional symphonic form, with its first and second subject groups, its exposition, development, and recapitulation, is not totally effaced, but is rendered more humanely (psychologically) basic: so that the Fourth Symphony can be christened the 'Inextinguishable' because intervallic integrity becomes a life-force that survives the batterings of self-willed, because improvising, percussion. The magisterial Fifth Symphony is also, in the same spirit, inextinguishable; indeed it resists attacks no less, perhaps more, savage for being notated. David Fanning's account of both these symphonies convinces, though Mark Devoto's substantial piece on the first movement of the Fifth disappoints, since he 'illustrates' sundry aspects of Nielsen's technical procedures without placing them in the context of the work. Organic process—"one thing leads into another", as

Nielsen guilelessly put it—thus fails to emerge. Since Devoto has written superbly musical analyses of the work of Berg, one must perhaps attribute this relative failure to lack of empathy with an un-Berg-like composer. Even so, given Fanning and Krebs's surveys, we cannot complain that these two symphonies are scanted in this compilation; while its treatment of the Sixth (and last) of Nielsen's symphonies breaks, in Jonathan Kramer's essay on unity and disunity in the work, new ground, justifying its startling claim that Nielsen's Sixth Symphony, written in 1925, may be the first "post-modern" musical creation—at least if one discounts Beethoven as the too-long-dead white male he spiritually isn't.

Kramer's paper is the longest in the book because, although it wastes no words, it needs time and space to make its case. The work has always been found puzzling, for the title Nielsen gave it—*Sinfonia Semplice*—belies its nature. To friends and professional performers Nielsen gave several contradictory accounts: which Kramer's unjargonistic analysis proves to be *un*contradictory, since contradiction, given the music's intervallic and motivic integrity, is the paradoxical essence of its 'simplicity'. Both the open, innocent-seeming lines *and* the outbursts of savagely dissonant harmony and of polymetrical ambiguity coexist without apparent precedence and consequence. Thus the several frisky fugues are all aborted, each sequent fugue being shorter than its predecessor, so that fugal unity subverts its ostensible purpose. Similarly, tonal goals are inoperative, often teetering around G, Ab and F ; while the fourth movement is a crazily inconsequential variation set, embracing a daftly lovely waltz and a footlingly funny fanfare. Kramer finds these bemusements 'pessimistic', though that is surely too simple an account. To me, the recurrent veerings and tackings, frustrations and startlements suggest vulnerability yet also an oddly vernal promise whereby, although defined themes and tonal aims prove inoperative, life is generated from the very unpredictability; we admit that having no end, in terms of theme, metre and key, is the only end of which, at this moment in history, we have inescapable need.

This is an inconclusion that so very different an artist-philosopher as John Cage would have approved of; yet it also makes sense in Nielsen's terms if we remember that the very first musical postmodernist was Beethoven himself, in a work like the A minor String Quartet opus 132. In this extraordinary piece things not only happen that did not have to happen, but which are indeed the opposite of what might have been predicted. No wonder Beethoven's late quartets puzzled his contemporaries, potently animated by aspirations and resolutions. This is not to say that Nielsen's Sixth Symphony is a rival to Beethoven's late quartets, only that the fact that it belongs in the same extremely rare category hints that it may be possibly the greatest, probably the most remarkable, and certainly the most enigmatically prophetic of Nielsen's works. That's how it seems to me, after I've read twice and hopefully digested Kramer's analysis, and have relistened to Nielsen's symphony three magical times.

The only Nielsen work that may be said to carry on from the Sixth Symphony is the Clarinet Concerto of 1928, his last substantial work. Cecil Ben Arnold writes of this piece—along with the earlyish Violin Concerto and the radiant Flute Concerto of 1925—in a manner so chart-ridden and 'preordained' that it fails to do justice to the diminishing twilights and burgeoning dawns that are the music's essence. Still more rebarbative is Richard S. Parks's vast Schenkerian analysis of 'Pitch structure in Nielsen's Wind Quintet', before which this old and perhaps old-fashioned but certainly not pre-Schenkerian reviewer can but quail. Parks admits that some of the work is not susceptible to this kind of analysis; but his editor, presumably knowing what to expect, commissioned the piece, so no doubt she and a few other hardy spirits find it helpful. I'd have welcomed, instead, a sizeable essay from the editor Mina Miller on the piano works, which she could approach with the scholarly knowledge of an editor and the imaginative percipience of a performer. Still, one shouldn't complain of what a book *might* have contained; this one is cherishable for the central analytical papers of Jonathan Kramer, David Fanning and Anne-Marie Reynolds; for the quasi-biographical material discussed by Tom Kristensen, Lewis Rowell and Jorgen Jensen; and for the appendix of Nielsen letters, well selected and newly translated by Alan Swanson.

Finally we owe a special debt to two Englishmen. Although Robert Layton's considerable critical gifts are not fully extended by his documentation of LP and CD recordings of Nielsen's music, there is no denying his chapter's usefulness. Robert Simpson contributes a 'personal view' the more valuable because it comes from the author of the best book on Nielsen in English, who is also a fine post-Beethoven, post-Nielsen, if hardly postmodern, composer of symphonies and string quartets. Looking back on the music sixty years after Nielsen's death, and after having himself attained his biblically allotted three score years and ten, Simpson's tribute is peculiarly moving, as he reflects on the "inexhaustible" strength of Nielsen's renewals whilst our desperate century totters (whereas Nielsen's Sixth Symphony floats) to its probably desperate but still inconclusive end.

MT, JANUARY 1996

HO, HO, HO

Constant Lambert: Concerto for piano and nine instruments; Piano Sonata;
Eight Poems of Li-Po; Mr Bear Squash-you-all-flat.
Nash Ensemble/Lionel Friend, Ian Brown (piano), Philip Langridge (tenor), Nigel
Hawthorne (narrator). Hyperion CDA 66754.

CONSTANT LAMBERT FIRST ATTRACTED ATTENTION IN THE LATE 1920S, along with Walton and Bliss. He thus grew up during the heyday of what came to be called the English Musical Renaissance, though his connections with it were oblique. Indeed he is not unambiguously a British composer, for his father was born in St Petersburg and spent his early years in Australia and Paris, where he functioned as a reasonably successful visual artist and as father of a 'Bohemian', Augustus John-style family of considerable liveliness. Constant himself was so intellectually precocious and so variously talented that it was a toss-up which art he would opt for. At the age of seventeen, however, he entered the Royal College of Music where he admired, among his teachers, Vaughan Williams and R. O. Morris, while being slightly contemptuous of George Dyson, whom he considered the representative academician. Typically, Vaughan Williams, though of very different background and interests, saw what Lambert needed and introduced him to E. J. Dent, then chairman of the International Society for Contemporary Music. With Dent's encouragement, Constant acquired an enthusiasm for (especially) Stravinsky, Satie, Ravel, Poulenc, and Milhaud that remained vivaciously constant throughout his career. When he was a mere nineteen he was offered, on a silver spoon, a ballet commission from the great Diaghilev, so that he started as a European rather than insular composer. Although his first two ballets (*Romeo and Juliet* and *Pomona*) are musically insubstantial, being Frenchified dance music lightly tinged with white-note Stravinsky and the eupepticism of Les Six, they pointed in what was, for him, the right direction. And Parisian polish was soon fleshed out with awareness of English musical traditions of the sixteenth and seventeenth centuries, imbibed from that great teacher (and good minor composer) R. O. Morris; and still more with the impact of Black jazz, which infiltrated Paris during the 1920s. Lambert responded with a readiness unusual among English musicians of the time, and arrived at an idiom more personal, and more topical and local, than might have been expected from his juvenile sophistications.

The Rio Grande, his choral and orchestral piece with solo piano, to an exotically evocative poem by the very twenty-ish Sitwell, was written at the age of twenty-two, became an instant success, and remains one of the most durable cross-over pieces in the repertory. Still frequently performed (it is a Proms favourite), it fuses dazzling jazz pianism (reflecting the authentically 'great', early Black jazz pianists) with an acute ear for choral and orchestral sonorities, and also with a profound sense of the passion of the blues. What has kept this artfully entertaining and entertainingly artful piece vernal is its plethora of haunting tunes, allied with a harmonic 'flow' such as Delius claimed to have "picked up from the darkies in Florida", as they improvised choral polyphony while the sun declined. In its hybrid state between art music and pop music, *The Rio Grande* has much in common with Gershwin's *Rhapsody in Blue* and Piano Concerto, works which Lambert, in his brilliantly written, dazzlingly clever, and often very funny if sometimes wrong-headed book, *Music Ho!* (1934), affected to despise.

The success of *The Rio Grande*, though later deprecated by its composer, released a small flood of creation; all the music by which Lambert is likely to be remembered was composed between his twentieth and thirtieth years. The pieces on this CD are admirably representative, and are superbly performed by the ever-reliable Nash Ensemble under the direction of Lionel Friend. Although I have known Lambert's music more or less from the days in which it appeared, I'd forgotten how original a composer he is, over and above his documentary and topical interest. No less than Walton, and considerably more than Bliss, he now seems a significant part of the then evolving tradition of 'new' English music, unprovincially aware of European and American affiliations. Two of the works on this disc stem from the jazz-art legacy of *The Rio Grande*, discovering in it unexpected startlements and darker depths. The Piano Sonata, written in Lambert's twenty-fourth year, has all the jazzy glitter of the earlier piece, but the first movement skates more dangerously through its rumboid and tangoid cross-rhythms, is harmonically more astringent, and is texturally even more effervescent. The second movement, a nocturne combining a blues with a skittery scherzo, exploits the passionate potential of false-related blue notes and of percussive acciacaturas. It gets closer to the heart of jazz than any piece by a 'straight' composer, even including Milhaud's *La Création du Monde*, which, though justifiably admired by Lambert, is artful in sophistication and elegiacism as compared with Lambert's urban, if also urbane, toughness. The sonata's finale justifies its rather grand gestures, being in the manner of white-note Stravinsky, yet patently and potently Anglo-American, redolent of big, dusty cities (during these years Constant often escaped to southern French sea-ports, lest he lose the common touch; the sonata he composed in Toulon, the concerto in Marseilles).

Impressive as is the Piano Sonata, the Concerto for piano and nine instruments represents a remarkable advance, achieved over a mere year, between 1924 and 1925. The overture, in toccata style with superbly laid out interludial cadenzas, recalls the pianism of *The Rio Grande*, albeit in denser and darker, though not less ebullient, vein. The 'Intermède' again telescopes a slowish movement, this time in wistfully pastoral woodwindy style, with a chittery-jittery scherzo; while the finale, marked *lugubre*, reveals painful disturbances beneath a funereal procession. The blue-black element in this music proves to be far more than homage to an ephemeral fashion; as early as 1929 Lambert anticipates the general, tragic import that, thirty or forty years later, Michael Tippett—born in the same year as Lambert, 1905—would discover in the blues. Arguably this concerto is Lambert's finest work and—tellingly though it is scored for its nine players—one slightly regrets that it wasn't given a more orthodox concerto set-up so that it could have secured more frequent performance. At least this recorded performance makes restitution, for Ian Brown is responsive to every excitation and subtlety, and the accompanying instrumentalists, especially David Corkhill and John Wallace on jazzy percussion and trumpet, reinforce the soloist's electricity.

Significantly, the concerto was dedicated to the memory of Peter Warlock, the composer, 'early music' scholar, and amateur wizard who mesmerized an entire generation of English composers, driving them, according to some reports, to "dissipation and despair". There can be no doubt as to the cataclysmic effect of Warlock's suicide, at the age of thirty-six, on Lambert who, according to Giles Easterbrook's liner notes, incorporated into his score—along with grimly parodistic references to his own *Rio Grande*—quotations from Warlock's masterpiece *The Curlew*, and from two magical late pieces, the choral *Corpus Christi Carol* and the bleak Bruce Blunt song 'The frostbound wood'. Although these quotations seem to me heavily disguised, they ought to be there, and no doubt are. Certainly the influence of Warlock is overt in the *Eight Poems of Li-Po* for tenor, flute, oboe, clarinet, and string quintet composed between 1926 and 1929. Chinese poetry in translation was fashionable in the 20s perhaps because its 'detachment' suited the mood of the post-war years, which mistrusted heroics. Lambert knew Warlock's settings of Chinese poems in his *Saudades* cycle, written very much 'under the influence'—to use an appropriately druggy metaphor—of van Dieren. Arthur Bliss, a friend of both Lambert and van Dieren, also produced some van Dieren-afflicted Chinese songs, of considerable charm, but without the aphoristic concision of Lambert's numbers, deliciously scored and as discreet in rhythm as the piano-dominated works are metrically complex and abrasive. At this date Lambert's verbally inflected vocal lines sound as English as Peter Warlock, or even as the late Fredegond Shove songs of Vaughan Williams himself. In this performance the instrumental ensemble is as suave as, in the jazzy pieces, it is sharply meticulous. Philip Langridge sings with his habitual musicality, though he would have profited from slightly more forward projection from the engineers.

In his thirtieth year Lambert wrote his largest work, *Summer's Last Will and Testament*, to magnificent verses of Elizabethan Thomas Nashe. This has some claim to be considered his greatest as well as biggest work, since its final setting of Nashe's threnody 'Adieu, farewell earth's bliss' transforms its remorselessly swaying sarabande into a triple-rhythmed funeral march that attains tragic grandeur. The poet's vision of plague-haunted Elizabethan London is nightmarishly metamorphosed into the twentieth century's manic-depressive post- and pre-wars London scene, involving too Lambert's own traumas. Although at its end *Summer's Last Will and Testament* becomes great music, it is perhaps less consistently inspired than the Piano Concerto, the inner grandeur of which belies its (surprisingly undated) surface.

After *Summer's Last Will* Lambert composed little music, partly because his health, undermined in childhood, was increasingly affected by his advancing alcoholism—which was itself in part occasioned by a residue of physical pain consequent on juvenile operations. Even so, the reasons for his creative decline had positive aspects, for his burgeoning career as a conductor—who did more than anyone to advance the cause of new British music—became a full-time job. Moreover, it involved his creation, musically almost single-handed, of English ballet, which produced among many good dance works for theatre an indubitable masterpiece in Vaughan Williams's *Job*. By all accounts Lambert was a superb conductor of ballet, which is hardly surprising since his rhythmic sense was so rich and ripe, at once Purcellian and Ellingtonian! Oddly enough, his own ballets are not among his most musically distinguished works, though *Horoscope*, written in 1937 for Margot Fonteyn, when the brilliant couple were lovers, expertly fuses *Rio Grande*-like jazziness with romantic-classical modes from the greatest of all dance composers, Tchaikovsky. Even so, this is music effectively concocted for theatrical use: whereas the Piano Concerto, the Piano Sonata and possibly the Li-Po songs define the identify of an exceptionally talented man, and of a generation of British musical life.

The remaining piece on this CD, *Mr Bear Squash-you-all-flat*, is a caper executed in Lambert's seventeenth year, which the composer did not publish and which hasn't been publicly performed. Its interest lies in its revealing, at so early an age, prescience and self-knowledge. Its relation to Russian fairy tales is a central orientation of Lambert's life, and his sharp ear is already operative. But the twenty minutes the piece occupies tend to dilute the impact of this remarkable and rewarding disc. Let us hope that the presence of Nigel Hawthorne as narrator successfully boosts sales, as is no doubt intended.

MT, JUNE 1995

PART FIVE

AMERICANA

The youth of America is their oldest tradition.
It has been going on now for three hundred years.
OSCAR WILDE, *A WOMAN OF NO IMPORTANCE*

America . . . where all the races of Europe are melting and reforming.
ISRAEL ZANGWILL, *THE MELTING POT*

Good Americans, when they die, go to Paris.
OLIVER WENDELL HOLMES, *THE AUTOCRAT OF THE BREAKFAST-TABLE*

Introduction

T HE AMERICAN DREAM' IS A WELL-ESTABLISHED POLITICAL CLICHÉ THAT can be traced back with certainty to the early nineteenth century, and is probably older. It evokes images of hard-working, fair-minded and prosperous citizens: it also suggests a characteristic open-mindedness, a welcome for both new people and new ideas, and a willingness to try anything. John Updike wryly suggests that "Americans have been conditioned to respect newness, whatever it costs them", and certainly we can observe a pioneering spirit and the driving forces of adventure in the works of composers such as Ives, Copland, Gershwin, Virgil Thomson, Lou Harrison and John Adams.

Wilfrid Mellers was the first British composer and musicologist to write extensively on the development of specifically American music in both its 'concert' and 'popular' genres. His *Music in a New Found Land* appeared in 1964, and was, in part at least, a product of his having been Visiting Andrew Mellon Professor of Music in the University of Pittsburgh, though his interest in jazz—a most important element of the book—goes back many years. His continuing enthusiasm for 'themes and developments in the history of American music' is evident in the articles that make up this final part of the book. As always, his commentary ranges widely: from the composers mentioned above, and others like them, to the strikingly individual qualities of Black American music—blues and ragtime, 'crossover' styles, the 'escape art' of the Broadway Musical, and the eccentricities of the 'Wilderness' composers, Harry Partch, and Paul Bowles, "detached from history" and uncompromising in their commitment to ideals. This is music of exceptional variety created by composers whose acceptance of what music is and what it might become displays, as often as not, a dramatic 'otherness' in its echoes of, and artistic independence from, Europe.

JP

LYRICS OF DEPRIVATION

Bruce Jackson, ed., *Wake Up Dead Man: Afro-American Worksongs from Texas Prisons.*
(Cambridge, Mass.: Harvard University Press, 1972)

THEL SMYTH, EDWARDIAN COMPOSER AND PROPHETESS OF FEMALE
emancipation, when asked what most impressed her about a spell in
jail on behalf of the Cause, tersely replied: "couldn't get out". That is
how it seems to most of us, in our relatively affluent, relatively free society;
we grow easily oblivious of the sense in which the world itself may be a
compound of many prisons, Hamlet's Denmark—or wherever—being one
of the worst.

The Black man in the United States, however, in his non-affluence and
un-freedom, has never been able to forget the world as prison: so the songs
he has made while incarcerated differ not at all in kind, nor much in degree,
from the songs he has created in the world outside. Both inside and outside
he has started from the rock-bottom reality of his physical body—the husk
that fetters his spirit—and of his voice through which, independent of
material circumstances, he may attempt communion with his fellow creatures. Inside and outside, he has sung of deprivation, of oppression, of
alienation, of persecution, of the fortitude and resilience that (just) keep
him going. Inside, of course, his instinctual belly-laugh is harder to come
by: he is more brutally aware of the alienation of Us and Them; and his
sense of deprivation is more acute, since it covers the basic hunger of sex,
the one positive satisfaction that 'unaccommodated man' might hope to be
left with. In such conditions, however, resilience and fortitude seem the
more impressive: so that one might almost claim that the Negro's prison
songs are the heart of his instinctual art. Certainly they are 'music of necessity'—to use the phrase helpfully applied to the creations of oral cultures—
in a peculiarly uncompromising sense. They are functional in that they
assist the rhythms of work; simultaneously they effect an emotional
catharsis that makes oppressive labour bearable.

Bruce Jackson teaches English at the State University at Buffalo, and is
interested in African-American prison songs as human documents rather
than as art. Yet he is justified in pointing out that this distinction is invalid,
and his book is as important for professional musicians as it is for social historians. Indeed both musicians and historians are human beings before they
are representatives of a profession; and it is difficult to imagine that anyone
concerned about the human spirit *in extremis* could be unmoved by *Wake
Up Dead Man.* Essentially, it is an anthology of songs, prefaced by material
that sets the songs in context. Mr Jackson spent many months living in

Texan prisons, getting to know both jail-birds and jailers; he describes this experience in a prose that is sober, tough, and unaffectedly compassionate: which qualities may explain why he was able to establish so rewarding a relationship with the 'inmates'. They too appear in interview, reminiscing; and the prose they speak has a rhythmic sonority comparable with that of the songs they fashion from their agonizing if exiguous experience.

These songs are worksongs, not songs about work. They exist—sung or shouted by a leader who is usually a penetrative tenor and answered in choric homophony or heterophony by the others—to stimulate physical activity; at the same time they discharge emotional pressure because they refer to specific human predicaments, introducing local characters and topical events. Prison guards apparently tolerate in song much that they would ferociously censor in spoken conversation; the deeper reality of art, being distanced, seems to them unreal and therefore sanctionable play. Presumably this is also why the convict is permitted to indulge in songs that have no functional purpose, but simply and profoundly offer emotional release. Prison moans and hollers may then become almost indistinguishable from, and hardly aesthetically inferior to, the blues.

It is interesting that, while the staple musical fare is the functional worksongs that are traditional but perpetually modified by local conditions, all the more talented leaders evolve personal songs that—like the dream-songs of many primitive peoples—become synonymous with the singer's threatened identity. His own song is his soul, which will remain inviolate: though the originally extemporized words will be transformed through the years as the singer's circumstances—usually dependent on the 'Captains' within and the women without the gates—almost imperceptibly change; and though the basic melody will be subtly metamorphosed and intensified by ornamentation that is misnamed as such, since the ornaments are precise manifestations of particularized passion, whether they are melodic arabesques melismatically extending a syllable, or elisions of rhythm or distortions of pitch springing from the communicable word or from prearticulate grief. What is created, from the improvised half-rhymes and assonances of the verse and from primeval melodic contours and rhythmic shapes that betray their African origins, is 'corporeal' music—to use the phrase coined by the American aboriginal composer, Harry Partch.*

A sigh or a cry, a moan or a groan, even a titter or a jitter, becomes a lyrical consummation; and the songs that seem most free often turn out to be those that are most tightly if intuitively disciplined. Mr Jackson does not attempt analytic commentary on the ways in which the monodic songs of a powerfully imaginative folk-artist, such as J. B. Smith, function; nor for the most part do professional music critics and folk-music experts. In this book he does, however, provide evidence which—especially if used in conjunction with the recorded sound—might serve as a basis for such commentary. One is therefore grateful that the transcription of the songs has been made by two musicians, Judith McCulloh and Norman Cazden, who are sensitive and conscientious enough to notate the near un-notatable; one's only criticism being that in the freer pieces there is some ambiguity about accidentals, other than that inherent in the singing. Other documentation is irreproachable; there is an excellent discography and bibliography; information about Mr Jackson's own tapes (which ought to be issued on commercially available discs); and a magnificent series of photographs.

These last are not merely intrinsically valuable; they also help us to understand how on the mark Mr Jackson is in reminding us that this semi-improvised verse and music is not something to be inspected on paper, nor even listened to on disc; it is to be fully experienced only in the context of the life or partial life from which it came, with the 'aural landscape' of cane-cutting or flat-weeding and the amorphous noises of man, bird, beast, and nature as part of the music. The great Charles Ives has made us aware of the relevance to the art-composer of such an attitude; this book should help it to percolate down to more pedagogic types. The version of 'Captain don't feel sorry for a longtime man', here reproduced complete, may seem minimal in melodic invention as compared with the glories of Western art music; clearly, however, it must have been a shattering experience as sung by Marshall Phillips as leader, with Theo Mitchell extemporizing on the Lord's Prayer as the choric antiphony begins impulsively to swing and sway. It is to the credit of the transcriber that the notation of microtonal blue notes and of overlapping entries enables one, however distantly, to recreate this experience.

Given the conditions that produced it, we can hardly wish to share in such potent musical activity other than vicariously, in the mind's ear or on tape; nor can we honestly deplore the fact that Black prison songs are a declining tradition. They are disappearing because they are no longer needed, since labour is less arduous because more mechanized; moreover prison conditions—especially, if surprisingly, in Texas—are inevitably if slowly growing less savage as the Black man's image as murderous outlaw is eroded by his still equivocal emancipation. Yet in no foreseeable future is the pain the Black man sang of or the resilience he embodied likely to be humanly incomprehensible. The paradox of American civilization is once more evident, since her industrial technocracy is responsible for most of the monstrous inhumanities of which the Black man sings, yet only the United States could have produced this splendid book, at once innocent in its passionate concern and sophisticated in its disinterested scholarship. It restores one's teetering faith in the dignity of man, whether that man be an average law-abiding white editor-author or a law-flouting Black man who is also an American citizen—no longer log-cabined, but cribbed, confined, if not quite coffined.

TLS, JULY 1973

THE RICHES OF THE EARLY RAGS

Vera Brodsky Lawrence, ed., *The Collected Works of Scott Joplin. Volume I: Works for the Piano, Volume II Works for Voice* (New York: New York Public Library, 1971)

THE ORIGINAL BLACK AMERICAN MUSIC WAS THE COUNTRY BLUES: wherein 'primitive' melodic modalities, folk techniques of pitch distortion, and rhythmic energies and dislocations inherited from the African "beauty of his wild forebears" came into contact and conflict with the metrical and harmonic prison of the White American march and hymn. The instrument used to accompany these vocal laments was the guitar which, while being chordally harmonic, lent itself readily to quasi-vocal techniques through its flexible intonation. When, in the shanty towns and lumber camps, the guitar began to give place to the harmonic and equal-tempered piano, the tension between Black African and White American impulses was inevitably intensified. Primitive piano blues tended to become fast and aggressive. The cross-accents between springing melody and boogie bass in barrelhouse piano style are a desperate assertion of sexuality—the *only* positive assertion the poor Black could hope for: while the rapidly pounding beat measures off time and space as furiously as the great American steam-locos that the pieces frequently celebrate.

Barrelhouse piano was a music of dispossession, a low-life urban folk art created in and for a low-life society. Yet by the first decade of the twentieth century a different if complementary tradition was developing: for the Black population wished to create its own 'art' music, capable of holding its own with, even of triumphing over, the entertainment music of the White man. This music came to be called ragtime; and the ragging was what the Black man did to his White material. Basically, rags are marches (usually with four sixteen-bar themes, sometimes with rondo-like recapitulations) of the type grandly epitomized in the work of Sousa; but they also absorb elements from directly European sources—French quadrille and valse, Spanish tango and habanera, Italian opera, English ballad, and music-hall minstrel song. Of course, barrelhouse piano and piano rag overlap. Rag composers usually started as barrelhouse pianists in the red-light districts, while barrelhouse piano thumpers used published rags as material for improvisation. The great Jelly Roll Morton was a literate composer of rags, drawing material from the European operas and social entertainment music that flourished in New Orleans; he was also one of the supreme masters of jazz improvisation.

None the less, the difference in approach between the instinctive blues and barrelhouse piano player and the composer-pianist who created rags is crucial; and it is significant that the most justly celebrated of rag composers, Scott Joplin (1868–1917), started his career when a boy of fourteen as a bordello pianist, but achieved fame and fortune through co-operation with a White, small-time music publisher who prospered in an environment pervaded by the gospel of free enterprise and Methodist Nonconformity. Joplin's equivocal success-story started, appropriately enough, at the turn of the century, in 1899, when he published *Maple Leaf Rag*. In its sheet-music form the piece created a furore only comparable—given the then inadequate means of publicity and mechanical dissemination—with that created by an early Beatles number; and it still sells today. Perhaps its success depends on its emotional ambiguity. Superficially, it incarnates the eupeptic optimism of the American march in two-step rhythm, and its regular sixteen-bar strains, based on the cornerstones of tonic, dominant, and subdominant, assert stability. Both the age-old melancholy of the vocal-guitar blues and the frenzy of barrelhouse piano are banished in favour of deadpan jauntiness. At the same time, however, this simple bonhomie is modified by the habitual syncopation—the Black body-rhythm, flexed against the pulse of Time, displacing metrical symmetry; by the occasional chromatic passing notes that may derive from the plantation singers' talent for ad hoc choral harmonization; and even by the dandified elegance of the keyboard figuration.

We may recall that the African American (as distinct from the White American) source of ragtime was the cakewalk, a grotesque prancing dance wherein the Black slaves had competed, in parodistic imitation of their White masters, for a prize of a cake. Something of this satirical flavour survives in Joplin's rags; and one is not sure whether it is parody of the white man, of the white man's image of the black, or of the African Americans themselves. In any case, the ambiguity imbues the music's merriment with an undercurrent of wistfulness; and it may well have been this that conquered black and white public alike. Through his rags the Black man yearned for the White man's presumably civilized sophistication: while the White man yearned for an Edenic innocence which, in his world-weariness, he only affected to despise.

Although *Maple Leaf* is a prototype from which Joplin did not radically depart, it would be untrue to suggest that his art is without development. He received conventional training from a (German) music teacher in his boyhood Texarkana, acquired a fairly wide knowledge of European operatic scores, studied counterpoint on his own initiative, and worked assiduously at his self-imposed task of creating a literate African American art-music. He used the techniques he acquired not to modify the basic convention, but to realize its limited emotional implications with deeper subtlety. This is evident even if one compares *Maple Leaf* with *The Entertainer*, a ragtime two-step composed only three years later. In this delightful piece the lingering syncopations on the upward leaping sixth and the chromatic oscillations between F major and minor generate a wide-eyed pathos as well as wistfulness. Five or six years later the richer textures of *Gladiolus Rag* or *Wall Street Rag* create a touching equilibrium between passion and tenderness: the cross rhythms and harmonic ambiguities lend a precarious vulnerability to the elegance, which is the mask the Black man—not to mention ourselves—presents to the world. A few pieces outside the rag convention—notably the tango, *Solace*, with its darkly sumptuous trio, and the concert-waltz, *Bethena*, with its surprising of naive modulatory capers—encouraged Joplin's attempts to intensify the ragtime form, and so led to the rags of the last few years; notably, in 1909, *Euphonic Sounds* (remarkable for its elliptical modulations in the second strain, and for the stop-time syncopations in which the beat is merely implicit); and, in 1914, *Magnetic Rag* (distinguished by its resonant disposition on the keyboard, its ripe appoggiaturas, its intensification through complex rhythms with a Spanish flavour, and even by a hint of sonata-like development in the third and fourth strains).

It would be going too far to compare these late rags, as artistic transmutations of popular dance forms, with the mazurkas of Chopin, for the legacy Joplin had to draw on, both in its sophisticated and its popular manifestations, was relatively crude. But in his preface to *The Collected works of Scott Joplin*, Rudi Blesch, the most knowledgeable authority on ragtime, hits the mark in implying that these beautifully written pieces are a more imaginative and moving testimony to the American spirit than ninety per cent of the portentously Teutonic music written contemporaneously by American 'art' composers; and it is both fitting and touching that at last, fifty-five years after his death, Joplin should have been awarded the accolade he longed for. His collected works are now published in the American Collection Music Series by the New York Public Library; and, although the collection is not quite complete (the copyright owner of three rags refused to release them, and the score of Joplin's first opera has defied attempts to unearth it), we are offered two substantial volumes, with index, dates of copyright, rollography and discography, and some illustrative material.

The first volume consists of piano music, clearly reprinted in photostat from the original editions, with the original covers charmingly inserted, though without a list of minor variant readings. The second volume contains the opera *Treemonisha*, for which Joplin wrote his own libretto, and on which he laboured obsessively during his later years, believing that it was his and the Black Americans' mission to graduate from rags to High Art.

Indeed, the literary theme concerns education and emancipation from error and superstition; not surprisingly, however, the qualities in the music that fascinate are those that relate to a 'primitive' Black past rather than to the White school or opera hose. Whatever Joplin's intentions, the piece is a play in music rather than an opera, for there is little recitative or arioso. The dances, however, incorporate some of Joplin's most gracefully seductive rags, notably the 'Real Slow Drag' to conclude; while the choral numbers draw on Joplin's recollections of spirituals, plantation songs, and even (in the 'Confusion' scene) on racial memories of African antiphony. (The notation of the vocal yells surprisingly if naively anticipates notational devices in the music of today's avant-garde!) Back-country animism appears in comic numbers like 'The Frolic of the Bears' and 'Wasp Nest'; sometimes (for instance, in the aria "I want to see my child") there is an authentic whiff of the blues.

Joplin published the vocal score of *Treemonisha*, here duplicated, at his own expense. After interminable delays and difficulties it was inadequately produced, without orchestra or scenery—and was a total failure. By this failure he was finally broken, and died young, in a lunatic asylum, his condition being in part syphilitic but also a consequence of the pressures a Black composer was inevitably submitted to in a White world. The best of his rags remain as a durable an unpretentious monument to his genuine achievement; and, if *Treemonisha* was a misguided enterprise, there's enough talent and imagination in it to suggest that, given the right encouragement, he might have made a significant contribution to that indigenous America form, musical comedy. Perhaps he might even have created a Black complement to *Porgy and Bess*, that great piece of musical theatre in which Gershwin, the White American Jew, reveals the parallel between his own (affluent) alienation and that of the African American (who had plenty of nothing except nothin'). According to Rudi Blesch's admirable introductory essay, *Treemonisha* is to be given its first proper performance later this year.

TLS, JUNE 1972

CHOPIN OF THE CREOLES

THE POPULARITY AND EXTRAORDINARY MUSICAL GIFT
OF LOUIS-MOREAU GOTTSCHALK

S. Frederick Starr, *Bamboula! The Life and Times of Louis-Moreau Gottschalk*
(Oxford: Oxford University Press, 1995)

A MERICANS ARE THE LAST 'FIRST' PEOPLE; THE RAWNESS OF THE AMERICAN scene in the early nineteenth century, combined with the rapidity and rapacity of the industrialization of the United States, meant that barriers between aristocratic art and democratic entertainment were hazily defined. Musical character and quality stabilized when the poles of European artistic tradition and American commercial enterprise fused and ignited: as they did with conspicuous flair in the person and work of Louis-Moreau Gottschalk. Intrinsically, Gottschalk is a good if not 'great' composer whose technical abilities were precisely matched to his experiential needs; historically, he is the earliest of the hybrid artists we now call 'crossovers'. On both counts, his life and work deserve investigation more committed than that he has so far received. Frederick Starr's fat book, thoroughly researched, documented and annotated, leaves few stones unturned, and is judiciously balanced between the life-enhancing Work and the brief but colourful Life.

Gottschalk's ancestry was polyethnic, for he was born in 1829, in New Orleans, a romantic Southern city affiliated to European France, Spain and Italy, with mercantile connections with Germany and England, and with an indigenous Black slave population outnumbering the whites by ten to one. He was the son of an intermittently affluent English stockbroker of German-Jewish descent, and of a beautiful young quadroon whose family migrated to Louisiana from rebellious Saint-Domingue, in the West Indies. He was blessed with being, as a pianist, a child prodigy, ripe for stimulation by the city of his birth which, in Starr's words, offered "the most stunning manifestation of Jacksonian democracy in the realm of culture to be found anywhere in America". Starr is slightly heavy-footed in niggling over just when and where the boy Gottschalk might have heard this or the other type of New Orleans music; but he gives a fascinating picture of the musical city where—given its wealth and European affiliations—opera was fostered with a fervour oblivious of class distinctions, and where each polyethnic stratum of society relished its own 'music of necessity'. White party-musics of all ilks flourished; and some may think that African American slaves made the finest music of all, sowing the seeds of the New Orleans jazz explosion. In any case, the boy Gottschalk, open-eared and open-eyed, responded electrically to this gallimaufry of aural stimuli. His mother, with pretensions to nobility, regaled him with the politer musical frivolities; his

Black nurse Sally crooned her haunting ditties to him; his brothers and sisters vamped hits of the day and yesterday, of ethnically *mestizo* parentage. His father, if not conspicuously musical provided business acumen, and supported—was perhaps proud of—his son's talents.

Given those talents, along with father's wealth and mother's 'connections', Gottschalk was sent at the tender age of thirteen to study piano and composition in Paris, while hobnobbing socially with the high and mighty. Starr makes the most of the lavish documentation of the Paris years, during which the boy earned the admiration of artists of the calibre of Chopin, Liszt, and Berlioz, Hugo, Lamartine, and Gautier. Although a mere teenager, he had no problem in consorting with them, both because his gifts were exceptionally precocious, and because he inherited his mother's fabulous good looks, was well-groomed sartorially and culturally, spoke impeccable French and was fluent in English, Spanish and Italian. But although he fluttered the hearts of innumerable Parisiennes, his triumph was not founded merely on glitzy glamour and pianistic pyrotechnics. Chopin, of all people, paid homage to the *sensibilité* of his pianism; his vivacity and intelligence are evident on every page of the notebooks in which he began to record his social contacts and international travels.

Gottschalk had begun to compose piano pieces even before he left for Paris, since creation was spontaneously stimulated by New Orleans's ragbag of white, black and coffee-coloured party-musics, including French quadrille and vaudeville, Italian romantic opera, Spanish tango, habañera and zarzuela, African-derived Negro rag, and the sundry Creole hybrids. In Paris he 'wrote up' these pieces literally, with skills increasing as his composition lessons with reputable teachers, though not with Chopin, prospered. His 'Creole' dances are unpretentious in aim, though he sometimes claimed that he was fashioning an art music as apposite to his homeland as were Chopin's mazurkas to his native Poland. Starr is slightly on the defensive as to how 'serious' a composer Gottschalk was: a defensiveness surely irrelevant, since his importance lies precisely in his crossover status. His Paris-reinforced technical facility enabled him to evolve a perfect recipe for 'light' music in an emergent democracy. Cliché and invention must weigh evenly in the scales, for a piece that is too cliché-ridden may tickle the ears momentarily, but won't preserve its savour: whereas a piece that departs too far from convention will disturb, rather than confirm us in, our conformities, and so won't function efficaciously as entertainment. Gottschalk gets the balance just right: his tunes are memorable, catchy without being outlandish; his Chopin-derived harmonies are piquant, yet not self-indulgent, since they are usually subservient to physical movement and may be prone to a witty unpredictability. His piano textures, if less adventurous than

Chopin's because more turned outward to the social world, are at once opulent and elegant. Grateful to play and gratifying to listen to, his pieces inculcate social bonhomie, making us feel good in our social contexts.

Today, we find most satisfaction in the dances Gottschalk made from memories and tunes of his Louisianian childhood. *Le Bananier* is a 'chanson nègre' in which lucid spacing enhances the wistfulness of the wide-eyed French-Creole tune, over an African-styled drone. *La Savane*, described as a 'ballade créole', offers a haunting tune, childish in structure and submitted to only the simplest type of variation; and if the third of these Louisianian sketches, *Le Mancellier*, is more sophisticated in combining a seductively rhythmed serenade with a love-story enacted under the sultry shadow of this poisonous plant, the textures are so cleanly handled that the relatively complex piece was no less a hit than its two innocent companions. *La Bamboula* and *Le Banjo* slightly americanize exotic material from the West Indies and Africa, exploiting patterned figurations and fetchingly repetitive tunes in bouncy rhythms to create, as far back as 1850, harbingers of a preminimal music which, having virtually no harmonic or tonal development, may function as aural wallpaper. No wonder these pieces, dashingly executed by a handsome virtuoso, caused a furore in Paris, which was repeated in Spain, where Gottschalk abandoned himself to the luxurious lilt of tangoid syncopation, henceforth a significant element of his idiom. At the same time he could, during these European years, turn out a *Mazurk* (*sic*) or a *Grande Scherzo* palpably modelled on Chopin and almost worthy, in elegance and occasional pathos, if not in density and emotional charge, of the master himself. He knew his public, which, in a world increasingly democratized, liked to feel cosily at home while being aware of extravagances in the wide world. The hysteria which Gottschalk evoked in Europe rivals that triggered by Liszt. Playing mainly his own music, he appealed to connoisseurs and amateurs alike; women battled for fragments of his clothing; potentates serenaded him with bands and bunting. Starr recounts the often lurid tale with a gusto leavened by irony; and has then to confront the fact that at the dizzy crest of his fortunes Gottschalk packed his trunks and reshipped his phalanx of pianos, heading for his native land—and not, moreover, to glamorous New Orleans, but to aggressively commercialized New York.

Gottschalk's gladiatorial progress through Europe had not been without hiccups, and fabulous success often teeters on the brink of the jitters. Starr establishes, however, that the main reason for Gottschalk's defection from Europe was a series of reverses in his family fortunes. Father's business deals proved vulnerable to the market's vagaries; and these disasters affected the father's health, and possibly precipitated his early death in 1853. Gottschalk's

Catholic mother and banker-father had instilled in their son a sense of family responsibility; so at the age of twenty-four, he found himself a foster-father to his mother and a small tribe of siblings. With American enterprise, the young man turned himself into a peripatetic Liszt transplanted into New World soil. Whether driven by desperate necessity or by an incremental workaholism nurtured by a starry-eyed belief in his embryonic nation, Gottschalk for some years virtually lived on the American railroad, playing not only in major cities but also in shanty towns and rural outposts. Small-town audiences no doubt relished his Creole and Latin American dances, while finding Chopin and Liszt beyond their ken. Though Gottschalk must have had an eye on material necessity, he was not being patronizing when he deliberately manufactured 'low' pieces celebrating topical and local events like the opening-up of the continent to the omnivorous railway; nor did he fail to record the progress of the Civil War, through which he gallantly persevered on his pilgrimage, often in conditions of extreme discomfort, and sometimes danger. Moreover, the war presented moral as well as physical problems. As a deep Southerner by birth, he was a Confederate; but the needs of his career (and therefore family), his purpose as a democratic educationist, and his hatred of slavery allied him to the Union cause. His 'paraphrases' on national tunes—on the analogy of Liszt's operatic fantasies—roused rabbles with their panache, but tempered portentousness with demotic hilarity. Technical ingenuity combines with ingenuousness in what Gottschalk called "the full fire of chromatic grapeshot and deadly octaves"; contemporary audiences must have responded not only with patriotic fervour but also, as do we, with mirthful amazement. The notorious *Grand Paraphrase on the Union*, a topical and local work if ever there was one, can still be heard with pleasure, being simultaneously predictable and startling—the basic Gottschalk paradox.

It is more tricky to decide whether Gottschalk wrote his sentimental ballads and 'meditations' addressed to his raw American public with his tongue in his cheek. If he did, it was again without condescension, since he had a love-hate relationship with the lower strata of his audience, and nursed a muse happy to be simultaneously sophisticated and naif. Typically if improbably, he claimed that the most ubiquitous among the pieces he referred to as 'tear-jerkers'—the meditation entitled *The Last Hope*—had been inspired at the deathbed of a Louisianian inamorata, in memory of whom he alchemically transmuted a much-loved Presbyterian hymn into a slow French valse, displaying the same sensuous yet disciplined luxuriance he lavished on his exotic dances. Starr is justified in reminding us that this is, in its genre, not only an exquisitely tailored but also a beautiful and moving piece. The heart of common humanity cannot, after all, be gainsaid: published in 1854, *The Last Hope* sold 35,000 copies in its first year, has been through more than thirty editions, and is still in print.

Starr's inevitably breathless account of the American years induces incredulous awe: how could one fairly frail man have weathered a concert a day, or sometimes three or four performances, while travelling, on his own estimate, 92,000 miles in painful and even hazardous physical conditions, aggravated by crooked managers and impresarios? Moreover, fantastic triumphs were punctuated by dismal flops in backwater states; monies vastly accumulated, only to dissipate in a puff of smoke. Yet when Gottschalk decided that he had to escape the treadmill it wasn't, according to Starr, so much because of financial difficulties as because of an amorous entanglement, or at least a mindless act. He was accused by a strict Californian seminary for young ladies of having seduced an adolescent inmate; and glumly concluded that the publicity would demolish his career (and therefore his family) in northern Protestant America. Apparently the charge was baseless; Gottschalk, although irresistible to women, was no womanizer, though he found it difficult to eschew flirtatious young females who were unlikely to pose a serious threat. In so far as he indulged in full-fledged 'affairs', he tended to be victimized by them, as in his relationship with the formidable Ada Clare, an actress who, adoring him, defeated her own ends by the pertinacity of her pursuit. She was still, several years after the affair was officially over, hot on his trail during this pathetic Californian episode. Running away to Cuba, and thence to Argentina, Uruguay and Brazil, initiated his best, or at least his happiest, years. The music he heard encouraged him to compose music similar to his early Creole pieces, yet richer and riper in sophistication. *Pasquinade*, a French gavotte tune over a stride bass, indulges in reiterated ornaments that presage the riffs of ragtime. *Suis-moi* fuses habañera with cakewalk, in a style to be explored, fifty years later, by Scott Joplin and the great Jelly Roll Morton; *O Ma Charmante, Épargnez-moi*, described as a 'caprice', enchantingly mates duskiness with elegance, to portray a tropical romance. Best of all these Latin pieces is *Souvenir de Puerto Rico*, an example of the popular 'patrol' that gradually swells from silence to fortissimo, then recedes into the distance. Starting with a bare hint of march beat, the piano decoration stimulates excitement as the harmony is chromaticized and the pulse generates a 3+3+2 rumba metre that effects a forward lurch, followed by stasis. This rhythmic spasm is very sexy, yet slightly comic, combining with colourful part-writing, symmetrical sequences and lucent textures to create music that is, in the jazz senses, both 'hot' and 'cool'.

This small masterpiece overrides distinctions between art and entertainment, suggesting that some such compromise is the essence of Gottschalk's achievement. It seems probable that Latin America was the right setting for his fulfilment. In Europe, he had been praised by great artists and honoured by royals and potentates; in North America, he had, through the grinding rigour of his concert schedules, generated euphoria among *hoi polloi*. On both continents, he was too intelligent to have been duped by legendary success; so it was fair enough that his sense of humour (well documented by Starr) should have carried him through toil and turmoil to a languorous *dolce fa niente* in Latin America, characteristically interspersed with frenetic bouts of energy. Boldly, even blithely, he rode over revolutions and riots, armed with a schematic Grand National Fantasy into which the appropriate national anthem could be slotted, as occasion demanded. Even his periods of ill-health and (perhaps consequent) melancholia acquired, in the cartoon fairyland of Latin America, an awesome preposterousness. In his memoirs Gottschalk recounts how, weary with the world and concertizing, he retired to the wilderness, living Crusoe-like in the crater of an extinct volcano, intermittently attended by a picturesque wild-man Friday. Each evening, he would wheel out his grand piano (an American Chickering, of course), to serenade the gibbering monkeys, parakeets, and the yowling jaguars, while the sun set. Alas, Starr's researches have revealed that the volcano wasn't all that remote from civilisation, and that the companion was no wild man but a mulatto student-disciple: which puts the damper on Gottschalk's resonant grand, but doesn't demolish the story's loony magic.

If this volcano episode is a grotesque parody of Gottschalk as Romantic Hero, the monster concerts he organized in Latin America complementarily parodied the commercialism of the massed piano festivals he had put on in North America, partly as mercantile enterprise in collaboration with Chickerings, partly as an anti-puritan, anti-German riposte to his archenemy, the Boston brahmin pedagogue John Dwight. With typical theatricality, the monster concert to end all monsters carried Gottschalk himself to his grave; for his collapse at the age of forty during the second performance of the great event, was attributed to emphysema and appendicitis, aggravated by the frantic preparations (in which Gottschalk fulfilled most administrative and managerial as well as artistic duties) for the *concerto mostro*. Estimates of the number of performers varied between 650 and 800; massed pianos collaborated with an immense orchestra with soaring strings, an ostentatious posse of ophicleides and serpents, an army of eighty drummers, and a parade of flower-bedecked drum-majorettes, or their contemporary equivalent. The climax was a *Grande Tarantelle* for Gottschalk's solo piano with the mammoth orchestra: music which, surviving in less gargantuan versions, is as riotously Italian as Rossini, though in total effect Judaic-French—an Offenbachian galop on the brink of a

Second Empire abyss, if not Gottschalk's subterraneanly growling volcano.

In his final Latin American phase Gottschalk was, like Brazil itself, larger than life and ripe for death: interestingly enough, a century later the leading Brazilian composer, Heitor Villa-Lobos, also organized monster concerts involving thousands of performers in a democratically educational-nationalistic spirit no less theatrical, if slightly less farcical, than Gottschalk's extravaganza. Starr hints that Gottschalk was planning, after the ultimate *concerto mostro*, to return to New York, and perhaps eventually to Europe, to embark on a career as a 'serious' composer of operas and symphonies. The aborted attempts he'd made in such directions hardly convince us that he was cut out for the role; I don't know whether Starr's speculation has documentary support, but would regret it if it did, since opera and symphony (if too 'seriously' cultivated) would have denied the nature of Gottschalk's gifts and would have misdirected his historical function. This doesn't affect my admiration for this fine book, which should remain 'definitive' for the foreseeable future.

TLS, JUNE 1995

ROME TO COPLAND SOUND
AMERICAN MUSIC'S PATH TO GRACE

Andrea Olmstead, ed., *The Correspondence of Roger Sessions*
(Boston, Mass.: Northeastern University Press, 1992)
Barbara B. Heyman, *Samuel Barber: The Composer and His Music*
(Oxford: Oxford University Press, 1992)
Aaron Copland and Vivian Perlis, *Copland Since 1943*
(London: Marion Boyars, 1992)

IF WE DISCOUNT THE AMERINDIANS, WE MAY SAY THAT THE FIRST GENER-
ation of American art-composers wrote eighteenth-century European
hymnody with interesting grammatical errors. The second, nineteenth-
century generation wrote more 'correct' church music and streamlined
instrumental music according to Teutonic recipes, flourishing or
floundering in polite parlours, genteel universities, and on the concert cir-
cuit. In the early years of the twentieth century emerged the first indigenous
American art-composers, the grand old Pioneers, Ives, Ruggles and Varèse,
backed by a second league of Riegger, Ornstein and Rudhyar, with Partch,
Nancarrow and Cage paradoxically bringing up a rear avant-garde. What
one might call an American Tradition defined itself as the neo-Europeans
and the Pioneers merged. The three composers featured in these books are
perhaps the most distinguished in this group.

The senior member, Roger Sessions, born in 1896, was a university composer, rooted in Europe. He came of a venerable New England family affiliated with the Law and the Church—though his parents were early divorced.
He himself was intellectually brilliant, entering Harvard at the age of fourteen, and proceeding to advanced studies at Yale. Years of his youth were
spent in Italy, France and Germany; he spoke the main European languages
with fluency, adding Russian for good measure. (He habitually wrote to his
correspondents in their native tongues, even when they'd become natural-
ized Americans.) Back home, he settled into the life destined for him,
teaching at the most prestigious universities—Harvard, Yale, Princeton and
Berkeley, with a brief, slightly condescending spell at the Juilliard School of
Music. Proud of his Harvard ancestry and his European training, he was
uninterested in attempts to define an American vernacular, though from his
outpost in Rome he rather desultorily helped Copland organize a famous-
notorious series of concerts of modern music. Sessions may have been
justified in maintaining that American worth would better establish itself
without conscious contrivance, but was surely wrong in thinking that a
New World called for no new awareness. Significantly, he was patronizing
about Ives, whose 'openendedness' now seems to make him the major figure
in America's story, and a potent one in world music.

Despite his reverence for his New England heritage, Sessions had no affinities with religious Puritanism, but carried ingrained protestantism to an ultimate end, in an anti-denominational, discreetly progressive spirit. As a citizen of Europe, he was first creatively inspired by Ernst Bloch, a Swiss Jew and expatriate, whose alienated state paralleled Sessions's own in the dubiously United States. With Bloch's example, Sessions explored Europe's past without being engulfed by it. His first work to attract attention, *The Black Masquers* (written in its original theatrical form at the age of sixteen), is a far cry from New England, both in its *fin-de-siècle* subject and its heady flirtings with the technical opulence of Bloch, Strauss and Mahler. It took Sessions a long time, and agonizing labour, to discover his own identity beneath the European accretions. He was a slow worker whose difficulty in meeting deadlines cost him dear in material as well as spiritual terms—as his interminable apologetics in these letters reveal. Two of his finest key works, the First Piano Sonata and the Violin Concerto, were each an elephantine nine years in gestation, while his biggest piece, the (very) grand opera *Montezuma*, was conceived in 1935, theatrically born in 1962.

In Sessions's mature work, the influence of Bloch gives way to a more generalized, less fevered, relationship to European, especially German Expressionist, traditions. His music grows more lucid, but also more complex; it would seem that the anguish of creation served to safeguard his integrity and ultimately to assure a kind of triumph. Works like the Second and Third Symphonies earned not only respect, but also admiration, at least from the technically initiated; and when Schoenberg, exiled from Nazified Germany, became an American citizen, Sessions realized that his goal had always been a chromaticism that could be 'absolute' in being disciplined by serial law. Since serialism was international, it was also American; and when Sessions espoused it, notably in his Violin Concerto, he and his music became a beacon for the sophisticated, university-trained young. The letters to Schoenberg from Sessions (awed and humble) and to Sessions from Schoenberg (prim and oddly touching) tell us much about musical creativity in the United States during the 1950s and 60s, the years of Sessions's glory. As usual, however, glory was ephemeral; and while it didn't matter to Sessions that he never made it with Us the People, he lived long enough to recognize that his thirty-year labour on *Montezuma* may have been abortive, and that the day would come, perhaps had already come, when chromatic serialism no longer seemed a gateway to truth.

This may be why a perusal of these letters—written over three-quarters of a century, meticulously edited and annotated by Andrew Olmstead, and most handsomely produced—leaves a residue of melancholy and bitterness. Given the distinction of Sessions's mind, the letters afford considerable intellectual stimulation. Even so, there's a priggish self-righteousness in the early letters, not least when he's addressing his apparently adored first wife, whom he eventually abandoned for a student. (A familiar tale, though, to be fair, the pupil became a second wife, and the marriage lasted.) Later on, when Sessions had become a father-figure to the then-young David Diamond, his morose and verbose heavy-handedness with his disciple sounds like pique over David's having stayed in Paris as a pupil of Nadia Boulanger, instead of returning home to daddy. There's something faintly distasteful in the way Sessions gnaws on his moral dubieties like a dog worrying a bone. Perhaps unfairly, this reflects on his music; one wonders whether Sessions's art— notwithstanding the manifest distinction of works like the Violin Concerto, the *Theocritus Idyll*, and the Second String Quartet—is ever likely to become part of a current, quasi-classical repertory. For all its compositional craft and care, the music does not stay memorable and is, today, not easy to love.

Samuel Barber, a relatively lightweight composer fourteen years Sessions's junior, *is* still spasmodically current. He too came from a genteel New England background, though his habitat was not in universities, but in the parlour, concert-hall, and the opera-house wherein his aunt was a singer of celebrity. He also had an uncle Homer who was a more than competent composer of drawing-room songs, and a wise guide to, and guardian over, Sam's boyhood; few children can have been so fortunate in an early mentor. Like Sessions, Barber was highly precocious, musically if not intellectually. At the age of nine, he announced to his mother that he intended to be a composer, and from that date onwards turned precept into practice. He joined the Curtis School of Music at the same age as Sessions went to Harvard. Within a few years, Sam—dazzlingly handsome, even beautiful, with silver spoons spilling from his mouth and prizes magnetically gravitating towards him—was doing the rounds of Europe with a sequence of boyfriends, studying mostly in Rome with Rosario Scalero, an ably conservative conservatory-teacher who kept his pupil's nose to the contrapuntal grindstone, thereby giving precision to facility. The music Barber needed to write adopted a nineteenth-century romantic idiom such as appealed to his 'loved ones' back home. Nostalgia was, in no discreditable sense, his impulse to creation: as is movingly testified in his setting of Matthew Arnold's 'Dover Beach', scored for baritone and string quartet when Sam was just twenty (and sweetly sung by the composer on an early recording of 1935). Arnold's cry of the young heart, lonely and afraid in an inimical world in which faith is extinct, was translated by Barber from its Victorian industrial environment to America during the years of Depression. But if the music wears its heart on a sleeve cut in a nineteenth-century fashion admired in Philadelphia, that visible heart rings true.

Because of his spontaneous romanticism, Barber became a repertory composer as Sessions did not. Intermittently, his music flickered into small flames that became middlebrow 'hits' almost comparable with the lollipops of Tchaikovsky or Rachmaninov, if without the fetching tunes. The most famous of these pieces remains the *Adagio for Strings*, which, originally the slow movement of a respectable string quartet, became a box-office titbit when rescored for string orchestra. Taken up by Toscanini in 1938, it achieved a fame in part extra-musical, since it became an elegy for the casualties of the Second World War, and subsequently graced ceremonies in honour of defunct presidents and political martyrs. The piece is a genuine, not Hollywooden, tear-jerker, in which finely spun cantilena gives to harmonic opulence a frail pathos, so that one is involved, but not emotionally bullied. This is an achievement echoed in Barber's loveliest piece, *Knoxville: Summer of 1915*, a setting for soprano and orchestra of part of a prose poem by James Agee that seems to have direct autobiographical import for Barber, no less than for its author. Agee, like Barber, had a musical aunt and a wise uncle, and a mother and father who were "good to me" in a familiar and well-beloved home, yet who could not, "not now, not ever, tell me *who I am*".

Such an intimately honest *recherche du temps perdu* was, though the deepest, not the main stream of Barber's creation. As a prize-winning glamour-boy, he was commissioned to write symphonic and theatrical pieces, and did so with a panache that sometimes became rodomontade, since the heroic vein was not his by nature. Sam, not knowing "who I am", could not grow up: which must be why the acutely perceptive Virgil Thomson wrote of the "well-bred attitudinizing and mincing respectabilities" of his more pretentious symphonic works. Still, these pieces were frequently played and were for the most part critically lauded, as well as relished by their public. It's also significant that Barber was the first twentieth-century American successfully to graduate into Grand Opera. *Vanessa*, prestigiously commissioned by the New York Met in 1958, is a romantic opera in Puccinian idiom, but with a distinctively American theme hinging on alienation and a love deep-frozen in the past. Its book, cunning in stagecraft, was by Gian Carlo Menotti, for thirty years Barber's lover and co-home-maker, and a composer with sharper theatrical instinct but less native musicality than Barber. Initially, *Vanessa* enjoyed a success that calls for the overworked adjective 'fabulous'.

Yet success wasn't durable. The opera's European press was patchy and condescending and the piece, once sunk, hasn't been convincingly resuscitated. And Barber's later attempt at an even grander opera was a total disaster. Since the subject of Antony and Cleopatra—in Shakespeare's own incandescent language—seems an improbable choice for a genteel New

England homosexual, the project points to a deficiency in self-knowledge outside the charmed circle of childhood; which, for Barber, was a refuge, whereas for Ives it was a recognition that "the child is father of the man". Unsurprisingly, Barber had even less use for Ives than had Sessions; his near-paranoid rejection must have sprung from fear of Ives's polymorphous 'reality'. Well, golden boys often have to pay a price, and Barber's last years were pitiful. The fiasco of *Antony and Cleopatra*—presented with extravagant hype, directed by Zeffirelli—coincided with the breakdown of Barber's long liaison with Menotti and the selling-up of their beautiful home. Barber's terminal cancer may well have been in part psychosomatic.

Even so, some of Barber's works continue to be played and replayed—not only the *Adagio for Strings*, the vernal Violin Concerto, *Knoxville*, and a handful of the songs he produced with unfacile spontaneity, but also a few tougher pieces that, justifying recourse to more 'contemporary' techniques, are more highly charged as well as densely textured. Especially impressive is the Piano Sonata written in 1949 and taken up by Horowitz, perhaps in part because Barber was a socialite composer who wrote expertly for the keyboard, but also because the music had substance enough to render repeated performances enlivening but not offensive. It is, however, absurd of Barbara Heyman to claim in her biography that Barber's is the 'greatest' piano sonata of the twentieth century; even in an American context, Barber's sonata, however fine, is in a lower league than the two magnificently rebarbative sonatas of Ives and the superb, uniquely American sonata of Copland. In general, Heyman has written a conservative 'Life and Works', appropriate to her subject. It is useful because thorough, with many well-produced music examples. But she weakens her case by pitching her claims too high; it should suffice that Barber, less ambitious, less influential, and less portentous than Sessions, still plays a modest role on the lower slopes of Parnassus.

It may not be fortuitous that there are, in Barber's best works, notably the Knoxville elegy, the Piano Sonata and the Piano Concerto, faint intimations of Copland: the man who among these three composers unquestionably 'made' American music—not from the haven of renowned universities nor from cosy New England parlours and concert-halls, but by entering American life at all points: significantly he, in contrast to Sessions and Barber, was a prime mover in the belated discovery of Ives. "I was born", he confessed, "in Brooklyn in 1900 on a street that can only be described as drab. Music was the last thing anyone would have expected in that street. The idea was entirely original with me." Copland's aboriginality conditioned his becoming, through his music's Russo-Jewish, Negro-Cowboy identities, the voice of polyethnic America. In the Piano Variations of 1930 he extracted from hard skeletonic textures and rigidly geometric organization a steel-girdered music intermittently capable of tenderness, mirth and grace. If this music has the hardness of the New York skyline, it is also aware of vistas, as it proffers a tentatively affirmative answer to its biblical question: Shall these bones live?

Throughout his long life, Copland composed other, scarcely less austere masterpieces—notably two more piano works, the Sonata of 1940 and the Fantasy of 1957. Such formidable statements court popular favour no more than does the music of Sessions, though by this date they are in the repertory of many responsible pianists, worldwide. Yet at the same time as Copland was making these 'abstract' works, he was also exploring more accessible forms of expression through his ballets and film-scores. The once canvassed view that these works were a denial, even a betrayal, of his earlier integrity cannot be sustained; for the folky vein of the ballets—especially the now classic *Appalachian Spring*, written for Martha Graham—does not evade the rigorous logic of the Piano Variations, since Copland sees the prairie as a symbol of the irremediable lonesomeness of big cities, the hymn as a symbol of the religious and domestic security that urban man had forfeited.

The Wild West ballet *Billy the Kid* (1938) is a parable about Law and the Outlaw, which musically redeems Billy's death in the twilit emptiness of the desert. The 'Copland sound' of that conclusion is immediately and irresistibly recognizable; and resounds in the scores to the films *Of Mice and Men* and *Our Town*, which are among the most beautiful, and are certainly the most functionally intelligent, scores ever made for cinema. The technique of the film 'clip' is here allied to Copland's balletic technique of 'frozen' moments and dance gestures. There is no music that more honestly conveys the simultaneity of the Big City and the solitudinous prairie than that of Copland; no music more compassionate in accepting spiritual isolation while embracing the feelings of 'ordinary' men and women; no music that attains, through tension, a tougher sanity, a wryer humour, a deeper calm.

This is why Copland's music has been played far more frequently than that of any other American. He was not embarrassed to enter the world at any level: approaching vivid showbiz music in his Latin American vein, and creating an 'occasional' piece like *Lincoln Portrait*, which has received many thousands of performances, with the speaking part declaimed by presidents and politicians innumerable (including, most recently, Margaret Thatcher), as well as, simply and affectingly, by Copland himself. The piece has survived its nationalistic popularity because, though less stark than the Piano Variations, it too is sturdily built, politically valid because valid in musical terms. Though never a 'party' man, Copland was political as Sessions and Barber, as much Europeans as Americans, were not, in that he was a quintessential New Yorker who travelled the world as cultural ambassador, not only in Europe, but also in the East and, especially, in Latin America. Wherever he went, his vigour never faltered, and his famous beaming smile disseminated sanity, amity, and also grace. When he decided that he ought to write an autobiography, his purpose was not to trace his turmoils and triumphs as artist, but to describe the evolution of the American musical scene for which, though he doesn't say so, he has been himself largely responsible. He solicited the help of Vivian Perlis in assembling the literary jottings he had made over many years. She transcribed the texts, interspersing them with historical glosses and with comments from the many people he had worked with in a multiplicity of cultural ventures. She comes up with a biography that functions at once from within and without its subject: a collage that persuades us that we are ourselves participating in New York's hurly-burly, presided over by Copland's 'plain' presence. As Bernstein put it, Copland was "the Dean of American Composers" not because he'd been around so long and virtually nothing had been done without him, but simply because he was, among American composers, the strongest and the best.

The first volume of this work appeared as long ago as 1984. This concluding volume has been worth waiting for, for it is no less lively in incident and opinion, and again demonstrates that Copland's plainness was a moral force and an act of love. It's significant that although Copland was, like Barber, homosexual and had at least two enduring relationships that gave him stability, we allow them to take their place, as we read the book, among all the persons and events coincident in his multifarious life. In contrast with the ingrowing psyches of Sessions and Barber, Copland's private life was charismatically marked by an outgoing generosity that, while not suffering fools gladly, always knew how to forgive. Related to this is the fact that his sometimes unavoidable combativeness was always countered by a sense of humour—a faculty deficient in Barber, and perhaps absent from Sessions. Only a sense of humour could have sustained Copland through the idiot bickerings of rivals and even colleagues, not to mention the obscenity of the McCarthy years, when Aaron, who had performed wonders in promoting the American cause at home and abroad, was arraigned as a traitor because some of his friends or acquaintances may have been communists. It seems fitting to end with a letter Copland wrote to the national press, when the worst of his ordeal was past:

This is the first time, as far as I know, that a composition [in fact, the overtly patriotic *Lincoln Portrait*] has been publicly removed from a concert program in the United States because of the alleged affiliation of the composer. I would have been a man of stone not to have deeply resented both the public announcement of the removal and the reasons given for it . . . I cannot for the life of me see how the cause of the free countries will be advanced by the banning of my works . . . No American politician has yet called for the banning of an American composer's work because of its aesthetic content, as is the case in Russia today. I'd a thousand times prefer to have my work turned down by a Republican congressman on political grounds (or because I voted for Stevenson) than have it turned down for aesthetic reasons. It is easy to see why this is so. My 'politics'—tainted or untainted—are certain to die with me; but my music, I am foolish enough to imagine, might just possibly outlive the Republican Party.

TLS, MARCH 1993

ALL THE THINGS THEY WERE

FROM JEROME KERN TO HAROLD ARLEN: THE 'GOING-ON-NESS'
OF BROADWAY'S BALLADEERS

Allen Forte, *The American Popular Ballad of the Golden Era, 1924–1950*
(Princeton: Princeton University Press, 1995)
Steven E. Gilbert, *The Music of Gershwin* (New Haven: Yale University Press, 1995)

A LLEN FORTE, CURRENTLY BATTELL PROFESSOR OF THE THEORY OF MUSIC
at Yale, is the foremost exponent of the technique known, after its prog-
enitor, as Schenkerian analysis. He has written a helpful introduction
to the subject, and in this big book of 366 pages, adorned with 354 examples
in straight or graphic notations, he brings the technique to bear on American popular ballads of the 'Golden Age': a project that, in the distant 1930s
when I was a student, would have been dismissed as risible. The book is
brilliantly planned and, despite an inevitable quota of jargon, lucidly, even
elegantly written. Forte assumes that his readers understand orthodox
musical notation and have a reasonable acquaintance with musical terminology; but he glosses any terms that might not be readily comprehensible,
and appends a survey of the specialist terminology employed in the music
industry, as distinct from academe. He also offers a clear account of the
Schenkerian principles on which his own analyses are based, explaining
how, when applied to tonal music, they help us to understand why, in a
musical composition, some things cohere and others don't. While Forte is
aware that it is dangerous to assume that coherence is necessarily a criterion
of value, he persuades us that Schenker's approach can help us to decide
that some pieces of music are 'better than' others, and to comment on what
is happening, at a given musical moment, in human terms.

The range of music examined is putatively simple, and limited; all the
songs commented on are brief, tonal and concerned with the kinds of experience that may be categorized as entertainment. This doesn't mean that the
academic dismissal of such music in my youth was justified. Then, pre-
dominantly rural folk music was regarded as the creation of anonymous
people working in long-established traditions, entangled in 'universal'
themes like love, war, sex and death; art music, by contrast, was made by
individual composers, often living in urban communities with complex
cultural traditions, who were more than usually sensitive to the problems of
human identity. Beyond 'folk' and 'art' music in these senses lay a third category of entertainment-rather-than-art music, addressed to the masses,
concerned not so much with the 'realities' of life and death as with escape
from them into wish-fulfilment. Such simple-minded distinctions between
art and entertainment have evaporated, mostly because Freudian psychology revealed that the categorization of 'real' and 'illusory' experience
tends to be slippery; but also because democratic correctness boggles at

condescending to so large a percentage of the population. Urban songs may have been produced by industrial technology for a mass audience, with the goal of material gain, but that doesn't alter the fact that the songs, dealing verbally and musically with adolescence, sex, love and loss (though not often with death), are about the things that make the world go round. Moreover, there is evidence that commercial success may often be proportionate to the degree to which words and music grapple, consciously and unconsciously, with the springs of feeling.

Believing this, Forte doesn't hesitate to conclude that the purveyors of commodities on Tin Pan Alley, Broadway and the Big Band circuits included among them composers capable of holding up their heads among classical artists. His Big Six is also mine and, I suspect, almost anyone's: Jerome Kern, Irving Berlin, Cole Porter, George Gershwin, Richard Rodgers and Harold Arlen, in chronological order. To each of these men Forte allots a substantial chapter, explaining the 'harmonic language', 'rhythmic features', 'melodic design' and 'lyric qualities' of the thirty-two-bar standard. He then proceeds to detailed analyses of a half-dozen or so songs by each composer, wherein he shows how irony and ambiguity may wittily, wittingly and unwittingly reveal 'reality'. Pop lyrics may seem acceptable, though trite or facetious, because audiences today are wary of Beethovenian assaults on destiny, or even of the Schubertian savouring of potentially suicidal loss. Nostalgia, wit, irony, even facetiousness, may be strategies for survival. Each composer of Forte's Big Six employs a slightly different technique to bring the strategy off.

The oldest of the group, Jerome Kern, was born in 1885 into a fairly well-off American-Jewish family with European antecedents. The family was dedicated to music, so Kern received conventional training in European techniques, and was especially well versed in operetta. He worked briefly in music-theatre in Edwardian London, but also learned his craft the hard way, as a publisher's song-promoter. Being exceptionally bright, he readily learned to adapt the conventions of 'light' European music to the American scene, and was quick to pick up hints from his younger contemporaries, especially Gershwin and Cole Porter. He never seems to have doubted that his destiny lay in 'show music', and no doubt thought of that as a democratically American ambition. In 1927, he proved that he was on the mark in creating *Show Boat*, a musical that combined nostalgia and escapism with an awareness of racial and political issues. The weight and substance of the piece have earned it a place in the repertory of 'legitimate' music-theatre—and Forte's analysis of 'Can't help lovin' dat man' confirms the work's stature. Similarly, Forte's account of Kern's quintessential nostalgia-balled, 'Smoke gets in your eyes'— with its scalp-prickling modulation from E flat major to B major in the middle eight—shows us how nostalgia fuses memory and desire.

The second of Forte's Big Six is Irving Berlin, born in Russia in 1888 as Izzy Baline, and reared in a Lower East Side New York ghetto. The son of a Jewish synagogue cantor, Berlin embarked on a show-business career more or less in childhood, working as a singing waiter. Unlike Kern, however, he remained musically illiterate in the sense that he never learned adequately to notate music, and played the piano empirically, mostly on the black keys. The well-rehearsed tale that, having acquired some success, Berlin designed and helped manufacture a mechanical means of modulation from F sharp major to any key in the tonal spectrum, is apparently true. Throughout his long life (he lived to be more than 100), he needed assistants to transcribe his inspirations on to paper and tape; yet Forte justifiably maintains that Berlin's success was as much artistic as commercial. Speaking of 'Isn't this a lovely day?', he points out how

The bass ominously moves down to G flat, pulling the tenor with it in parallel tenths. As a result of the voice leading, the harmony in this bar is the traditionally ambivalent augmented triad. In this instance, the change from G flat to F yields the B flat triad of bar fifteen, and the resultant change in harmonic colour is clearly a very effective instance of text-painting in the popular idiom. Not only does the harmony momentarily attain a higher pitch level, with pictorial implications, but also the B flat triad is symbolic of the pun on 'broke' and 'break': the storm breaks, and the suitor receives a break.

Next on the chronological list is Cole Porter, born in 1893, remote from the Jewish ghettos, to a fabulously rich tycoon-father. Berlin's polar opposite, he was as highly educated, widely travelled and world-weary as Berlin was rudimentarily naive; yet both men were show-business professionals, and each admired the other's music. Just as Berlin's superficially artless ditties reveal unsuspected depths, so Porter's dizzy rhyme-schemes and verbal and musical puns hide intense passions and even violence, as in 'Night and day'. Here the beat of the tom-tom and the ticking of the clock generate obsessive melodic repetition and blue major-minor harmony, verbally compounded by internal rhymes on 'yearning', 'burning' and 'turning'. In no popular ballad composer is the disparity between the tinsel of the Jazz Age and the tragic farce of private experience more potent.

Porter's life, though busily inventive, was far from conventionally happy, being complicated by the fact that, homosexual by nature, he was married to a beautiful woman with a fortune of her own; at a more prosaic level, he was often in physical pain as the result of a riding accident. Moreover, his playboy life occurred against the backcloth of the years of Depression, and of war and rumours of war. Such was the background to the Golden Age of popular song in general; but nowhere was its effect more acute than in the case of Cole Porter. Forte gets to the heart of this in his analysis of 'Everything I love', revealing it to be a supreme example of the use of popular song as a 'technique for survival' a state of 'going-on-ness' (to use Percy Grainger's term) that is as primitive as it is sophisticated. Consider, too, the zest crazily inculcated in the virtuosic rhyming and hyperbole of Porter's famous 'list' song, 'You're the tops', and contrast it with the suave simplicities of Berlin's 'Cheek to cheek'.

George Gershwin, born in New York in 1898 of a Jewish working-class family, has long been accepted as the supreme American show-business composer, and was the only one of Forte's Six to graduate from the music industry and establish a second identity as a concert composer. He transformed an American musical, *Porgy and Bess* (based on a novel by DuBose Heyward*), into a great, as well as grand, opera; but, two years after its launch in 1935, he died of a brain tumour, aged thirty-nine. Gershwin, like Porter but unlike Kern and Berlin, was musically and intellectually precocious, though neurotically divided between his identities as a glamour-boy and ambitious Artist. Composition lessons with Edward Kilenyi, counterpoint lessons with Henry Cowell, and a toying with Joseph Schillinger's briefly fashionable do-it-yourself kit for aspiring composers, may all have aided his facility; but when Gershwin sought advice from Ravel, whose sensuously delectable music he revered, the Frenchman refused to teach him on the grounds that he already knew all he needed to know. Successful in show music and (after *Rhapsody in Blue*) in concert music, Gershwin worked himself to death in the composition of *Porgy*. We don't know what 'caused' his brain tumour, but we do know that, despite his ebullience, he was not a happy man. A compulsive womanizer, he avoided any serious commitment to woman or man, as though success in life, as well as in art, would have been too much to expect, or cope with.

Allen Forte devalues Gershwin's extraordinary achievement, not so much because he ignores the concert works (which are not his subject), as because he omits the *Porgy* songs, on the grounds that they are arias dependent on their operatic context. Admittedly, this is what makes the songs uniquely powerful; yet that they also function as 'numbers' is indicated by the fact that they have proved so fertile a source for jazz improvisation. And in his commentary on the 'late' songs, Forte points out how Gershwin, more than most popular balladeers, had the faculty for growth and maturation usually associated with art composers. Forte's uncovering of the pentatonic formulation (based on Big Ben's chimes) that underlines 'A foggy day' relates that teasingly wistful number to the major issues of innocence and experience explored in *Porgy and Bess*; while even the cynical audacity of 'Nice work if you can get it' yields unexpectedly metaphysical insights, since "the music and lyric finally get together at the beginning of chorus 2, where the initial B7 chord, laden with accoutrements, now expresses the lyric's 'Loving'". At bar three, the bass begins a chain of fifths that mimics the one in bars one to three, reinforcing the plaintive twist in the lyric: "Won't you tell me how?" The question, which adds a disturbing extra bar to the standard thirty-two-bar formula, remains unanswered; the unusual shape of the song hints that it may be unanswerable.

Like Cole Porter, Richard Rodgers was born (in 1902) into an affluent New York family and college educated, at Columbia. He was not, however, as glamorous as Porter or, in his way, Gershwin, but was rather a middle-of-the-road professional, who, while at college, teamed up with the lyricist Lorenz Hart, forming a duo hardly less intimate than the Gershwin brothers. The critic Alec Wilder has maintained that Rodgers's numbers display the "highest ever level of consistency, excellence, inventiveness and sophistication"—impressive attributes that cannily avoid the question of value. The more cautious Charles Hamm reckoned that Rodgers's songs, while being "superb examples of a song style developed by several of his older contemporaries, failed to break new ground". Either way, there can be no question that Rodgers deserves his place among the elect; and Forte's account credits him with some of Gershwin's ability to grow and to develop. An early number like 'Thou swell' (1927) juggles ingeniously with verbal and musical rhythms; but two years later, Rodgers is capable of producing a number like 'A ship without a sail', the title of which immediately suggests a more dangerous voyage. Rodgers liked the song's "unusual metrical construction" and Forte admires its opening, with two descending major sixths. The tune, written before the words, provokes nautical imagery in Hart's lyric which Rodgers capped with a 'Tristan' chord, on the word "love".

Harold Arlen, the junior member of Forte's Six, was born in 1905; his father was cantor in a Buffalo synagogue. Arlen spent his apprenticeship years in New York, writing songs for Harlem's Cotton Club and working with bands led by Cab Calloway, Jimmy Lunceford, and the great Duke Ellington. His instinctive musicianship and Jewish acuity made him just the man to fuse Black spontaneity with White know-how—a sleight of hand and voice that marked him out as the natural successor to Gershwin, presenting confrontations between innocence and experience in 'a darker shade of pale'. The best-known example of this is the superb torch-song, 'Stormy weather', which Forte doesn't discuss; but he comments illuminatingly on the "remarkable melodic design" of 'Last night when we were young', which depends on the way in which, in the second chorus, "the ubiquitous chain of bass fifths still holds sway, bringing the progression to rest on the tonic note which, at this terminal moment, and after all the rich chromatic harmonies, supports an unadorned tonic triad. What could be a more expressive close?"

It was probably Arlen's deep awareness of the blues that made it possible for him to create his supreme success—in white and pink. 'Over the rainbow' was written in 1938 for *The Wizard of Oz*, in which it was performed by the seventeen-year-old Judy Garland. Forte subjects its open-eyed simplicities to detailed analysis, commenting especially on the bridge passage that some have thought too guileless to be true. In suggesting that it is precisely this bridge that puts the seal on what he calls the song's 'perfection', Forte pays another tribute to genius, as distinct from talent. Sophisticated musicians who have marvelled at this apparently infantile song's power to move us may find themselves, after reading Forte's account, a shade wiser.

The chapter on Arlen forms a climax to Forte's study, but the remaining sections are not otiose. A long chapter on selected songs by other composers makes no mistakes; the numbers considered are all intrinsically interesting. Some—for instance, those of Hoagy Carmichael, whose most famous number, 'Stardust', started off as a wordless piano piece—are of considerable historical and documentary importance. Forte ends with a chapter dedicated to women composers working in the world of show-music, especially Gershwin's collaborator and close friend, Kay Swift, who died three years ago, aged ninety-five. Forte is good, too, on Anne Ronell's 'Willow weep for me', though this may merely mean that I welcomed such enlightening commentary on a number that has always 'fetched' me.

The Music of Gershwin, written by a pupil of Allen Forte, is also Schenker-orientated, and serves to show how Gershwin's concert works have held their place in the repertory not because they embrace sequences of good show tunes held together by Lisztian candyfloss, but because they have their own structural, if unacademic, coherence. Steven Gilbert writes persuasively of the best of these pieces, *An American in Paris*, though he doesn't consider why the two still later works, the *Second Rhapsody* and the *Cuban Overture*, haven't become repertory pieces. Could it be that their tunes aren't vintage Gershwin, even if the symphonic sections accord with Schenkerian analysis? The chapter on *Porgy and Bess* is a let-down. Although it discusses the opera's long-range structure and comments in Schenkerian terms on the individual songs, it doesn't relate these events to what happens musically and experientially. In dealing with opera, musical analysis that doesn't tell us what happens, when and why, misses the boat—tiresomely, rather than tragically, as do Bess and Porgy. There is a real need for a substantial book on the *music* of George Gershwin; ironically, this one fails because it is too exclusively musical.

TLS, JULY 1996

A VOICE IN THE WILDERNESS

Jeffrey Miller, *In Touch: The Letters of Paul Bowles*
(London: Harper Collins, 1994)

O N SEVERAL OCCASIONS, PAUL BOWLES WROTE TO FRIENDS AND PUB-
lishers proffering chronological information about his extraordinary life. In a letter dated September 1958, addressed to James
Michie of Heinemann, he recounts that he was "born in New York City
during the age of Prohibition". Leaving secondary school at sixteen, he
enrolled in an art school but, finding it "silly", relinquished it at the end of
his first term. He moved to the University of Virginia because Poe had been
there; but abandoned that (also silly) institution half-way through his first
term. He went off to Paris, where he encountered sundry surrealists and
latched on to, and modestly contributed to, *transition*, that landmark of
avant-gardism. When Paris too palled, he

started walking round Western Europe; briefly returned to the University of Virginia,
only to escape again: this time to Berlin, where I first met Isherwood and Spender.
Then Gertrude Stein suggested I should go to Morocco. So I did, and wandered
about Morocco, Algeria, the Sahara, and Tunisia for four years, then went to the West
Indies. After that, South America and Central America. In between I came back to
write scores for Broadway shows, of which I have done about two dozen, among
others the first William Saroyan play and the last Tennessee Williams play. When the
war finished I went back to Morocco where I bought a small house . . . Then I went
back to the Sahara, where I wrote *The Sheltering Sky*. After that I went to India, where
I began *Let it come down*, then to Ceylon, where I saw a little island I liked. I laid the
grounds for an eventual purchase and heard in Madrid the following autumn that I
could buy, which I did that very day. Again I went to Ceylon, and wrote *The Spider's
House*. Then I went to Japan. Then back to Morocco, where I put together the book
called *Yallah*. Then I went to South Africa . . . and back to Ceylon, where I arranged a
Rockefeller Grant to record indigenous music in Morocco . . . Back to Tangier, where
my political past caught up with me. Troubles ensued. I settled in Portugal for a few
months and was in Albuferia when a telephone call came from New York asking me
to return immediately, to aid in staging a [Lorca] play I had adapted from the Spanish
and written an extensive score for. I didn't want to come back but I came; I'm also
doing a score for the new Tennessee Williams opus.

From that bald summary of a summary it's obvious that Paul Bowles is,
among artists, an, or even the, ultimate expatriate. Characteristically, however, in listing the 'facts', he makes no surmises as to motivations behind
them; nor does his autobiography of 1972 indulge in interior speculation—
indeed, William Burroughs maintained that it should have been called

"Without telling", rather than *Without Stopping*. Yet, paradoxically, Bowles's faculty for not telling was an incentive to his creation. His father was rigorously repressive; his mother was too feeble to oppose her husband. Horrendous anecdotes about father's harshness surface in Paul's childhood dreams and in his juvenile story-telling and picture-making; in some stories of his maturity—especially in the chillingly but appropriately titled 'Pages from Cold Point'—anecdote acquires the status of myth. Whether or not it was factually accurate, the tale of Paul's being exposed by his father to the bleak midwinter as punishment for some presumptive misdemeanour, or, perhaps, merely to toughen him up, freezes our marrows as well as Paul's. No wonder he wanted to be everything his father, a prosperous dentist, wasn't; and no wonder that he 'got away', on his limited resources, as fast and as far as possible.

Yet that negative process had positive consequences. The parents, after all, must have contributed to the boy's exceptionally precocious talents, in both intellectual and imaginative terms. From the age of four or five, in the cocoon of his private life, Paul read voraciously in English, and soon acquired other European languages that were spontaneously developed during his teenage travels. It would seem that Paul's Poe- and Machen-style dreams had disturbing affinities with New York and dentistry; while his first notated stories prove that fairy-tales both seductive and scary could be woven out of Freudian guilts as well as Jungian achetypes. If Paul decided that music was the art in which he would invest his potential, that may have been because music, being the least intellectually articulate of arts, could most readily disguise, without betraying, dangerous reality. Bowles's role as "invisible spectator"—not committed to but recording experience *ex periculo*—was already implicit in his choosing music as a channel of creativity, though not for 'self-expression'.

Significantly, Bowles knew, back in his early days at the University of Virginia, that the music that would turn him on was not that of Western tradition. Writing to a college friend, William Treat Upton, he remarks that,

art music will get what it needs not from new subjects to sing about, nor from new technical devices... but from new ways to sing, which will be increasingly conscious of folk musics of all corners of the globe, particularly the unfamiliar corners. When one considers the potentialities of the endless variety latent in the human throat and hears the miserable and pitiable sounds from a concert hall during a famous singer's recital, one realizes the size of the task that lies ahead of the composer and the truly creative interpreter to keep this form of art alive beyond the time of the present dying generation.

What looks like a technical comment turns out to embrace an aesthetic and a philosophy: for the "dying generation" referred to is not merely the people currently alive in Bowles's society, but the industrialized West itself. A musical technique stands for an alternative life, inverting a famous precedent in inviting Bowles to "go East, young man"—as far as possible, both physically and metaphysically, from the Christ-ridden, industrially despoiled place of his birth. Bowles's formidable strength is attested in the fact that, while being only hazily aware of the cost, he obeyed the prompting of his heart.

Paul's apartness, as a child and a young man, inevitably had a sexual as well as artistic dimension. In a letter to his college friend Bruce Morrissette, written in 1929 when he was nineteen, Paul confesses, in juvenile breathlessness, that

homosexuality is a thrilling subject for me, just as sanguinary killings are, and rapes, and tales of drug addicts . . . Moi, I should like to know all forms of pleasure . . . knowing beforehand that to all I should remain equally indifferent . . . I have a feeling that bestiality, or whatever one calls it, would be more idyllic than human intercourse. There has never been a person, même my mother, for whom I felt the affection I feel for almost any cat.

Later, Bowles hazarded that his homosexual or bisexual drive was of low voltage, this being itself an aspect of his outsider-status.

The two men who initiated Bowles into music were both gay. Henry Cowell, who introduced Paul to the Arabic music of which he was to make, decades later, so impressive an anthology of tapes, was rewardingly married, but spent a spell in prison, during the McCarthy years, for homosexual offences; the great Aaron Copland, as empathetic a man as he was distinguished composer, became Paul's teacher, and significantly accompanied him on his first pilgrimage to Morocco, though it is improbable that they were lovers. The list of Bowles's correspondents over a long lifetime embraces a dazzling array of homosexual talents: lesbian Gertrude Stein, who first sent him to Morocco; Beat poets and novelists such as Ginsberg, Kerouac and Burroughs; powerfully cultish writers like Truman Capote, Tennessee Williams, Carson McCullers, and Gore Vidal.

Perhaps the most potent influence on Bowles's formative years was the Parisian collaboration of Gertrude Stein and Virgil Thomson on their 'opera' *Four Saints in Three Acts*, created in 1928, but first performed, in Paul Bowles's presence, in New York in 1934. Despite its Parisian chic, *Four Saints* portrays in rock-bottom terms *The Making of Americans* chronicled in Stein's interminable novel of that name.* That the opera also seems interminable is the point, since its anti-climax is St Ignatius's vision of Pure Being in the famous "Pigeons on the grass Alas" episode, wherein homely homing pigeons are metamorphosed into holy doves. Stein had conceived the libretto as one of her 'landscape' plays in which people, things, and stories, being coexistent rather than consecutive, are in concept non- or even anti-Western.

The aesthetic of *Four Saints* pervades much of Bowles's music, which is either 'occasional' in being devised for specific circumstances or 'incidental' in being an accompaniment to theatre. Musical devices inherited from Thomson and Copland, and behind them from Satie and the 'cubist' Stravinsky of the 1920s and 30s, establish links between Bowles's music and the 'music of necessity' manifest in the sung and danced rituals of the Arabic and Latin American musics he picked up on his travels. Bowles's music liberates in the vivacity of present moments, eschewing expressionist intentionality. 'Ephemeral' theatre music that scored strongly in the 1930s and 40s still packs a punch, reminding me that during the Second World War the late Marc Blitzstein, in this country as a composer to the US Forces, remarked to me that "If ever Paul Bowles gets round to writing a Work, it'll be a *humdinger*". He never did, the reason being that his centre of creative gravity shifted from music to words: a shift itself a consequence of his bifurcated nature. Although he did not consciously pursue the unconscious, seeking psychological if not sexual penetration, he couldn't remain content with a Steinian child's-eye-view. In physically separating himself from the social world, in deliberately seeking homelessness, in globe-trotting, and in his final acceptance of a (telephoneless) wilderness and desert, he needed articulate words and musical sounds to explore motivations as well as, or rather than, moments of being. This bears on his sexual orientation, for in 1938 he married Jane Auer, a young Jewish girl of remarkable elfin vivacity, and a burgeoning writer of dazzlingly original fiction.

Jane was a lesbian who relished casually promiscuous encounters as a warm refuge from an inimical world. When she had long-term relationships, as with white Helvetia Perkins and with her fiercely greedy Moroccan servant, they amounted to obsessions as much neurotic as erotic. Paul, as usual reluctant to tell his own tale as distinct from other people's, offered no weightier explanation of his marrying than that it was something people usually did: just as, later, he gave as his reason for joining the Communist Party the fact that lots of his contemporaries seemed to be doing so. In the normal sense, Paul's and Jane's marriage didn't amount to much; they lived mostly in separate apartments, often in different places and even different countries, pursuing in Jane's case a search for identity manifest in her exiguous stories and plays, and in Paul's case, a clinical analysis of mores and manners in worlds as remote as possible from his birthright. Yet, at a deeper level they needed, were indeed devoted to, one another precisely because their roles were complementary. Though neither wanted sex from the other, Jane needed social status as the Wife of Paul Bowles, while Paul perhaps unwittingly needed Jane's emotive desperation as proof that human communication might still be possible. Eventually, Jane's genius earned her fame as well as cult-status, though she killed herself, mostly by way of alcohol, in the process.

The first of a series of strokes ended her writing career at the age of forty, after which she declined into intermittent lunacy, and ultimately into a near-vegetative state. Paul's 'coolness' made it possible for him to cope with this with something approaching efficiency, though, of course, he never let on at what cost to himself. He now had no choice but to confront, in personal terms, the abyss which he had celebrated (and that is the appropriate word) in his ruthless alienation. Even after her decline, everyone remembered Jane in her pristine ebullience; after her death Paul virtually abandoned original creation to become a mouthpiece for—or a recorder, transcriber, and translator of—texts by Arabic story-tellers whose art was oral and aural rather than literate. Thus Eastern and Western worlds fused, barriers were broken: a synthesis inherent too in the way Bowles wrote his novels, in which the initial themes were planned out on the bases of 'reality'—often in the form of quite trivial occurrences—while the resolution of the people and plots was handed over to unconscious process. Even in his first novel, *The Sheltering Sky*, Bowles knew that the death would be irremediable, but did not know how it would occur until it happened.

Bowles's finest years predated his work as an oral-story-teller, for he achieved literate fulfilment in those early short stories that drew mythically on childhood experience, and in *The Sheltering Sky*, which, though not directly autobiographical, played painful variations on Paul and Jane, death and desert. In this novel, published in 1949, the horror that juvenile Paul had relished in Poe and Machen is no longer a game, but a revelation of the Heart of Darkness no less shattering than that of Conrad's Mister Kurtz, an achievement made feasible only by Paul's non-commitment. Whereas Jane had to kill herself in her acts of self-discovery, Paul survived in the laconicism of his cool prose, and perhaps even in his fetishes about grammatical and linguistic correctness. Thus he faced the terror of the sheltering sky that sheltered nothing but emptiness; and given the book's "terrifying honesty", it was predictable that, though first acclaimed as a cult-book issued by a cult-publisher, it became a best-seller, proving that to some degree his horror was also ours.

Bowles's later novels were respectfully, even enthusiastically, received, though *The Sheltering Sky*'s success was not repeatable. *Let it Come Down* (1952) turns a glassily amoral eye on human relationships, and finds a perverse euphoria in the acceptance of catastrophe. *The Spider's House* (1955) expands the theme of culture-clash and creed-clash into the labyrinths of Eastern-Western politics, leaving orientals bemused and occidentals bamboozled. *Up Above the World* (1966) turns Western morality topsy-turvy, in a way that is no less scary for being described, though not dismissed, as an 'entertainment' in Graham Greene's sense. There is point in the fact that, whereas Jane destroyed herself by way of the Western drug of alcohol, Paul found salvation through kif.

Some of Bowles's letters describe in painstaking and pain-inducing detail the effects of kif, hashish, and mescalin; occasionally, in offering documentary evidence, they amount to works of art that help us to understand how Bowles's fictional nihilism could be supportable. In an extraordinary letter to the composer Ned Rorem, written from Asilah in August 1963, Paul, high on mescalin, inverts reality and illusion:

See where you are. Look around. This is what it's like. Can you stand seeing it, touching it? Fortunately, one draws no conclusions, since everything is far too real to mean anything. Disgust is what one would feel if one were alive. But disgust is something that ought to be felt *for* someone, by someone. But of course there is not even anyone to experience the disgust, so it remains there, unfelt, but around one— unregistered loathing, inattainable nausea.

It's half past one now. The room is full of insects, borne on the stench of the ocean. Ever since the first day of May the smell has got a little stronger, the stains on the cement have grown blacker and thicker as layer dries on layer. The fishheads crawl with maggots and bristle with flies. Sometimes I take a litre of gasoline and pour it over a particularly lively pile of garbage by the front door. The neighbours stick their heads out of the windows above and watch. They think it is something to do with my religion, and very likely it is. *Don't we all want to be cremated—we who no longer have any connection with the earth?* [my italics].

Though this is hardly an inspiring message to leave to posterity, it was the condition of Bowles's survival: he 'came through' what he believed to be the end of Western civilization to confront, from the empty desert 'out there', the interior desert left by Jane's self-destruction.

The American characters in Bowles's stories tend to be detached from history and from narrative sequence. They exist in 'landscapes' of their currently contradictory moments, as do the creatures inhabiting Stein's and Thomson's saintly opera; and if being 'lost' is the source of their despair, it is also a condition of their momentary gaiety, in more than one sense. Does the same apply to the stories Bowles has created or compiled over the 1970s and 80s, in the mask of an oral story-teller like Mohammed Mrabet, who, through Bowles's agency, has become a successful literate author in a non-literate society? The answer is yes and no, in that Mrabet's tales sometimes describe the divisions and destructions wrought between human beings, especially husbands and wives, by alcohol, while also envisaging amiable, even comic, reunions and renewals engendered by Eastern hashish. If this means that Bowles believes that happiness can never be more than illusory, that is no reason for being ungrateful for it. In a letter written to Peter Garland in 1977, Bowles tells him that the lovely, gamelan-influenced music of the Californian, Lou Harrison, played by Paul on tape to attentive Moroccans, inspires them to transports of delight, since they consider it the music of Paradise. We may recall that Bowles's own music, during the years in which he made it, was, if not paradisal, usually happy, and sometimes funny, as his fictional prose seldom or never is.

How wonderful it would be if Bowles could, in his eighty-fifth year, return to music to create that 'humdinger' of a work which, half a century ago, Marc Blitzstein thought him capable of. This being improbable, we can none the less get a notion of what such a music might sound like from a marvellous letter that Paul addressed, in 1947, to Peggy Glanville-Hicks, the Australian-born, California-adopted composer with whom Paul had a relationship which, though probably not sexual, was intimate enough to fan flames of jealousy in lesbian Jane. The aural paradise here evoked is

compound of the natural sounds of Fez, that fill the spaces that would otherwise have been only silence. Wind, water, birds, animals, and (here) human voices make a fine auditory backdrop. The human voices make the most beautiful sounds of all, when the muezzin calls during the night . . . They preface the actual mouddin with religious remarks sung in freely embroidered florid style, each man inventing his own key, mode, appogiature and expressive devices. And when you have a hundred or more of these incredibly high, birdlike voices doing flamenco runs in different modes and rhythms from different minarets, against a background of cocks crowing, you have a very strange and special sound.

Having over many years little access to modern communication techniques, Bowles was a prolific letter-writer, with a large circle of correspondents, among whom the most rewarding tend to be composers such as Virgil Thomson and Peggy Granville-Hicks. A 'biographical chronology' helps us to sort out the lesser known among Bowles's famous or infamous acquaintance, though a few photographs would have lent lustre to his paradoxical fusions of illusion and reality. Still, Jeffrey Millar has judiciously selected material from a vast storehouse; and the book is handsomely produced.

TLS, JANUARY 1995

UP THE MARSHY CREEK

John Barth, *Once Upon a Time: A Floating Opera*
(London: Sceptre, 1994)

JOHN BARTH WAS A PHENOMENON OF THE 1960S: AND SINCE (GOOD) LITER-
ature IS, in Ezra Pound's phrase, "news that STAYS news", he still is. Like
Pound, Barth too "made it new"; and what he made still matters to us. He
had several false starts before evolving a prose style at once precise and flexible enough to create imagined worlds that are so vividly embodied that
they can seem truer than truth. By the time of *The Sot-Weed Factor* (1960),
his medley of historical know-how, pristine invention and poetic discovery
seemed irresistible, and in 1966, his *Giles Goat-Boy*, a long, intricate, disturbingly funny book, not only achieved cult status, but unexpectedly
became a best-seller. With hindsight, we can see that its mythical themes
turned on all the issues (of consciousness and unconsciousness, of intelligence, natural and artificial) that pressurized people then and still concern
us today. Barth himself, in this new novel, looks back and tells us that *Giles
Goat-Boy* presented

the world as one big University, divided by cold war polarities into rival campus
blocs. The hero is sired somehow by the *West Campus* mainframe computer on a
virginal librarian no longer in her first youth. To hide the scandal, the baby is put out
with the prize goats on one of the University's remote experimental livestock farms
and through his kidship he's raised by the goats as one of themselves, watched over
by a maverick old genius named Max Spielman.

The story of *Once Upon a Time* enacts the basic myth of the eternal
return, involving a quest and a perilous journey: from a mysterious birth, initiation, exile, confrontation with demons of sundry sorts, to a return by way
of death and transfiguration. Such patterns of behaviour were outlined by
key writers of the 1960s, such as Joseph Campbell, Northrop Frye and Marshall McLuhan, all of whom play vicarious roles in this book. But it is not an
anthropological, let alone a theological, tract, and what matters is the identity
it achieves between the present reality of narration and its putative, sometimes contradictory meanings. *Once Upon a Time* tells its author's personal
story, or parts of it, while at the same time admitting, by way of its title, that
the true story is also a fairy-tale. Barth started the book in the year devoted to
the (sometimes denunciatory) celebration of Columbus's discovery of the
New World; and he has produced a 'memoir' which re-creates not only himself, but also a world. He sees all facts as fiction in so far as facts have mythic
implications; and it is significant that Barth gives his 'true fiction' a musical

266

context that overrides verbal meaning. In doing so, he returns to his first published creation, *The Floating Opera*, which made a fantasy world out of the riverboat musical shows popular during his provincial youth.

This new 'opera' floats on a sea of memory and desire, tracing its archetypal quest. The Overture (which is very long in proportion to what turns out to be a less-than-three-act-opera) is set in the present moment of writing (1990–92), in the Maryland Barth lives in and from which he and his second wife are about to embark on a voyage in their boat, punningly named US. Their home, the marshy creeks they start from, the vagaries of light and water, are evoked with startling immediacy, as are the tools of Barth's trade, in this case old-fashioned pens. This factual pilgrimage is counterpointed against an ideal pilgrimage undertaken by a friend and his wife, reversing Columbus's voyage of discovery, and carrying it beyond its source. This friend, Jerry (Jerome) Schreiber, also known as Jay Scribner, may be compounded of several mates from Barth's childhood and adolescence but is, as his names indicate, an *alter ego* for Barth himself.

Back in the Maryland marshes, Barth and his wife, in their craft, are engulfed by a savage hurricane; the two lovers are separated from one another. Lost and alone, the Barth figure encounters, or imagines he encounters, a vision of his remote past in the person of his twin sister: historical memory confronts present fact and timeless myth. This interweaving of levels of reality makes for a 'tapestry', that is rich, but also arbitrary, as is made clear when the Overture's preview of themes and motives emerges into the opera proper.

Act One relives the traumas of childhood and adolescence, with goat-boy Barth, his parents, twin sister and elder brother and the mythical Schreiber or Scribner, acting as Virgilian guide to the author's Dante. Disorderly narrative is interspersed with reflections after events, described as arias, ariettes, duets or trios; but pithy footnotes intermittently establish where we stand in relation to the present. 'Events' include both what happens to us in relation to other people and the world, and what happens in our minds and sense, by native wit and by way of the books, papers and letters we read, the movies we watch, and the music we listen to and make. Jazz proves significant in the lives of the twins, Jack and Jill, and of their ghost-friend Jerry/Jay; and the jazz sections of the book offer an unusually, perhaps even uniquely, perceptive account of the jazz experience. But, despite the spiritual as well as physical alleviation of jazz, the First Act of this 'opera' ends in a Fall such as is endemic to childhood. The parodic analysis of the Jack and Jill nursery rhyme, here, is as acute as it is hilarious, and leaves us in no doubt that this mini-fall foreshadows the author's real (if temporary) loss of his real wife in the real marshes. The Entr'acte that follows Act One is called 'In the Dark'.

Act Two of the opera—with the Hero grown up, youthfully married, three times a father, in and out of colleges, studying and teaching, improvident, impecunious, always stringing words together—is even more pluralistic that the First Act. Jack and Jerry (Jerome, Jay) evolve from brat-brawling childhood to enjoy varying degrees of success in academia and varying levels of affluence. Real but also legendary figures, among them Theodore Roethke, Charles Olson, Dos Passos, Lukas Foss, and George Boas (Barth's teacher at Johns Hopkins) are hardly less central than the main protagonists; while the world itself—crowded with wars and rumours of war, political tyrannies at home and abroad, and media heroes who make fantasy barely distinguishable from 'reality'—becomes more bewildering the more we are conscious of it. The shifting kaleidoscope of external events and internal occurrences makes Act Two of the novel no less comically ebullient, but more turbulent that the First Act. Even so, chaos pays off, for the next Entr'acte summons not darkness but light.

This light centres, with no suspicion of corniness, on the young woman who becomes Barth's second wife, and the sea-mate of the voyage presented in the Overture. Yet the promised Third Act does not, 'in fact', occur, for the sound reason that the new love (who has in fact lasted more than twenty years) refuses to play a fictional part in it. Her mythical influence remains, however, and the reader can rejoice in Barth's distillation of—from a catalogue of life's evasions, ambiguities, deceptions and self-deceptions—a faculty for love.

Barth's strings of sentences may often alarm, but their impetus is in the deepest sense poetic. When, at the end of the book, though not of the unfolding story, Barth says a farewell to his *alter ego*, he calls him "my vigilant, virtual Virgil": a joke that spreads slow circles over a very deep pool. The 'fireworks' of his prose are a tribute to the sometimes virulent virility of the American language, but since the writing is "as natural as breathing", the popular comparison with the dandyish Nabokov seems misplaced. His achievement, he believes, is simply that "the sentences get written", making factual fiction and fictional fact. His *alter ego*, Jerry/Jerome/Jay, enquires: "What makes you think you have it man?" To which Barth retorts:

It was an honest question not an interrogative criticism. "I guess I don't think anything, Jay: just put one word after another, and the next after that." Hands in his hip pockets, elbows winged out, he regarded me. Have I mentioned that it was a delicious Baltimore late April night, glistening from a warm rain shower, azaleas just opening but dogwoods and tulip magnolias in full bloom. It now was. I shrugged and smiled. I shrug and smile.

TLS, NOVEMBER 1994

ON THE OLD EXOTICISM TRIP

Carol J. Oja, *Colin Mcphee: Composer in Two Worlds*
(Washington DC: Smithsonian Institution Press, 1990)

T
HE NOTION OF WORLD MUSIC HAS BECOME A COMMONPLACE. NOW-
adays, horizons are wider; in particular, the seraphic sounds of the
Balinese gamelan have become familiar throughout thousands of
schools and colleges in the United States, and are beginning to proliferate in
Britain and in other outposts of industrial civilization. It's easy to say that
the culture and philosophy implicit in Balinese music are so remote from
those of our Western industrial technocracies that such an obsession can be
no more than an escape. But there's also a positive aspect to the cult of Balinese music, in that it is a non-competitive communal activity in which
anyone may democratically join. With no imposition of ego and will, one
may participate to the level of one's ability. Small wonder that the young
take to the gamelan so naturally. By now there's a group of West Coast
American composers, led by Lou Harrison, who construct their own oriental but indigenous gamelans, and make for them modern American
music which does indeed, like the ancient Balinese art, "cherish, conserve,
consider, create".

This tradition, so different from, yet not radically opposed to, Western
progress, stemmed mostly from work accomplished during the 1940s and
50s by Lou Harrison in association with John Cage. They had, however, a
precursor in Colin McPhee, the subject of this handsomely produced book
in the Smithsonian Institution Press's series of monographs on (mostly forgotten) American composers. The author, Carol J. Oja, thinks McPhee is
unjustly forgotten, and to a degree she is right, for he has considerable documentary importance. Canadian-born in 1900, he had ancestors from the
isle of Islay in the Outer Hebrides where—ironically enough, as we'll see—
the whisky comes from. He spent his boyhood in Toronto where, being
musically precocious, he soon acquired local celebrity as a pianist of dazzling virtuosity, especially dedicated to the music of Liszt. He also composed fairly prolifically, and was soon harried by a need for more
sophisticated and cosmopolitan standards. Unharried, however, by strin-
gent financial circumstances, he followed other American composers of his
generation to Paris, where he became a pupil not of the redoubtable Nadia
Boulanger, but of Paul Le Flem, a student of Roussel. Under the aegis of literary figures like Stein, Joyce, Hemingway, Crane and Cummings, and
encouraged by composers like Copland, Marc Blitzstein, Roy Harris, Virgil
Thomson, and French disciples of Satie and Stravinsky, McPhee was not

short of intellectual stimulation. He recrossed the Atlantic in 1926 and settled in New York, eventually becoming and American citizen.

Before long he was accepted as a leading figure in New York's glittering
musical scene, though his rate of production was not impressive. In 1928,
however, he composed a concerto for piano and wind octet, in which he
played the solo with considerable éclat. Although the piece deserved its success and is still occasionally heard, it seems at this date of historical rather
than intrinsic interest, for there is little in it that hadn't been better done by
Stravinsky in his Wind Octet of 1923 and his concerto for piano and wind of
1924. With hindsight, we may decide that the interest of McPhee's concerto
is not so much in its qualities as a work of art as in its being a harbinger of
later developments. For its geometric pattern-making and glittering
metallic sonorities acquire, retrospectively, distinctly non-Western if not
specifically Balinese characteristics; and it may be no accident that
McPhee's next work, the *Sea Chanty Suite* for baritone solo, male chorus,
two pianos and two sets of timpani, exploits similar sonorities while also
encroaching on the oral, rather than literate, conventions of folk-music.

Moreover, it was precisely at this time, the end of the 1920s, that McPhee
heard newly released recordings of Balinese gamelan. Enchanted with the
sounds, he asked "who were the musicians? How did this music come
about? Above all, how was it possible, in this late day, for such a music to
have been able to survive?" He determined to find out. Although homosexual by inclination, he married Jane Belo, an intelligent and talented
woman rich enough to take him to Bali and to support him while he
researched its music. Perhaps the end justified the means: for although
McPhee did not become a great or even a very good composer, he wrote two
books that have become classics. One, *A House in Bali*, tells the tale of the
beautiful house Jane built for them, and of the life they lived in it, potentially as part of the native community; this is a superior travel book which
is really, and crucially, about what makes life worth living. The other book,
Music in Bali, is a large-scale study which remains authoritative, even
definitive. Though scholarly, it is without pedantry, since McPhee's concern
is not only how the instruments and music function, but also with why
their effects are as they are. He writes very well; and although the big book,
thirty-odd years in gestation, wasn't published until 1966, the 'McPhee
experience' was a significant factor in the Balinese reorientation initiated by
Cage and Harrison. The McPhees lived in Bali between 1931 and 1934, and
were back again, living separately, in 1937 and 1938. In the intervening years,
1935–6, McPhee was in New York consorting with progressive musicians
and trying to launch what he believed to be his masterpiece, *Tabuh-
tabuhan*, a work for large orchestra based on his piano transcriptions of

Balinese gamelan. But although Copland, Blitzstein, Paul Bowles, Wallingford Riegger and many others encouraged and extolled him, the piece
didn't get performed in New York. That was left to Carlos Chávez in Mexico
City, where *Tabuh-tabuhan* was a momentary sensation. Momentary, however, it was; and the reasons for its non-survival, not spelled out by Oja, are
inherent in the painful tale her book tells.

Of course *Tabuh-tabuhan* has some historical importance; in its own
terms it is brilliantly written, and we shouldn't forget that McPhee's Balinese transcriptions had some influence on Benjamin Britten's much more
creative use of Balinese devices in *The Prince of the Pagodas* and even in the
later church parables. Yet one has only to compare McPhee's *Tabuh-
tabuhan* with the magically beautiful Piano Concerto written by Lou Harrison for Keith Jarrett in 1985 to realise that McPhee's piece founders on a
deceit. For although the main reason for the superiority of the Harrison
work is that he is the better composer, there is also a matter of principle
involved. McPhee, transcribing Balinese gamelan for equal-tempered
modern instruments, destroys the music's soul—which is inherent in its
relatively *just* intonation. Any system of temperament must be to a degree a
fall from grace, though some declensions are steeper than others. There is
little evidence in this book that McPhee, though he had written expertly of
the traditional tunings, was much bothered by their philosophical and even
psychological implications. This may be why *Tabuh-tabuhan*, whatever its
virtues, remains a part of what Steve Reich called "the old exoticism trip";
whereas Harrison's concerto, in which the piano is tuned in a subtle compromise between East and West, is an aural revelation to, and a spiritual
experience for, us divided and distracted twentieth-century creatures.

Nor is it entirely fanciful to relate this technical matter to the disastrous
story of McPhee's life. While he intermittently exhibited a charm that
beguiled well-wishers other than his long-suffering wife, his jeremiads
about the state of the wicked world (especially in reference to his own talents), his self-absorption and his infantile petulance prove increasingly tiresome. One suspects that it was in part his own fault that his 'masterpiece'
wasn't played in New York, and that his late creative flowering—in the 1950s
and after the success of his books—proved abortive. Oja's analyses of the
Second (Pastoral) Symphony and of the *Nocturne* for chamber orchestra
are persuasive enough to make us want to hear them; but not to convince
us, or even herself, that they are major contributions. By the time McPhee
produced them he was a sick man, with an alcohol-damaged liver. Drink
may have been his craven answer to the neglect he thought he suffered
from—and to the loss of the beautiful brown boys of Bali, who were no
doubt as solacing as the tintinnabulations of their bells and gongs. Of

course it wasn't the sexually permissive Balinese but McCarthyite WASPS who eventually drove him from his island paradise. At least he made his own memorial, for McPhee will be remembered for one great book unlikely to be superseded; and perhaps for another small book that charms as it tells us what was wrong with *his* life, not to mention those of the rest of us.

TLS, MARCH 1991

AN AUTHENTIC AMERICAN COMPOSER
HOBO MUSIC FROM THE GLOBAL VILLAGE

Harry Partch, *Bitter Music: Collected Journals, Essays, Introductions and Librettos*, edited by Thomas McGeary (Champaign: University of Illinois Press, 1991)

O NE OF THE MOST MYSTERIOUS WAYS IN WHICH GOD PERFORMS HIS wonders is the anomaly whereby the absolute consonance of his 'perfect' fifth won't exactly tally with the cycle that makes harmonic, modulatory music possible. In the harmonic systems of Europe's classical musics octaves, fifths and thirds are incommensurate in their pure forms; 'pure' intonation is feasible only in the monophony of presumptive angels, and of some savages and orientals. If Harry Partch (1901–74) is the most radical among the grand old pioneers who sought for a distinctively New World music, the reason is that for him Just Intonation was not merely a technical matter, but the profoundest possible criticism of our Western life. For Partch, the equal temperament that, since Bach, has made the glories of Western music realizable, was literally a fall from grace to disgrace. We Europeans have created musical artefacts of extreme sophistication; for so-called primitive peoples, on the other hand, there is no artefact in the form of a score. The discovery of sound-sources in the world out there, and their metamorphosis into *instruments* through which natural and supernatural forces may speak, is itself an act of creation: in which sense the medium is indeed the message.

Harry Partch, reared in the parched wastes of the Californian and Arizonan deserts, was favourably placed to begin again, *ab ovo*. He disowned such music as he had composed in conventionally Western guises because he came to believe that Western man, along with Western music, was on the wrong track. His renovated new music was about as old as music could get: for Partch, like the Amerindians among whom he lived, based it on instruments designed and built by himself, out of materials from his local environment. The extremely beautiful instruments project the spirit of place, and speak truth in that their intonation is as pure as may be, with minimal deference to harmonic exigencies. The players, moreover, need to be worthy of the instruments, for how they stand and move is almost as important as the sounds they utter. This would have been entirely intelligible to Partch's Amerindians; if for him as a white West Coast American the music was inevitably a 'mask', it was far from being passive imitation of Indian chants and dance ceremonies, or of the Japanese kabuki theatre, the Chinese operas, and the African song-and-dance rituals he knew and loved in San Francisco. Partch's instruments, glamorously named Cloud Chambers, Diamond Marimba, Kithara, Harmonic Canon and the like emit sounds relatable to that globally Californian scene, being as distinct in timbre as in tuning from those produced in Western music.

For Partch, music was his life-work in a literal sense. His rediscovery of the word and the body in a 'corporeal' music countered the pretensions, and still more the cheats and deceits based on commodity and consumer ethics, of Western civilizations; and he had the courage of his convictions, abandoning Western civilization for some years to ride the roads and rails as an itinerant hobo. This was not a gesture conformable with the Beat poets and novelists of his generation, but was genuinely a consequence of the Depression years; workless, he bummed around, washing dishes while mulling over the new-old theories of music-theatre for which he could find no material support. Eventually, he garnered financial backing to produce his book, *Genesis of a Music* (1949),* which expounds in vigorous and lucid prose the sociological, ideological, mathematical and acoustical bases of a justly intoned monophony opposed to the artificial temperaments of Western music, and to the (as he thought) bogus civilization that had produced it. Support for his music did not accrue on a comparable scale, and he could hardly have expected it to, since the fulfilment of his ideals would have implied the demise of the society from which he sought succour. People are reluctant to commit suicide: which is what Partch himself did in so far as there was a flaw in his own 'philosophy', as well as in that of the maligned Western world.

This gradually becomes evident in *Bitter Music*, a collation of Partch's miscellaneous writings and lectures, edited by Thomas McGeary and published by the University of Illinois Press with the unPartched elegance typical of their admirable series, Music in American Life. A basic American life features large in the two autobiographical journals, *End Littoral* being an account of Harry's hard hike through the solitudinous coastal mountains of California, while *Bitter Music* describes his years as a travelling bum. Both are written in tough, flexible prose, without self-pity. *Bitter Music* leaves us in no doubt that for Partch life and music were one; personal reflection intermingles with snatches of hobo speech and song, presented in rudimentary notations that demonstrate how "words *are* music", in rockbottom America no less than in ancient Greece, in Gregorian chant, or Provençal troubadour song. Partch's start as an authentic American rather than pseudo-European composer occurred when in 1941 he refashioned some of these aural graffiti into a piece, *Barstow*, named after the place that spawned it, and scored for his own intoning voice, accompanied by his adapted microtonal viola and by *ad hoc* percussion, all played by himself. Never did music spring more basically from word and body.

More ambitiously, Partch capped this in 1943 with *US Highball*, an account of his hobo rail-journey from San Francisco to Chicago, in which the text consists of the names of fleeting railway stations, interspersed with fragments of bum-dialogue, and snatches of advertisements, wayside graffiti, pop tunes, hill-billy and bar-tunes. Partch's instruments impersonate both the trains and the hoboes as characters. In later works the positive and negative aspects of this outcast's journey-to-no-end are more sharply differentiated, (pre-Christian) vitality being opposed to the mechanization and bureaucracy-ridden sterility of the modern world.

Partch epitomizes this duality in calling his theatre-pieces satyrs, since they are satires in the modern sense on the (negatively) barbarous present while also reinvoking the satyrs who were (positively) barbarous sources of potency. This he explains in his prefaces, here reprinted, to his sundry 'plectra and percussion dances', produced in the early 1950s. "Music and dance enter the consciousness through the gate to illusion . . . This might be considered as autobiographical by almost anyone, in darkly humorous moments." Partch defines the sense in which what he does is aligned with jazz and tribal pop, and also the (in his view more significant) sense in which it differs from, or is opposed to, them.

Partch's most sustained, extremely well-written statement of aims comes in his verbal prelude and postlude to *The Bewitched*, first performed on the University of Illinois campus in 1956. The text contains few articulate words, and the instruments effect the action as much as the mimes and dancers. A group of Lost Musicians, aided by an Ancient Witch or Prehistoric Seer, dadaistically and unmaliciously debunk fake products of twentieth-century mechanization and intellectuality—'A Soul Tormented by Contemporary Music finds a Humanizing Alchemy', or 'The Cognoscenti are plunged into a Demonic Descent while at Cocktails'. At the end, the Lost Musicians find that, in their clownish innocence, they already know the only truth that is humanly apprehensible, for "truth is a sandflea", and another moment must seek another flea. So twentieth-century satire merges into what Partch calls slapstick, linking contemporary non-values to values so old they seem eternal. Humans who microtonally yell, moan or grunt in jazzy abandon or hysteria may become indistinguishable from hooting owls, barking foxes and the wild cats of the woods; in returning to Nature they may rediscover their real selves. The long wailing chant at the end of the Prologue evokes, with therapeutic effect, an age-old quietude that is none the less pregnant with longing. Significantly, it is based on a chant of the Cahuilla Indians who live in the southern Californian deserts.

Partch followed *The Bewitched* with three other 'satyrs', all with introductory essays reprinted in this volume. *Revelation in Courthouse Park* (1960) transplants the Bacchae of Euripides to suburban American life;

Water, Water (1961) presents an American city which, afflicted by drought, desperately appeals to a Water Witch: a dangerous course, since the floods released by a very Black jazz band prove so copious that a baseball game has to be abandoned, and Civilization topples in rain and ruin. *Delusion of the Fury* (1969), the last of Partch's Global Village musicals, grimly lives up to its title, and is world-wide in reference. In all these pieces words are semi-articulate, while the instruments are makers of magic, as were the first strings ever plucked or stroked, the first horns ever blown, the first bells or drums ever resonated.

All Partch's works, whether blessings on the house or assaults on our technocracies, are magic that is supposed directly to affect our personal behaviour and communal discourse. Herein lies the rub: for the sharp intelligence of Partch's approach cannot disguise a damaging naivety. It is true that post-Renaissance science and technology have much to answer for in terms of the human weal; but it is also true that post-Renaissance 'consciousness' alone made possible a Shakespeare and a Beethoven, and that when once they've been 'invented', one cannot pretend they never existed. Although Partch said that he had no wish to oust other notions of music (and life), that, given his premises, can only have been self-deceit. There is even an inconsistency in his *wanting* to give set, complexly notated form to a concept that is in principle 'performance music'. In a sense, the dreary distrust of Western values currently rampant in some American universities might be construed as Partchian doctrine carried to the ultimate of imbecility. No wonder Partch was left with a sense of failure—the 'bitterness' in the title to this book.

There were crudely practical reasons why Partch's 'corporeal' ideology could not reach fruition. For his instruments could be developed only in rich (usually industrially sponsored) academic institutions such as were philosophically anathema to him, so that his Global Village, aboriginally a home for Everyman, was rendered élitist. The more inescapably this came home to him, the more curmudgeonly he became in response to the institutions (including the University of Illinois) that had, however inadequately, supported him; and the more his well-wishers (including this reviewer) suffered from his jeremiads about the malignancy of the society he was willy-nilly heir to. One of the consequences of this is that it is now difficult to know just *how* good Partch is. The designedly semi-articulate texts of his theatre pieces do not, on the evidence of their reprinting, offer much purely literary nourishment, for the obvious reason that they were not meant to exist apart from their visual and musical extensions. Equally, the music, though all recorded, wasn't intended to stand as concert music *per se*. In musical terms there are arid stretches as well as marvellous moments (mostly in *The Bewitched*); and even the marvellous moments need theatrical projection for total effect. It would seem that the 'flaw' in Partch's philosophy lay in its simplistic nature, notwithstanding the sharp vigour of his mind. What he asked for could never happen, in the conditions of life as it is; and he wasn't prepared to accommodate what is to what might be.

This is a minor tragedy, for which Partch was himself partly responsible. Still, this book offers occasion for gratitude, for it reminds us that (in the words of Lou Harrison, the Californian composer who has to a degree assumed Partch's mantle): "Harry told the truth about tune, as Kinsey did about sex. In ancient things we hunt eternity—their dust is incense, and beyond them we hear old melodies surely learned from angels." That in turn reminds us that Partch may genuinely claim to have something in common with Yeats, a much greater artist whose translation of Sophocles's *Oedipus* was to provide a text for his first venture into music-theatre. Perhaps the most fascinating item in this collection is Partch's account of his solitary meeting with Yeats: who approved of Harry's 'corporeal' view of the nature of music-theatre, while reciprocally Partch hazarded that Yeats's reported and self-vaunted unmusicality—his inability to 'hold a tune'— was really evidence of his aural acuity, which would not tolerate the 'false' intervals of Western tradition! Well, may be; but not even for Yeats's ear could the entire heritage of Western music be thrown on the trash-heap; and Harry Partch was no Yeats, nor even, as a corporeal composer, a Tippett or Birtwistle.

TLS, MAY 1991

OLD VALUES, NEW DEALS

John Dizikes, *Opera in America: A Cultural History*
(New Haven: Yale University Press, 1996)

O PERA IN AMERICA IS AN ODD PHENOMENON BECAUSE THIS COMPLEX art was a creation of Old Europe at its zenith, when post-renaissance men and women sang paeans of glory to themselves in the highest, proud enough of their indomitable will and irresistible reason to play God. Of course, the great opera composers—notably Monteverdi, Handel, and Mozart—owed their eminence to their recognition of humankind's limitations, as evident in its normality and consequent vulnerability. Even so, opera continued to hymn human courage, if not omnipotence, and to that end called on extravagance of musical, mimetic, and theatrical technique, involving almost superhuman ingenuity, vast material resources, and immense sums of money—mostly provided by the mundane potentates whose glory was the subject of celebration.

Against this European backcloth, America's New World cut a sorry figure. As raw communities were hacked out of the wilderness, there could be no inherited traditions, little aesthetic awareness, a minimum of artistic expertise. Yet 'opera in America' struck roots quickly, and that the art so improbably prospered would seem, on reflection, to make sense. For most Americans were refugees from Old Europe; those who conquered the wilderness were often men and women of character and charisma, as well as of corporeal and mental toughness. One might even say that the pioneers were challenging God much as had the opera-making denizens of Europe, but in far more hazardous conditions. For opera, of all fanciful flowers, to flourish in the wilderness would testify to the triumph of the durability, far-sightedness and 'stickatitiveness' that were the signal characteristics of a New World. Operatic projects became feasible because, paramount among native American virtues, was the will to power and, ancillary to that, the knack of making money. Early American tycoons promoted opera as evidence that they, too, could be mini-gods and world-leaders. Such opera was a social gesture rather than an artistic enterprise; the New World must excel the Old in whatever it did best: so the notion that Americans might one day invent their own kinds of opera was toyed with only marginally, if at all. This remains true: for although opera houses have proliferated all over the States, and the New York Metropolitan thinks it's the greatest, as well as the richest, opera house in the world, the list of indigenous American operas that can stand alongside their European forebears is still microscopic. Ultimately, American music-theatre logically turned into the democratic

American Musical: which, though indigenous, is hardly collateral to the glories of European opera over four centuries.

John Dizikes calls this big book a 'cultural history' of opera in America, and displays both intelligence and imagination in tackling so large a theme. His approach is roughly chronological, though vividly written 'cameos' of key figures—usually singers but occasionally impresarios—appear preludially and interludially, making us aware of what it felt like to live at this moment or the other. Thus the Mozart-singing Garcia family serve to introduce the first section, which embraces the European heritage 1735–1836 and its impact on America. The first American cultural centre to be explored is predictably New Orleans, with its Latinate-European culture and its inextricable mingle of Spanish, Italian, French, German, Hebraic, and English elements, darkly tinged with Black African strains inherent in the slave trade. New Orleans pluralism was prophetic of the shape of things to come: even though America's global power was dominated by her New England Puritan traditions, which directly nurtured the money market. Philadelphia is Dizikes next port of call, where the New World and the Old meld in pursuit of artistic excellence and ethical probity. The allegorical 'interludial' figure is here the beautiful Maria Malibran, a consummate artist who became the ultimate romantic diva: not merely a singer but also a legendary icon worshipped by thousands in a world wherein class distinctions, though not extinct, counted for less than they did in Europe.

Philadelphian society boasted a core of citizens who, having experience of European culture, wanted to replicate it in their new world. That so sophisticated an art as European opera from Mozart to Rossini and Bellini should have excited hysterical fervour not only in an élite, but also in a not highly literate democracy seems surprising: but becomes credible when Dizikes, moving into his next phase, called 'Expansion, 1836–63', gives a vivid account of the furore released by Balfe's *The Bohemian Girl*. Musically this piece, though simpler than its Italian prototypes, was recognisably within their tradition; its 'fabulous' success was due to the fact that it carried the bonus of the vernacular language, and offered a theme that was a harbinger of American musical comedy, with a Gypsy Outsider standing as surrogate for American pioneers who have tamed the wilderness in becoming part of it. The piece still earns an occasional revival, a tribute to its English-American immediacy; but it was the Gold Rush that sealed its American fortunes, since the gold mania was a pioneering enterprise that changed the world. Significantly, Dizikes's next allegorical interlude is devoted to Jenny Lind the Swedish Nightingale, whose apparently childish simplicity and blond blandness was an opposite pole to encroaching material greed. She became an icon no less potent than a twentieth-century pop-

star such as Sinatra, the Beatles, or Madonna; moreover, she owed her outlandish success not to her however magical voice, but to what we call promotion: for J. F. Barnum, of circus fame, concocted her image, which in
turn generated her (and his) fabulous fortunes. People thronged, and savagely fought, to get into her concerts, even if they'd never heard her sing,
but knew of her only as an image of blond Nordic beauty and (no more
than presumptive) chastity.

The Jenny Lind mania was possibly the ultimate zenith of operatic
American pop-star frenzy. After that, the story bifurcates: an evolution that
Dizikes intelligently charts by taking as his next interludial symbol not an
opera star, nor even an impresario, but Walt Whitman, quintessential
American poet whose 'barbaric yawp' both experientially and technically
symbolized a New World. Yet he saw his almost pathological devotion to
romantic Italian opera as an aspect of his newness; he likened the flowing
lines and surging rhythms of Rossini and Bellini to his verses, and found no
contradiction in the fact that his 'free verse' had its most direct source in the
rhythms of the Authorized Version of the Old Testament. Always his
explorer's zeal for the New (including unorthodox areas of sexuality,
though at the time Walt was understandably cagey about this) fused with
respect for old European values. Henceforth, the streams diverged, Boston
being associated with the preservation, even embalming, of conservative
traditions, while Chicago accepted the capitulation of art to commerce,
seeing in the process profit—not merely in material terms—as well as loss.
Within the Bostonian tradition a few native (mostly university) composers
tentatively concocted indigenous operas within unambiguously Italo-
German conventions. At a broader, more commercial, level, the legendary
success of *The Bohemian Girl* was ballasted by a dizzier vogue for Offenbach
and, in due course, for the more middle-classical hedonism of Gilbert and
Sullivan. When native Americans began to emulate these theatre musics the
American Musical was imminent, if not born,

The Yorkshire mayor who promised a potential public that the forthcoming Festival would embrace everything from "Brass Bands in the Park
to the 'Ighest Cultural Art" might have been speaking of developments
nationwide in the United States; certainly the building of New York's Metropolitan Opera House was a signal victory for the 'Ighest Cultural Art
engineered—to use an appropriate metaphor—by impresarios who had
alike the power of money and know-how. The world's most scintillating
stars, such as the radiant Patti, shone in the great masterpieces of Italian tradition; while Walter Damrosch craftily steered the 'difficult' Wagner into the
corridors of power. Metropolitan opera became multi-lingual, as was New
York's urban society; at the same time the opera house of Chicago asserted

brash American energy, revelling in the democratically potent operas of Puccini, Italianate aftermath of Wagner.

Dizikes's next interlude, on Lillian Nordica, highlights this evolution towards the century's end, for she was distinguished even more by her human charisma than by her vocal talents. Bifurcation between 'old' music and 'new' theatre was encouraged by this tendency towards realism; and paradoxically the 'escapist' art of the American Musical gradually won its place, being 'people's music', alongside the fully-fledged productions of the opera house. Musicals were 'real' because they were 'new'; interestingly, the really real American composers (the grand old American avant-gardistes like Ives, Ruggles, and Varèse) had no truck with the 'social' world of opera, and when genuine American art composers began to make American operas they were peripheral. One of the first, indeed, was Black: Scott Joplin, professionally a composer of notated piano rags who, in his *Treemonisha*, made a near-opera on a racial theme: which predictably didn't get sung and played, let alone produced, until forty years later. Even the first white composer to score an operatic *succès de scandale*, if not *d'estime*, was far from being a mainstream WASP: for Virgil Thomson's *Four Saints in Three Acts* was created in Paris, during the twenties, in collaboration with the American expatriate writer Gertrude Stein, and was eventually produced a decade later, in New York, and with an all-Black cast! The quirky zaniness of the piece—as of Thomson's later collaboration with Stein, *The Mother of Us All*— nonetheless carries social and even political implications, and a case can be made that *Four Saints* is the first authentically American opera to become (almost) a repertory piece.

By the time these operas were produced in the States the New Deal was radically transforming the conditions that had made opera in America feasible. Marc Blitzstein's 'plays in music'—produced very much 'off' Broadway—were patent political statements of considerable verbal pith, musical punch, and theatrical flair, and still survive—especially in *No for an Answer* and *The Cradle will Rock*—in the tradition of 'alternative theatre'. When central American composers like Aaron Copland and Douglas Moore entered the operatic field they too eschewed conventionally operatic glamour, writing of fairly low American life, if without overt political intentions. Significantly, one of the most cataclysmic failures in all operatic history was Samuel Barber's *Antony and Cleopatra*, prestigiously composed for the reopening of the New York Met, with a Shakespearean text telling a torrid love story, garnished with 'a cast of thousands', and a phalanx of camels and elephants. Barber, a good and sensitive composer, was a Philadelphian, American but genteel; his attempt to fuse the artistic and the demotic was doomed from the start.

It wasn't, however, beyond George Gershwin, a White Jewish Negro who had been trained on Tin Pan Alley and in the Broadway musical. His opera on DuBose Heyward's novel *Porgy and Bess*, starting as a Broadway musical, turned into an opera on the quintessential American theme of the dichotomy between innocence and experience, Black and White, Jew and Gentile, ruralism and urban commerce. I suspect that it is still the only great, as well as grand, opera produced by an American, and regret that John Dizikes, in recounting other people's contradictory opinions of it, underplays its importance. Still, his account of the mid-twentieth century is farsighted, and he explores how the maturation of the Broadway musical from Kern to Bernstein to Sondheim bears on the evolution of a new audience for American opera, both within traditional venues and in *ad hoc* conditions. His interludial heroes and heroines—Italian Caruso, African American Marian Anderson, Greek Maria Callas—mark developing stages in this process; while a final chapter on the fortunes of Mozart in America surprisingly but effectively ties up the ends. This big book had started with the enterprising Garcia family introducing Mozart to the American backwoods; it ends with the gradual, inevitable, heart-warming, mind-stimulating growth of love for Mozart in America's vast urban democracy—a process which, he points out, wouldn't have been possible without the technological advances in recording, radio and television. Old-fashioned opera buffs are prone to deplore technological advance. They (we) should think again on the evidence of this book, which is the more cheering in that it appears in a society wherein the criminal imbecility of the human race (to which we all belong) seems hell-bent on self-destruction. *Opera in America* deserved its award, three years ago [1993], from the National Book Critics Circle, for it is brilliantly planned, engagingly written, and unambiguously on the side of life. Its many hilarious anecdotes tell us something about the world we live in. Odd that we've had to wait so long for so generous a work to reach our country. We, too, are in need of cheer.

MT, NOVEMBER 1996

COSMIC GERSHWIN

John Adams, *I Was Looking at the Ceiling and Then I Saw the Sky*
(Royal Lyceum Theatre, Edinburgh, 1995)

N TERMS OF NUMBERS OF COMMISSIONS AND PERFORMANCES, OF CRITICAL notice (if not always approval) and of pecuniary reward, John Adams must be among the handful of 'most successful' composers currently active. This pleases him, for he likes to be liked; and it pleases me because he is a good composer, who seismographically mirrors our global village while at the same time enhancing the quality of life.

He is often called a minimalist and certainly came to the fore in the wake of composers such as Steve Reich and Philip Glass, who did not so much assert identity as seek identification with the world and the tribe, helping us to survive and even flourish in our asphalt jungle, much as indigenous peoples used art to habituate themselves to the fright of the forest. Reich achieved international celebrity because his new start sprang from an adaptation to urban industrial technocracy of techniques he picked up, 'in the field', from African, Balinese, Moroccan, and Jewish 'musics of necessity'. Adams, growing up a decade or two later, hasn't needed so uncompromisingly to reject Western traditions. Not only is he 'open' to the multifarious experience of a pluralistic society, he can also relish his polyethnicity, pointing out in one interview that,

I'm inclined to think that stylistic evolution has reached a point where it's going to relax for a while, like it did in Bach's or Brahms's day, and that composers are just going to feed like cattle in a great big pasture, which is the way I work. I'm feeding not just on minimalism but Berg, Stravinsky, rock n' roll, doo-wop music, Arabian music, Jewish music. It makes it really fun to compose now, if you don't let these theoreticians get you down.

Living in racially and culturally polymorphous California, Adams makes music that is implicitly theatrical, whether or not one calls it opera, and that inevitably reflects the way we live now, whether in naturalistic or in mythological terms. His first two operas, *Nixon in China* and *The Death of Klinghoffer*, made in collaboration with the director Peter Sellars, were at once documentary, in that they dealt with real people, and ritualistic, because these people had acquired mythic dimensions.

Adams's new theatre piece, presented as the opening event of the 1995 Edinburgh Festival, features no legendary figures but is still semi-documentary in that the stories it weaves together are based on fact. The libretto is by June Jordan, a Black 'people's poet', whose art is public in being devised for singing or for speaking out loud, rather than for reading. In this piece, *I Was Looking at the Ceiling and Then I Saw the Sky*, her characters are young people victim-ized by the repressive new laws imposed by the Californian constitution, which spends vastly more on the erection of new prisons than on education, let alone welfare. These particular young people are Leila, a Black graduate student and worker in a family-planning clinic; her lover, David, an upwardly mobile Baptist minister; Consuela, an 'undocumented' refugee from El Sal-vador and single mother with two children; their father, Dewain, a reformed gang-leader who steals two cans of beer in an affray precipitated by the immi-gration authority's attempt to abduct Consuela's son; and the white cop Mike who, 'doing his duty', arrests Dewain, in company with his own girlfriend, Tiffany, who photographs 'true crime' for a tabloid television show. Her pic-tures of cop and victim flash across the continent, whose audiences relish the new, tough-on-crime laws, whereby the theft of a can of beer, combined with two trivial previous convictions, can land a man in gaol for life. The remaining character, Rick, a prospering Asian-American attorney, who conducts Dewain's defence, provides a loophole, and is himself a hybrid between worlds. He seems to win Tiffany from Mike, which may be a sign of grace.

But there are no heroes and villains in this Los Angeles, only confused people living in a world they didn't make and can't comprehend. In this sit-uation, God (or something) intervenes in the form of an earthquake—the opera's title is a 'documentary' quotation from a survivor. For the piece's artistic purposes, this Act of God divides the two acts; what the young people see through the shattered ceiling is a sky that changes their lives. Although the issues involved are patently political, this is not a political parable; on the contrary, it suggests there's not much point in identifying with the tribe if you've no idea what your own identity is. Nothing is quite what it seems: the coloured characters are confused by deracinations over which they have no control; even the white cop is on the verge of admitting that he fancies the Black minister; and Tiffany may end up with the lawyer. Yet there are no real endings, only hard-won tolerances and acceptances since, as Auden put it, "we must love one another or die".

In this production, the television clichés of camera-flash and sound-bite are brilliantly adapted, not in chronological narrative but in a sequence of twenty-two numbers sung (and, sometimes, spoken or mimed) by actors backed by the Finnish rock band *Avanti!* The band, consisting of electric keyboards, saxophone, clarinets, string bass and percussion, improvises some of the music in accordance with Adams's prescriptions; certainly in conjunction with the solo singers it mates opera, theatre and tribal ritual, so that we enjoy the kind of life-in-process that theatre was for the ancient Greeks. The singers, all under twenty-five, trained in theatre and in musicals rather than in opera or concert-hall performance, are charismatic.

Ceiling/Sky's sense of unpredictability and danger depends on the physicality of these 'performance artists'; but they, in turn, depend on Sellars's startling, funny-alarming direction, Jordan's vernacular text and, above all, on Adams's music. The evocation of disorder and confusion by way of set 'numbers' might seem hazardous, but it works, precisely because Los Angeles is disconnection epitomized—at least until cosmic catastrophe lets in the sky. In Act One, the songs—each illustrated by cartoon graphics— serve to reveal unconscious motivations. Adams says that he aims to be a successor to the Gershwin of *Porgy and Bess* and the Bernstein of *West Side Story*. He may not have produced a sequence of songs to rival Porgy's tragic love song or the threnody of the Edenic innocence of 'Summertime', but he has triumphantly used the idioms of his generation in a way comparable with Gershwin's adaptation of the show songs of the 1920s and 1930s, and more than measures up to Bernstein, whether in the 1950s cool of Dewain's 'Solo in Sunlight', in Consuela's touching 'Dream', or in the superb ensemble number that ends the first act, 'Song about the Sweet Majority Population of the World'. No less subtly, 'Rick's Awkward Love Song', addressed to Tiffany, is spoken, not sung, and provides the moral hub for much of the action.

The Earthquake itself, in an entr'acte for the Band alone, makes its loud point while having less character than most of the music. This may merely mean that I, being of Bernstein's generation and not so far off Gershwin's, cannot readily empathize with this music's idiom, though I can hear that it works as a transition to Act Two, when the sky comes through the roof. Earthquakes, though not themselves anthropomorphic, can affect human destinies and, since music needs time to effect changes within the psyche, the numbers in Act Two are fewer but longer than those in Act One. Three consecutive numbers work out the fates of David and Leila, and of Mike and Tiffany, while the comparable three numbers for Dewain and Consuela attain an almost Gershwin-like tragic grandeur, especially in Dewain's accurately titled 'Song of Liberation and Surprise'. These final three numbers are powerfully moving as well as viscerally thrilling.

Its superior detractors are bound to accuse *Ceiling/Sky* of being politically naive and artistically brash. They may be right, but shouldn't forget that naivety may be a condition of courageous veracity, while brashness may testify to the desperate necessity for moral conviction. Of his approach to composition, Adams has said: "I never have a day when I wake up and say 'O God, I don't feel like composing today'. I always want to do it, and there's always something interesting out there." A similar resilience, which comes across in *Ceiling/Sky*, gives cause for mirth in both the medieval and the modern senses.

TLS, SEPTEMBER 1995

EPILOGUE

NEW WORLDS FOR OLD

RUTH CRAWFORD-SEEGER
THE PERIL AND THE POWER OF CULTURAL BIFURCATION

Judith Tick, *Ruth Crawford Seeger: American Composer*
(New York: Oxford University Press, 1997)

ORN IN 1901, RUTH CRAWFORD BELONGS WITH THE GRAND OLD PIONEERS
of American music, notably Ives, Ruggles and Varèse, alongside a
larger, less grand, second team including Dane Rudhyar and Henry
Cowell, who were formative influences on her early composing. Her immediate background, however, was oppressively insular, for her father and
grandfather were Methodist ministers in Old Virginia, while her mother
was a pioneer only in being one of the earliest 'female stenographers' in the
labour force. Ruth's childhood was peripatetic, since puritan pastors moved
from church to church and town to town. In the major part of her adolescence was spent in Jacksonville, Florida, a town and state hardly dedicated
to culture, let alone to the avant-garde.

Yet Judith Tick, in this model biography to which she has devoted more
than twenty years, makes it credible that Ruth, from her small-town background and prissy evangelicism, was a girl who dreamed dreams and scrib-
bled reams of verse neither conspicuously good nor bad, while developing
pianistic talents that far outshone the scope of this often provincially girlish
occupation. She established herself as a piano teacher in the community,
and earned local fame as an embryonic virtuoso. But although a red-
cheeked girl without airs or graces, Ruth knew that she needed and
deserved horizons wider than those of Jacksonville; and in 1921 she boldly
moved to Chicago, then the haunt of (often affiliated) tycoons and gang-
sters, but also the home of a fine symphony orchestra, and a temporary set-
tling-place for singers and instrumentalists of international calibre. So for
her the Windy City was also a Wonder City: wherein the music of Mahler,
Debussy , Ravel, Stravinsky, and Scriabin stimulated her creativity. While
eking out a precarious livelihood as a piano teacher and occasional soloist,
Ruth studied with Adolf Weidig, a professionally competent though not
notably inspiring theory-teacher; and herself composed small piano pieces
that pointed (in 'A Little Waltz') towards her ultimate destiny in American
folk music studies, but also (in 'Kaleidoscopic Changes') towards an immediate, experimental cult of modernism.

It's hardly surprising that the exoticism of her musical experience in
Chicago should have effaced her dour American puritanism: the more completely because her piano teacher in Chicago was Djane Lavoie-Herz, a
charismatic woman reputed to be the greatest interpreter of the 'shockingly'
fashionable, theosophically *recherché* Scriabin. Under Herz's tuition—which

may have embraced emotive, if not overtly sexual, undertones—Ruth read Madame Blavatsky as well as the Bhagavadgita and Lao-tse; and entrancedly met Dane Rudhyar, a composer who, born in Paris in 1895, emigrated to New York City in 1916, the same year as Varèse. A poet and painter as well as composer, Rudhyar was also an internationally celebrated astrologer, and a student of various brands of oriental mysticism; in 1924, looking the part, he played Jesus Christ in a movie! A real, if slightly mad and totally humourless minor composer, he offered Ruth what she imagined she needed, and was certainly light-years away from Jacksonville, Florida. At the same time Ruth was brought down to earth by the effervescent Alfred Frankenstein, who introduced her to black jazz and the freedom of pitch and rhythm typical of an improvised, primarily melodic, music: she profited from this when, in her second career, she worked in American folk musics.

But the most significant 'contact' she acquired through Djane Herz was Henry Cowell, born in 1897, still experimenting with his upright piano stored in a shack in the woods, soon to become an advocate of what we now call World Music. It was he, in turn, who introduced her to Carl Sandburg, the raw poet of American plains and small-town life: who was a harbinger of her second career in folk art and an immediate stimulus to 'modernist' creation, since a cycle of settings of his verse stands, with her *Piano Preludes*, as the most distinctive fruit of her Chicago years. Sandburg's tough, homespun humour—and perhaps his frequent identification with childhood—countered the airy, sometimes windy theosophy she imbibed from Herz and Rudhyar; indeed one might say that Sandburg and Rudhyar represented the two opposite but complementary poles that fuelled Ruth's creativity; and that the homey and exotic streams met in the polymorphous, polyethnic figure of Henry Cowell, who at this stage changed Ruth's life, as well as her 'career', by maintaining that, given her exceptional talents, she needed to spread her wings in that epicentre of modernism, New York City.

A spell at the MacDowell Colony in New Hampshire steered her on her way: for in the Colony, which was in the world but not of it, Ruth met illustrious literary figures like the poet Edwin Arlington Robinson, the largely autobiographical prose-writer Ed Dahlberg, and the playwright Thornton Wilder, as well as Mrs Amy Beach, the most 'successful', if not the most innovative, of American women composers. Alongside all this Art, Ruth had a (self-aborted) love-affair, such as is endemic to Summer Music Schools, with a young journalist-poet. Resident, if hardly settled, in New York, Ruth was, at 1 West 68th Street, within walking distance of the Carnegie Hall and the New York Met. Through her friendship with Marion Bauer, a composer affiliated to arty French traditions rather than to Ruth's conscious Americanism, she met Carl Ruggles, whose orchestral *Portals* she considered "an outstanding work, closer to greatness than any American music I have heard": though she rebuked him for his hermetic chauvinism, maintaining that "amalgamation will be a great thing; out of all the races will spring the true American". The dynamic Varèse also came her way; as did the then fashionable ethnic musicologist Joseph Yasser, and the theorist Schillinger, from whom George Gershwin picked up technical tips. Before long, Cowell himself came to live in New York, and Crawford joined the musically and politically radical group he formed with Aaron Copland and Marc Blitzstein, with the sharp-witted Virgil Thomson as catalyst between American brashness and Parisian chic. Ruth kept her head above this heady world through the Copland-like 'plainness' of her character, the hard edge of her intellect, and the embracing vigour of her musicianship. We cannot know what would have happened had Ruth continued to live alone in this cultural hurly-burly, since at this point Charles Seeger, a patrician American and well-healed Ivy Leaguer from Harvard, moved from Boston to New York to become, with Cowell as intermediary, Ruth's teacher, friend, lover, and eventual husband. Seeger was himself a composer who knew and admired the likes of Ives, Ruggles, and Varèse, though he did not creatively emulate them. He became however, their spokesman, endowed with wide and deep historical and philosophical knowledge; having given up composition in 1919, he aimed to shake up a stuffy New England musical establishment with an injection of the then avant-garde music of Europe, from Debussy and Scriabin to Schoenberg and Berg, and from them to Bartók, Stravinsky, and Satie—though neo-classicism was a doctrine that Seeger, and still more Crawford, mistrusted since it substituted European role-models for New World libertarianism.

Seeger recognized Ruth's exceptional gifts, and proved an inspiring teacher. He had evolved—or was in process of evolving by way of a big (unfinished) book—a system for the making of American avant-garde music: which differed from the European brand in having virtually no past. In the implicit 'rules' of Seeger's system, if that is what it was, tend, like those of Schoenberg's serialism, to be negative: pitches should be minimally repeated, to discourage tonal orthodoxy; harmonies should be derived from pre-invented linear rows rather than from harmonically conceived cells or sets. This encouraged 'horizontal' thinking by way of the motivic evolution of intervals and metrical patterns, creating what Seeger called 'dissonanted polyphony'. This accorded with Ruth's already-formed instincts, since in her Chicago works she had favoured far-flung, wide-spaced, irregular-rhythmed lines interacting with naggingly reiterated motives based on very small intervals, often functioning as ostinati. These two types of melody are broadly analogous respectively to Schoenberg (or more accurately to Ruggles as an American, open-air free-atonal Schoenberg), and to Bartók (who will acquire a different significance for Ruth when she enters into her second, folk-founded life). Yet what is most remarkable about Crawford's music is its American aboriginality. Her idiom—which benefited from, though it was beyond the range of, Seeger's or anyone's system—sprang new-minted from her nerves, blood, and bones: until it culminated in the string quartet she started in Europe, in 1931, but revised soon after her arrival in New York. This masterpiece packs into four movements, lasting *in toto* around ten minutes, maximum content in electrical melodic impulse, intricate rhythmic energy, potent harmonic change, and dazzling textural variety. The strenuous linear polyphony of the first movement and the eel-like whirligig of the scherzo have little in common with Hindemithian busy-ness or Schoenbergian chromatic *angst*, though there are affinities with the paradoxically dense but open polyphony of Ruggles and, to a lesser degree, that of Ives and Wallingford Riegger; and with the motivic evolution that Varèse likened, in his own music, to crystal mutation. (In reference to her own music Crawford favoured a metaphor from the weaving of Persian rugs.) Sometimes Crawford's rhythmic procedures anticipate the 'metrical modulation' that Elliott Carter explored twenty years later; while in the finale, scored in two parts for the first violin and the other three instruments in muted unison, the two voices function in inverse metrical proportion, creating a mathematical structure comparable with those investigated, thirty or more years later, in the pianola music of Conlon Nancarrow. The slow movement works by infinitesimally slow exfoliation and contraction from nodal clusters, making for a canonic polyphony of dynamics rather than pitches, though the climax metamorphoses into linearity. Sonorities such as these, familiar in the sixties, were totally unknown in 1931; but what matters is not chronological precedence, but the fact that Crawford's soundscapes are still, in 1997, "news that STAYS news"—to use Ezra Pound's appositely *memorable* phrase. Fortunately, the string orchestral version of this movement is one of the few examples of Crawford's music currently available on CD (Decca 443 776–2).

In a full-scale biography of an eventful life, Judith Tick cannot be expected to offer exhaustive critical analysis of this extraordinary music, though everything she says about it is worth the carrying. Moreover, the musical commentary bears directly on the disturbing human story she has to tell; for although Seeger's tuition helped Crawford intellectually to know what she was about, there's little doubt that she would have found her way without him. His graduation from teacher to friend to lover to husband

292

changed her life, for better or worse. It would seem, from Tick's vivid account, that Charles's chilly upper-class reserve veiled unexpected depths of passion; and at least the marriage lasted until Ruth's premature death, despite the inevitable clashes between career and family responsibilities. These problems were compounded by the fact that Charles's lofty social status didn't prevent his losing most of his money in the Depression—a social phenomenon which, ironically enough, was intimately associated with the pressures that imbued Ruth's music with its formidable intensity. Joseph Straus, in his analytical study of Crawford's music published in 1995, suggests that the force of her work stems from its tension between "the highly structured and the rhapsodically free"—which is, after all, one of the familiar, basic oppositions of Western musical thought. At first it seems that this inner conflict must be irreconcilable; "only gradually does one become aware of the subtle ties that bind the disparate parts", offering "a healing vision in which the seeming dualities of our lives can be heard to melt, thaw, and resolve themselves, if not into a transcendent synthesis, then at least into a respectful coexistence". Although this healing vision is hardly comparable with that of Beethoven in his late quartets, it is a therapeutically social, and even religious, act and is, given its time and place, a remarkable and heroic achievement.

In the light of Straus's critical insight we may understand why Ruth Crawford's life, after she'd been metamorphosed into Crawford-Seeger, was at once fulfilment and tragedy. One suspects that Seeger, before he met Ruth, had relinquished composition because he'd come the conclusion that the making of an authentically 'modern' American music was unlikely without a change in social structure. This must be a reason why this patrician American improbably threw in his lot with Marxist philosophy and politics, and collaterally with People's Music in the form of folk song and dance. During the New Deal, Seeger's radical politics unexpectedly alleviated his depression-induced economic vulnerability, since he was offered jobs fostering the American Heritage, as manifest musically and anthropologically in folklore. This entailed a move to Washington, and later to Maryland, where the Seegers, although far from affluent, not only survived, but also reared a new family that became a dynasty of folk musicians and scholars, some of them still active today. In the oldest, Pete, was an offspring of Charles's first marriage, still fraily extant when he and Ruth first nervily lived together. As for Ruth, she seems to have loved Charles deeply (though Virgil Thomson characteristically opined that Charles worked her too hard and made her cook too much); and while keen to preserve her autonomy as a composer, she was no less eager to "compose babies" as well as, or even rather than, music, in the process sacrificing her 'dissonanted polyphony'. Even so, there is evidence that she saw her dichotomy as real, and painful: to the point of tearing up the manuscript of her violin and piano sonata, the most ambitious work of her Chicago years, recently performed with acclaim in glamorous New York City. Although her destructive act was no more than a gesture, since the sonata had already been published by the indefatigable Henry Cowell, gestures still count when made by a Ruth Crawford.

Yet Ruth welcomed her new life; though apolitical compared with her husband, she wasn't reluctant to be involved in his politics, and positively relished the folk music that followed in their wake. If 'her' music, being sparsely performed, was forgotten except by the few (choice) spirits in the know, she was happy to embark on an alternative career, assisting Charles in his collection and codification of indigenous American songs and dances. At first Charles was gratified by and grateful for this: though it was crass, as well as cruel and fallacious of him to tell Ruth that her folk-music 'versions' were more important (and 'better'?) than her string quartet. Perhaps one should be a shade sorry for Charles too, for he had always known that as a 'modern' composer he was not in the same class as his wife; so it must have given a sharper twist to the knife when her work as collector, editor, and arranger of folk tunes made her, in *his* field, a celebrity in her own right. During the forties and early fifties Ruth published several anthologies of tunes, mostly associated with and directed at children, usually with her own piano arrangements that combined discreet scholarly authenticity with commercial viability. Working in schools herself, mostly with young kids, she became a wonderful teacher, having the common touch alien to her husband, and earning the reward of a personal spot on TV. By hindsight, we can see that Ruth's career in music education parallels that of Bartók and Kodály in Hungary, and of Villa-Lobos in Vargas's Brazil. That she was able to bring this off in a vast industrial technocracy, rather than in a relatively self-enclosed, still in part agrarian community, testifies to her toughness of character, acute intelligence, and comprehensive musicianship. Tick's account of Ruth as an 'educational' composer convinces us—with the help of well-produced music examples—that Crawford deserves a place alongside Bartók and Kodály, her truth to experience in her notations being commensurate with her skill in making versions practically useful in our alien environment, as well as in that of the original juvenile singers. Marc Blitzstein puts this succinctly when, reviewing, in 1942, one of her compilations in Minna Lederman's periodical *Modern Music*, he wrote that, "Mrs Seeger *hears with extraordinary precision and love.* If it was sung like that, that's the way it gets notated. Mrs Seeger lets us in on an *alive* musical moment, from which we can reconstruct the variations and possibilities" [my italics].

When Ruth crossed the barrier between folk-musicology and folk music as performance-art (which in America merged into Country Music), it was in collaboration with Alan Lomax, the first folk-musicologist to become, in no discreditable sense, an entrepreneur. Why they worked so well together is not difficult to understand: for Lomax described Ruth as "the fairest person I ever met, the most non-prejudicial, the most balanced". The numinous dimensions in her own music were not incompatible with the 'balanced' plainness of her folk-image: which is why Alan Lomax saw (as Charles Seeger possibly didn't) that Ruth was "a modernist composer who regarded folk-song as a very, very interesting musical literature she needed to master", both for intrinsic reasons and in the interests of her own, temporarily aborted, art. She made one attempt to combine the two in *Rissolty Rossolty*, a five-minute work for high-school orchestra, in sub-Ivesian style, two folk songs and a fiddle tune. Though it doesn't have the spontaneous vivacity of Ives's comparable ventures, nor the startling audacity of Ruth's 'own' music, it is a life-enhancing piece that ought to be much used in schools and colleges—and perhaps is, in America. Even so, Ruth was worried that she'd overestimated youthful abilities; though the piece would be literally 'child's play' to the youth orchestras of today. In any case, the enterprise was not repeated, and Pete Seeger commented that "Father and Mother kind of sloughed it off, felt that it wasn't important". One has an uneasy suspicion that this was not so much on account of Ruth's technical dubieties as because Charles resented the fact that his wife's folky pieces were more honest in hearing, and more effective in performance, than his own. Commenting, on another occasion, on a folk-song-setting game or contest the Seegers indulged in, Pete remarked that his setting was "OK", his father's "rather good", his mother's "Perfect".

In 1951, with her children launched in the folk-orientated world, Ruth Crawford made an attempt to return to her dissonanted music, composing a wind quintet that unsurprisingly gathered together threads from her Chicago and New York years. Also unsurprisingly, it is not a uniquely potent masterpiece like the string quartet written when she first arrived in New York, though it would have been good enough to serve as a launching-pad for a *renouvellement*. We'll never know whether that is what it genuinely was; nor whether the cancer of which she died at the age of fifty-three was a consequence of the spiritual and cultural bifurcation she suffered. Nor, for that matter, can we be sure that 'suffered' is the right word. In the aboriginally American property of 'her' music depended on a pristine quality relatable to the truthful innocence with which she approached her years of folk song collating and—both musically and in physically diurnal fact—of child-nurturing. Among her children, Mike and Peggy kept the flag flying and torch flaming, admitting to and conquering the hazards of commercialization.

Her daughter Peggy, still active today, confessed that she couldn't understand

how the woman I knew as my mother created something like that 1931 string quartet. It is like someone crying; it is like someone beating on the wall. And I don't want to think about this as regarding my mother, because my mother always seemed to have it all together, to have gotten a life that pleased her.

Well, perhaps these two opposed views, far from being antipathetic, are the heart of our 'post-modern' condition, which Crawford-Seeger prophetically envisaged. Listen again to that string quartet and wonder whether it may not entail Straus's "healing vision" in and through its contradictoriness. Then sing, and maybe dance to, Ruth's recreations and re-creations of folk music and wonder if there may not be a comparable fusion of hurt and healing in them also. At least through her early death Ruth escaped the attentions of the obscene Committee for UnAmerican Activities, who wouldn't have approved of her profoundly patriotic work any more than they sanctioned the great Aaron Copland's. It cannot have approved of Charles Seeger either, though it let him off with a warning, and he lived, honourably enough, to the age of ninety-three.

Judith Tick, author of this great book, has qualities comparable with those of the book's subject, being clever, perspicacious, wide-eyed and open-eared, yet also 'plain', like Ruth Crawford and Aaron Copland. In the book, cool yet committed, proffers the information one needs, remains scrupulously fair in discussing divided loyalties, never proselytizes, always remembers Pilate's unanswered question: What is Truth? It is incumbent on the Oxford University Press to issue a British edition without delay: for although Crawford is a quintessentially American phenomenon, no subject could more powerfully reveal how 'America' is germane to us all. In my distant youth I must have been a bit like Ruth Crawford: not in being a composer of genius but in being concerned with the New—which meant Stravinsky, Bartók, Schoenberg, and especially the supreme composers of the New World: Ives and Copland—and at the same time, given the basic *need* for newness, with the new-old art of urban jazz, and with rural folk musics, White and black, as evidence of 'eternal' human verities we shouldn't lose sight or sound of.

MT, NOVEMBER 1997

A Select List of Works by Wilfrid Mellers

BOOKS (in chronological order)

Music and Society: England and the European Tradition. London: Dennis Dobson, 1946
Studies in Contemporary Music. London: Dennis Dobson, 1947
François Couperin and the French Classical Tradition. London: Dennis Dobson, 1950 (2nd ed., London: Faber and Faber, 1987).
Music in the Making. London: The Bureau of Current Affairs, 1951 (2nd ed., London: Dennis Dobson, 1952).
The Sonata Principle, vol. 3 of *Man and his Music,* and *Romanticism and the Twentieth Century,* vol. 4 of *Man and his Music.* London: Barrie and Rockliff, 1957 (new edition, Barrie and Jenkins, 1988).
Harmonious Meeting: A Study of Music, Poetry & Drama in England, 1600–1900. London: Dennis Dobson, 1965.
Music in a New Found Land: Themes and Developments in the History of American Music. London: Barrie and Rockliff, 1964. Rev. ed. 1975. Revised paperback ed., with new foreword, London: Faber and Faber, 1987.
Caliban Reborn: Renewal in Twentieth Century Music. London: Gollancz, 1968.
Twilight of the Gods: The Beatles in Retrospect. London: Faber and Faber, 1973.
Bach and the Dance of God. London: Faber and Faber, 1980.
Beethoven and the Voice of God. London: Faber and Faber, 1983.
A Darker Shade of Pale: A Backdrop to Bob Dylan. London: Faber and Faber, 1984.
Angels of the Night: Popular Female Singers of Our Time. Oxford: Blackwell, 1986.
The Masks of Orpheus: Seven Stages of Musical Experience in the West. Manchester:Manchester University Press, 1987.
Le Jardin Retrouvé: The Music of Frederic Mompou 1893–1987. Limited edition, with illustrations by Robin Hildyard. York: The Fairfax Press, 1989.
Vaughan Williams and the Vision of Albion. London: Barrie & Jenkins, 1989 (rev. ed. London: Albion Music Ltd., 1997).
Percy Grainger. Oxford: Oxford University Press, 1992.
Francis Poulenc, Oxford: Oxford University Press, 1993.

ARTICLES AND REVIEWS

Wilfrid Mellers has been writing musical journalism since the 1930s. His earliest pieces were published in *Music and Letters, The Music Review, The Listener, Counterpoint, Scrutiny, The Kenyon Review, Tempo,* and *The Musical Times.* In recent years he has written mainly for *The Times Literary Supplement* and *The Musical Times.* The following is a very limited selection from his total output and it is given in chronological order. It includes articles published as chapters of 'symposium' books.

'Hollywooden Hero: *The Fifth Column* by Ernest Hemingway', *Scrutiny* VIII, 1939. Reprinted in F. R. Leavis, ed., *A Selection from Scrutiny.* Cambridge: Cambridge University Press, 1968, vol. 2, pp. 89–97.
'Petulant Peacock: *Letters on Poetry, from W.B. Yeats to Dorothy Wellesley.*' *Scrutiny* IX, 1940. Reprinted in F. R. Leavis, ed., op. cit., vol. 1, pp. 96–99.
'Magic and ritual in the junior school', *The Musical Times* (May, 1964), pp. 342–45.
'The teenager's world', *The Musical Times* (July, 1964) pp. 500–05.
'Stravinsky and Jazz'. *Tempo,* no. 87 (1967), pp. 29–31.

'The scope of school music: notes on a university course'. *Music in Education* (1968) no. 32, pp. 130–133.

'The new troubadours: reflections on pop and modern folk music'. *Musicology* (1969), no. 2, pp. 3–12.

'The resources of music'. *The Times Literary Supplement* (special issue on education), 10 July 1970.

'The key and the kingdom: reflections on music, childhood and education'. *Australian Journal of Music Education* (1971) no. 9, pp. 13–16.

'The Duke at 70' [on Duke Ellington]. *Music and Musicians*, March 1972.

'Modern Minstrel' [on Bob Dylan]. *The New Statesman*, 8 December 1972.

'Music in a modern university: a question of priorities'. *Studies in Music* (1972) no. 6, pp. 1–9.

'Pop, ritual and commitment'. *Royal Society of Arts Journal*, January 1974, pp. 80–91.

'Where occidental meets oriental' [on Bartók]. *The Times Literary Supplement*, 5 August 1977.

'God, modality and meaning in some recent songs of Bob Dylan'. In *Yearbook: Popular Music*, vol. 1. *Folk or Popular? Distillations, Influence, Continuities*, edited by Richard Middleton and David Horn. Cambridge: Cambridge University Press, 1981.

'The hermetic and the democratic' [on American music]. *The Times Literary Supplement*, 28 October 1983.

'Paradise and Paradox in the Sixteenth Century'. In *The Cambridge Guide to the Arts in Britain.* Vol. 4. *The Seventeenth Century*, edited by Boris Ford. Cambridge: Cambridge University Press, 1989, pp. 179–221.

'The aristocrat as pirate: the Byronic legend in the music of Berlioz and Tchaikovsky.' Music Matters, in *Music & Musicians* (ed. Basil Ramsey), July 1989.

'Music and worship: towards the twenty-first century'. Music Matters, in *Music & Musicians*, September 1989.

'The Wagner Phenomenon'. Music Matters, in *Music & Musicians*, October 1989.

'Eden, South Carolina and New York'. Music Matters, in *Music & Musicians*, December 1989.

'A letter before leaving America'. Music Matters, in *Music & Musicians*, January 1990.

'A musical bestiary.' Music Matters, in *Music & Musicians*, February 1990.

'Le cas Satie'. Music Matters, in *Music & Musicians*, March 1990.

'Fidelio and Leonora: the demoncratic hero and the female principle.' Music Matters, in *Music & Musicians*, April 1990.

'Exulting in monotony: Steve Reich and the meaning of minimal.' Music Matters, in *Music & Musicians*, May 1990.

'Percussion as therapy.' Music Matters, in *Music & Musicians*, June 1990.

'Sacred and profane: reflections on Bach in the 90s'. Music Matters, in *Music & Musicians*, July 1990.

'Schnittke, death and deconstruction.' Music Matters, in *Music & Musicians*, August 1990.

'The jungle and the screen: *Charles Keochlin: His Life and Works* by Robert Orledge'. *The Times Literary Supplement*, 2 March 1990.

'New worlds, old wildernesses: Peter Sculthorpe and the ecology of music'. *Atlantic Monthly*, August 1991.

'The music of loss: *Letters from a Life: Selected Letters and Diaries of Benjamin Britten,*

edited by Donald Mitchell and Philip Reed'. *The New Republic*, 20 January 1992.
'The pilgrim's pleasure: *Gabriel Fauré: A Musical Life* by Jean-Michel Nectoux.' *The New Republic*, 8 February 1993.
'The two faces of an artful entertainer: *Leonard Bernstein* by Humphrey Burton'. *The Independent on Sunday*, 29 May 1994.
'The flesh became word: Purcell and the church re-formed'. *The Musical Times*, October 1995, pp. 12–15).

COMPOSITIONS
Publishers include Lengnick, Novello, and Ashdown.

1944
Four Short Shakespeare Songs for women's voices: 'Mariana's Song'; 'Ariel's Song'; 'Ophelia's Song'; 'Ariel's Song'.

1945
Two Motets for mixed chorus and brass: 'The City of Desolation'; 'The City not forsaken' (words from Isaiah).
The Forgotten Garden. Cantata for tenor and string quartet (words by Henry Vaughan).
Trio for violin, viola, and cello.

1946
Four Carols for boys' voices with optional celesta: '*Virgo, Rosa virginum*'; 'Lullaby'; 'Alleluya'; '*Jesu, fili virginis, miserere nobis*' (words anonymous).
Sonata for viola and piano.

1948
The *Lysistrata* of Aristophanes. A play in music with three singing parts and chamber orchestra.
The Song of Ruth. Cantata for soprano, mezzo-soprano and baritone soloists, chorus and orchestra (words arranged by R. J. White from The Book of Ruth).

1949
Three Songs for counter-tenor, flute, and guitar: 'On a Gentlewoman walking in the snow' (Strode); 'Elegy' (Nashe); 'To Mistress Isabel Pennell' (Skelton).
News from Greece. Cantata for mezzo-soprano, mixed chorus, three trumpets and percussion (words by R. F. Willetts).
Extravaganza for speaker, counter-tenor, piano, harpsichord, celesta, guitar and percussion (words by Aristophanes, translated by R. F. Willetts).
Some of Gravity, Some of Mirth. Song cycle for soprano and piano: Rondeau: 'Now welcom somer' (Chaucer); Dirge: '*Timor mortis conturbat me*' (anon.); Scherzino: 'Joly Jankin' (anon.); Elegy: 'Fair summer droops' (Nashe); Rondeau: 'O the month of May' (Dekker).

1951
Yggdrasil. Cantata for SATB soloists and chamber orchestra (words by Christopher Hassall).

Five Invocations for counter-tenor and piano: 'A Loss at Sea' (Anacreon); 'The Ceryl' (Alcman); 'Peril and Prayer' (Simonides); 'Drinking Song' (Alcaeus); 'Paen to Peace' (Bacchylides) (words translated from the Greek by R. F. Willetts).
Galliard for trombone and piano.

1952

Carmina Felium for soprano, clarinet, bassoon, violin, viola, cello and piano: 'A Cat' (Edward Thomas); 'Comfort' (Walter de la Mare); 'The Cat and the Moon' (W. B. Yeats); 'Earthy Anecdote' (Wallace Stevens); 'The Song of the Composed Cat' (George Moor).

1952–53

Symphony for large orchestra.

1953

Fool's Paradise: Six Shakespeare Songs for baritone and piano: 'When daffodils begin to peer'; 'Come away, death'; 'O mistress mine'; 'I am gone, sir'; 'Take, O take those lips away'; 'When that I was and a little tiny boy'.

1954

The Shepherd's Daughter. Chamber opera for soloists, chorus and small orchestra (libretto by George Moor).

1955

Indra and the Lark. Cantata for ATBBB soloists, piano and percussion (words by George Moor).

1956

Pax Dei for chorus, semichorus, and brass (words from the Epistle of St James and Jeremiah).

1957

Peacock Pie. Unison songs for girls' voices and piano (words by Walter de la Mare): 'Full Moon'; 'Song of the Mad Prince'; 'The Song of Shadows'; 'The Pigs and the Charcoal Burner'; 'Andy Battle'; 'John Mouldy'; 'The Buckle'; 'Alas, alack!'; 'Summer Evening'; 'The Barber's'.
Mary Easter. Ballad opera for actors, soloists, chorus and small orchestra (libretto by David Holbrook).

1958

Samson Agonistes. Ritual music for woodwind, brass and percussion: *Introitus et Cantus Potentiae; Traductio Lasciva; Oratorio et Conturbatio; Cantus Opacus et Exitus Ululantium.*

1959

The Borderline. Music drama for young people: actors, soloists, chorus and small orchestra (libretto by David Holbrook).

1960

The Hedge of Flowers. Masque for girls' voices and small orchestra (words by David Holbrook).

Primavera. Six canzonets for women's voices: 'Spring Canticle' (anon); 'Christmas Canticle' (anon); Scherzino: 'I have a gentil cock' (anon.); 'Epithalamium: Now hath Flora robbed her bowers' (Campion); Lullaby: 'Ye spotted snakes' (Shakespeare); Nocturne-Benediction: 'Now, until the break of day' (Shakespeare).

Lacrimae Amoris. Two monodies with refrain, for counter-tenor solo and three male voices: 'Dialogus Profanus' (Raleigh); 'Monodia Sacra' (anon.).

Canticum Incarnationis, for six solo voices (words by Kathleen Raine).

Spells for soprano, flute, oboe, viola, and percussion (words by Kathleen Raine):'Invocation'; 'Love-spell'; 'Spell against sorrow'; 'Spell to bring lost creatures home'; 'Spell of Creation'; 'The Unloved'; *'Amo ergo sum'*; 'Epilogue: Spell of safe-keeping'.

Journey to Love. Song cycle for soprano and piano (words by William Carlos Williams):'A Negro Woman'; 'View by colour photography'; 'The Lady Speaks'; 'Shadows'.

1961

Missa Brevis for mixed chorus and chamber organ.

Ex nihilo and *Lauds* for unaccompanied chorus (words by Kathleen Raine and W. H. Auden).

Three Resurrection Hymns of Emily Dickinson for mixed chorus and organ.

Chants and Litanies of Carl Sandburg for male chorus, piano, and percussion: 'Spring carries surprises'; 'Cool tombs'; 'Summer grass'; 'In tall trees'; 'Ripe corn'; 'Finish'.

Cantilena e Ciancona for solo violin.

Fantasia, Burletta e Pensieri for solo cello.

1962

Rootabaga Story for story-teller, children's voices, tenor solo, piano and percussion (words by Carl Sandburg).

A Ballad of Anyone for soprano solo, chorus and piano, with optional percussion (words by e. e. cummings).

Early Light. Two part-songs for young people (SATB) and piano (words by David Holbrook).

Voices and Creatures. Declamation for voice with flute and percussion (words by Theodore Roethke): 'The Small'; 'The Siskins'; 'Snake'; 'Interlude'; 'The Song'.

Alba in 9 Metamorphoses for solo flute and orchestra.

Three Lullabies for tenor, viola and piano—'Birthday sleep' (Vernon Watkins); 'That laddie's a long, long way from home' (George Barker); 'Love Song' (George Barker).

Threnodies from the Waters. Four dirges of Thomas Lovell Beddoes for soprano, piano and percussion.

To Mistress Isabel Pennell. Madrigal for unaccompanied voices (words by Skelton).

Eclogue for treble recorder, violin, cello and harpsichord.

Sonatina for treble recorder and piano.

1963

Trio for flute, cello and piano: Eclogue, Estampie, Threnody.

Laus Amoris. Suite for symphonic strings: Canticle; Rounds; Chorale; Ductia; Canticle-Epilogue.

1964

Cat-Charms. 'Three times three' easy pieces for piano.

The Happy Meadow. Cantata for speaker, children's voices, recorder consort, glockenspiel, xylophone and percussion (words by Robert Duncan and Yvor Winters).

Runes and Carolunes for children's voices and miscellaneous instruments (words from Pygmy and Eskimo dance-songs plus two poems by Caroline Mellers).

Rose of May: A Threnody for Ophelia for speaker, soprano, flute, clarinet and string quartet (words by Shakespeare): Invocation: Ballad I; Cadenza: Ballad II; Cadenza: Ballad III.

1965

The Ship of Death. Cantata for soprano and tenor voices, clarinet, bass clarinet and string quartet (words by D. H. Lawrence).

1966

A May Magnificat for mezzo-soprano and chamber orchestra (words by Gerard Manley Hopkins): 'Spring and Fall: to a young child'; 'May Magnificat'; 'God's Grandeur'.

Te Deum for SATB chorus and organ.

Christmas Eve. Carol for unaccompanied mixed voices.

Noctambule and Sun Dance for woodwind, brass, percussion, and piano.

1968

Natalis Invicti Solis for piano.

Canticum Resurrectionis for sixteen solo voices (words by Gerard Manley Hopkins).

1969

Cloud Canticle for double chorus (words by Ronald Johnson).

Life-Cycle. Cantata for young people—for two choirs and orchestra (words from dance-songs of Gaban pygmies and Eskimos).

Yeibichai. A night-chant for coloratura soprano, scat singer, soprano and baritone soloists, mixed chorus, two speakers, jazz ensemble and large orchestra (words by Gary Snyder).

1970

The Word Unborn. Cantata for sixteen solo voices, two percussionists (one notated, one improvising), flute, clarinet, trombone and cello (words by Ronald Duncan).

The Ancient Wound. A monodrama for singing actress, two actors, improvising chorus, three instrumental trios and tape (text by Peter Garvie).

De Vegetabilibus et Animalibus for soprano, clarinet, violin, cello, and harp (words from Ronald Johnson's *The Book of the Green Man*).

1971

Venery for Six Plus. A music theatre piece for singing actress, flute, trombone, double bass, piano and tape.

1972

Ghost-Dance for flute, viola, and harpsichord.
Opus Alchymicum for organ.

1974

The Gates of the Dream. A masque of Thel—for two trios of solo voices and four instrumental trios, with speakers (words by William Blake).

1975

The Key of the Kingdom. A love-spell for high soprano, piano, percussion, and improvising flute/clarinet (words anonymous).
White Bird Blues for soprano and free-bass accordion (words by Poppy Holden).
Threnody in Memoriam E.W. for eleven solo strings.
Dwight's How Long for solo piano.

1976

Orisons and Oracles for soprano, violin, clarinet and piano (words by Poppy Holden).
A Blue Epiphany for J. B. Smith for solo guitar.

1976–8

Sun-Flower: the Divine Quaternity of William Blake for coloratura soprano, soprano, baritone and bass soloists, two choruses and large orchestra: 'Urizen'; 'Los', 'Beulah'; 'Jerusalem'.

1978

Rosae Hermeticae for two sopranos, two violins, cello, two clarinets (doubling bass clarinets), guitar and chamber organ (words from Blake, Yeats, Gertrude Stein and the Song of Songs): 'The sick Rose'; 'Hymn of the Golden Rose'; 'White Rose Song'; 'White Rose Dance' (*ductia*); 'Black Rose Song'; 'Red Rose Dance' (sarabande); 'Red Rose Song'; 'Hymn of the Blue Rose'; 'Envoir'.

1979

A Maze of Nothing. Six runes to ballads of Helen Adams, for soprano, flute, viola, cello and guitar: 'In and out of the hornbeam maze'; 'Silver and gold'; 'Goose-girl's song'; 'The chestnut tree'; 'Dog-star run'; 'Away'.

1980

Shaman Songs for Jazz Paraphernalia (flutes doubling saxophones, keyboards, electric bass, percussion): 'Little-Water Chant'; 'Beseeching the Breath'; 'New-Moon Chant'; 'The Praises of Sun and Falling Water'.
Three Shakespeare Songs for soprano and flute: 'Under the greenwood tree'; 'Blow, blow thou winter wind'; 'It was a lover and his lass'.

The Dream of the Green Man. A masque for church performance—for soloists, chorus, semi-chorus and small orchestra (words by David Holbrook, adapted from Ronald Johnson's *The Book of the Green Man*).

<hr>
1981
<hr>

Glorificamus for double brass choir.

An Aubade for Indra for clarinet and string quartet.

The Wellspring of Loves. Concerto for solo violin and string orchestra, with optional percussion: 'Aphrodite Akraia'; 'Aphrodite Paregoros'; 'Aphrodite Ambologera'.

A Desart, with Girl and Lyons. Scena for soprano and piano (words by William Blake).

Three Songs of Growing for soprano and piano (revised and adapted from *Mary Easter*, 1957).

The Pentagle Song for mixed chorus, piano and percussion (words by David Holbrook).

<hr>
1986
<hr>

Hortus Rosarium.

<hr>
1997
<hr>

Two Blake Songs for soprano and recorders: 'The Sick Rose'; 'Ah! Sunflower'.

Notes

PART ONE

INTRODUCTION

p. 6 This and the following statements by Wilfrid Mellers come from an unpublished interview with JP.

p. 13 "However far back . . . the first attempts": Curt Sachs, *The Rise of Music in the Ancient World East and West* (London: Dent, 1944) p. 20.

p. 13 "Music in the background": Hans-Werner Heister, "Music in concert and music in the background: two poles of musical realization". In John Paynter *et al*, *Companion to Contemporary Musical Thought* (London and New York: Routledge, 1992).

WHAT IS MUSIC FOR?

p. 16 Emperor Chuan Hao "struck the bell . . .": Percival Price, *Bells and Man* (Oxford: Oxford University Press, 1983), p. 1.

p. 16 "for the Glory of God and the Instruction of my Neighbour": see Bach's epigram on the title-page of the *Orgel Büchlein*:

> Dem Höchsten Gott allein zu Ehren,
> Dem Nächsten, draus sich zu belehren.
> [For honour of the Highest God alone,
> For my neighbour, that he may learn from it.]

Bach, when teaching figured bass, was in the habit of dictating to his students a maxim adapted from words of the composer and theorist Friedrich Niedt (1674–1708): "consonances and dissonances [should] make a well-sounding harmony to the Glory of God and the permissible delectation of the spirit". See Hans T. David and Arthur Mendel, eds., *The Bach Reader* (New York: Norton, 1945), pp. 32–3.

p. 19 Progressive pop and minimalism often share the racks in record shops: "[Glass's] *Heroes Symphony* . . . was inspired by the David Bowie-Brian Eno album of the same name . . . The Funeral Music from *Akhnaten*, too,is invigorating: lively drum rhythms, crashing dissonant chords in the bass, a tonality of its own, a real sense of ritual theatre rising to an exhilarating climax." Helen Wallace, *The Times*.

p. 19 the "marriage of instrument and bow": see Herbert Whone, *The Hidden Face of Music* (London: Gollancz, 1974), p. 72.

p. 21 our young don't believe in time as future . . . : from 'Essay on Poetics', in A. R. Ammons, *Selected Longer Poems* (New York: Norton, 1980).

p. 25 symbolic representation of the ideal organization . . . : by A. R. Ammons, ibid.

SINGING AND DANCING IN THE UNKNOWN

p. 26 "an infantile form of the human ability to . . . master reality by experiment": see Erik Erikson, *Childhood and Society* (London: Vintage, 1965).

p. 26 initiated at the end of the last century by Lady Gomme: Alice Bertha Gomme, *The Traditional Games of England, Scotland, and Ireland: With Tunes, Singing Rhymes, and Methods of Playing*, 2 vols. (London: David Nutt, 1894–98).

IN THE MOOD

p. 35 "the appalling popularity": see Constant Lambert, *Music Ho!: A Study of Music in Decline* (London: Faber & Faber, 1937), p. 63—Part Four: The Mechanical Stimulus, (a) The Appalling Popularity of Music: "Music has an odd way of reflecting not only the emotional background of an age but also its physical conditions. The present age is one of overproduction. Never has there been so much food and so much starvation, and . . . never has there been so much music-making and so little musical experience of a vital order."

p. 36 4´33″: the single-sheet publication (Edition Peters/Henmar Press, 1960) indicates that the work is in three parts, in each of which the instrument is *tacet*. There is also a note that the first performance took place at Woodstock, NY, 29 August 1952, and was given "by David Tudor, pianist, who indicated the beginnings of parts by closing, and the endings by opening, the keyboard lid". In choosing this particular length of time as the title of the piece, Cage may have had in mind the standard duration of one side of a 78 rpm record. That is, if people were used to listening to musicians *playing* in blocks of 4´33″, why not listen to a musician *not-playing* for the same amount of time? That would be a new kind of attentive-listening experience:

"The classic and pure piece of non-music . . . may be taken as a frame for the natural sounds of life, a segment of time isolated and defined in order to trap, for a moment, the experience of the haphazard, 'real' world." See Eric Salzman, *Twentieth-Century Music: An Introduction* (Englewood Cliffs, NJ: Prentice-Hall, 1967), p. 165.

"Clearly this is an end; it may also be a beginning, in that in possessing so completely blank an innocence Cage can be, like Gertrude Stein and Paul Klee, 'as though new born, entirely without impulse, almost in an original state." See Wilfrid Mellers, *Caliban Reborn: Renewal in Twentieth-Century Music* (London: Gollancz, 1968), p. 137.

COMPOSERS' THOUGHTS

p. 40 **the first volume, published in 1956**: see Victor Zuckerkandl, *Sound and Symbol: Music and the External World*, translated by W. R. Trask (New York: Bollingen Foundation Inc., Pantheon Books, 1956).

p. 43 **a *tâtonnement dirigé***: "a purposive groping"—Teilhard de Chardin's description of the development of living things. See Victor Zuckerkandl, *Man the Musician*, ([place]: [publisher], 1973, rev. ed. 1976), p. 328.

MAKING SPIRITUAL CONTACT

p. 45 **the pioneer work on epic ballad by Milman Parry and Albert Lord**: see Milman Parry 'Studies in the epic technique of oral verse-making. 1. Homer and Homeric Style', and '2. The Homeric language as the language of an oral poetry'. *Harvard Studies in Classical Philology* 41 (1930) and 43 (1932). See also Milman Parry and Albert B. Lord *Serbo-Croation Heroic Songs – I Novi Pazar: English Translations* (Cambridge, Mass., and Belgrade: Harvard University Press and Serbian Academy of Sciences, 1954).

THE BLUES IN HISTORY

p. 62 **a breach—far deeper than any sociological division between cultures**: see J. Chernoff, *African Rhythms and African Sensibility* (Chicago: University of Chicago Press, 1979), p. 33: "African music is not just different music but something that is different from 'music'. For a westerner to understand the artistry and purpose of an African musical event, it is necessary for him to sidestep his normal listening tendencies."

PART TWO

LITTLE TIME TO SPARE

p. 80 "true friendship among persons . . . at a perpetual distance": Anderson, *The Constitutions of the Free-Masons* (London, 1723).

p. 81 "deemed nothing human alien" to him: *Homo sum, humani nil a me alienum puto* (I am a man, I count nothing human alien to me). Terence, *Heauton Timorumenos* [*The Self-Tormentor*], I. i. 25., c. 163 BC.

p. 82 "without Contraries [there] is no progression": William Blake, *The Marriage of Heaven and Hell*, plate 3.

p. 83 "I need not tell you with what anxiety . . . fellow men": see Emily Anderson, *The Letters of Mozart and His Family Chronologically Arranged, Translated and Edited with an Introduction, Notes and Indexes* (London: Macmillan, 1966; revised 1985), p. 907 (letter 546).

REBEL WITHOUT APPLAUSE

p. 92 Mum and Dad "fucked him up": Philip Larkin, 'This Be the Verse', in *Collected Poems*, edited by Anthony Thwaite (London and Boston: Faber & Faber 1988), p. 180.

p. 98 The book on Gesualdo: Cecil Gray and Philip Heseltine, *Carlo Gesualdo Prince of Venosa: Musician and Murderer* (London: Kegan Paul, Trench, Trubner & Co, 1926; reprinted, Westport, CT: Greenwood Press, 1971).

BLUE REMEMBERED HILLS

p. 100 Housman described himself . . .: A. E. Housman, *Letter* (5 February, 1933): "I am not a pessimist but a pejorist (as George Eliot said she was not an optimist but a meliorist)". See *The Shropshire Lad*, LXII:

> Therefore, since the world has still
> Much good, but much less good than ill,
> And while the sun and moon endure
> Luck's a chance, but trouble's sure,
> I'd face it as a wise man would
> And train for ill and not for good.

p. 100 "Take my hand *quick* and tell me . . .": the italic is WM's, emphasizing the pun on 'quick', ie. alive, as in 'the quick and the dead'.

LOU HARRISON AT EIGHTY

p. 114 "Cherish, Conserve, Consider, and Create": Lou Harrison's "lifelong motto". See notes by Alan Rich, music critic of *The Los Angeles Herald Examiner*, for the CD recording of Harrison's *Piano Concerto* and *Suite* (New World Records NW366–2)

p. 115 "We must love one another or die": W. H. Auden, 'September 1, 1939'. See Humphrey Carpenter, *Benjamin Britten: A Biography* (London: Faber & Faber, 1992) p. 135.

p. 115 strictly tuned to Javanese *slendro* modes: the Javanese gamelan consists of two sets of instruments, each with its own *lara* (tuning system): *slendro* and *pelog*. *Slendro* is an anhemitonic pentatonic mode (five notes without semitones), while *pelog* is a seven-note mode which includes semitones and has more variety than *slendro* in the size of intervals. See N. Sorrell, *A Guide to the Gamelan* (London: Faber & Faber, 1990), p. 55–57.

p. 115 **practically the Human Song**: Lou Harrison's words, cited by WM who, in the original publication, added the following footnote: "Research work with children, carried out during the 1960s (especially by John Paynter), confirms the basic 'humanity' of pentatonicism. The children, left to improvise music on fully chromatic metallophones, tended to ignore the non-pentatonic tones and to play in a ludically pentatonic Eden!" See John Paynter, 'The role of creativity in the school music curriculum', in *Music Education Review* edited by Michael Burnett (London: Chappell, 1977), p. 13ff.

p. 116 **"going-onness" and "long flow form"**: see Wilfrid Mellers, *Percy Grainger* (Oxford: Oxford University Press, 1992), p. 49.

p. 117 **retuned in compromise between Eastern and Western traditions**: see the notes by Alan Rich, referred to in note [p. 114] above: "the black keys are tuned to produce the mathematically precise 4ths and 5ths beloved of medieval theoreticians; the white keys come off resembling the 'just intonation' of the Renaissance and Baroque . . . each group [of the orchestra] tunes to different facets of this system."

PART THREE

INTRODUCTION

p. 123 ". . . **opera and ballet productions on giant screens in parks . . .**": *The Times*, 7 July 1997.

p. 124 **'haecceity'**: from the medieval Latin of Duns Scotus, *hæcceitatem*—the quality described by the use of the word 'this', as in 'this person' but also implying 'hereness and nowness'.

OUT OF ARCADIA

p. 126 **the 'First Practice' of polyphony**: *Prima prattica* and *seconda prattica*: terms which derived from controversy between Monteverdi and Artusi early in the seventeenth century. In effect they describe old and new styles, the *prima prattica* being the established polyphonic techniques of the sixteenth century, and the *seconda prattica* the 'modern' style, characteristic of the madrigals, which dictated that the words should govern the music.

p. 126 *Il Pastor Fido*: a pastoral drama by Giovanni Battista Guarini (1538–1612). Drafted in 1583 but not published until 1601, it had great popularity during the seventeenth century, particularly in England. Notably, it introduced the dramatizing of lyric sentimentality (i.e. imitating real human action) and was dependent for its effect upon the addition of music. See Maria Maniates, *Mannerism in Italian Music and Culture, 1530–1630* (Manchester: University of North Carolina Press and Manchester University Press, 1979), pp. 26–27, 77, 228–9.

FIDELIO AND LEONORA

p. 133 **deemed nothing human alien to him**: see note for p. 81 above.

NEW LIFE IN A NEW WORLD?

p. 152 **a fabulous *succès de scandale***: *The Times* on 24 January 1928, reporting on a performance in Vienna, observed that: "No opera produced for the first time in Vienna lately has aroused more controversy than Krenek's 'jazz' opera *Johnny Strikes Up* . . . [it] proved a musicianly, amusing, and highly enjoyable evening's entertainment. The musical world and the Press, however, are sharply divided in their criticism of the opera, half of them maintaining that it is a 'sacrilege' that such a work should have been allowed in the Opera House, the others championing the opera as a work of genius."

p. 152 **Another reason . . . was its eclecticism**: again, *The Times*, 24 January 1928: "The opera has blended the elements of melodrama, cinema, and revue to a remarkable degree, yet the conception is that of grand opera."

INNOCENCE DROWNED

p. 154 **his now celebrated letter**: W. H. Auden to Benjamin Britten, 31 January 1942, from Ann Arbor. See Carpenter, *Britten*, p. 163–64.

WRONG BUT WROMANTICK

p. 157 **the failure of Britten's only 'occasional' opera**: see Carpenter, *Britten*, pp. 325–26.

RESTORED BY INNOCENCE

p. 161 **The original 1957 production . . . was not greatly esteemed**: See Carpenter, *Britten*, pp. 374–75.

MONOTONOUSLY MINIMAL

p. 173 **Children always say "Do it again"**: from 'The Ethics of Elfland' in W. H. Auden, ed., *G. K. Chesterton: A Selection from His Non-fictional Prose* (London: Faber & Faber, 1970) p. 186.

PART FOUR

INTRODUCTION

p. 178 **historically and contemporaneously** *transeunt*: it is interesting to recall Stravinsky's statement that, in composing *The Rite of Spring*, he had no antecedents—"I heard, and I wrote what I heard: I was the vessel through which *Le Sacre* passed". Surely it is as illogical to have made such a claim as it would have been to suggest that *The Rite* would not or could not, in varying degrees, influence composers who were Stravinsky's contemporaries or who would come later.

A SINGLE-MINDED PURSUIT

p. 179 **'wordless analysis'**: subsequently, Keller used the term 'Functional Analysis' (usually abbreviated to 'FA') to define this process:

> "Most striking . . . was the evolution of Functional Analysis ('FA'), which burst upon the world in 1957 to an astonishing welter of publicity and documentation, mainly Keller's. These aimed at demonstrating the listener's experience of a work in purely musical terms, without commentary or explanation, and revealing 'the unity of contrasting themes and movements'."

Christopher Wintle, ed., *Hans Keller: Essays on Music* (Cambridge University Press, 1994), Introduction, p. xvi.

THE COMPOSER AS WOUNDED BIRD

p. 184 the (now much dimmed) writings of Jean Paul: Jean Paul Friedrich Richter (1763–1825). There is a useful introduction (in English) in J. W. Smeed, ed., *Jean Paul des Feldpredigers Schmelze Reise nach Flätz* (Oxford: Oxford University Press, 1966). See also, W. Hecht, ed., *Jean Pauls Werke*, 2 vols. (Berlin and Weimar: Aufbau-Verlag, 1973).

p. 187 *Hoffmann's scary tale 'The Sandman'*: see E. T. A. Hoffmann, *The Tales of Hoffmann*, selected and translated by Michael Bullock (New York: Frederick Ungar Publishing Co., 1963).

p. 187 **Tom Moore's *Lalla Rookh***: Thomas Moore, *Lallah Rookh: an oriental tale* (London, 1817). In fact, a series of four verse-tales linked by a prose account of the journey, from Delhi to Kasmir, of the emperor's daughter, Lalla Rookh, who is to be married to the king of Bucharia.

PART FIVE

LYRICS OF DEPRIVATION

p. 231 **'corporeal' music**: "For the essentially vocal and verbal music of the individual—a monophonic concept—the word Corporeal may be used . . . The epic chant is an example, but the term could be applied with equal propriety to almost any of the important ancient and near-ancient cultures—the Chinese, Greek, Arabian, Indian, in all of which music was physically allied with poetry or the dance. Corporeal music is emotionally 'tactile'. It does not grow from the root of 'pure form'. It cannot be characterized as either mental or spiritual." Harry Partch, *Genesis of a Music: An Account of a Creative Work, Its Roots and Its Fulfillments*, 2nd (enlarged) edition (New York: Da Capo Press, 1974), p. 8.

ALL THE THINGS THEY WERE

p. 256 **DuBose Heyward**: (1885–1940), South Carolina poet and novelist. A dramatized version of *Porgy* (1925), a novel about black people in Charleston, made by Heyward and his wife, was awarded a Pulitzer Prize and became the basis of the opera *Porgy and Bess* (1935).

A VOICE IN THE WILDERNESS

p. 261 **Stein's interminable novel**: Gertrude Stein, *The Making of Americans: Being a History of a Family's Progress 1906–1908* (New York: Something Else Press, 1925, reprinted 1966).

AN AUTHENTIC AMERICAN COMPOSER

p. 274 *Genesis of a Music (1949)*: see note for p. 231 above.

Index